11.12.15

For my best colleague Bob Liebman — who knows that getting thro's half the fun!

David A. Horowitz

Getting There

AN AMERICAN CULTURAL ODYSSEY

David A. Horowitz

in association with

PORTLAND • OREGON
INKWATERPRESS.COM

Copyright © 2015 David A. Horowitz

Cover and interior design by Emily Coats
Grunge ripped paper USA flag pattern © Andrey_Kuzmin. Bigstockphoto.com

All rights reserved. Except where explicitly stated, no part of this book may be reproduced or transmitted in any form or by any means whatsoever, including photocopying, recording or by any information storage and retrieval system, without written permission from the publisher and/or author.

Publisher: Inkwater Press

Publisher's Cataloging-in-Publication
    Horowitz, David A. (David Alan), 1941-
        Getting there : an American cultural odyssey / by
    David A. Horowitz.
        pages cm
        Includes bibliographical references.
        LCCN 2015930450
        ISBN 978-1-62901-203-2 (paperback)
        ISBN 978-1-62901-204-9 (paperback)

    1. Horowitz, David A. (David Alan), 1941-
2. Historians--United States--Biography. 3. College teachers--United States--Biography. 4. United States--Civilization--1945- 5. United States--Politics and government--20th century. 6. United States--Politics and government--21th century. I. Title.

E169.12.H676 2015   973.92092
                            QBI15-600031

Paperback
ISBN-13 978-1-62901-203-2 | ISBN-10 1-62901-203-3

Kindle
ISBN-13 978-1-62901-204-9 | ISBN-10 1-62901-204-1

Scan this QR Code to learn more about this title

Printed in the U.S.A.
All paper is acid free and meets all ANSI standards for archival quality paper.

1 3 5 7 9 10 8 6 4 2

ride the line of balance and hold on by just a thread
– B. Springsteen

To my life partner Gloria, who knows that a fine woman deserves a good yard man

ACKNOWLEDGMENTS

Portions of *Getting There* appeared in earlier forms in "An Eight-Day Week in Nicaragua: A Personal View," *North Coast Times-Eagle* (May-June and July 1987); "Antioch at the Dawn of the Sixties," *Antiochiana* (Winter 2011); and "The Sicuro File: A Personal Perspective on the Struggle over Portland State University's Most Controversial President," *Oregon Historical Quarterly* (Summer 2011).

As a project spanning more than a decade, this book received invaluable encouragement from colleagues in the Portland State University Department of History and the Oregon Cultural Heritage Commission. OCHC President David Milholland deserves particular thanks for his thoughtful responses to an early version of the manuscript. Nathan Cogan, Peter N. Carroll, and Michael G. Horowitz provided additional feedback along the way.

Andrea Janda digitized the photographs that appear on the cover and first page of each chapter and provided vital technical assistance during preparation of the manuscript. The staff at Inkwater Press, including Acquisitions Editor Sean Jones, Copy Editor Martha Swain, Creative Director Masha Shubin, Senior Graphic Designer Emily Coats, and Marketing Director John Williams, literally brought the book to life.

Finally, Gloria E. Myers, to whom the author has dedicated this work, remains his sole inspiration.

CONTENTS

ACKNOWLEDGMENTS VII
PRELUDE 1
BREAKING AWAY 5
BRANCHING OUT 29
CANOPY 53
ESTUARIES 75
WESTWINDS 97
FIREWEED 121
FERMENT 141
PRIMROSE 163
HABITAT 185
CREVICE 203
FOLIAGE 225
CLEARING 243
CONIFERS 267
MEADOWS 287
LEADING EDGE 307
SALAL 325
PRECIPICE 345
PINNACLE 367
WAITING FOR #17 385
SELECTIVE LIST OF AUTHOR'S PUBLICATIONS 397
CREDITS FOR PHOTOS AND SONG LYRIC EXCERPTS 403
INDEX 406

PRELUDE

what do you do with the sands of time?
– D. W. Poythress/L. Satcher

Woody Allen famously observed that 80 percent of success is showing up. Yet the real tale lies in getting there.

Getting There: An American Cultural Odyssey traces the personal, professional, and public ventures of a historian, teacher, journalist, musician, and activist over the past half-century. In describing a serendipitous attempt to fashion a creative, socially redemptive, and independent identity, the narrative intersects many of the significant political and cultural moments of a period characterized by extraordinary political and cultural ferment.

The action opens in New York City in 1959 with the abandonment of a middle-class Jewish home life and immersion in the work-study program of Ohio's progressive Antioch College. Several flashbacks provide glimpses of family history, childhood, and growing social awareness. After describing a productive period of study, work, and travel in the United States and abroad, the chronicle proceeds to the adoption of history as a chosen area of inquiry and the rigors and distractions of a graduate school apprenticeship in mid-1960s Minneapolis.

As the story approaches 1968 and a teaching career at Oregon's Portland State College (later University), *Getting There* details the attractions of counterculture values and antiwar radicalism. At the same time, a series of personal and academic influences interact with a faltering economy to arouse a renewed interest in the experience of what populists call "ordinary Americans." Succeeding chapters chronicle the publication of scholarly works placing the 1920s Ku Klux Klan, World War II noninterventionists, Cold War anticommunists, civil rights opponents, and latter-day culture warriors within an insurgent tradition defying "left and right." Meanwhile, a second vocation in journalism leads to explorations of topics ranging from Watergate and the CIA to post-Vietnam stalemate, Middle East politics, and the allures of popular culture.

The populist slant of these endeavors encourages an iconoclastic style of teaching that avoids excessive jargon, incorporates an unconventional approach to cultural diversity, and insists upon the democratic traditions of humane learning. Outside the classroom, stints as a political activist, social critic, and organizer of public forums reinforce the maxim that a cultural historian's work is never done, as do performances as a café pianist and theatrical accompanist as well as efforts to commemorate the literary and artistic heritage of the Pacific Northwest.

Getting There depicts the challenge of blending academic, personal, and public pursuits into a coherent life strategy. It asks whether learning can embrace tools of reason and intellect with intuition, empathy, and a playful appreciation of creative expression and beauty. The narrative further explores prospects for combining rational inquiry with a passion for social justice. Can one play a role in the national conversation, it inquires, while evaluating the value of such contributions? Is it possible, in the end, to move past cynicism and defeatism, restate progressive values, engage succeeding generations, and play a part in healing society's wounds?

Each of the segments of *Getting There* stands as a self-contained unit with little reference to subsequent events. Characters normally take their place within the context of the narrative, not in terms of later accomplishments or misdeeds. Although relatively prominent individuals occasionally play a role in the story, most of the book's characters were not in the public eye. Respecting their privacy, the text often limits itself to their first names. In a few cases, alternate identities appear with quotation marks at first mention. The author sees no value in pillorying others for vulnerabilities he failed to detect when wisdom or foresight might have dictated otherwise.

Portland and Arch Cape, Oregon, 2015

BREAKING AWAY

(1959-1960)

why wait any longer for the world to begin?
  – B. Dylan

As I descended the steps of New York's dusky Grand Central Station a month past my eighteenth birthday, I gave little thought to the prospect of inaugurating the adult stage of my life. After dutiful hugs to parents and a quick handshake with younger brother Michael, I made my way down the darkened platform. It was September 1959, the last season of a decade that had taken me from a protected childhood in the West Bronx to the awakenings of suburban adolescence. Without hesitation, I put one foot ahead of the other and stepped into the future with no idea of the extended odyssey awaiting me.

OLD GROWTH

A bespectacled and rather gangly graduate of Long Island's Wheatley High School, I was bound for an initial year at Antioch College, a small, progressive liberal arts institution in southwest Ohio. Urged to chart out an educational plan, I had discovered that nearly all the "A" listings in the directory of American colleges addressed "Christian men and women." Since I was unmistakably Jewish, at least in cultural identity, this would not do.

Coming across the entry for Antioch, I experienced a sense of a relief at the focus on a secular and inclusive brand of humane learning. Here was a school without fraternities or sororities, intercollegiate sports, or compulsory chapel. Rather than speaking to the parents of prospective students, the profile appealed directly to applicants with promises of intellectual exchange; a democratic, self-governing campus; and a program geared to individual growth and a spirit of social service.

Founded as a denominational college in 1852, Antioch had been one of the nation's very first racially integrated and co-ed colleges.

Getting There

Under the leadership of New England educator Horace Mann, the school had embraced a reformist orientation.

"Be ashamed to die until you have won some victory for humanity," Mann instructed.

As Dayton hydraulic engineer and conservationist Arthur E. Morgan assumed its presidency in the 1920s, the college adopted the individualized general education curriculum and five-year work-study program that would make it one of America's innovative seats of liberal learning. Although my father dreamed of sending his sons to the Ivy League, I clung to Antioch as my first preference with quiet determination. In truth, I was hardly a candidate for Columbia or Brown. Although a second-round honor society inductee, I had not earned exceptional college aptitude scores, and my grades ranked a modest sixteenth in a class of ninety-six.

Besides, so much of my family and personal background seemed compatible with Antioch's unconventional appeal, and to some extent, its progressive social values.

My father's parents, Barnett Ariovich and Rifka (Becky) Golub, had been next-door neighbors in the Jewish village or *shtetl* of Radun in "Russian Poland," later Belarus. As Barnett faced conscription in the czar's army, he set out in 1901 for East London's Jewish quarter in Whitechapel, where he sent for his fiancée. Two years after their marriage, they welcomed their first child, Samuel. At the hospital, Hebrew charity officials anglicized the couple's last name to Horowitz. Not long after, the Jewish Colonization Society secured them a free booking in steerage to Halifax, Nova Scotia. From there, the immigrants made their way to Manhattan's Lower East Side, where on September 11, 1908, my father Nathan was born on the kitchen table of a Cherry Street tenement. His sister Gussie, later "Teddy," arrived two years later.

While Becky cooked, washed, and saw to the needs of several boarders, Barnett put in twelve-to-fourteen-hour days as a garment trade presser. A committed socialist, he joined the Amalgamated Clothing Workers Union and cursed "the bosses." In the early

1920s, Becky relocated the family to a series of airier East Bronx flats with indoor plumbing. Partly due to poor progress in his first year at the High School of Commerce and anxious to help support the household, Nathan dropped out of schooling at age fourteen. He would take on an assortment of menial jobs until landing a position in 1927 as a summer social director at a small hotel in New York's Catskill Mountains. Yet once the Great Depression took hold in the early 1930s, his only employment would consist of combing the Manhattan garment factories for workers' compensation referrals for a shady medical clinic.

My mother's background was slightly more impressive. Her father, Nathan Levine, was born in Russian Minsk in 1891. At fourteen, he fled to Brooklyn, New York, to live with cousins and avoid the czar's draft. After high school, Nathan worked at the family restaurant on the Lower East Side. There he met waitress Bessie Hertzig, who had recently emigrated from southwestern Poland. Once married, the couple had two children: a son, Milton David, and my mother, Dorothy, born in 1917. Nine years later, the Levines bought a Chinese restaurant in Honesdale, Pennsylvania, an industrial town in the Pocono Mountains. Milt's Irish schoolmates dubbed him "Mickey," a handle he maintained for the rest of his life. When the Honesdale business failed, the family took over a Chinese eatery, cocktail lounge, and dancehall in Lake Huntington, a seedy resort on the edge of the Catskills.

Radical politics captivated the Levine family. A secular Jew whose family had beaten her as a child when she tried entering school, my grandmother Bess rallied to labor causes in the 1920s, became a close ally of Socialist Party leader Norman Thomas in the '30s, and campaigned for liberal and reform candidates and issues the rest of her life. Meanwhile, daughter Dorothy studied journalism at New York's public Hunter College and followed Mickey into the Socialist Workers Party. As admirers of exiled Russian revolutionary Leon Trotsky, the two opposed Josef Stalin's Communist regime in the

Soviet Union while participating in marches and demonstrations to denounce the evils of fascism, capitalism, and imperialism.

Joining his brothers-in-law and mother on a retreat to Lake Huntington as sister Teddy recuperated from a miscarriage in 1935, Nathan Horowitz met the love of his life. He was nearly twenty-seven; Dorothy Levine was eighteen. Unaware that she was an accomplished swimmer, he broke into one of her political treatises with a challenge to race across the lake, only to lag far behind when they swam back to shore. When Nathan won the house raffle at Nat Levine's Broadway Casino that evening, where Dorothy waited on tables, however, he knew she liked him.

Both New Yorkers had produced poetry, short stories, and plays since they were children. Nevertheless, their courtship was problematic. Nathan liked to write humorous verse, character studies, and skits, often in ethnic dialect. Dorothy focused on the Depression's human drama and suffering and romantic poetry. Having absorbed her mother's religious agnosticism and affinity for social criticism, she could not understand why this romantic but unemployed son of the East Bronx remained an observant Jew with little class-consciousness or political commitment.

When Nathan left with two friends on a cross-continental auto trip in 1936 to seek his fortune as a Hollywood screenwriter, the couple's future seemed in doubt. Yet after returning several months later, he scraped together two thousand dollars to buy the coatroom concession of a Manhattan restaurant owned by Bess's brother Charlie. The promise of financial security evidently facilitated marriage plans. In February 1938, a month after Dorothy graduated college, the couple celebrated a wedding dinner at Charlie's eatery. In deference to the prospect of tips at the coatroom, they held the event the day after the Washington's Birthday holiday.

As the "Roosevelt Recession" intensified that year, the newlyweds moved on to Minsky's Burlesque at Miami, Florida's Million Dollar Pier, another of Charlie's ventures. Nathan served as a souvenir barker while college-educated Dorothy ran the box office.

The following spring, they relocated to the Congress of Beauty, an attraction Charlie's son managed at the New York World's Fair of 1939. Months after the exposition closed, my father began driving a diaper service truck and the couple moved into a rent-controlled studio apartment in the West Bronx.

NURTURE

On August 17, 1941, not long after taking over a three-room spread in the same building, the Horowitzes announced the arrival of a son. My father proposed to call me David Alan in memory of his maternal grandfather, Avrum Duvid; my mother agreed because Davidovitch was the given middle name of Leon Trotsky. Although I carried a weighty lineage, both parents took note of my "sunny" disposition.

As the United States entered World War II four months after my birth, my father received a military deferment as a punch press operator at a New Jersey defense plant, a four-to-five hour round-trip commute from the Bronx. By then, he had collaborated as a lyricist with composer and friend Charles Kingsford on four "Negro dialect" spirituals under the pen name Nathaniel Harris. The best of the lot, "Chicken Dinnah!" would merit a radio performance by popular tenor Nelson Eddy. During the presidential campaign of 1944, meanwhile, my mother beat out young playwright Arthur Miller in a contest sponsored by the CIO (labor's Congress of Industrial Organizations) for the best radio script on public housing.

On September 2, 1945 – VJ (Victory over Japan) Day – the family welcomed a second son, Michael. Within months, my father undertook a twenty-eight year sales career with the West Disinfecting Company (later West Chemical), a manufacturer of commercial sanitary products. Two years later, he and my mother began work on a play about a frustrated shoe clerk coming to terms with his mediocre artistic talents. Copyrighted by "Nat Harris," *Tin Waltz* would run for two weeks in an off-Broadway church basement in 1954. Under the name Nady Horowitz, meanwhile, my father channeled his love of dialect verse into an amateur theatrical production for one of the Catskill Mountain summer bungalow colonies the family patronized during the first half of the decade. A take-off on the Jewish wedding ceremony, these cross-dressing mock marriages featured bawdy Yiddish and English parodies to familiar popular and ethnic tunes.

Without the burdens of a family, Mickey embraced political activism. After Pearl Harbor, he overcame socialist objections to "imperialist" war by volunteering for the Army to fight Hitler. Ultimately stationed in Hawaii, Mickey became a founding member of the American Veterans Committee (AVC), the first mainstream service organization to open its doors to African-Americans. With Bess Levine and AVC associates behind him, he rose to the leadership of the Upper West Side Manhattan chapter of Americans for Democratic Action (ADA), the influential postwar organization of anticommunist liberals who supported expansion of the New Deal social welfare state.

Elected national chair of AVC in 1955 on a civil rights platform, Mickey undertook a one-man tour to document discriminatory racial practices in Veterans Administration hospitals in the Deep South. The trip resulted in a 2,500-word report to the House Veterans Affairs Committee. Appropriately, ADA co-founder Eleanor Roosevelt delivered the keynote address at Mickey's second AVC inaugural in 1958. I still have the framed photo that shows me listening in rapt attention as the former First Lady and premier human rights advocate speaks from the dais.

Despite the secure and protected nature of life in the postwar West Bronx and my father's Depression-era anxieties over assuming a mortgage, his status as his company's number one sales representative nationwide introduced the prospect of a move out of the city. Five years after the broadcast of my mother's radio script on public housing, New York City built nine fifteen-story structures to serve eight hundred families on the grounds of a former convent a half-block from our building. The project brought increased congestion to the area, a dire shortage of parking, and a new ethnic mix that included Puerto Ricans and African-Americans. Whether the neighborhood's changing demographics or my parents' dream of having their own home provided the central motivation, the arrival of a new Studebaker sedan permitted weekend jaunts in search of a suburban refuge. Five years later in 1956, our middle-class family would join the historic "white flight" from urban America and abandon its Bronx roots for a three-bedroom ranch house in Long Island's Roslyn Heights.

Dutifully completing the *New York Sunday Times* crossword puzzle each week, my self-educated father continued to pursue literary interests with a steady output of poetry and parodies. His masterpiece was "Bewitched, Bothered, and Bar-Mitzvah-ed Am I," which my brother sang to my piano accompaniment as near-hurricane force winds and rains battered the backyard tent that housed the September 1958 reception marking Michael's elevation to Jewish manhood. The move to Long Island also coincided with the start of my mother's career as a grade school instructor in Corona, Queens, where she organized a chapter of the United Federation of Teachers while taking evening courses in preparation for certification as a guidance counselor.

Suburban life did not detract from the intensity of table banter during family gatherings for Passover Seders and other holidays. Uncle Mickey loved to relay the Yiddish jokes the rabbis told at the Federation of Jewish Philanthropies, where he served as an executive assistant. Conversation ranged from iconoclastic takes on the Old Testament to the crimes of Josef Stalin and Adolf Hitler, the injustices of southern racial practices, the corruption of New York's Tammany Hall political machine, and the social significance of Broadway musicals such as *South Pacific*. Battered by the former struggles of his working-class family and economic survival, my father nurtured a deeply conservative strain within his temperament. Yet the constant give-and-take over politics and culture enabled me to absorb a critical spirit and learn that people could engage even the most divisive issues in a spirit of amiability and tolerance.

My own intellectual development had begun to accelerate back in the Bronx when a witty and compassionate seventh-grade social studies teacher inspired my interest in history and politics. By then, I had gravitated to the irreverent late-night radio broadcasts of humorist Jean Shepherd, who mixed nostalgic tales of Indiana boyhood and recordings of old-time blues and jazz classics with barbed critiques of conformity and political banality. A plug on the show even moved me to become a founding subscriber to Paul Krassner's satirical magazine *The Realist*. Once in Roslyn Heights, I fell under the influence of high school literature teacher Howard Storm. As he sat cross-legged on the front desk with shoes kicked off and heavy white socks exposed, this curly-headed, wisecracking Beat generation hipster mixed studies of Shakespeare with spontaneous rants at suburban complacency, materialist posing, and unthinking piety.

Stimulated by authors such as Somerset Maugham, Theodore Dreiser, and Sinclair Lewis, I developed an early ear for hypocrisy and cant. When I chose Vance Packard's *The Hidden Persuaders* for a book report during senior year, I fixated on the exposure of the advertising industry's psychological manipulations of consumer motivation. A chance reading of *1919*, the second volume of Depression radical John Dos Passos's historical trilogy *U.S.A.*, provided an emotional immediacy to the struggle for social justice and the dignity of working people.

These radical proclivities received encouragement from my friend Ken, a "red diaper baby" offspring of former activists who habitually called for me on the way to the school bus stop. Years earlier, a former bohemian high school friend of my mother's had treated me to a pair of ten-inch Folkways recordings by cowboy and railroad balladeer Cisco Houston. Ken now introduced me to Pete Seeger and the Weavers, whose folk music incorporated the struggles of radicals, labor organizers, peace activists, and ordinary people from every culture.

I now became a regular at "hootenanny" sessions at the home of Nancy Kurshan, another Wheatley High student from a political family. Sitting in Nancy's pine-paneled suburban recreation room, we combined the latest calypso hits with calls for revolutionary solidarity in standards such as "We Shall Not Be Moved," "Joe Hill," "The Klan," "The Midnight Special," "Union Maid," and "If I Had a Hammer." Ken also brought me to the high school for Saturday morning sessions led by biology teacher John Lineweaver. A North Carolina liberal, Lineweaver exposed us to the critiques of radical sociologist C. Wright Mills and to discussions of poverty, the population explosion, racial justice, imperialism, and other pressing issues.

INITIATIONS

Once the overnight train pulled into Springfield, Ohio, the contingent from our specially designated car headed for a short, wiry, and red-bearded figure with a handwritten "Antiochians" sign high above his head. Introducing himself as Mac, without another word he beckoned us to follow and unceremoniously waved us into the back of an old flatbed truck. Within minutes, we found ourselves hurtling down a winding two-lane highway, allowing only furtive glimpses of the rolling countryside speeding by. As we rushed past the two traffic lights of tiny Yellow Springs, nine miles south, Mac screeched around a corner to the tree-shaded campus.

"Everybody out!" he yelled.

No one was going to baby us around this place, I thought.

As we waited in line for housing assignments, it seemed that just about every student came from a major city or cosmopolitan suburb. Still, for someone who had never been west of New York State or New Jersey, it felt exhilarating to meet people from exotic locales such as Pocatello and Louisville. My roommate, a strapping and good-natured biology major, was from Cincinnati; Frank

Maurer's father had graduated from Antioch and had roomed with a fellow named Horowitz.

No, that was not my dad, I answered politely, thinking about my father's proletarian upbringing and early struggles in the work force.

Boy, does he have the wrong number, I mused, a variant of the punch line to the old Jewish joke about the patrician on the telephone who asks Sadie Rosenbaum if he's reached the Anderson residence.

Orientation Week's battery of aptitude tests indicated that I had scored an abysmal 2 percent in spatial relations, quite possibly the lowest on record. Yet the results in social studies and humanities exempted me from many entry-level classes. Flushed with self-confidence, I approached the curriculum as if it were a board game and decided to bypass courses such as the History of Western Civilization as well as introductions to sociology, geography, political science, philosophy, English literature, and psychology, the last my intended major. I ultimately regretted this strategy. Yet I felt a tinge of excitement as I began my college career.

How different the mood seemed from my first venture in schooling.

On that terrible September morning in 1946, my father dutifully escorted me to kindergarten past the iron fencing of P.S. 104, an imposing white structure that looked like a prison. To this day, I recall the pungent odor of freshly applied wax on the institutional floors and the intimidating aura of the framed portrait of haughty George Washington in the hallway. As I sensed that the freedom of my timeless childhood and cocooned family life were forever gone and that I had fallen into the hands of uncaring strangers, a wave of panic engulfed me.

Quivering in complete terror, my eyes began to tear.

Then I encountered Miss Mahon, the enormous Irish-American principal.

"There'll be none of that nonsense here, young man," she commanded.

Reacting like a cornered animal, I delivered a hefty kick to the huge woman's behind.

Moments later, as the inevitability of the forces arrayed against me sank in, I meekly succumbed to my fate.

Beyond learning how to hold scissors and carry chairs, I never did master the handicrafts of kindergarten nor develop any affection for the regimentation of schooling. By first grade, moreover, difficulty in reading the blackboard required an eye exam and, to my dismay, a pair of glasses. Even so, I took well to print writing until a second-grade classmate and I decided to learn cursive script on our own. My penmanship never recovered. Monitoring my careless habits, my father brought me a "THINK" placard from his new IBM sales client. Although my father's intrusions could be imperious, I followed his advice to complete my homework on Friday evenings to free up the weekend, although my pals and I usually competed to finish the task during class. Beyond building replicas of African villages and other onerous construction projects, however, I refused to compromise my independence by tolerating parental help.

Experimenting with a self-styled curriculum for my first two years of college, I signed up for exotic-sounding classes such as Physical Science and the World Picture, the Social Psychology of Utopian Communities, and Workshop in Small Group Functioning. In the last, our final project team drew from the text of *Alice in Wonderland* to devise a completely fabricated theory of "inverse communications," although one of the three instructors insisted he was on to the scheme from the beginning.

My most valuable course during this period was Mickey McCleery's Introduction to Political Behavior. I immediately took to the plain-talking, working-class World War II veteran who wore Hawaiian shirts in all weather, sported an ever-present cup of black coffee, and turned out to be the most frenzied softball catcher I ever encountered. An advocate of the "consensus" school of political science, McCleery assigned a textbook by the distinguished V. O.

Key, which preached that societal stability depended upon a plurality of "socio-economic elites" competing for influence within a non-ideological, interest-group framework. We also absorbed the lessons of former dockworker Eric Hoffer, who denounced fanatical "true believers" who discarded political realism for ideological purity. Although McCleery's approach lacked the idealism that motivated many of us, his emphasis on critical reflection and intellectual discipline revealed a profound commitment to his students.

"There is no substitute for thought," a sign in his seminar room proclaimed.

McCleery certainly was no knee jerk liberal. When the subject of the American Legion came up in one after-class consultation, I reiterated Uncle Mickey's view of AVC's rival as a collection of conservative ultra-patriots and defenders of racial segregation.

"Aw hell," the professor countered, "all these guys are interested in is a chance to get a drink down at the Legion Hall on Sundays."

I chose to do my term paper on the Industrial Workers of the World (IWW), the freewheeling early-twentieth-century radical labor organization celebrated in *1919*. Coming from a home where writing was second nature, I usually found it easy to express myself on paper. It was a shock, then, when I received a D+ on the first draft. McCleery patiently explained that my work was far too narrative and lacked sufficient analysis. Overcoming a weakness for theoretical constructs, I revised the essay with the proposition that the relative isolation of western mining and lumber camps increased the militancy of IWW labor activism.

I wound up with an A- for the course.

OF FAITH AND SOUL

During orientation, a speaker suggested we check out the houses of worship in Yellow Springs to sample local culture. This idea appealed to my curiosity about people removed from my own upbringing. My parents had provided a living lesson about tolerance by acclimating to each other's religious beliefs. By this arrangement, my mother, a proclaimed agnostic, was free to stay at home while my dad brought my brother and me to the Orthodox synagogue a half-mile from our West Bronx apartment during the Jewish high holidays. Yet the agreement required that at age thirteen both Michael and I would have bar mitzvahs. In preparation, I began a three-year apprenticeship in religious lore and ritual in the fall of 1951, a matter of tedious after-school sessions Monday through Thursday afternoons as well as Sunday mornings.

I never anticipated that Hebrew School would offer an unanticipated lesson in faith. For East Coast Jews, prowess on the softball field provided an important avenue to acculturation. The Horowitz family scrapbook, like countless others, contained innumerable snapshots of my brother and me with a bat in hand or a glove poised for the staged play at third. Identification with Major League Baseball offered another aspect of Americanization. As late as the 1950s, New York boasted three professional franchises – the Brooklyn Dodgers, the Yankees, and the Giants, the last my father's team since childhood. By coincidence, my appearance at Hebrew School came just after I had followed in my father's footsteps and become a Giants fan.

Despite enormous excitement over rookie Willie Mays during the summer of 1951, the Giants dropped thirteen and a half games behind the first-place Brooklyn Dodgers in mid-August. Yet the club managed one of the greatest comebacks in sports history, tying for the National League lead on the last day of the season and forcing a three-game playoff. With the series evened up at a victory apiece, I raced home from school to catch the televised finale, only to experience complete devastation when the Dodgers surged to a three-run lead in the top of the ninth inning. Unable to continue witnessing my misery, my mother pleaded with me to end the agony and go to my scheduled class at Hebrew School, advice I followed with a heavy heart.

As fellow students and I gathered in the center's gymnasium for a songfest late in the afternoon, I suddenly heard a commotion at the entrance, only to see my mother, with my brother in tow, bursting into the crowded room.

"Davey, Davey!" she screamed. "The Giants won! The Giants won! They won! The Giants won the pennant!"

Before I knew it, she had me in her arms leaping for joy across the creaky floor.

My diamond heroes had staged the ultimate bottom-of-the-ninth-inning comeback, climaxed by a three-run walk-off home run by third baseman Bobby Thomson, a feat that would be immortalized as the greatest moment in the history of organized baseball.

The Giants eventually lost the World Series to the rival Yankees, whose magnificent stadium was barely a mile from our front door. Beyond the ribbing of all my friends, I had to contend with the quiet satisfaction of Uncle Mickey, a lifetime supporter of the Bronx Bombers. Yet the experience taught an invaluable lesson about never letting anyone, even a loving and caring parent, tear you away from a deeply held faith. Three years later, I delivered a seamless rendering of Hebrew Scripture at my bar mitzvah ceremony, supplemented by a light-hearted speech my father wrote for the afternoon reception in a nearby catering hall.

Despite the scripted jokes about a squeaky-voiced thirteen-year-old coming into "manhood," my father took Jewish identity seriously. Time after time in a period shadowed by ghosts of the Third Reich, he urged both Michael and me never to forget who we were or where we came from. I had no problem with this admonition. Yet I had little interest in religion. When President Dwight D. Eisenhower placed the words "under God" in the Pledge of Allegiance in 1953, I refused to recite them on principle. By the time I got to high school, I found it hard to take seriously any belief in a personal God when every society and sect seemed to insist its own deity was supreme and universal.

Since my interest in the Yellow Springs churches was mainly cultural, not inspirational, therefore, I soon tired of bland services, watered down coffee, and stale donuts. Besides, I found other ways to spend free time. This included serving as a proofreader for the weekly *Antioch Record* and co-hosting "Around the Town," an innocuous five-minute spot on the college radio station devoted to announcements of community cultural events, potlucks, and benefits. The Little Art Theater, the eight-seat-wide local movie house featuring exotic foreign films by Ingmar Bergman and the French New Wave, provided a slightly more elevated diversion.

Fortunately, Yellow Springs featured far less pretentious venues. Friday and Saturday nights often found me sharing 3.2 percent beer with my dorm mates at the Trail Tavern. The selections on the classic Trail jukebox ranged from the sounds of Mose Allison, whose sparse country phrasings and staccato jazz piano were considered the ultimate in late-'50s hip, to Miles Davis, whose understated and muted trumpet epitomized the "cool" jazz of the period. The jukebox at legendary Com's, a fried chicken joint and tavern on the west side of town catering to a more adventurous crowd, offered early "soul" hits by Ray Charles, Lloyd Price, and others, accompanied by ample portions of the house specialty served by the congenial and maternal black co-proprietor "Goldie," nicknamed for her fillings.

YPSILANTI COUNTY

Just as Antioch's first-year students acclimated to the routines of campus life, half the class had to choose winter-term cooperative work assignments. Beyond training for an academic specialty, the program sought to provide general experience as part of a liberal education. Merging my interests in psychology and social studies, I accepted a position in the editing department of the Survey Research Center at the University of Michigan at Ann Arbor. For forty dollars a week, four of us from Antioch were to code consumer-sentiment questionnaires for processing by IBM computers.

The job program sought to compensate for the insular nature of a small college by forcing students to engage the world at large. This included learning how to land on your feet and survive in a strange city. I was glad when biology major Eric Knowles agreed to share lodgings with me. As elderly rooming house proprietors led us up one musty, carpeted stairway after another in Victorian rooming houses adorned with over-polished mahogany railings, however, we despaired of finding the bohemian-styled quarters our free souls demanded. Finally, we stumbled upon a dilapidated building scheduled for demolition. Delighted that we could rent a barely furnished upstairs room at nominal cost and walk to a nearby meals cooperative, we decorated the space with free travel posters and set up my new portable record player.

By now, Joan Baez was the rage among folk music fans who contrasted her pristine renditions of traditional British and southern American ballads with commercial pop culture. In what my brother later described as my "Brandenburg period," I also developed a taste for the Baroque classics. During evenings, however, Eric and I fused our folk music aesthetic with more mundane longings. Almost nightly, we took to hanging out at a run-down house rented by a mixed-racial couple who hosted hootenannies jammed with wispy bohemian college girls decked out in the black skirts, turtlenecks, fishnet stockings, and white tennis shoes favored by Baez devotees. I even escorted one of these beauties to a university hockey match, although when I clumsily tripped over my date's metal folding chair, the evening was never the same.

With one exception, the job at Survey Research was the first and only 9-to-5 position I ever held. Mainly, it taught me how small a percentage of Americans had personal savings and the enormous indebtedness of most families. Beyond that, the center provided an important lesson on electoral politics. Several co-workers were the spouses of University of Michigan faculty. One day during break, I made a caustic comment about President Eisenhower.

"Why don't you help us do some organizing for the Democrats?" the wife of a prominent political scientist challenged.

At a loss to come up with an excuse, I consented.

That Saturday, I found myself riding around rural Ypsilanti County with a reticent old farmer in thigh-high rubber boots. As a canvasser, I was to encourage prospective voters to take Democratic Party literature and ask their opinion of the leading presidential contenders. At one weathered farmhouse, a bedraggled young mother came to the front door with several dirty children in tow. When I asked if she supported John F. Kennedy, the first Roman Catholic frontrunner for the nomination since 1928, she looked me directly in the eye and responded with a gentle demurral:

"Oh, no – we're Baptists, you know."

DEEP IN MY HEART

Back on campus in the spring of 1960, my earlier experience as a proofreader for the student newspaper qualified me for minor reporting assignments. The first involved a talk by David McReynolds, a Socialist Party and War Resisters League organizer on tour for the Student Peace Union, recently established on thirty midwestern campuses. Addressing a crowd of thirty people, the speaker introduced the concept of the Triple Revolution, encompassing the massive upheavals in industrial, technological, and social class relations predicted for the 1960s. McReynolds had faith that society could devote itself to human needs rather than merely material ones. In this regard, young people would play a crucial role. Because the older generation could not grapple with issues such as the escalating arms race, he warned, students should not believe that someone else would solve their problems.

Attracted as I was to the Student Peace Union's call for unilateral U.S. nuclear disarmament, I hesitated to become a full-fledged activist. This led to a compromise – I would approach the issue as a journalist. On Memorial Day, I joined a march of 150 demonstrators, including forty Antioch students, on a thirteen-mile "Walk for Peace" from nearby Wright-Patterson Air Force Base to the Dayton Public Library. My story described the protest beginning with a prayer at the base entrance and the singing of "We Shall Overcome."

Getting There

The hymn, I noted, was "quickly becoming the theme song of social protest in America."

I had ample cause to make such an assertion. Earlier that term, I had run into Assistant Editor Vic Moll at the college coffee shop. If I could find a camera, Vic said, I could accompany him to Nashville, the site of lunch counter sit-ins that had dominated the news for months.

Like most Americans, I had a textured relationship with the realities of race. My mother remembered how a kindly older woman had stopped to admire my curly brown hair and long eyelashes as I toddled along the sidewalks of the Bronx at age four.

"What a lovely little boy!" the stranger exclaimed, "But sweetheart, what are you doing in *this* neighborhood?"

As my mother realized the woman had taken her dark-skinned and kinky-haired son for a "Negro," she bristled and abruptly grabbed my hand. At home, I had won the devotion of Agnes, the elderly Jamaican woman who cleaned our apartment once a week after my mother developed an allergy to detergents. During an elevated subway ride across Harlem on an excursion one day, my father had instructed me never to use disrespectful language to describe the poor "colored" people on the sidewalks below. Like many of my friends, I was under strict orders to substitute the phrase, "catch a *tiger* by the toe," for the derogatory racial slur normally employed in choosing sides in street games.

Whatever my intentions, I remained frightened by Joe, the huge, gruff, slow-moving black building janitor who wore oversized denim overalls and never uttered a word. As Joe hosed down the front sidewalk one day, his bulky hand grabbed a lifeless robin. The bird probably had crashed against a windowpane. Yet my peers and I imagined the giant had suffocated the creature out of pure malevolence.

One Saturday around Christmas, I accompanied my father as he mounted my Lionel model train tracks onto a piece of plywood in the basement workroom. Not long after he left to retrieve a tool, I heard Joe shuffling out the door of his adjoining quarters. Cursing under his breath and likely furious at the pounding that had interrupted a midday weekend nap, he overturned the plywood with a resounding crash.

Infuriated by this outrage, I delivered a forceful kick to the intruder's rear. Enraged by the attack, he turned around and began stumbling toward me like a zombie, emitting guttural sounds as his arms reached out to grab me. I retreated in complete panic – screaming, crying, and nearly tripping over my legs as I frantically ran down the dingy central passageway toward the storage room.

Just then, my father emerged from the elevator.

"I left you alone for two minutes!" he yelled, as if holding me responsible for the sight before his eyes.

By seventh grade, my horizons had begun to broaden. I distinctly recall my social studies teacher's solemn announcement that on May 17, 1954, the U.S. Supreme Court had declared racial segregation unconstitutional in public schools. Subsequently keyed into civil rights by Uncle Mickey's activities, I responded in my senior year of high school when Nancy Kurshan chartered a bus to Washington, D.C., and recruited volunteers to attend a national youth mobilization to support public school integration. We returned in May 1959 with twenty-six thousand others to hear a host of speakers, including a youthful Rev. Martin Luther King, Jr. Yet the most inspiring moment of the trip came when groups of black people on the streets of Washington waved to us in support as our bus made its way to the Capitol Mall.

I never did find a camera, but Vic said there was room in his VW bug if I wanted to go to Nashville. Since February, over seven hundred black students from local colleges and seminaries had submitted to arrest for refusing to leave segregated lunch counters. Trained in nonviolence by civil rights leader Rev. James Lawson, activists including John Lewis and Diane Nash had created a grassroots student movement. Once the local African-American clergy organized a "selective buying" campaign, the city government permitted retail outlets to integrate their luncheonettes.

Once in Nashville, Vic and I stayed at the home of Dave Crippens, a black student at Antioch whose father taught at one of the historically African-American colleges. The next morning, our team paid a visit to Alexander Looby, the black lawyer who had orchestrated the legal defense of the arrested students and had his house dynamited in response. When we left the office, the VW had disappeared from its parking space. Once we flagged down a passing motorcycle cop, he circled around us slowly before coming to a stop.

"Y'all most likely been towed," he drawled, mentioning the name of a garage.

When we asked where that might be, he responded with an uncontainable grin:

"Oh, that's way over in n----r town."

We politely thanked the officer and headed across town to reclaim our wheels.

From there we visited a white liberal theology professor at Vanderbilt University.

In unmistakable terms, he described the college as a "smug, white, middle-class institution where smug white southerners sent their smug white children to meet smug future husbands and wives to produce smug white little southerners."

To appreciate the importance of the local black pastors, we attended a Baptist church service on Sunday morning and discreetly took seats in the rear. To our embarrassment, however, the minister insisted that we stand up so that the congregation could applaud our "courage" in coming down to support their young folk, a tribute we saw as completely unwarranted.

The most exciting part of the trip involved conversations with protesters themselves.

"We didn't break any law – only southern tradition and policy," one activist told us. "The essence of racism is the refusal of the white man to treat the Negro as a person."

The sentiments of the civil rights crusade seemed so self-evident and the dignity of its leaders and participants so inspiring that it was impossible not to feel like a convert. Any pretension of objectivity completely evaporated on our last day when we gathered at the seminary. With the young men in white shirts, solid-color ties, and conservative dark suits and the women in modest Sunday attire, it felt as if we were in church. Then the meeting reached a peak of quiet fervor when Guy Carawan, a white folksinger in blue denim and shirtsleeves, drew the assembly into a circle to clasp hands and lead us in "We Shall Overcome."

This was the first time I had heard the hymn.

"Deep in my heart, I do believe ..." we joined in unison in trembling voices.

It felt as if the serene solidarity of that moment would stay with us forever.

BRANCHING OUT

(1960-1963)

take these sunken eyes and learn to see
— J. Lennon/P. McCartney

Riding back from Nashville in the spring of 1960 with my compilation of notes, I thought of how John Dos Passos had incorporated newspaper headlines, speech excerpts, and popular culture snippets into the documentary "Newsreels" of his trilogy *U.S.A.* Once on campus, I assembled a suitable collage of quotes, which the *Antioch Record* ran as a sidebar to Vic Moll's lead feature.

"The Nashville Story – the story of race clash, of violence, of victory," read the promo, "*told in the words of those who were there as recorded by RECORD staffer Dave Horowitz.*"

PASSIONS

I had published my first creative work of historical prose. Yet my commitment to civil rights did not proceed smoothly. Two of my dorm mates commented that Nashville had ruined me by turning me into one of Eric Hoffer's ideological true believers. The teaching assistant in my spring term social psychology class may have agreed: when my final paper sought to use the sit-ins as an example of a utopian community, I received a lackluster C+.

That summer, I pursued my interest in psychology as a counselor at a Federation of Jewish Philanthropies summer camp for emotionally disturbed boys. Back at Antioch in the fall, however, my focus began to waver. Sharing a suite in an old house on the edge of campus with history majors Chris Lutz and Ade Bennett, I learned about Louis Filler. Fresh from receiving a B.A. from Columbia University in the late-1930s, Filler had published the definitive study of early twentieth century Progressive reform journalists. My roommates described how the professor mesmerized his classes with anecdotes and stories that humanized historical figures.

"You ought to come and listen," Chris advised in understated New England cadence.

Attending Filler's lectures was unlike any classroom experience I ever had encountered. About thirty seconds late, a full-figured fifty-year-old blur of motion rushed into the hall, sheaves of papers protruding from notebooks and loose-leaf binders, glasses slipping from his nose, his short hair in disarray. Without missing a beat, he began, as if in the middle of a sentence. Filler brought unknown figures such as Josiah ("Cigarette") Flynt to life, describing the turn-of-the-century journalist who rode the rails, dined with European royalty, and wrote about urban America's growing crime and vice syndicates.

"Crime is like water," Filler quoted Flynt, "it seeps from the top."

I particularly relished hearing about "muckraking" journalist Lincoln Steffens, who insisted that common thieves, underworld bosses, and lowly politicians could be just as noble as high-minded figures such as tenement housing reformer Jacob Riis or even Theodore Roosevelt (his best friends called him "Theo," never "Teddy," Filler warned). It was intriguing to learn that Steffens had reassured a dying political boss he would go to heaven despite his sins. Enchanted by Louis Filler's charm, intellect, and theatrics, I attended the course regularly. The lures of history had captured me.

Outside class, the presidential election dominated the news. At the behest of former dorm mate Phil Schaefer, a stocky, bespectacled, and friendly fellow from Queens with a booming voice and a passion for politics, I had joined a campus group supporting the abortive presidential primary campaign of civil rights liberal Hubert Humphrey. Now, with Democratic nominee John Kennedy set to address a rally at Springfield's Wittenberg College, I accompanied 150 protestors from Antioch and nearby African-American colleges to press the candidate to speak out on racial segregation and disenfranchisement. Given the moral purity I now brought to these issues, I learned something about the art of politics. To everyone's surprise, Kennedy praised the demonstrators for invoking the American right to protest in a commendable cause and promised to make federal appointments without regard to race or ethnicity.

MUSIC MEN

I listened to President Kennedy's inaugural address over the radio in Rochester, New York. It was January 1961 and I had just become the first Antioch co-op job student assigned to the Baden Street Settlement House in the heart of the city's black ghetto. Reporting early on my first day, I scouted the neighborhood – the first suggestion my supervisor made at our initial meeting. One of my responsibilities was to enroll a half-dozen ten to twelve year olds in a boys' club designed to enhance cultural horizons through weekly field trips to the symphony hall, local museums, and colleges. I also agreed to play piano for a boys' singing group.

Although I always had struggled to carry a tune, music had been a constant presence in my life. Family lore held that the black swing musicians at my grandparents' Lake Huntington establishment had serenaded me on their shoulders on my first birthday. My parents recalled that at age three, I used to sway back and forth to Beethoven and Brahms symphonies in my little rocking chair. I soon moved on to vocals by Al Jolson, Bing Crosby, Burl Ives, and especially Judy Garland, whose bluesy rendition of "The Atchison, Topeka, and the Santa Fe" became a favorite. When Uncle Mickey and Grandpa Nat became the proprietors of a bar on Manhattan's Upper West Side following World War II, I fixated on the bass lines of the rhythmic tunes on the booming jukebox.

Seeking to cultivate my musical tastes, my parents had bought me a children's classical record album called "Rusty and his Piano." Yet my keyboard interests did not blossom until I was eight, when the staff at my East Bronx summer day camp put on a season-ending show. As I watched the counselor at the upright keyboard feeding sparsely placed chords to a striking female balladeer delivering a languid torch song, I knew I wanted to be a piano player.

Under the tutelage of "Uncle Charlie" Kingsford, my father's musical collaborator, I began taking lessons in the fall of 1949. Each Saturday, my dad escorted me on the subway to Charlie's studio, located on the top floor of a West 57th Street walk-up above the Russian Tea Room next door to Carnegie Hall. I began practicing at home with a toy keyboard. Once my parents bought a pre-World War II studio upright, I rehearsed my lessons with a wind-up clock inches away. I had stipulated that if no one pestered me, I would devote an hour a day to practicing. Although Charlie warned my father that I had no sense of rhythm, he sustained my interest by teaching me a popular song at the end of each session. A sixth-grade friend had shown me how to improvise off chord names. My father now treated me to two fifty-cent popular sheet music selections each week at the Carl Fischer store across the street from Charlie's studio.

Then I discovered rock 'n' roll.

The awakening dated back to the summer of 1954, the third season our family spent at a Catskill Mountain bungalow colony near White Lake. Once my friends and I made the half-mile trek to Jo-Jean's crossroads ice cream stand, I watched the girls in tight pedal pushers sway to pulsating jukebox hits. Bill Haley's "Shake, Rattle, and Roll" was my favorite. Invited to Bronx pal Tommy Schumacher's apartment the following New Year's Eve, I heard the rhythm and blues originals that Haley and other white artists were imitating. The rough, murky, and smoky songs coming over the radio, rendered by hoarse black voices, moaning saxophones, sparse rhythm guitars, and offbeat accents, hinted at a strange new world that completely intrigued me.

We were listening to the Alan Freed Show.

By the end of the evening, I was a rock 'n' roll fanatic. I could not get enough of Chuck Berry, Fats Domino, Little Richard, and the "late, great" Johnny Ace. A year later, my best friend Ira Stein and I made it to the Brooklyn Paramount for one of Freed's live stage shows. Not surprisingly, this newly acquired taste devastated my parents, who still insisted on subjecting the family to radio broadcasts of New York's Metropolitan Opera every Saturday afternoon. I was far from a rock 'n' roll rebel, since I had no experience with dancing or girls. Yet I was proud of the fact that only three of us in an eighth-grade English class debate had the courage to defend our generation's music against the accusation that it contributed to juvenile delinquency.

My dedication to rock 'n' roll waned during high school amid a sea of bland white posers. Then classmate and trombone player Dave Lubin, my partner in a summer yard care business, introduced Richard Koppleman, a bespectacled and wiry clarinetist who had contacts for dance band gigs. For thirty dollars, Koppleman secured me a copy of the two-volume "fake book" serving professional musicians with melody lines, lyrics, and chord names for pop standards. Then Dave came up with a drummer – blond-haired Wheatley High classmate Stu Anderson. My father christened us "The Music Men," a play on the title of a current Broadway musical. True to his word, Koppleman produced dates for his mother's office party under the Jones Beach boardwalk, a cousin's West Bronx bar mitzvah, an Irish-Czech wedding party on the top floor of a Long Island firehouse, and a youth group dance at the Temple, where Stu caused a sensation among the Jewish girls.

CHOICES

With leads from the Rochester settlement staff, I recruited six boys into my vocal group. Seeking to expand their tastes beyond the classic rock 'n' roll I banged out on the piano, I introduced a set of folk songs and railroad ballads. This only confused matters.

"Are you black or what?" one of the crew finally asked.

When I answered, he had difficulty understanding what I was doing there.

Later that winter, the local newspaper ran a story on Baden Street that featured a photo of my singing group gathered around the piano.

My most important assignment, however, was to administer the tutorial program initiated by O. H. Lester, the settlement's African-American social worker. O.H. wanted to use university students to help inner-city high school youth pass basic subjects such as math and English and motivate them to go on to college, which he saw as the best route out of the ghetto. I began by decorating the tutorial room with giveaway travel posters, scored several second-hand lamps and tables, and even brought in a portable phonograph for quiet classical music. Then I took out a free advertisement in the University of Rochester student newspaper that announced the program's acceptance of "a few applications" for additional tutors. Within a week, the program had as many mentors as it would need.

I returned to campus in the spring of 1961 as national political developments intensified. By then, a Fair Play for Cuba Committee had attracted several of the most highly energized Antioch politicos. Even my friend Margie Ross, a fellow Survey Research editor and black political moderate, was sympathetic to the cause. When I confessed I was ambivalent about Fidel Castro's suppression of civil liberties, Margie delivered a tongue-lashing.

"Come on, David," she scolded, "don't be such an old lady. This is a revolution!"

One morning in April, my dorm mates and I heard a radio news report about a dramatic landing of invading exiles on Cuban shores and the imminent demise of Havana's pro-communist regime. A subsequent broadcast even described a Fidel Castro sighting in Mexico City. Days later, Chris Lutz showed off a letter his father had published in New York's *Village Voice* with the first reference I had seen to the "Bay of Pigs" and CIA involvement in the operation. Meanwhile, campus civil rights groups were seeking volunteers to join a set of Freedom Rides to test federal rulings to desegregate interstate bus travel in the South. At this point, however, I decided to keep my focus on studies. I would pursue a commitment to racial justice by returning to Baden Street for an anticipated second stint in the summer, I reasoned. Yet even this plan encountered obstacles.

Having overcome a lackluster history in the work force with belated success as a sales rep, my father fretted that the settlement house experience would set me up for a low-status career as a social worker. In the end, the unrelenting pressure from home wore me down until I agreed to request another assignment. Co-op job supervisors responded with a position as a psychiatric aide at McLean Hospital outside Boston with the stipulation that I return winter term.

Although the McLean post did not offer the autonomy I enjoyed in Rochester, it provided a lucrative learning experience. During the two-week training session conducted by a well-seasoned psychiatric nursing supervisor, we learned there was no distinct line between sanity and insanity. Mental illness, she insisted, was nothing to be ashamed or frightened of and was just as pervasive as any physical ailment. Aides were to assist the professional staff without making independent diagnoses and were to be supportive of patients' needs but not play favorites or get too close. Finally, our blunt trainer was adamant about the need for apprentices like us to forget about psychiatric labels and rely on common sense instead.

Unlike nursing assistants, psychiatric aides did not clean rooms, make beds, service bedpans, deliver meals, or dress patients. We were to escort people to appointments, engage residents in light conversation, and participate in ping pong matches or board games while helping to coordinate social activities. Assigned to a women's unit, where most everyone suffered from depression, I was surprised to find how patients looked after each other. Their leader, a middle-aged Jewish woman on to my youthful inexperience, was superb at bracketing cheerful references to "Mr. Horowitz" with good-humored but relentless teasing.

Like the Federation camp, McLean complemented my interest in psychology just as my mother prepared to start a career as a grade school guidance counselor. Yet academic ventures in the field baffled me. In my Social Psychology of Utopian Communities course, I had felt frustrated by the Buddha-like professor who sometimes sat silently before the class waiting for students to say what they wanted to know. Discussion sections involving the teaching assistant and a few souls left me baffled by obtuse concepts such as the "I-Thou" relationship in the works of Jewish theologian Martin Buber. My second psychology course, Approaches to Human Behavior, featured a young instructor who wore neatly ironed button-down blue-denim work shirts, thin ties, and tasteful sports jackets to match his trim blue jeans. Unfortunately, the professor's emphasis on behavioral science failed to engage me, leaving me with a mediocre C for my efforts.

After two years of college, I began to realize that my real concerns centered on social history and the world of ideas. The term paper for my Conservation course, for example, portrayed free-market criticism of the public power projects of the New Deal's Tennessee Valley Authority (TVA). In art history, my final essay focused on the "Ashcan" School of urban realism among early twentieth century American painters. To inaugurate my third year, therefore, I decided to enroll in Louis Filler's Intro to American Civilization.

The primary text for the course was Charles and Mary Beard's *Rise of American Civilization* (1927), a progressive classic whose portraits of ordinary dirt farmers, artisans, and democratic icons such as Tom Paine, Thomas Jefferson, and Andrew Jackson read like fiction. Filler filled in the narrative with a dash of cynicism, referring repeatedly to "the horny-handed sons of toil" who provided the mythic material of the American Dream and agrarian frontier. The term's work climaxed with the reform era of 1830-1860, Filler's new specialty. Profiling the single-mindedness of figures such as Ralph Waldo Emerson, Henry David Thoreau, and abolitionist William Lloyd Garrison, we got the impression that giants walked the earth in the tumultuous days before the Civil War and the ultimate assault on slavery.

"I will be heard!" the mighty Garrison had declared.

Back at McLean that winter, a new assignment placed me on a men's unit named for late-nineteenth century purity crusader Anthony Comstock. Part of my duties required me to accompany an eighteen-year-old jazz musician on retreats to the cellar where he whaled away at a drum set in hour-long practice sessions designed to vent his rage. Sometimes I escorted people on field trips, including one in which a patient about my age visited friends in Cambridge.

"This is my shrink," he nodded toward me as we entered an apartment full of bohemian characters who could easily have been my classmates.

I spent a good deal of time on the floor with a gentle blonde-haired albino man in his early forties who taught me jazz-styled piano chording. Returning after a weekend off, I learned he had committed suicide by smothering himself to death with a pillowcase. My most pressing challenge arose the day I heard a crash of glass coming from the room of a nineteen-year-old, self-styled hipster. As I came through the door, he glared and asked what I was doing there.

The next thing I knew, he had the jagged edge of a broken coke bottle against my throat.

Sensing he meant no harm, I somehow relaxed and remained silent.

Within seconds, the patient's favorite nurse rushed in and quietly indicated she would take care of things. At that, my captor allowed me to make a discreet withdrawal.

HOUSE OF FRIENDSHIP

Filled with anticipation, I trudged across the gangplank of the student ship *Aurelia*, the smallest passenger vessel on the Atlantic, onto the docks of Le Havre, France, at 4:30 a.m. It was June 1962. As part of Antioch Education Abroad, I was on my way to a co-op job in the French countryside as a prelude to a year of study at England's University of Leeds. Relishing the prospect of new experiences, I imagined that the port signs and animated commands of the beret-clad stevedores were a theatrical set created by an energetic French language instructor. Soon fellow history student Jeff Brooks and I were on a train speeding through the Normandy countryside. By late morning, we had arrived at the North Paris depot, where we purchased a map and found our way on the Metro to the city's Latin Quarter – the Left Bank of the Seine.

It did not take long to learn how to negotiate for rooms in the student district's cheap hotels, many still with squatting toilets. We soon adapted to breakfasts of flaky croissants and whipped-cream-topped *café au lait*, thirty-cent lunches of Algerian *couscous* (bowls of lamb and rice), and veal or chicken dinners served with bottles of wine at half the price of a small coke. Exploring the city by foot, Jeff and I acclimated to the frenzied rhythms of European traffic and discovered the semi-enclosed urinals on public squares. When we tired of walking, we rode the open-air platforms of the diesel buses. On Bastille Day, we followed a student mob celebrating in the streets until the crowd descended upon a flashy American convertible. Fearing the worst, we laughed in relief when the owner turned out to be a large smiling black man who elicited cheers and calls for a speech as he drove off with a wave. Rocking cars and exploding firecrackers, the students proceeded to taunt the police with cries of "to the sewers."

After ten days in Paris, I left by train for Chambon sur Cisse, a small village in the Loire Valley wine country. I was bound for the Foyer Amitié (House of Friendship), a Quaker home and watchmaker's apprentice shop for socially maladjusted boys. I was to serve as an itinerant Big Brother and do assorted tasks for the director, Monsieur Marcel Fourget. As I descended from the train at Blois, a friendly-looking woman in wire-rimmed glasses tapped me on the rear shoulder and introduced herself as Madame Fourget.

Driven to the Foyer in a sputtering *Deux Chevaux* (two-horsepower Citroën), I followed my hosts to a suite above the kitchen. Suddenly, a rapid-fire argument broke out. As I gazed self-consciously at photographs on the wall, Mme. Fourget smiled and explained, *"problemes."* Minutes later, she escorted me down the road to an ancient stone structure, a former chateau guardhouse, where a toothless old woman led us up narrow stairs to a huge door with a metal key extending from the bolt. Behind it was a spacious room with a weathered tile floor, a disused fireplace, a single electric bulb dangling on a cord from the high ceiling, and a porcelain washbasin resting on a rickety table. This was to be my home for the next two months.

My primitive French language skills (I had managed only a C- in third term French) prevented me from realizing that the room above the Foyer kitchen provided a rendezvous for M. Fourget's sister and the watch-making instructor, a Roman Catholic the Quaker family deemed unsuitable for marriage. In return for my lodgings, I would spend half the summer scything a nearby pasture for eventual conversion to an athletic field. At first, only two apprentices remained on the grounds: Bernard, a fifteen-year-old streetwise Parisian, and Omar, a somewhat younger Algerian. Our first task was to erect a tent for visiting work campers. This involved clearing and leveling a large space on a steep and rocky hill, constructing a stairway of small branches and packed dirt, digging a drainage ditch by picking through solid rock, and mounting the canvas tent and supplying it with beds and tables.

The most ludicrous part of the assignment involved attempts to motivate Bernard and Omar to work.

"C'est necessaire," I helplessly repeated in fractured French to their undisguised howls.

Energizing fourteen teenage work campers from English Quaker schools proved no less difficult. All the same, we finished clearing the field, began digging a three-foot pit for an indoor furnace at the Foyer, and started construction on a two hundred foot water line. Asleep by eleven, I arose well before breakfast to the crowing of roosters and strolled down the hill to play classical music on a portable phonograph. Pocket French dictionary in hand, I made my way each morning through the pages of Romain Rolland's epic novel, *Jean-Christophe.*

The summer routine generated a new sense of serenity and self-confidence. I attributed much of this inspiration to Marcel Fourget. A slightly built, balding man of perennial optimism and energy, Marcel was completely sure of who he was, utterly selfless in his intentions, and capable of taking any problem in stride. On my twenty-first birthday, a milestone I chose to keep to myself, I wrote my parents that I had learned that peace of mind was far more important than material reward, an untested statement of faith that would resonate throughout the decade.

RED BRICK

Mid-September found me leaping out of the cab of a huge lorry and bidding farewell to the friendly Yorkshire driver who had brought me from the outskirts of London to the industrial hub of Leeds. I had spent the past three weeks traveling through France with Judy, an Antioch friend who taught me the ins and outs of hitchhiking and finding reasonable accommodations. Now, however, it appeared that my free-spirited adventures were on hold. Because university dormitories were full, I would have to lodge off-campus. This meant rooming with Stan, a former Antioch hallmate, in the undistinguished brick duplex belonging to a childless, penny-pinching middle-aged couple who took in only Jewish students. To compensate for the "middle-class" surroundings, I bought a colorful Renoir print and hung it on the wall of the bedroom.

Whatever the letdown from my quest for exotic experience and the grayness and frequent fogs of Leeds skies, I relished the university's intellectual life. I found to my delight that a recommended criminology course offered a historical overview of concepts of crime and punishment rooted in Enlightenment notions of rehabilitation and the advent of the penitentiary. When the class addressed juvenile delinquency in Britain and the United States, moreover, the casual pipe-smoking instructor wanted to hear about my experiences at

Baden Street. Most of my work, however, revolved around two British history courses, providing the chance to devour the highly readable narratives of social historians such as George M. Trevelyan.

Letters home now outlined an interest in the historical context of human endeavor and a scholarly career. I imagined that academic communities fostered the individual freedom and tolerance of unconventional values I had come to cherish. Much of my euphoria had to do with the vibrant political culture at Leeds. The university was a provincial "red brick" institution that catered to northern England's working class and had a reputation as one of the most politically active schools in the country. This became clear when two women presiding at the Labour Party's Registration Day information booth invited me to their table for coffee. A year earlier, Antioch students Mike Ross and geology major Stephen J. Gould (then just "Steve") had organized the Leeds anti-nuclear arms movement. This coincidence opened the door to an assortment of social democrats, liberals, Marxists, communists, peace activists, and antiracists.

Taking advantage of new friendships and enhanced mobility afforded by the purchase of a used Lambretta scooter, I dove into a vast array of political meetings, films, lectures, and social events. This included membership in the Leeds Folk Music Club, which held boisterous weekly meetings in the upstairs loft of a downtown pub. Sampling huge quantities of English room-temperature beer, we sang Negro spirituals and work songs, American bluegrass, Woody Guthrie Dust Bowl ballads, Scots-Irish tunes, Renaissance airs, and political ditties. My folk music exposure in Roslyn Heights and at Antioch now served me well.

The Cuban missile crisis of October 1962 conveyed a far more serious tone. I found myself among a hastily mobilized group intent on drafting telegrams to both Soviet and American embassies with the heading, "No War Over Cuba." When someone asked for writing paper, I volunteered my notebook. In a letter home, I agreed that President Kennedy was justified in calling for the elimination of Soviet missile bases in Cuba but warned that the risks a U.S. blockade posed to nuclear confrontation were too great. From the relative safety of Great Britain, I declared that America's "holier than thou" obsessions were in danger of destroying the world.

My cavalier dismissal of U.S. concerns did not go down well at home. Michael may have spoken for the family when he invoked the political realism he had absorbed in high school with a defense of Kennedy's efforts to protect American national security. In truth, my espousal of radical generalities could not hide the fact that I frequently found the posturing of Leeds cohorts rather burdensome. When I accompanied several friends to Cambridge for a conference on educational reform, I cringed when I heard a speaker vow that England would never be free until its ancient centers of learning were no more. As a would-be populist, I found it hard to bear the condescending taunts our group attracted from a table of Cambridge upperclassmen at a local pub. I also sympathized with the desire to overhaul the British policy of "streaming," which selected elite students for university training and consigned the rest to vocational pursuits. Yet destroying some of the world's most illustrious centers of knowledge did not seem helpful.

The vulnerabilities of Marxist ideology surfaced in a debate between a British sociologist and an American philosophy of science professor.

"What 'science' has remained unchanged for one hundred years?" the American asked.

On another occasion, a conversation about avant-garde African-American jazz pianist Thelonious Monk left me wondering. I had once read an account of the crowded Manhattan apartment where the musician and his family lived, partly a result of Monk's refusal to make artistic compromises. When a socialist friend accused the performer of being in it for the money, I attributed the comment to complete ignorance. Not long after, I witnessed the excesses of sectarianism at a party thrown by a wealthy Ceylonese biochemistry student and abstract painter who also was a communist.

Asked to lead the crowd in American "proletariat" songs, I easily obliged. Then around midnight, a brick sailed through the front window, followed minutes later by the arrival of a local contingent of Trotskyists, the communists' historic socialist adversary. After some pushing and loud banging of doors, the "Trots" vanished into the thick mist taunting their rivals with cries of "traitors to the working class."

OLD WORLD/NEW WORLD

Christmas break brought me to the Continent, where I caught an opera in Paris before moving south to Italy. After hiking across the hills of sunny Genoa, I took in the Renaissance art classics of Florence and stayed at a youth hostel once serving as the palace for fascist dictator Benito Mussolini's mistress. My next stop was Venice, where I absorbed the mysterious ambiance of the canals with nightly walks along the city's shadowy alleys. From there, I caught the train to Munich, where I spent hours trying to reconcile the apparent normalcy of the bustling and youthful city with its role as the site of Adolf Hitler's largest rallies. At that point, Germany's Third Reich was a bare seventeen years in the past.

Back in Leeds for winter term, I moved to a room in a newly renovated student building, where I shared a kitchen and bathroom with two Turks and their exquisite live-in British girlfriends. Within days of moving in, I received a visit from Antioch's Phil Schaefer, about to begin a stint at the London School of Economics. On twenty-four hours' notice, I improvised a housewarming event, enticing some seventy friends from the political Left to the crowded room where Phil became the focal point of the evening.

For five boisterous hours, the energized visitor single-handedly held off revolving hordes of socialists and radicals in continuous debate. As I sliced servings of cheese and fruit, I could hear familiar voices talking of the "working class" while Schaefer's rich baritone countered with defenses of "American democracy" and "our fine President."

"Oh, we had fun!" Phil exclaimed as he rubbed his hands at the evening's conclusion.

I felt compelled to acknowledge my former dorm mate's tour de force as the best that American liberalism had to offer. At the same time, the rigid class structure of British society helped to explain the radicalism to which many of my friends clung.

One evening, I answered a knock at the front door of the flat to find two well-dressed gents standing with a short, pert elderly woman.

"How do you do," one of the men began.

"Did Mr. Auden tell you we were coming? This is Lady Morris."

I gulped.

Rubbing shoulders with British nobility was a long way from the West Bronx.

I had heard about the vice chancellor's wife paying a visit to the residence but assumed the inspection already had taken place. She was there to see how students lived in the new university digs. After responding to a request to demonstrate the use of the vacuum cleaner, which none of us had yet deployed, I invited the contingent into my newly cleaned room.

Lady Morris wanted to know how I compared the unit to a hall in America.

"You know, we were there in the Twenties," she explained.

My mind instantly conjured up an image of the well-mannered noblewoman and her husband attending a soirée in the company of F. Scott and Zelda Fitzgerald in what seemed the distant past. When the party left, I heaved a sigh of relief and imagined that the two officials accompanying Lady Morris had done likewise.

As I immersed myself in several classics of British history during winter term, a psychology major seemed more remote than ever. I found R. H. Tawney's monograph on the ties between the Protestant Ethic and the rise of capitalism in seventeenth century England and Holland particularly inspiring. Another gem, G.M. Young's *Portrait of an Age,* rendered the history, ideas, and imagination of

Victorian England in elegant prose. At the same time, my criminology class provided insights into social process through readings that saw delinquent subcultures rooted in the failure of working-class youth to achieve status in conventional society. Despite my efforts at intellectual independence, many of these works seemed to reinforce the critical perspectives conveyed by my friends on the Left.

During spring break, I made it to Rome and found my way to the Foresteria Pellegrino, a converted church serving as a youth hostel. The facility featured tiny cardboard cubicles with bare mattresses and a series of cots along the corridors. Yet accommodations depended upon the whim of the shady operators who ran the place and spoke no English. After waiting an hour with another American, I followed one of the managers through an alley where a door opened to a half-furnished room with two beds and a bathroom. When I returned late one night from a side-trip to Naples, however, there were no vacancies. One of the Italians now led me to the back seat of a Volkswagen Beetle parked on a narrow side street. Without hesitating, I threw my raincoat over my body, used my sleeping bag as a pillow, and curled up my legs for the night. The next day, I awoke at 8 a.m. to secure a cot in the corridor for my last evening in Rome.

After showering that next morning, my heart sank when I discovered that my watch and return train ticket to Paris were gone. Furious at my carelessness, I vowed to hitchhike the entire distance. As I painfully made my way through the spring rains of the Italian Riviera, however, fate seemed to turn when I got a ride in a late-model Chevrolet from a French woman and her daughters who said they once had lived near Roslyn Heights. They had picked me up because they figured French customs would not look through a foreigner's duffle bag to see the Italian purchases they wanted to bring into the country duty-free. My assistance earned an invitation to a birthday party at the family villa in Cannes. To my consternation, however, no one paid any attention to me and I soon thanked my hosts and moved on down the road.

I caught my next ride from a battered station wagon carrying a young house painter and his wife, a schoolteacher dressed in a well-worn rabbit fur coat. They drove me to a communist youth hostel, where I came in on an after-dinner conversation dominated by a striking young Venezuelan woman defending the Cuban revolution. When I intruded with a brief comment in basic French, the fiery Fidelista turned to me.

"*Vous etes un Castroist, monsieur?*" she asked.

Tempted by her ravishing beauty and fervor, I nevertheless clung to my principles.

I supported the *idea* of the revolution, I replied weakly, but had reservations.

At that point she resumed her conversation and never turned my way again.

VINTAGE MOVIES

Returning to London at the end of spring break, I met up with a contingent from Leeds for the annual Aldermaston March for nuclear disarmament. The idea was to work the experience into a community studies paper on the British student Left for Antioch work credit.

"Though I don't have too much faith in appeals for morality in political affairs," I explained in a letter home, "I somehow feel it's important that some people put nuclear-war politics into perspective." Yet I also relayed the reaction of a Trotskyist friend who mocked the "bourgeois" anti-nuclear arms movement and extolled the glory of a "Workers' Bomb."

On the Aldermaston March I was part of an army of fifteen thousand protesters who averaged twenty miles a day on foot, sleeping along the way in tents or school corridors. Amazingly, no trash remained at any stopover while organizers of this virtual city on the move coordinated luggage transports, campsite buses, dispatchers, first-aid workers, radio broadcasters, and newspaper staffers. There was even a group called "Spies for Peace" who distributed alleged "official secret" documents detailing how Britain would set up an underground government following a nuclear war.

Back in Leeds, I prepared for the final exams Antioch required for my un-graded history classes. Since my tutors had responded to my periodic essay assignments with understated but favorable comments, such as "not bad," I had little anxiety about my mastery of the subject matter. With the exams completed, moreover, I had a free block of time before summer. At that point, I came up with idea of a scooter tour to Edinburgh.

My traveling companion was Ruth, a sociology student and regular at the Leeds Folk Music Club. Ironically, Ruth turned out to be the person who reawakened my interest in popular music by introducing me to BBC radio's "third channel," which in 1963 devoted the bulk of airtime to up-and-coming British bands that included Gerry and the Pacemakers, the Dave Clark Five, and the Beatles. The trusty Lambretta soon took the two of us through the picturesque fishing villages of the Northumberland Coast. From there we headed north to Scotland and the sights of Edinburgh before circling back through the stark moor country of the Yorkshire Dales.

After closing up shop in Leeds and accompanying Ruth to her family home in Kent, I was on my way to the Continent again. My destination was a volunteer work camp in northwestern Greece to earn Antioch co-op credit. The trip offered two memorable moments. In German Bavaria, I caught a ride with a congenial middle-aged driver in an upscale sedan. He was on his way to a reunion with former members of his World War II army platoon, a disclosure he conveyed to the American beside him without any self-consciousness. Proceeding south along Italy's Adriatic coast, I slept on the beach near Pescara. Early the next morning, I awoke to the sound of someone urinating against a nearby retaining wall.

It was an old vagrant. Staring at me in curiosity, he asked where I was from.

When I answered in sparse Italian, he shook his head.

It "was not possible," he protested: no American would ever spend the night that way.

That evening, I caught the overnight ferry from Brindisi. Onboard, a series of white-uniformed attendants ceremoniously ushered me to my accommodations, a solitary reclining chair on the outer deck. I was bound for the small Greek port of Igoumenitsa in the northwestern province of Thesprotia to join twenty-five international volunteers affiliated with Britain's United Nations Organization, a non-profit development agency.

My first assignment teamed me up with a thirty-five-year-old Canadian pacifist sandpapering and whitewashing the exterior of the new regional administrative center. Fortunately, the routine afforded ample relief from the mid-summer heat. Breaks included a morning session of Greek lessons, two daily swims in the Adriatic, and convivial group meals with fresh vegetables supplied by "Grandma," a toothless old woman named Normo who wore torn, full-length black leggings and rode a mule into camp each day to sell the garden produce tied to her back. Word was that Normo spoke a Turkish dialect and loved to curse like mad.

Evening walks into town were a particularly attractive part of daily life. We customarily stopped at a stand to sample five-cent glasses of *ouzo,* the licorice-tasting, highly intoxicating national drink served with tiny slices of tomato or cucumber. The locals invariably treated us amiably. Yet on one stroll, an agitated older man approached our group, cursed "the Americans," and spat in my direction. Everyone quickly hustled me down the roadway. I surmised that the outburst stemmed from U.S. support of the pro-British monarchy in the bitterly fought Greek Civil War of 1948, a reminder, once again, of the power of history.

Volunteers were free to use weekends to explore nearby islands, such as Corfu, or proceed northward. After the village grocer acted as a translator at the bus line, several of us joined a group of swarthy farmers for a trip to Filiates, a regional center resting amid the dry limestone mountains immortalized in Lord Byron's poetry. As giggling children stole shy glances at the strange-looking foreigners in their midst and the vehicle negotiated the hairpin turns of a winding, single-lane dirt mountain road at 10 mph, the driver spun Greek folk songs on a portable phonograph and led everyone in boisterous group sings. When we reached the military zone five miles from the border with communist Albania, we had to pass inspection. The bloody history of the region seemed evident in the cliff-hanging "flying monasteries" from which Greek Orthodox villagers had flung themselves during repeated invasions by Muslim Turks. Outside Filiates, we learned about a cave that had been the last communist holdout during the civil war.

During my third week at camp, I joined a team of seven charged with constructing an auxiliary water pipeline to Gera Meri, a small mountain village whose young people had fled for work in Germany. We were to tap a spring three miles away and a thousand feet up the slope – a good three hour's climb. Our cook, a Scots history teacher, prepared our meals on a portable gas stove in the remnants of a stone hut with natural flagstone as flooring. After digging a toilet pit a good distance away, several of us cleared the brush of an old goat pen for sleeping quarters. Our only company was a lone goatherd who provided us with milk and cheese and secured our bread and vegetables on mule treks to the village. We reciprocated with evening card games and ample servings of hot chocolate.

The most magical moments at camp occurred as the sun set thirty miles out to sea and only the tingle of goat bells interrupted the complete silence. Yet by August, I was off to Rome to meet my parents, whom I had not seen for over a year, on the return leg of their first trip to Israel. The posh accommodations of their hotel presented a sharp distinction to open beaches, deck chairs, goat pens, and full days of hard manual labor. Yet the adjustment proved surprisingly easy, especially when the three of us flew across the Alps to Paris and settled in at the Grand Hotel at the Place de l'Opera. More than the luxury, however, my father relished the long walks the two of us took through the city's teeming streets and

Getting There

neighborhoods. Whatever our differences, both of us shared a taste for what I simply called "the oldness of things."

Once my parents returned to the States, I rendezvoused with Ruth for a planned vacation in Spain. We wound up at Benicarlo, a fishing village along the Mediterranean's Costa Brava, where, for forty-five cents a night, we settled into a small rental with whitewashed walls of stone, an overhead grapevine, and a kitchen half-exposed to the sky. Immersed in the languid ambiance of the surroundings, I pored through the pages of Lawrence Durrell's mystical *Justine* amid sensual days on the beach, leisurely ambles through town, extended seafood dinners, *horchata* liquid ice-cream drinks, local pastries, and Spanish folk music in the cafés.

At the end of August, we retreated to Paris, where I had to catch the train for Rotterdam and the ocean voyage back to the States. I dreaded leaving Ruth. Sure enough, when we pulled out of the station and I struggled to wave good-bye with moist eyes and a racing heart, I felt like a soldier leaving for the front in one of those vintage European war movies.

I vowed to make it my business to return to the Continent as soon as possible.

The next day, September 2, 1963, the eighteenth anniversary of Victory over Japan Day and my brother's eighteenth birthday, I set forth for the United States on board the *Groote Beer*, a World War II Dutch transport.

CANOPY

(1963-1965)

there is no reason and the truth is plain to see
— K. Reid

Sitting on the deck of the *Groote Beer*, I took stock. Fifteen months in the Old World had introduced me to an incredible variety of people, a wealth of experience, enhanced self-reliance, and an evolving sense of personal values. My contacts had extended from the rich to the poor, from the industrial working class to the peasantry. I had met communists, social democrats, and conservatives, though my sojourns in autocratic Greece and Franco's Spain suggested that political ideology did not always dominate everyday life. Indeed, working in a French village, surviving on a Greek mountaintop, and extensive study and travel had sensitized me to the norms and rules of particular cultures, enabling me to develop a better understanding of my own. Detailed letters home, in addition, had honed basic narrative writing skills.

At the same time, I was unclear about the future. Could I readjust to American society and the materialism I thought I had outgrown? Was I intent on joining academia as a scholar, and would I choose history and the United States as my field of interest? If I did, I would have to pass muster with Louis Filler, known for eviscerating those who took their obligations too lightly. Even if I gained Filler's support, would I succeed in finding my way to graduate school? Would that, in turn, lead to the sort of academic career I had imagined back in Leeds?

MINUTES AGO

Days after my ship steamed through New York Harbor on September 11, 1963, my father's fifty-fifth birthday, the two of us set out for Yellow Springs in the family car. Once settled in at my new dorm, the first order of business was to visit Louis Filler.

"If you want to *live* and really live – not subsist on social security or something," Filler instructed, "you've got to beat the deadheads at their own game. You've got to have more facts than they, be smarter than they, and do everything they do better. Then you can rebel."

"You have a lot of potential," he responded when I asked him to be my advisor, "but you have many rough edges. We're going to polish off those rough edges."

Through four years of college, I had always chosen a subject that interested me for term papers. To my delight, Filler now agreed to supervise a twelve-credit senior research project on the history of organized crime in the United States.

In November, a visiting political scientist addressed the Antioch community on the application of creative non-conformity to American politics. The speaker received the loudest applause when he taunted New Frontier officials in Washington, D.C., for not sending their children to public schools. Despite President Kennedy's support for a civil rights bill to desegregate public accommodations following police brutality against peaceful black protesters in Birmingham, Alabama, the previous spring, his slow response to the moral imperatives of racial justice had tarnished his record among many liberals. Beyond that, Kennedy's Cold War posturing during the Bay of Pigs and the Cuban missile crisis had not been popular in academia, even in England.

"But of course, Mr. Horowitz, you Yanks are still fighting the Reds," my conservative Leeds tutor had quipped during one discussion of international policy.

During the summer of 1963, Kennedy proposed to limit nuclear arms arsenals and signed a test-ban treaty with the Soviet Union. Yet a degree of intellectual snobbery and radical superiority at Antioch compromised the president's standing.

Days after the political scientist's talk, I had a routine consultation with Louis Filler at his office in Old Main, the college administration building. When we were done, I took my normal shortcut to cross the building along the front seats of the auditorium balcony. There I spotted Robert, a music major classmate, at the grand piano on stage.

"Damn!" he yelled, gazing toward me with a grim smile and shake of the head.

"They're gonna cancel my recital. The goddamn president's been shot."

My mind had difficulty processing what I had just heard.

I immediately imagined a minor wound to the foot, similar to a shooting Theodore Roosevelt once survived.

When I stepped outside the darkened building into broad daylight, however, everything appeared absolutely still.

All I could hear were the sounds of a news broadcast coming from a loudspeaker someone had placed on the fire escape of South Hall, the adjoining women's dormitory.

Almost immediately, TV anchor Walter Cronkite's somber delivery reverberated across the empty plaza.

"Minutes ago," announced Cronkite with a slight crack in his voice, doctors had pronounced President John F. Kennedy dead in Dallas, Texas.

It was November 22, 1963, and it seemed as if the world had turned upside-down.

For hours, I paced the trails of Antioch's nature preserve in Glen Helen.

If *this* could happen in a world in which everything appeared so predictable, I thought, *anything* was possible.

Horrified at the sudden extinction of the president's young and vibrant life, I nevertheless gravitated to a glimmer of hope. To say that nothing was forever set in stone, that the universe was a plastic entity in which chance, accident, and the unforeseen could take place, offered the ultimate prospect that substantive change for the better could occur more rapidly than anyone had anticipated.

Inadvertently, I had stumbled upon the key to the remaining years of the decade.

BARGAINS AND BATTLES

With the assassination occurring in the midst of my reading on violence and criminal activity in American life, the project took on enhanced immediacy. Repairing to Roslyn Heights for Christmas break, I produced a ninety-eight-page paper entitled "By Bargain or By Battle: Organized Crime in the United States, 1880-1917."

Underworld criminality in the modern United States, I argued, arose as a response to state regulations on gambling, prostitution, and liquor consumption. Yet as illegal activity expanded by 1910 into corporations, labor unions, frontier communities, and urban gangs, white-collar crime, racketeering, and extortion became equally as important. American culture helped to facilitate the spread of these activities, I suggested, because customary social restraints and law were relatively relaxed in a society given to a rights-oriented political philosophy and an emphasis on economic individualism. The uprooted nature and rapid pace of change in the United States, I concluded, contributed to the social disorganization manifested in lawlessness. Hence, it was not surprising that underworld crime accounted for 10 percent of gross national income by the 1960s.

The key to understanding persistent violations of law, I insisted, was the realization that segments of "respectful" society were willing to cooperate with it.

"If there was one thing the student has learned from this inquiry," I surmised, "it is that the values, practices, and mores of the so-called underworld precisely mirror those of the society it exploits."

American individualism, I noted, offered the hope that a person could be more than just a cog in the machine of state and industry. Yet I wondered if the nation needed to examine whether hostility to law and social controls fit the needs of modern society. Under the demanding regimen of my mentor, I had broadened an investigation of underworld criminality into a speculative essay on the practice of criminology as well as the strengths and limitations of American culture.

"Great stuff," Filler scribbled on the front page of the completed work.

As promised, my mentor had whipped me into shape, bringing discipline to my work by insisting that typed drafts contain absolutely no errors and that all assertions come with examples and proper citations. In short, Filler made an honest historian of me and honed the skills demonstrated by my personal correspondence into the expository style of professional scholarship. Perhaps his greatest gift was the freedom to deal with the larger issues of inquiry and general matters of culture. If you did your homework, he seemed to imply, the sky was the limit in terms of the questions you could address.

TWO NATIONS

On the train back from New York, I met Lucy Gilbert, a literature major who told me about Bob Dylan, a rising folksinger whose earthy ballads and poetically rendered lyrics conveyed complex emotions and a tortured sense of social justice. I soon picked up a copy of *The Freewheelin' Bob Dylan*. One of the tracks – the apocalyptic "A Hard Rain's A-Gonna Fall" – seemed starkly appropriate after the Kennedy assassination. Not long after, Dylan showed up at the Antioch cafeteria, reportedly looking for women. He appeared shorter than I had imagined.

By early 1964, however, the Beatles, whose name and sound had reminded me of Buddy Holly and the Crickets when I first heard them on the BBC, were calling many "folkies" back to pop music. When the group made its second appearance on the *Ed Sullivan Show* in February, I crowded around the Student Union TV with nearly two hundred others, more than had taken part in the Kennedy vigil. Soon, the esoteric jukebox at the Trail Tavern was playing almost nothing but Beatles tunes. Meanwhile, Friday night "twist" sessions broke out in the cafeteria to the rhythms of Ray Charles "soul."

Beyond the attractions of popular music, Antioch provided generous samplings of folk, jazz, and blues. In addition to the recorded music at outdoor Friday night folk dances, you could run into a bluegrass banjo picker on almost any doorstep or in any hallway. Pickers and strummers showed up to jam at the downtown bakery on Friday nights as patrons waited for fresh loaves of bread to emerge from the ovens at 3 a.m. Antioch "white blues" performers, including Mississippi Delta stylist John Hammond, Jr., also had their following. Meanwhile, late-night jazz sessions with my former roommate Frank Maurer on standup bass soon found their way to the college coffee shop.

At progressive Antioch College, politics were never far behind. Following a year dominated by the Birmingham protests, the admission of two black students to the University of Alabama, the assassination of Mississippi NAACP leader Medgar Evers, the massive March on Washington, and the murder of four black Sunday school students at Birmingham's Sixteenth Street Baptist Church, civil rights continued to be the main story on campus. In April 1964, a student group sponsored a talk by "a militant Negro rights agitator" who predicted it was "gonna be a long hot summer."

By then, Antioch activists already had brought the struggle to Yellow Springs. During winter term, police had deployed riot sticks, tear gas, and fire hoses to attack and arrest forty-two students and sixty-six others when protesters violated a court injunction against demonstrating in front of Lewis Gegner's Barber Shop for its refusal to serve black customers. Ever since I had patronized black barbers in Rochester to cut my curly hair, I had taken my business to the black barber shop in Yellow Springs. Before then, however, I had used the more centrally located Gegner's and received service without trouble. When the white proprietor said he did not know how to cut "kinky" hair, therefore, I knew that was not true. Nevertheless, I did not join the protests.

Intent on meeting requirements for graduation, I had all I could handle in Liberalism and Conservatism, Louis Filler's senior history thesis seminar.

Although most of the class chose presidential figures as the subjects of their project, I focused on John Dos Passos, the leading American radical novelist of the 1930s whose work I had sampled in high school. Running 107 pages, my thesis used the author's fiction and essays as primary sources to chart his ideological odyssey from World War I to the 1960s.

"America our nation has been beaten by strangers who have turned our language inside out who have taken the clean words our fathers spoke and made them slimy and foul," Dos Passos declared in the emotional climax to *The Big Money* (1936), the final work of his classic Great Depression trilogy, *U.S.A.*

Nevertheless, the man who saw his country divided into "two nations" found it difficult to acclimate to the bureaucratic Soviet Union or to the American Communist Party, which he viewed as using the working class for its own purposes. Wary of Party attacks on socialists and anarchists, particularly during the Spanish Civil War, Dos Passos gradually rejected Marxist aesthetics and wound up joining former radicals such as Max Eastman in denouncing dictatorships of both the left and right. Well before the United States entered World War II, Dos Passos had returned to the democracy of the American and English-speaking tradition. From that point on, he insisted that the modern state posed organized society's most powerful threat. Big Labor and Big Government, concluded Dos Passos, were more dangerous to human freedom than capitalism.

THE NEXT STEP

To my relief, Filler treated my scholarly efforts with generosity. Years later, my brother would ask my mentor if I had been one of his best students. There were brighter minds, acknowledged Filler, but I had a "dogged" quality that set me apart. No doubt, the assessment had something to do with my joy in studying history. Learning about the passions associated with the human condition and the contorted path to social justice inspired my imagination and appealed to the appreciation of theatricality I had absorbed from my family. Since written expression was an essential component of the discipline, moreover, I felt comfortable working within its confines.

At the same time, Filler had imparted a humanistic approach to history that involved analyses of cultural developments in the study of human behavior. For that reason, classes outside the field contributed significantly to my understanding of social process. During my last term, I signed up for a seminar on the work of British novelist D.H. Lawrence. Working within an interdisciplinary spirit, the class infused literary studies with psychoanalytic and social science theory. Accordingly, I focused my term paper on Lawrence's contention that the roots of mid-twentieth century fascism lay in the alienation generated by the over-rationalized societies of the industrial world.

Toward the end of spring term, I followed up my interest in cultural studies by agreeing to provide background piano accompaniment for the final screening of the Saturday night silent film series a literature professor hosted in Old Main. The movie in question was Erich von Stroheim's legendary *Greed* (1925), a two and a half hour epic based on literary naturalist Frank Norris's *McTeague*. Over the years, I had managed to find accessible pianos at various co-op job sites and availed myself of the battered upright in the sparsely furnished student union lounge. On one occasion, I had even jammed with a blues harmonica player at a late-night session at the college coffee shop. Creating a motion picture soundtrack, however, proved to be a daunting task.

During a preview of the feature, I compiled a detailed set of notes. The trick was to amplify the emotional essence of each scene by devising distinct musical themes for each character and situation without calling undue attention to the accompaniment. To accomplish this, I compiled a cue sheet of selections from my dance band fake book. For the youthful McTeague, I chose "I'm a Ding Dong

Daddy from Dallas." I filled in other scenes with my own compositions or improvised existing melodies. When the camera panned outside the window of the hall where McTeague's marriage took place to a passing funeral procession, I changed the Wedding March I was playing to a minor key. Two nights after the preview, I sat at the auditorium grand piano lit by a bare stage light and provided 150 minutes of cinematic accompaniment for an audience of five hundred.

I would leave Antioch with a modest B average, ranked sixty-fifth in a class of 216. Thanks to a background in U.S., British, Chinese, and Russian history, however, I had placed in the top 12 percent nationally in the history Graduate Record Exam. Aware that pursuing an advanced degree would most likely ensure a student deferment from the military draft, and with no other conceivable plans in mind, I applied to graduate school.

My most important priority was a program offering immediate financial support. With this in mind, I applied, at my parents' urging, to the University of Minnesota, where Josef Altholz, the son of old family friends, taught British history. Josef warned that the history department rarely extended graduate teaching assistantships to first-year students. After it placed me on a list of alternates, however, Minnesota came through with an appointment that included a $2,200 annual stipend and a highly discounted in-state tuition rate.

On a sultry, southern Ohio afternoon in June, the Antioch class of 1964 received its diplomas in an outdoor ceremony as my parents and Michael, now a student at Brandeis University, looked on. True to form, Antioch did not require caps and gowns, although my parents insisted that I wear one of my father's baggy dark suits for the occasion. Nearly five years of work, travel, and study had generated a degree of personal confidence, and thanks to Louis Filler, self-discipline. Perhaps most significantly as I approached the age of twenty-three, I could taste the pleasures of financial independence.

It was time to proceed with the next step.

Getting There

UP ON THE ROOF

Weeks after commencement, I found myself on the subway to Lower Manhattan. Sporting a new pair of steel-toed boots, I was on my way to a summer job with a construction company owned by my Uncle Bernie and his brother. After returning from Yellow Springs, I had sought to build up financial reserves for graduate school by finding work at the New York World's Fair. Then I had driven up to the Catskills in a futile attempt to sign on with one of the resort hotels. My father pretended to commiserate with the failure to market my services. At the same time, he could not resist the chance to restate his often-repeated mantra that the only route to economic independence came through a profession. It was a great relief, then, when Bernie came through with the job.

After a stint on the Lower East Side, where I vainly tried to follow the directions of a supervisor with a heavy Italian accent who assumed I knew more about the trade than I did, I served as an unskilled laborer at Greenwich House, a historic West Village settlement agency currently under renovation. Fortunately, I wound up working with Pete, an experienced young carpenter who hired on half the year and spent the remaining months collecting unemployment to support an art career.

Our first task involved "Eleanor," a bathtub from the apartment that formerly served President Roosevelt's First Lady on overnight visits to social work colleagues in New York. Moving the bulky fixture down several flights of stairs consumed about a week's labor. From there, Pete and I graduated to guiding new deliveries of building blocks down a slide for storage in the basement.

As long as I was under Pete's wing, things went smoothly. Then I received an assignment to operate a pulley to lower building refuse from an open window to an inner courtyard three stories below. One day, I inexplicably lost my grip on the rope.

To my horror, the load plunged to the ground with sickening speed.

Moments earlier, a team of black workers had shown up to collect discarded debris. Alerted by my panicked screams, the foursome managed to scurry to safety. Nevertheless, their leader cursed out the supervisor, gathered his men, and abruptly stormed off the site, a reaction no doubt associated with the city's racial tensions during the summer of the Harlem Race Riots.

It would take weeks to purge that scene from my mind. Thankfully, the daily routine offered lighter moments. At lunchtime, everyone repaired to the cool breezes of the rooftop. The constant banter of the break never let up. When attractive women on the sidewalks below elicited whistles and catcalls, however, I felt a tinge of discomfort. In time, nevertheless, I began to see these unsolicited compliments as attempts at something of an "equalizer" between the working-class crews and the upscale women of the district.

TWO WORLDS

Taking leave of my construction comrades, I flew to Minneapolis in mid-September 1964. Years of Antioch co-op jobs had taught me how to find my way in a strange city. First, I checked in at the downtown YMCA. Then I began the search for lodgings on the streets of the West Bank, an area of older, frame houses and shops targeted for university expansion and freeway development. Although situated across the Mississippi River from main campus, the district housed the newly constructed Social Science Tower, home of the history department. I soon came across a spacious one and a half room layout above a vacant storefront slated for demolition. The rent was only sixty-five dollars a month. Better still, the location on South 2½ Street, a dead-end adjacent to the parking lot for the West Bank university complex, was perfect.

After obtaining a twenty-dollar couch from a nearby junk shop, I balanced the intended bed on my head and carried it four blocks down the main drag to my new home. By a stroke of luck, my digs were around the corner from The Mixers, a legendary West Bank cocktail lounge and student hangout. On my first night, I spotted a striking young woman sitting with a friend in the darkened interior. Overcoming a habitual difficulty in breaking the ice, I struggled to begin a conversation, only to have one of the two respond.

"I suppose you just came off the road with your Harley?" Karen challenged.

Thrown off guard, I had no recourse but to reveal my academic stripes, adding that I was from New York and had just moved in around the corner. This aroused sufficient curiosity on a dull night to garner an invitation to join the table.

Days later, Karen's friend Crystal, a blonde-haired Norwegian-American photography student from upstate Minnesota, introduced me to George and Gretchen Tselos. A history graduate student, George had been born into a Greek-American family in the Bronx; Gretchen was, of all things, a North Dakota Jew. The couple now briefed me on the history department and its professors. Meanwhile, Crystal and Karen provided entry to the West Bank's bohemian and university "hangers-on," a significant segment of campus life in the expansive days of 1960s higher education. I met Maury Bernstein, a public radio folk music host who had known Bob Dylan as Zimmerman when the young Minnesotan had enrolled at the "U" for six months. Maury insisted that Dylan's nasal voice was so grating that people used to walk out of parties when he pulled out his guitar.

Several days after settling in, I took a deep breath as I often do in moments of transition and approached the ground-floor entrance to the Social Science Tower. George Tselos had explained that I would be one of forty teaching assistants assigned to either The History of Western Civilization or the U.S. History Survey. With four hundred undergraduates in these huge lectures, each TA (teaching assistant) would lead three discussion sections of thirty-five students each and grade exams. I soon discovered I was one of four assistants who would service the U.S. History course under the supervision of Robert Berkhofer, Jr.

"So you're a Progressive!" the cerebral Berkhofer nearly shouted at our first meeting, a response, no doubt, to my Antioch lineage and association with Louis Filler.

My first thought was that I was dealing with a political reactionary. Nor was I reassured when the professor boasted he had a legend among students for being "nuts."

Trained in the 1950s, Berkhofer was part of a generation overturning the Progressive paradigms of historiography that had shaped my education. Instead of defining American history as a struggle between the virtuous people and selfish interests, these Counter-Progressives emphasized complexity of motive and focused on psychological and cultural conflicts instead of economic or political ones. A similar spirit pervaded my first graduate seminar, David W. Noble's U.S. Intellectual History. Back at Antioch, Ade Bennett had told me about this theatrical Minnesota professor, whose summer school lectures he had audited. As my advisor, Noble had little interest in bureaucratic details, voiced no objection to my plan to bypass the master's degree and go straight for a PhD, and showed no hesitation in admitting me to his seminar.

During our conversation, I noticed that my new mentor remained on his feet. The opening day of the seminar, he explained that he had a chronic back problem that compelled him to stand or lie down instead of sitting. Accordingly, Noble would be leading our discussions from a prone position on the conference table. At first, the seminar seemed like a cult where devotees obediently awaited the words of the spiritual master. Yet it soon seemed perfectly natural to address a professor lying flat on his back.

Noble's classes incorporated an American Studies approach that linked the history of ideas to politics, social structure, philosophy, and diverse forms of expressive culture. Weekly readings covered recent classics in the field that countered the "agrarian myth" by focusing on how American leaders strove to portray the pristine New World as a refuge of innocence and natural simplicity from Old World Europe's tyrannies and corrupted institutions. Noble was then completing *Historians Against History*, in which he argued that America's leading historical narratives had incorporated this Metaphor of Two Worlds into a national faith. Disposed to irony and eager to counter the orthodoxies of the profession, Noble seemed to be laughing to himself as he reflected on each formulation.

BLACK AND WHITE

My exposure to critical perspectives deepened in Allan Spear's U.S. Race and Nationality, one of the first courses in the nation to trace American attitudes toward both ethnic and racial minorities. The enthusiasm and energy of this rather short, plump, and balding recent Yale PhD was infectious. After exposing us to the sorry details of the Atlantic slave trade, Spear posed a classic "chicken-and-the-egg" question: which came first, slavery or racism? Anticipating the work of historian Winthrop Jordan, we concluded that ethnocentric prejudices predisposed North American planters to enslaving Africans, while slavery reinforced and legitimized their views. We also learned how black Americans had been antislavery activists, held political office in the post-Civil War South, resisted racial segregation, and sought civil rights justice and cultural autonomy.

The climax to my study of African-American history came in the spring of 1965 in a final exam question soliciting comment on White House advisor John Roche's statement that the American Dream now lay in reach of African-Americans. As works such as Charles Silberman's *Crisis in Black and White* (1964) and *The Autobiography of Malcolm X* (1965) made clear, however, blacks outside the racist South continued to experience disproportionate amounts of discrimination, poverty, and marginalization. Responding to Spear's question, I constructed a furiously rhetorical essay that echoed the emerging anger and frustration of black nationalists and radicals such as Malcolm X.

Professor Roche should find a soapbox in any big-city ghetto to deliver his barren platitudes, I wrote. The result would provide a fascinating footnote to social history.

Addressing me as "David X," Spear noted that he probably should hold me accountable for an excessive polemic but loved my passion and concurred with it.

WEST BANK

Although I had entertained only modest expectations for graduate school, professors such as Noble and Spear sparked my intellectual curiosity. To my surprise, I found that I also enjoyed leading my weekly U.S. History sections. I had only limited previous public speaking experience. While in high school, my attendance at a national Jewish youth conference prompted an invitation to address the local temple on the concept of the Chosen People. During a visit home in 1961, I had spoken to my mother's grade school class about the Baden Street Settlement. Oral research summaries in Louis Filler's seminar provided my only other ventures in public discourse. Now, however, my students seemed reasonably tolerant of my efforts in leading group discussions.

As satisfying as academic life appeared, however, I would not have survived graduate school without the enticements of the West Bank enclave. As a former rock 'n' roll fanatic, Jean Shepherd admirer, and follower of the folk music scene, I had no trouble relating to people with alternative sensibilities, whether at Antioch, on co-op job assignments, or traveling through Europe. Transfixed by underground films including John Cassavetes's *Shadows* (1959) and the French New Wave classic *Jules and Jim* (1962), and Bob Dylan's turn to metaphysical balladry, I balanced intellectual interests with a taste for unconventional people, innovative perspectives, and new experiences.

The Mixers proved to be the perfect place to pursue such interests. Retreating to the lounge around ten each evening after forcing myself to complete reading assignments, I encountered "Red," the former proprietor of the Minneapolis coffee house where Dylan had performed. Red now managed a run-down apartment building, where he held weekend "rent parties" featuring twenty-five-cent bottles of cold Budweiser and live performances by local folk luminaries Dave Ray, Tony Glover, and Spider John Koerner.

"Horowitz, I've been watching you," he said as he approached me one evening. "First I thought you were a narc but I guess you're all right. Interested in a spot on the insurance run? It's a Benson and Hedges lid every month. Best stuff you'll ever try."

I had been turned on to marijuana by Danny, a young friend of Crystal's and the stepson of an esteemed older poet and literature professor. Growing out his hair and already versed in "with-it" street talk, Danny joked that the West Bank was getting full of "hippies," the first time I remember hearing the term. In 1964 aspiring hipsters still related to jazz. Danny introduced me to Cathy, a wiry, bespectacled, and intense pre-med student who followed the jazz scene. When she told me that Cannonball and Nat Adderley were in town with avant-garde tenor sax man Charles Lloyd, I jumped at the opportunity to hear them.

Advertised by word-of-mouth, the event took place at Big Al's, a hotspot fronting the railroad tracks alongside the South Minneapolis grain terminals. The lounge normally served as a meeting ground for vice trade professionals and a downtown clientele of visiting business travelers. On "Blue Monday," the trade's customary night off, however, the club opened the upstairs space for live jazz and special events. Cathy and I watched in awe as the exquisitely dressed African-American crowd greeted each other as if gathering for Sunday church. The good-humored give-and-take between the hard-working musicians and a completely tuned-in audience was an inspiration.

As fall term ended, I anticipated the demolition of my building by finding a somewhat seedy, half a single-floor duplex several blocks away. The flat lacked a window in the sleeping alcove and shared a bathroom with an adjoining unit. Yet the rent was low, it had an adequate space heater, and an inside wall provided the perfect location for an old piano the Tseloses had donated. As I set up my towel-draped trunk as a coffee table in bohemian style, I anticipated prospects for an active social life.

Through Red's rent parties, I had fallen in with a crowd of hipsters who had begun to bridge the gap between the Beat Generation of the Fifties and a liberation-minded counterculture. This was a period when "cool" young men slithered through gatherings without saying a word, thereby attesting to a disdain for superficial chatter. I learned you never asked what people did for a living, an irrelevant matter compared to their inner make-up. For a while, I tagged along with Max, a large balding man who wore oversized fur coats and told outrageous stories, and Joanie, a dark-haired beauty who favored heavy mascara, used furs, and high-heeled boots. A chance meeting at the Laundromat, however, resulted in a more successful liaison with Judy, a Minneapolis native and political science major who lived across the street from my duplex.

TRADITION AND CHANGE

For the next several months, I juggled academic responsibilities with overnight stays at Judy's flat. Yet as summer approached, I decided to prepare for the PhD's second language requirement by entering a crash program for international students in Perugia, a picturesque medieval hill town in central Italy. Not anticipating the use of a foreign language for a U.S. history dissertation, I had chosen Italian mainly out of admiration for Rome's neo-realist cinema. At any rate, Perugia's dollar-a-night *pensiones* and inexpensive restaurants, including a municipal cafeteria run by the town's communist administration, offered a perfect setting for summer studies.

With a student body of Americans, Europeans, and Middle Easterners, many of whom required Italian language skills before attending medical school in Bologna, the university was a veritable melting pot. One classmate, a congenial Syrian, endeared himself to our lunch table by volunteering that *all* our governments stank. My most frequent companion, however, was a quiet-spoken young Perugian native who often joined me for dinner at my favorite *trat-*

toria. A fervent anticommunist and professed fascist, he sparked my taste for debate by insisting that free enterprise was the only system serving ordinary people and by supporting President Lyndon Johnson's recent escalation of the war in Vietnam.

Not long after my brother visited Perugia on his way to a year of study in Stockholm, I arranged for a ride with a classmate to London, where I flew back to the States. When I returned to Minneapolis, however, I learned that my duplex had sustained smoke and water damage from a fire and that Judy had moved and left no address. Fortunately, the building's owner had stored my belongings in a vacant storefront. After scouting the neighborhood on foot, I found a spacious two and a half room apartment on the second floor of a four-unit clapboard structure on the western edge of the West Bank district.

To begin my second year of graduate study, I decided to audit Dave Noble's Intellectual History lectures. Presenting himself as a "royalist," Noble resorted to generous doses of personal narrative, irony, and drama. He described the central myth of American culture as a national covenant in which Providence assigned the New World to a Chosen People. English Protestants favored by this gift could experience "progress" by returning to simple structures of religious worship and social life and rejecting Old World institutions such as the Roman Catholic Church, feudal aristocracy, and monarchy.

Given to theatrical impersonations, Noble thought nothing of donning a Puritan hat or Civil War uniform. To illustrate how American fiction reflected male reluctance to deal with community, the professor messed up his hair, unbuttoned the top buttons of his shirt, and paraded around the stage in a hilarious parody of literary bad boy "Stormin' Norman" Mailer. Inspired by the emphasis on literature in the class, I enrolled in an American Realism seminar that focused on late-nineteenth century novelists William D. Howells, Mark Twain, and Henry James.

To my surprise, Howells's fiction depicted the amoral nature of the corporate market. Likewise, Twain's *A Connecticut Yankee in King Arthur's Court* presented a stark parody of the destructive potential of modern industrial capitalism and perfectionist creeds. These writings paralleled the distrust of reform and distaste for rationality in the work of Henry James. In fact, the skepticism conveyed in James's novels seemed consistent with so much of my father's outlook while simultaneously reinforcing Dave Noble's emphasis on irony and paradox.

I supplemented the emphasis on cultural studies with a political thought seminar. The professor, Mulford Q. Sibley, was a Quaker pacifist and socialist who had provoked the condemnation of several state legislators by calling for campus intellectual diversity and the creation of dissident political and cultural organizations, including a nudist society. Despite the fact that almost the entire class consisted of consensus-oriented political science students, Sibley reinforced my long-held fascination with radicalism, which he defined as an approach penetrating the *root* of prevailing issues.

Inspired by this approach, I completed a research paper on Randolph Bourne, the World War I peace activist and bohemian immortalized in John Dos Passos's *1919* and treated in a Louis Filler biography. My essay pictured Bourne as an advocate of social democracy, cultural pluralism, and the cooperative ideal. As a self-declared nonconformist, the journalist and author had pleaded for rational policymaking instead of unconscious yielding to the forces of inertia and habit. He held out hope for Youth because he believed a new generation could marshal reason against the rigidity of tradition and absolutism, which he equated with feudal militarism and regimentation.

War, Bourne insisted in an iconic essay immortalized by Dos Passos, was "the health of the state."

My second paper for Sibley offered a profile of grassroots organizer Saul Alinsky. The direct-action philosophy of this urban populist encouraged the poor to take matters into their own hands. Alinsky talked in terms of power and organization, not ideology. He insisted that freedom and equality were not gifts but resulted only when people asserted their rights. Because new constituencies always threatened existing power arrangements, he explained, conflict was an essential ingredient of social change. Through Alinsky's notion of "mass *jiu jitsu*," I noted, activists could deliberately provoke establishment forces into recklessly denouncing their efforts, thereby broadening support.

Rather than creating mere rage, organizers were to channel existing fury into cold anger, calculated strategy, and deliberate action.

These were important lessons for anyone with an interest in social justice, and I never would lose sight of them.

ESTUARIES

(1965-1968)

let us not talk falsely now, the hour is getting late
— B. Dylan

Saul Alinsky offered a welcome alternative to the consensus-oriented graduate students in Mulford Sibley's seminar who saw mass-based organizations as inherently irrational. A further stimulant to radical analysis accompanied my service as a teaching assistant for Allan Spear, whose U.S. History lectures focused on the social and cultural issues I found most compelling. Bent on nurturing informal relationships, Allen invited his section leaders to join him at a back table at The Mixers to compose midterm and final exams.

OPEN DOORS

Creating exams was far more enjoyable than grading them. To ease the tedium, a group of U.S. History TAs began getting together to process the bluebooks. The arrangement had the advantage of allowing everyone to recite particularly amusing student responses. Beginning in the fall of 1965, these all-night marathons invariably took place at Bruce Goldstein's place. Sporting dark wavy hair, a brooding moustache, a Mexican poncho atop his towering frame, and leather sandals, Goldstein was a striking counterculture missionary. Raised by a Jewish family in Omaha, where his father operated the Hertz car rental franchise, Bruce had recently graduated from the University of California at Berkeley, where he had joined the Free Speech Movement against administration censorship of campus political activities.

Although Goldstein never seemed to complete term papers, he liked to rip apart our professors' grand schemes with an apt, "but what if ..." or "but then again." Then he would laugh sardonically, a mockery of attempts to impose order on an incomprehensible universe. Bruce also liked to hint that shadowy conspiracies, particularly those attributed to the CIA, framed history more than our mentors might admit. Although Goldstein was convinced that the political establishment was on the verge of collapse, he was not any clearer than the rest of us what might take its place. Meanwhile, he initiated us into the hippie lingo of the Haight-Ashbury counterculture and the psychedelic rock of Bay Area performers including Janis Joplin, Country Joe and the Fish, the Grateful Dead, and the Jefferson Airplane.

Bruce always seemed to have ample supplies of smoke to share with the TAs and younger instructors. His parties were famous for bringing academics together with poets, artists, old-line political revolutionaries, labor activists, folk musicians, working people, and even business sorts. Women found him irresistible. He seemed fascinated by them, baffled by their apparent contradictions, and forever hooked by their allure. Bruce Goldstein conveyed a tragic sense of love that resonated within my heart, and we soon became good friends.

About the same time, Bob Dylan's turn to electrified rock shook up the folk scene. One day, my neighbor Gerry and her wild-eyed boyfriend Eric insisted without explanation that I pick up a copy of the new Beatles release, *Rubber Soul*. Once I heard George Harrison's sitar on "Norwegian Wood," I realized the Liverpool gang had crossed over from appealing pop to rock as art. The introspective lines of "In My Life" and the Baroque phrasing of "Girl" suggested that the band had a "heavy" component I never suspected when first hearing them on the BBC. I soon proselytized the Beatles to everyone. Yet many academics and "folkies" still rejected anything related to commercial culture. When I sent a copy of *Rubber Soul* to my brother in Stockholm, however, he reported that fellow students clamored at his dormitory door to sample its contents.

By the winter of 1966, when the owners hired Wild Bill Lucas, a toothless and soulful elderly black blues vocalist and piano man for weekend entertainment, the Triangle Bar had become the center of West Bank nightlife. One evening, a reporter for the *Minneapolis*

Tribune spotted Crystal in the crowd and requested her help on a feature on the city's latest hot spot. When she engaged me in the project, the resulting Sunday magazine layout included a photo of the two of us standing at the bar with bottled beers in hand. Not long after, Crystal volunteered to shoot some pictures of me. Sporting my Navy pea coat and cowboy boots and dangling an unlit cigarette from my lips, I posed in Dylanesque fashion by the steps of an empty train car at the South Minneapolis railroad yards. The framed photo still sits in my hallway.

Although I had let my hair grow out and begun to identify with the liberating ethos of the counterculture, my love life lagged. The truth was that I had little self-confidence when it came to romance. I had not even had a steady girlfriend until my third year at Antioch, when I entered an affectionate but predominantly platonic relationship with a first-year art student. Over the years, subsequent attempts at physical intimacy proved clumsy at best. At the same time, fortune was not always on my side. During the fall of 1965, I managed to date a dark-haired graduate student whose well-fit dresses and black high heels presented a striking image, only to have her confess that although she enjoyed my company, she was involved with a married professor.

My fortunes seemed to improve that winter when a night at the Triangle led to Vicky, an undergraduate art student. Yet my inexperience in personal relationships made me excessively demanding of her time. Trapped by my own insecurities, I initiated a break-up and then fell into a deep funk over my foolishness. It took weeks before I returned to the Triangle. Eventually, however, I struck up an acquaintance with a hip young couple who liked having me to dinner, after which we usually shared some smoke and talked culture and politics. One evening, they introduced me to a friend, a fast-talking, funny New York Jew who had studied dance at the University of Wisconsin.

"Good move," Bob volunteered when I called to get Ellie's number.

"She's got everything she needs, she's an artist, she don't look bad," he sang in a parody to one of Dylan's songs.

On our first date, we saw a documentary on the Spanish Civil War. Ellie's uncle had served in the Abraham Lincoln Battalion and was one of 2,800 American volunteers who had fought in a losing attempt to defeat the fascist uprising of the late 1930s. Viewing footage of the war's atrocities, Ellie clung intently to my arm. As things progressed back at my place and I tensed up, she admitted feeling nervous herself. At that point, our relationship prospered.

To my delight, my witty new friend had an engaging grasp of history. When I described Allan Spear's presentation of Woodrow Wilson's World War I foreign policy as a synthesis of the economic and moralistic aspects of American capitalism, she instantly exclaimed I just *had* to read Bill Williams. Ellie had taken a graduate seminar from Wisconsin's William Appleman Williams, the former University of Oregon historian and author of *The Tragedy of American Diplomacy* (1959). In fact, she had become one of the professor's drinking pals. I now recalled that Spear had made a passing reference to *The Tragedy*. Inspired by the personal connection, I scored a copy of the book and quickly devoured it.

Williams was expressing the merger of material forces and ideology to which my study of history long had led me. He described U.S. foreign relations as the product of an open door policy that tied humanitarian desires to capitalism's economic imperatives. By connecting U.S. Cold War postures to the need for a world free of communist economic and political blocs, he was providing an implicit explanation for the expanding conflict in Vietnam. To top it off, the book assumed an essay form without the clutter of footnotes.

I faced a test of my interest in Williams's ideas in Mulford Sibley's seminar on American radical thought. To my consternation, I found that when we considered *The Tragedy*, the political science students dismissed the work as a Marxist screed of economic determinism. In response, I insisted critics were grossly misinterpreting the author or not bothering to read him. Williams had described the reformist elements of American opposition to European colonialism, I argued, but emphasized how America's economic empire prevented progress toward a just distribution of resources at home. The "tragedy" of U.S. foreign policy lay in the fact that overseas expansion was supposed to rectify domestic social and economic instability but merely generated further cycles of war, depression, and internal conflict. Worse still, attempts to impose American political and economic models produced negative responses in developing countries.

UPSIDE-DOWN

With no specific agenda for the summer of 1966, I returned to Roslyn Heights to catch up on reading and look for yard care jobs. Since Ellie was staying at her family's home in the North Bronx, I saw a great deal of her. I felt grateful for my friend's ability to elicit my self-confidence. Yet the relationship had its problems. Fashioning herself a psychoanalytic tutor, Ellie often took me to task for not coming to terms with the "uptight" repression of my personal and family life. Things came to a head when I dragged her to a Mets game. Anxious to engage her interest, I foolishly insisted that the movement of baseball athletes approached the artistic grace of ballet. This did not go over well with someone who had just completed a graduate program in modern dance. Lashing out without mercy, Ellie responded she could never take anyone seriously who was so completely unaware of the difference between art and a stupid game.

My case received no help from the fact that the Mets lost 11-0.

The relationship with the mercurial woman from the Bronx seemed to be one in which I was always a step behind. A weekend at her family's summer cottage in the Upper Hudson Valley provided the fatal blow. The setting was similar to the Catskill bungalow colonies I knew as a boy, but most members of this community were former communists or contemporary progressives. One was labor historian Stanley Aronowitz. Although not much older than I, Aronowitz already had published a seminal article on the labor movement in *Studies on the Left*, Wisconsin's radical history journal. Somewhat intimidated by the surrounding political and intellectual "heavies," I contented myself with being Ellie's sidekick. By failing to offer sufficient challenge, however, I had become a drag on the relationship.

"Did you really think you could hold me once I got back to New York and my friends?" she finally asked.

I retreated to Long Island in painful silence.

Despite the setback, I remained loyal to the optimism of the counterculture and radical politics. Having tasted a modicum of sexual freedom and engaged in my share of diversions, I identified with hip consciousness as an alternative to materialism and emotional repression. As my hair grew out further and street talk entered my speech, it became exciting to discover old friends who also were "into" major changes. By the summer of 1966, New York City had spawned a variety of FM rock radio stations. Venturing beyond the pop music formula, deejays now featured extended LP cuts that included the Beach Boys' opus "Good Vibrations," as well as work by youth culture idols such as Simon and Garfunkel, the Lovin' Spoonful, the Rolling Stones, and the Beatles. At the same time, Bob Dylan's two-disc *Blonde on Blonde* introduced a dream-like world of subconscious imagery and symbolism that defied linear time or logic.

Like pop culture, politics had turned upside-down. As civil rights groups assumed a more confrontational stance, leaders such as Stokely Carmichael now talked of Black Power. Despite the resulting media frenzy, I saw nothing wrong with black people asserting a collective political identity. Meanwhile, increased draft calls had brought four hundred thousand troops to Vietnam, the U.S. Senate had held televised hearings on the war, and protests had intensified. In August, I joined Uncle Mickey and five thousand others in a peace march to Times Square. Skeptical about the power of demonstrations, we nevertheless believed it important to denounce a war that inevitably targeted civilians in bombings and search-and-destroy sweeps. Both our generations believed that Hitler's atrocities involved the complicity of the "good Germans," law-abiding citizens who ignored their government's evil deeds and concentrated on their own affairs.

When President Johnson mocked "nervous Nellies" who opposed U.S. efforts in Vietnam, my mother sent the slogan, "I'm a Nervous Nellie – I'm Afraid of War," to the Committee for a Sane Nuclear Policy (SANE), which distributed it as a political pin. It no longer was possible to ignore the conflict in Southeast Asia. Invited to dinner at high school pal Dave Lubin's house, I met the uniformed ROTC navy graduate engaged to my friend's sister. When the officer expanded upon U.S. military strategy in Vietnam, Dave's sister and mother treated the assessment as a reflection of real-world expertise. Just then, Dave's grandmother spoke up.

"*Oi vey*, vhy do they keep killing, more and more killing?" she muttered to no one in particular with a shake of her head.

It was the only redeeming moment of a tedious evening.

PROMISE

Having taken custody of my parents' five-year-old Chevrolet Impala, I began the return trip to Minneapolis in the fall of 1966 by driving my brother up to Cambridge to search for off-campus lodgings for his last year at Brandeis. After teaching Michael a few tricks, such as asking the local mail carrier about vacant units, we found a suitable rooming house in the area. In the habit of reading bulletin boards, I called my brother's attention to a flier soliciting writers for *Crawdaddy*, a new rock magazine. I then headed north for the Canadian route west. In Sudbury, where nickel ore processing had contaminated the air and left the skeletons of dead trees for miles, I stayed in an aging rooming house where late at night my door creaked open and an enormous trucker cheerfully greeted me and plopped into the next bed.

Resuming studies at Minnesota, I enrolled in Josef Altholz's seminar on Modern England. The class provided the chance to work out the connections between economics and ideology highlighted by William A. Williams. A year earlier, I had produced a European History paper that outlined the conservative critique of free market commerce and liberal individualism associated with British authors Thomas Carlyle, John Ruskin, and William Morris. I now prepared a research essay that tied Britain's nineteenth-century overseas military activity and the desire for low tariffs to the willingness of political leaders to legislate an income tax.

A second seminar on the twentieth-century United States, led by Clarke Chambers, introduced revisionist works such as Gabriel Kolko's *Triumph of Conservatism* (1963), which argued that Progressive Era business regulation often coincided with market priorities. This was a variation of Williams's idea of "corporate liberalism," by which forward-looking firms sought to achieve social stability by accepting labor and social welfare reforms. Yet my main interest lay in the cultural revolution of the Jazz Age. Perhaps as a reflection of the times, I saw the real significance of the 1920s in the critique of Victorian sexual propriety and moral authority.

Following Chambers's research interest in social work professionals, I devoted my spring-term paper to the manner in which cultural attitudes shaped contemporary approaches to poverty. Sampling several studies, I cited arguments that found strength among the poor in the matriarchal family. At the same time, I used a conference paper by my former Baden Street Settlement supervisor O. H. Lester that Clarke Chambers had deposited in the Social Welfare Archives he administered. Lester chronicled how tutorials and visits to local colleges sought to enhance the school performance of inner-city black students by enabling them to broaden cultural interests and observe the "fun of college life." Only five years after my participation in the program, I questioned the effectiveness of using the promise of college to motivate northern ghetto youth when society seemed unable to let them compete on their own terms.

By now, my radical inclinations extended to a philosophy of history that incorporated the counterculture perspectives of LSD guru Tim Leary. In a letter to my brother, I described the study of the past as an artistic process that brought a closer understanding of the human condition and inner man. Historians, I argued, needed to "trip out" of their own imprinting. Meanwhile, my circle of TAs and West Bank associates provided ample entry into the counterculture. Mike Kopp, a Minnesota-born colonial history student, often joined me at the Money Tree, an all-night coffee shop where we rubbed shoulders with male wrestlers, off-duty cocktail servers, journalists, musicians, and a lively assortment of gays and lesbians. Mike and I soon befriended a philosophic nightlife habitué named Marlys, who liked to ruminate on life's absurdities and found the attentions of neophyte intellectuals somehow rewarding.

Sometime during the fall of 1966, I learned that my downstairs neighbor Sandy had succumbed to the brain cancer that had hospitalized her for months. Accepting a ride to the funeral with a friend of building-mate Gerry, I shared the back seat with a short-haired, trim, and pert stranger introduced to me as Rita, a history undergraduate. Rita sat cross-legged in a decidedly languid manner, a short skirt revealing her patterned white tights. As we drove on, her body seemed to move closer; at one point, I casually leaned an elbow on her knee.

To the utter dismay of Sandy's friends and admirers, the Catholic service mandated by the family depicted our unconventional and spirited compatriot as just another child of Christ. For me, however, the demoralizing day presented a hint of promise.

SUMMER OF LOVE

As Minnesota began thawing out in April, Rita, Bruce, and I drove to Chicago for a meeting of the Organization of American Historians. The main attraction was a panel pitting John Braeman of the University of Nebraska, a defender of U.S. Cold War policy, against William Appleman Williams, now heralded as the dean of "New Left" scholars. Before a tense standing room crowd, Braeman castigated Williams as a dupe of Stalinist tyranny and dismissed any effort to equate Soviet expansionism and the U.S. global agenda. Declining to take the bait, Williams offered a low-key response. On the train down from Madison, he said, he had written a few thoughts on a paper bag holding his bottle of Scotch and discussed them with the porter. Then Williams launched into a profile of an early 1920s State Department officer who had called for a creative response to the communist Soviet Union. As the session ended, neo-Marxist historian Eugene Genovese strode to the podium and embraced Williams in a full bear hug.

By the spring of 1967, Bruce Goldstein and I were sharing the first floor of a comfortable South Minneapolis duplex where Rita often stayed overnight. Goldstein continued to exert a major influence. As a cultural maven, he could offer explications of the metaphysical themes of a John Fowles novel or point out that folk lyricist Leonard Cohen had borrowed the spiritual insights of Greek author Nikos Kazantzakis in the enchanting "Suzanne" when describing Jesus as "forsaken almost human." Bruce now introduced Rita and me to the edgy sounds of rock groups such as Cream and The Doors, although the two of us seemed to prefer the more lyrical Beatles and the acoustic harmonies of Simon and Garfunkel.

After completing the last of my coursework, I began serious preparations for comprehensive PhD written exams scheduled for the fall. At the same time, I worked on developing lecture material for the U.S. History Survey I was to teach in summer school, the first opportunity to shape my own class. Fortunately, the two reinforced each other. I soon immersed myself in a substantial collection of journal article reprints as well as a set of published U.S. History lectures. On the hot, humid days of Minneapolis summer, I did my reading on the shores of nearby Lake of the Isles, where the widower of my former neighbor, Sandy, repeatedly confronted me.

"Horowitz," the jazz trumpeter liked to say when I politely declined his offers of free smoke, "when are you going to give up all this and enjoy life?"

I had no answer other than a mild shrug.

Getting a PhD was my trip and I was going to see it through after coming so far, even if I had little idea why.

As summer school ended in August, Rita and I embarked upon a trip to Oregon to visit her father, stepmother, and half-brother. A published economic historian of the mid-twentieth century United States, Harold Vatter had taught at Minnesota's Carleton College before accepting a position at Portland State College. Barbara Vatter was working on a University of Minnesota PhD dissertation on the early economic history of southern Oregon's Douglas County. I felt energized by the drive west and marveled at the lack of speed limits on the broad, two-lane highway crossing eastern Montana. When we passed through the dramatic Columbia River Gorge and reached Portland, it felt as if we had entered a place of true enchantment. Then Harold and Barbara drove us to the mountain and sea vistas of the rocky Oregon Coast and I saw my first view of the Pacific Ocean.

Since Rita's part-time job required a return flight to Minneapolis, I was free to extend the trip to California and visit Bruce in Berkeley, where he was staying with old friends. It was 1967 and the Summer of Love. Accordingly, my inaugural trip across San Francisco Bay included a pilgrimage to Haight-Ashbury and a tour of Fisherman's Wharf. Near the cable car terminus, a heavy-set hippie girl with a painted face called out "I love you!" Although I found the encounter somewhat ludicrous, I identified myself as a free spirit and maintained the faith that an alternative culture based on spiritual values might someday lead the country in a better direction.

When I drove back to Minneapolis, I relished the sight of Rita on the front steps of the duplex in tight-fitting jeans. By now, she had decided to find a place where we could nest. This soon led to a reasonably priced ground-floor unit in a well-maintained working-class neighborhood in Northeast Minneapolis. After we spent several days nailing free carpet sample squares to the floor, Rita bought some second-hand furniture and took in a grey kitten that she named "Che" after the legendary Latin American revolutionary. We were now a family.

$9,300

Having won a fellowship for the 1967-68 year, my teaching assistantship no longer qualified me for a state resident's tuition. Then I learned I could keep the lower rate if I went to see a former history professor, now an administrator. My contact was a World War II Navy veteran and one-time military historian who was not happy to see me. He was upset that the graduate students took him for granted, expecting him to extend them favors as if it were a privilege.

Then he proceeded to rage about my long, unkempt hair. "Why do you have to go around looking like that?" he asked impatiently.

"I'll tell you what," he snapped. "You come back looking like a man and we'll see what we can do for you."

I left the meeting infuriated at the arbitrary demands and power games of the straight world. Yet I had no intrinsic right to a discounted tuition, a matter of over a thousand dollars. Ever the pragmatist, I concluded there was just too much money involved to stand on principle. After all, my hair would grow out again. When I returned to the office properly shorn, I left with the precious waiver and the realization that, like most anyone else, I had a price.

In November, I was ready for the history comprehensives. Graduate students had formerly been responsible for four separate two-hour exams covering their geographical fields of specialization. This year, however, the department decided to combine the entire process into a single eight-hour session, requiring responses to three general essay questions and a historiography treatment of one of the

Estuaries

topics. I took the exam with another former TA, Fred Morgner, an ex-football player and Mixers' regular from working-class Newark. For some reason, the department placed us in the windowless anteroom of the seventh floor women's bathroom, where we could bring a typewriter, dictionary, packed lunch, and thermos of coffee.

Fred and I never took a break. Instead, we downed our sandwiches and coffee while furiously pounding away at our mechanical portable typewriters. The pressure to cover the required scope of U.S. History was enormous and only grew more intense. Impacted by the fever pitch of the Vietnam War, the frustrations of the peace movement, and the ordeal of an exam in a self-enclosed space with an eight-hour deadline, I vented all the rage building up inside me.

In response to a question on the New Deal, I acknowledged President Franklin Roosevelt's positive accomplishments through Social Security and labor legislation. Then I recycled the William Appleman Williams critique of liberal expansionism. Roosevelt also gave Americans the privilege of dying in a war to create a U.S. imperial empire, I insisted. Because I knew black history best, I saved the question on Race and the American Dream for the last twenty minutes. Racial minorities never had a chance in a society built on the most virulent forms of racism and prejudice from the very start, I concluded.

Apart from these outbursts, my essays demonstrated a decent knowledge of U.S. history. Yet my treatment of Roosevelt and World War II deeply offended one of the three examiners, an elderly nineteenth-century economic historian who had served as a Navy officer during the war. When I received my grades, Clarke Chambers and colonial specialist Darret Rutman each awarded me a "High Pass." The third professor failed me. Curiously, the result averaged out to a "Pass," possibly making me the only PhD candidate in academic history to receive both the highest and lowest possible results on the same exam. When Rutman asked to see me, he shook my hand, apologized for his colleague, and assured me my work did not deserve an "F." A few years later, he moved on to a prestigious appointment at the University of New Hampshire.

Having survived the comprehensives, I returned to Long Island for a visit and the start of my dissertation research. I was interested in merging William Appleman Williams's notion of corporate liberalism and Dave Noble's emphasis on American mythical tradition into a description of 1920s business thinking. Conventional accounts portrayed the period's political and corporate leaders as "irresponsible" and "reactionary" defenders of a one-dimensional ideology reflecting narrow economic interests. I wanted to examine how key "New Era" figures embodied a desire for social stability and harmony by endorsing elements of Progressive reform and humane capitalism. Using the New York City Public Library, I began compiling an extended note card bibliography of sources that included reformers, government officials, popular writers, public relations experts, and corporate managers.

The trip east also included a visit to the American Historical Association convention in Toronto to test the job market. The Vatters already had alerted me to a slot in American Intellectual History at Portland State. Consequently, I had arranged to meet Ann Weikel, a Yale English history classmate of Allan Spear, who had recently joined the department herself. Ann made me feel completely welcome as a potential colleague. My second appointment, an interview for a position at New York City's John Jay College, did not go as well. I was supposed to explain how I would relate to a largely black and Puerto Rican student body. Caught off guard, I stammered something about making adjustments for people who might not have all necessary college skills. The proper answer, I learned, was that John Jay students received the same treatment as anyone else.

Acknowledging the disastrous outcome of the John Jay interview, I feared for my future prospects. Yet I had diligently filled out the Portland State application form, even exaggerating when I said I hoped to finish my PhD dissertation by fall. I could not have been more surprised, then, when I received a phone call one wintry night as Rita and I listened to the stereo while lounging on the floor in an induced state of euphoria. It was Whitney Bates, Portland State's colonial America historian. Speaking in an officious manner that sounded as if he were continents away, Bates announced that the department had chosen me to fill the Intellectual History position.

If I accepted, the starting instructor's salary would be $9,300.

THE CAUCUS

With the assurance of a job, I spent the winter of 1968 devouring an extensive array of New Era business thinking. Yet as the Vietnam War continued, it was difficult to bury my head in dusty volumes. Critiques of the conflict were nearly unanimous in academic circles. When a group of TAs had taken in a Minnesota Twins baseball game the previous spring, the opening ceremonies included a swearing in of military recruits. As the crowd stood for the national anthem, accordingly, we sat silently in our seats. In February, as the U.S. Embassy in Saigon fell under attack during the Tet Offensive, I swung by the student union and came across a crowded meeting. The speaker was a diplomat from the South Vietnamese government who insisted that the communist insurgency had been fully repelled and that the enemy was on the run.

"That's not what I saw on CBS News!" I shouted from the back of the hall.

Immediately, I found myself surrounded by a belligerent crowd of war supporters. Thinking quickly, I resorted to a lesson learned in the Bronx: when overextended in the face of stronger forces, talk your way out of the situation, even if you have to back off a little. Extricating myself from the confrontation, I nevertheless took pride in having made at least a small dent in my antagonists' unquestioned certainty over the war's progress.

Not long after, I had another chance to turn antiwar sentiment into political action. Having registered with the Democratic Farmer-Labor Party (DFL) of Minnesota, Bruce and I received invitations to a precinct caucus and ward conference to choose delegates to the party's state conference and ultimately the Democratic National Convention. As some thirty members of our precinct met in the classroom of a nearby school, Bruce realized that everyone supported Minnesota Senator Eugene McCarthy, who had agreed to contest Lyndon Johnson's bid for a nomination for another term.

"We've got this thing wired," Bruce whispered as he drew me aside, literally rubbing his hands.

"Let's introduce some resolutions!" he exclaimed.

What did he have in mind? I asked.

"How about immediate withdrawal from Vietnam?" Bruce shot back without hesitation.

"How about an end to the bombing – unconditional amnesty for draft resisters?"

I had no idea why my friend chose me for the mission. Yet as he predicted, all three resolutions passed our caucus without a dissent. We then had to bring the proposals before the entire ward. Speaking without notes, I did my best, improvising an impromptu speech about the Vietnam War's devastating impact on American society. To my amazement, no one seemed to object. After all, the DFL was the historic power base of Vice President Hubert Humphrey, a former Minnesota senator who had solid backing from Twin Cities organized labor, a loyal war supporter. It was not a complete shock, therefore, that just as we seemed to be carrying the day, an old-timer stood up at the rear of the hall.

"Folks, let's wait a minute before we rush into any resolutions," he pleaded.

"What kind of message are we sending to our troops?"

Within minutes, the assembly tabled the proposals for further consideration.

My moment in the political spotlight had passed. Yet McCarthy went on to win a surprising 42 percent of the vote in the New Hampshire primary in March, while sixteen of the delegates from our South Minneapolis ward ultimately represented him at the national convention. The caucuses even nominated my friend Red for city parks commissioner.

INTERSTATE 94

Not long after McCarthy's shocker in New Hampshire, Rita and I watched Lyndon Johnson deliver the TV address that announced his withdrawal from the presidential race. Four days later, North Vietnam agreed to preliminary talks. Yet sometime during that second evening, we received a breathless call from Gretchen Tselos.

Someone had shot Martin Luther King.

King had gone to Memphis to support a strike of black public sanitation workers in a city dominated by a conservative white political establishment. His murder was a devastating blow to hopes of progressive social change – a brutal rejection of the creed of nonviolence, of aspirations toward racial harmony, of prospects for a humane and democratic America.

The King assassination and the inner-city violence that ensued held out bleak prospects for America's future. Only days later, however, I pushed aside these forebodings and flew to New York for the first stage of a long-planned dissertation research trip.

My first stop was the Columbia University library, where I examined correspondence between 1920s political reformers and several progressive corporate figures. On a break, I noticed a number of students sitting astride the windows of an adjoining building with placards in their hands, the initial phase of the Columbia antiwar protest of 1968. Yet nothing could deter me from my mission. When a late-night raid of police forcibly evicted hundreds of people who had taken over the university administration building in late April, I was on the road pursuing archival material in Cambridge, Syracuse, and western Pennsylvania.

Days after returning to Minneapolis, I phoned my parents to thank them for the 1967 Impala they had signed over to me at the start of the trip. Then I announced I would be getting married at the end of June before heading for Portland.

"Does Rita know?" my mother cracked, a reference to the single-minded Dustin Hoffman in *The Graduate* (1967) who insists he will wed his future bride before he even proposes.

In reality, my parents were not excited about the news. During their time in suburbia, my father had strengthened his Jewish identity, and my mother, an agnostic who supported Israel, had followed suit. Neither was comfortable, therefore, with the fact that while Rita was technically Jewish by virtue of her mother's lineage, her Gentile father and secular mother had raised her outside Jewish tradition. Seeking to assuage these concerns, I promised to secure a Reform rabbi for the ceremony. Then my mother called two weeks before the event to say that my brother Michael, scheduled to be best man, would not be making the trip to Minneapolis.

Rita and I had been among the minority of Minnesota academics who rallied to Robert Kennedy's belated entry into the Democratic presidential nomination race after the New Hampshire primary. The New York senator, we believed, combined an articulate opposition to the Vietnam War with compassion for the poor and a hardened understanding of politics. We took comfort in the fact that Kennedy laid claim to a broad political constituency that went beyond the confines of the reformist middle class and people like ourselves. When Bobby promised that he could bring together black and white, the young and the old, and the poor and the affluent, Rita and I dared to believe that a polarized and violence-prone America still might have a chance to redeem itself.

Moments after we finished watching Kennedy's victory speech following the California primary late on June 5th, the phone rang. It was Gretchen Tselos again. This time she delivered another round of horrifying news – Robert Kennedy was on the verge of death from an assassination attempt by a Palestinian nationalist enraged at the senator's support for Israel's occupation of the West Bank.

Estuaries

The two of us sat before the television weeping for hours, unable to speak, in utter despair for the future of the country a mere two months after losing Martin Luther King. We both felt drained of any hope or faith that in the end, things would turn out for the best. It would take exactly forty years before I could say I had recovered from the blow.

If Robert Kennedy's demise destroyed progressive aspirations for a better world, it nearly obliterated my brother's desire to live.

Michael had become part of the hippie scene in Cambridge, where he had written about the alternative press for *Crawdaddy* and engineered the birth of *The Living Children*, an ambitious counterculture magazine. Growing his hair long, donning granny glasses, and adopting hipster lingo, my brother saw himself as a generational spokesperson. After graduating from Brandeis, Michael returned to New York, where he became an assistant editor at the underground *Cheetah* magazine. Enrolling in the graduate political science program at the New School for Social Research, he found an old walkup in trendy Chelsea. Yet deadline pressures for a prospective *Esquire* piece on rock musician Jim Morrison of The Doors and an anguished response to the near fatal shooting of cultural icon Andy Warhol placed Michael's world in crisis.

The last straw was Bobbie Kennedy.

As Uncle Mickey remained in New York with Michael, my distracted parents showed up at Bruce's Minneapolis duplex for the wedding. Finding a Nehru jacket and white turtleneck to match mine, Bruce Goldstein cheerfully filled in as best man while Crystal served as the official photographer. Two days later, Rita and I packed our sparse belongings into a U-Haul trailer, placed Che the cat in the back seat of the Impala, and headed west on Interstate 94.

Once again, I was on the move. Married to a bright and witty soulmate, I looked forward to completing my dissertation and initiating my professional life. Imbued with a radical approach to history, I had yet to find my own voice. I was not even sure I was fit for an academic career. Despite the uncertainties as to what lay ahead, and the realities of a war-torn and polarized nation, however, I felt vaguely hopeful as we left the nurturing Middle West.

WESTWINDS

(1968-1970)

the man of a thousand voices talking perfectly loud
– J. Lennon/P. McCartney

D RIVING THROUGH THE SPARSE HILLS OF NORTHERN MINNESOTA, I TOOK stock once again. Graduate school had provided a foundation for the work ahead. Stimulated by the grand overviews of Dave Noble and William A. Williams, I had developed a critical perspective on American culture and history that offered a promising approach to teaching and scholarship. Despite a grounding in the conservative skepticism of writers such as Thomas Carlyle and Henry James, I saw myself as a progressive and a radical opponent of the Vietnam War. A prolonged course of study had rescued me from the draft. As I looked to my twenty-seventh birthday – the cut-off for compulsory military service – I remained determined to compensate for my class privilege with full support for the antiwar cause.

A NEW LIFE

Portland in 1968 seemed a cultural backwater compared to the cosmopolitan Twin Cities. Local health ordinances inexplicably prohibited outdoor café seating, liquor laws prevented dancing in taverns, and rock music venues and record shops were almost nonexistent. Yet the nineteenth-century riverfront and nearby West Hills, where Rita's father and step-mother owned a two-story turn-of-the-century home, offered a picturesque scene. We soon found a $120-a-month two-bedroom rental on a dead-end street in blue-collar North Portland, which we outfitted with cheap furnishings and an old piano.

Most of the summer found me in the unfinished attic, furiously pounding out lecture notes on a portable typewriter. By late-August, however, television broadcasts of the Democratic National Convention in Chicago intervened. Rita and I bore silent witness as delegates mourned the murder of Martin Luther King and paid tribute to Robert Kennedy with a rendition of "The Battle Hymn of the Republic." Then we watched party regulars defeat a resolution for a negotiated settlement of the Vietnam War.

The real action occurred outside the convention hall.

Led by Abbie Hoffman, Jerry Rubin, and Yippie (Youth International Party) cadres, thousands of protesters had descended upon Chicago for an alternative Festival of Life embodying antiwar politics and a counterculture sense of play. As the roll call for the presidential nomination began, the networks forwarded feeds from the downtown streets, where the police were unleashing violent attacks on journalists, bystanders, and anyone in sight. When Vice President Hubert Humphrey swept to anticipated victory, we sat in fury as half the screen showed my former idol dedicating his presidential campaign to a "politics of joy" while the other half depicted the police rampage. Both Rita and I would cast ballots in November for the Peace and Freedom third-party ticket, the only vote I ever have regretted.

For opponents of the Vietnam War like Rita and me, 1968 marked a turning point. Carried away by the appeal of the early civil rights movement, toughened by Black Power rhetoric, alienated by the establishment's inability to find a way out of the war, and emboldened by the counterculture's liberating ethic, we imagined ourselves on the cutting edge of authentic social change. Police brutality and murderous raids against Black Panther Party leaders only convinced us that the political system was tottering. Having a respect for history and human complexity, I never believed the Revolution was imminent. Yet I looked to a gradual shift in national consciousness toward more cooperative ideals. As the study of the past made clear, change was constant despite the permanent appearance of particular arrangements.

Rita's father was not so sure. As a runaway during the Great Depression, Harold Vatter had ridden the rails and marched for radical causes. Yet he had little patience for so-called revolutionaries with no strategic sense. He loved to recall with deadpan irony how student participants in 1930s protests wore denim pants and plaid shirts while working-class demonstrators, desperate for middle-class respectability and markers of success, favored dark suits and ties. Where were we high-minded idealists, my tough-minded father-in-law never tired of asking, going to get our engineers, teachers, and nurses?

Reluctant to relinquish romantic aspirations, I was not impressed when newly installed Portland State President Gregory B. Wolfe used the faculty convocation to chart the institution's future as a center of urban planning and applied technology. The desire to raise Portland State's stature likely stemmed from its historic status as the stepchild of Oregon's public universities. The college's origins lay in 1946 with the Vanport Extension Center serving World War II veterans. Wiped out when a railroad dike failed in a devastating Columbia River flood two years later, the facility rotated through several sites until the state legislature granted it the use of the former Lincoln High School building on Portland's downtown Park Blocks. It was not until 1955 that state officials overlooked opposition from rival higher education institutions, renamed the center Portland State College, and authorized its expansion to a four-year program.

Portland State's charter designated the institution as "a downtown city college" rather than a residential campus. Yet enrollment continued to expand as the metropolitan area prospered, permitting the recruitment of a large cohort of new faculty in 1968. As faculty retired to the cafeteria for refreshments following that fall's convocation, I met Gary Waller, a new member of the sociology department. Waller mixed an impatient disdain for "bourgeois" academics with a Missouri drawl and a self-deprecatory wit. Once he learned that I identified with William A. Williams, Gary acknowledged he was a New Left radical who had worked with SDS (Students for a Democratic Society) in graduate school at the University of North Carolina. A day later, I met sociology graduate student Joe Uris, a fast-talking former student body president and long-time activist. When Uris brusquely asked who I was and I said I was a Williams disciple, he seemed satisfied.

"I'll see ya, man," Joe called out as we parted, a customary salutation, I subsequently learned, for people he decided to tolerate.

As part of my acclimation to the Pacific Northwest, the Vatters insisted that I read Bernard Malamud's *A New Life*, the story of a New York Jew's introduction to the English department at Oregon State University in the 1950s. One of the book's anecdotes described a drive to the Coast through the interminable fog of a winding, two-lane mountain highway. The tale that left a mark, however, recounted the day every word of Malamud's lecture brought a mirthful reaction from amused students until he realized his fly was open. From the very first day, I made it a habit to check this detail before each class and still do. Besides relative punctuality and prompt recording of grades, the only other protocol I took to heart was erasing the board at the end of each session.

Utilizing some of my teaching assistant experience, I supplemented the textbook for my U.S. History Survey with a "people's history" anthology that included accounts of Quaker abolitionists, Revolutionary War merchant seamen, writings by Tom Paine, and other samples "from the bottom up," a phrase coined by New Left scholar Jesse Lemisch. My American Thought and Culture class explored the themes of New World Exceptionalism raised by Dave Noble. A weekly seminar, held across the street at the campus ministry, embodied the late-1960s mantra of social relevance by exploring the development of American attitudes toward race, minority groups, poverty, and social welfare. Yet the tendency of students to engage in sincere but uninformed moral posturing left me uneasy. I greatly preferred the use of an informal lecture style with the opportunity for some class participation to the open-ended seminar format.

WORDS

For Christmas break, Rita and I flew to Roslyn Heights. Neither my parents or new wife seemed able to do much about the emotional distance marking their relationship. Yet when Uncle Mickey and

Rita's mother, Ethel, came to dinner one evening, I received a first-hand lesson on the distinctiveness of historical perspectives.

"It was a terrible time," my mother recalled with my father's assent, as conversation turned to the Great Depression, a reference, no doubt, to the quashed hopes of the economic catastrophe and the rise of European fascism.

Yet Ethel, who as an economics student had compiled research for a Senate committee investigating corporate labor abuses, saw the 1930s as an era of political possibility and hope, an assessment Mickey seconded. I marveled how four individuals of relatively similar backgrounds could have such opposing views of the same period.

As a teacher, I took pride in placing contemporary issues within a historical context. Yet I longed to participate in debates outside the classroom. By the time Rita and I returned to Portland in January 1969, the White House was in Republican hands. Partly due to the third-party disaffection of antiwar sympathizers, including ourselves, Richard Nixon had defeated Hubert Humphrey in the presidential election by less than 1 percent of the popular vote. To my dismay, Nixon indicated no willingness to pull back from Vietnam, the Justice Department indicted eight antiwar activists for inciting the previous summer's riots in Chicago, and the FBI appeared to be intensifying its assassination program of Black Panthers.

With this backdrop, I sought to work out a radical perspective on the role of violence in the historical process when I participated in a spring student forum on civil liberties.

"The situation in the 1930s forced the labor movement to take the action they did," I told the audience.

"There were strikes, burning, and killing, which the police and state militia were frequently involved in with violent results, but it won them the New Deal, which everyone looks back on as well worth the price.

"We must pay for social change today," I continued, "and some of that payment won't be pretty. We'll have to go outside the laws and traditions held sacred by Western civilization to bring about the needed changes."

To my surprise, the *Portland State Vanguard* reprinted every word of this inelegantly phrased rant.

Not choosing to teach summer school, I had ample time to pursue my dissertation and even corresponded with Bill Williams over its direction. Yet progress was inexorably slow. I am not sure if I had lost interest, saw the task of translating notes into text as tedious, or simply been distracted by the culture's numerous temptations. Having learned that the history department had denied tenure to my Intellectual History predecessor for failing to produce a PhD, my behavior seems curious. Perhaps it had something to do with the social circles in which Rita and I now traveled.

Having served as a "temp" secretary, Rita had met the purchasing manager of an electronics firm who planned to open the alternative record store that would become Music Millennium. We now hung out with a crowd that followed the artistry of acoustic guitarist John Fahey, frequently reveled in hazy smoke, and relayed personal accounts of "astral projection" through space and time. In August 1969, the same month the Woodstock Festival took place back East, we joined our friends at Clackamas County's MacIver State Park for Bullfrog II, one of the region's first outdoor rock concerts. Here, tripped-out and mellow fans partied to a lineup of bands that included San Francisco's Jefferson Airplane, who landed by helicopter for a special set at 3 a.m.

When classes resumed in late September, Portland State had received university status due to the addition of several graduate and professional programs, and I was an Assistant Professor. By now, the impact of radical politics had begun to create a generational fault line among the predominantly liberal faculty, some of whom were World War II veterans skeptical of departures from formal democracy. Not long after registration day, the *Vanguard* reported the formation of a PSU Radical Studies Center. Accusing the university of excessive ties to the dominant forces of society, a group of dissident professors demanded that the institution assume a more critical social role and exert a more humane impact on the surrounding community. As a first step, the consortium announced publication of a catalog of courses taught by participating faculty and promised to promote discussions about radical change in university life.

Radical Studies spanned a variety of offerings in film, music, philosophy, speech, psychology, sociology, and history, including my three classes. As the group's initial statement acknowledged, not everyone agreed on what it meant to be a radical. Rather conventional in pedagogy and educational philosophy, I certainly had few thoughts about the place of the university in the broader community or new methods of teaching and grading. Instead, I clung to the faith that it was possible to construct a relevant synthesis of the American Experience through historical analysis. Mainly because I hoped to penetrate to the root of society's problems and because I advocated social change, I considered myself a radical. Consequently, I gladly accepted an invitation to the organizational meeting for a campus chapter of the New University Conference, a faculty activist group informally known as "the grownup SDS."

Beyond the presence of one English instructor, the composition of the early NUC was exclusively male. Confronted by a strange group of heavily bearded, intense, and serious-looking individuals I gathered were movement "heavies," I felt an initial sense of discomfort. As I became familiar with characters including Steve Kosokoff (speech), Hugo Maynard (psychology), and Roger Dexter and Mike Phillips (philosophy), however, my apprehensions quickly passed. With the added presence of Joe Uris and Gary Waller, it was easy to feel I had become part of the most animated, intellectually alive, and entertaining segment of the Portland State community. Even President Wolfe engaged us by passing on a *New Yorker* excerpt of Charles Reich's soon-to-be-published countercultural treatise, *The Greening of America*. In December, I wrote my brother that I had taken on the role of New University Conference ideologue when I

105

composed a position paper stating a preference for student admissions by lottery instead of grade-point competition.

After expending an enormous amount of energy on the case of a radical public school teacher whose admission and grant support the PSU School of Social Work had rescinded three days before registration, I immersed myself in the developing controversy over campus military recruiting. Joining a panel that followed an SDS protest against the presence of the Marines, I declared that the controlling interests in the United States had fashioned a polluted empire. The armed forces were part of that problem, I argued, and the university should break from the military and imperial structure. At the time I adhered to the prevailing radical notion that the powerful and coercive institutions of corporate capitalism prevented a free market of ideas. In response, Marine officer Judd Blakely asked if there was anyone I admired in America. Then he elicited a huge wave of laughter from the audience by noting that all my heroes happened to be dead.

My performance improved at a Vietnam Moratorium rally at Mt. Hood Community College in November. The PSU faculty senate had endorsed the first Moratorium in October. When it declined to do so for the following month's protest, campus organizers dispatched Philosophy's Mike Phillips and me to the conservative east-county MHCC campus. We arrived to find fewer than thirty people nervously occupying a corner of the gym bleachers as the cheerleading team practiced at the other end. After Phillips delivered a point-by-point critique of the war, I took the podium. In a conversational tone, I assured the crowd their small numbers meant nothing.

"All over this country there are people like you who are saying 'no' to this war today," I declared. "You are a part of history, and we will prevail!"

I had stumbled upon one of the secrets to public speaking, which is to assess the circumstances of your audience and address their needs and sensibilities, not your own. I sensed that the small contingent of would-be peace supporters felt isolated in a hostile environment and needed to hear they were important. In delivering the message, I also discovered that the most elegant formulations are often the most simple. Aware that I had struck a chord, I still was unprepared for the pale young man who approached the speaker's platform with his mother at his side at the close of the event.

"I'd like to thank you," he stammered. "You told the truth, and it means a lot to me."

He said he had suffered brain damage in Vietnam.

This time I was at a complete loss for words.

NONCONFORMIST

The community college experience marked an exhilirating point of my political activism. Yet troubling signs had emerged in my personal life. I remember climbing the stairway to the history department in my London Fog raincoat one dreary morning and feeling as if I had become a tired replica of my father, now over sixty. To my dismay, the lively intellectual and engaging relationship between Rita and me had become essentially platonic, a particularly painful development amid the liberationist promises of the counterculture. During Christmas break of 1969, I withdrew into a deep funk. Shortly after New Year's, I realized the marriage was over.

Within a week, a mutual friend of Rita's and mine had prevailed upon Gene, an urban studies graduate student, to provide me temporary refuge in a spare room in his compact North Portland rental. As I painted the walls of my sleeping quarters, newly inaugurated FM rock station KINK highlighted selections from the recent Crosby, Stills, and Nash album, which Gene described as the most perfect record ever made. Feeling a mix of post-separation melancholia, uncertainty, and emotional vulnerability, I was haunted by a single line from "Judy Blue Eyes."

"Will you come to see me on Thursdays and Saturdays?" Stephen Stills sang.

The lyric conveyed an ominous feeling that left me wondering about the new decade. Two months later, however, a fellow historian and New University Conference colleague told me about a vacancy on the second floor of an early twentieth-century wooden structure on Montgomery Street, two blocks up the hill from Portland State. For thirty-three dollars a month, I could share a kitchen and adjoining bathroom with two students. The flat's vacant front room faced south through a large bay window, although its only furniture was a beat-up, pale green half-sectional. Following a quick paint job and transfer of my desk and a few personal items, I resumed a single life amid the artists, musicians, and political activists attracted to the area's cheap housing.

Meanwhile, my spring-term seminar, "The Legacy of Slavery," assigned several new "people's history" collections that included ex-slave narratives and treatments of black folklore, humor, storytelling, and spirituals. I was most interested in the work of Eugene Genovese. During the summer of 1966, I had driven over to Long Island's Hofstra College to attend a debate at the Socialist Scholars Conference between Genovese and Herbert Aptheker, both Marxists. Reading crisply from his paper in a manner I have always tried to emulate, Genovese argued that ruling-class economic interests had ideological components and that Marxists needed to understand the relationship between materialism and ideas, the conceptual approach I had pursued in graduate school and sought to integrate in my dissertation. I was pleased, therefore, when I got to discuss my research on the New Era business community in a widely enrolled Radical Studies course.

Seeking to engage the audience, however, I indulged in a rare instance of pandering when I extracted a quote from a 1920s booster with a clear double meaning.

"What more could a young man aspire to in life than a future dealing in chemicals?" I recited to hoots.

I instantly regretted the gratuitous attempt to curry favor with the obvious drug reference.

As I drew closer to the NUC radicals early in 1970, Gary Waller organized support for a strike at a Northwest Portland roofing materials company that simultaneously faced grand jury indictments on two air pollution counts.

"Who says there's no longer any industry in this country?" Gary exclaimed as we gathered at the bleak site at 7 a.m.

Sometime later, a speeding car disrupted our picket line.

"Scabs!" someone yelled, as if we were in a 1930s movie.

Things now moved swiftly. As several strike supporters surrounded the car, a company guard threw one of them to the pavement, leaving his head perilously close to the front wheels. My Bronx upbringing had left me with a fear of seeing people run over. In a panic, I started swinging wildly at the two strikebreakers emerging from the vehicle. Then I quickly ducked as someone on the loading dock deployed a two-by-four within inches of my head. When I turned around, a cop was behind me.

"All right," he said. "Break it up."

Instantly relaxing, I fell back into the crowd.

Not aware of the terror in my heart, Waller expressed respect for my performance. Even in the polarized climate of the Vietnam era, it was unusual to see academics take to street fighting. Not long after, Gary suggested that we organize a Radical Social Science Union. The idea would be to support students whose critical approach to studies could benefit from supplementary reading lists, discussion groups, and even separate courses. Although rumors spread that we planned to "monitor" other classes and instructors, this was never our intention. Nevertheless, Gary could not hide contempt for milktoast professors he accused of moral hypocrisy or tepid reformism.

"Every liberal academic's nightmare is to be found out!" he liked to say.

Waller saw the university as a great marshmallow where nothing ever changed. Yet his cockiness could be tiresome. Following New Left historian Walter LaFeber, I suggested that the term "imperialism" required a narrow definition when dealing with the origins of U.S. expansionism in the 1890s. Gary accused me of mincing words. Seeing myself as a *nonconformist* radical, I decided to play with the minds of the Radical Social Science seminar by wearing a tie to class, an aesthetic affectation I continue to this day. I also declined to award blanket A's in any of my classes.

MAY 1970

The Radical Social Science Union often addressed the continuing conflict over military recruiting on campus. In March 1970, the Portland State SDS forced the Navy out of the student union, prompting the university to obtain a temporary restraining order against Gary Waller and fifteen activists. Insisting on the community's right to debate the moral implications of military involvement in an "orderly process," President Wolfe invited the recruiters back to campus. In a second wave of protests in late April, the White Panthers, a small group of street-wise allies of black liberation, led a hundred protesters in breaking into a room in Smith Center, forcing Navy recruiters to retreat to another building. In response, PSU administrators summoned twenty-four helmeted riot police to restore order.

Student discontent across the entire country reached fever pitch once President Nixon went on television to announce he had ordered U.S. troops in an "incursion" into Vietnam's neighbor, Cambodia. On May 4, 1970, the situation took a fatal turn when Ohio National Guardsmen opened fire on demonstrators at Kent State University, killing four. These events occurred just as I met Penny Allen, a snappy French language instructor and recent NUC recruit. Slightly built, Penny wore her hair down in counterculture fashion. I was taken by my new friend's energy, the lightning-speed of her mind, and her ability to size up any person or situation.

"David, we have to *do* something!" Penny insisted as the Kent State news broke.

We soon learned that the National Student Association had called for nationwide protests and that a strike committee had been formed at Portland State. As Penny and I trudged across the campus in those first hours, we shared the unspoken conviction that "the system" had crossed a proverbial line. Days later, news reports would describe the shooting of two unarmed black students at Mississippi's Jackson State University. No one who followed the struggle for racial justice would be surprised by such a development. Yet in the hours after Kent State, the shooting of white college protesters seemed a new departure. We could only believe that the Nixon administration's obsession with proving its strength was leading the country toward the creation of a fascist state. My commitment to the antiwar cause faced its ultimate test.

Dedicated to reason and nonviolence, President Wolfe announced that PSU would remain open during the strike but that faculty and students were free to act according to their conscience. Some 134 professors – one-fourth the total – endorsed the walkout and signed a statement calling for a belligerent level of non-violence. Meanwhile, half the student body honored the protest on its first day. On that morning, I strode down Montgomery Street in my fur-lined cowboy boots and reported to strike headquarters on the Park Blocks, where student leaders urged supporters to encourage those in class to join the action. Convinced that the country was facing a historic crisis requiring immediate response and wanting to do my part in the struggle, I instantly accepted the assignment. A few minutes later, I entered a building in the company of an unfamiliar compatriot.

Our first class turned out to be a Russian language course taught by an older female instructor, a Soviet émigré, I later learned. Despite Richard Nixon's move toward détente, this was not the place to rally opposition to a war against Moscow's communist allies in Southeast Asia. Not aware of these circumstances, I explained to the class that the normal routines of university life no longer could be maintained during the emergency produced by Kent State. Viewing the intrusion as unfair bullying of an older woman, however, one of the students moved to the front to protest our presence.

"I don't give a s--t what you think!" I told him, an intemperate outburst that may have had more to do with my lack of coffee that morning than anything else.

The challenger then pushed me away.

"Where I come from, if somebody pushes you, you push back!" I replied.

As I followed through, the heavy set woman who had accompanied me started screaming "f-----g fascist pigs" at everyone in sight.

Not long after my companion and I had moved on to a second room, a towering figure grabbed me from behind and effortlessly lifted me into the hallway. I subsequently learned he was the speech instructor of the class about to start in the room and a National Guard officer. I had experienced an uncanny run of bad luck in selecting appropriate venues for the urgent message to Portland State students.

Offering no resistance to superior force, I returned to the Park Blocks and joined a crowd of three hundred protesters deploying wooden benches to blockade traffic on S.W. Broadway, the nearby arterial route. The intention was to demonstrate that society would not be permitted to function in a normal manner when students were arbitrarily shot and bankrupt political leaders misused their power to perpetuate a pointless and bloody war. Yet there was something ludicrous about terrorizing ordinary homemakers and business people who were not necessarily our opponents. Fortunately, I missed two of the seamier incidents that followed that day, the food fight that accompanied a late-afternoon effort to "liberate" the university cafeteria and the trashing of the Student Center by drunken non-students later in the evening.

Sensing the university was no longer under his control, Wolfe formally closed the institution on the first night of protests. The next day brought what I saw as the only redeeming moment of the strike. As twenty of us sought to close the downtown military induction center, we clasped hands as a small contingent of police moved in to disperse us. Their intended point of entry turned out to be the space between strike leader Doug Weiskopf and myself. Holding on to each other as tightly as possible, we miraculously maintained our ground, and to my surprise, the officers retreated. Then, in a stroke of genius, somebody suggested that we declare victory and return to campus. Doug and I never could figure out why the police hadn't simply clubbed us to gain entry.

That night, over three hundred parents, faculty, staff, and students attended an off-campus meeting. In a voice trembling with intensity, German history professor Frank West rose to remind the packed house that war and repression had been the hallmarks of the Nazi state. My own thoughts were captured by Philosophy's Mike Phillips, who said the only way to bring an end to Vietnam was to make it too expensive for the government to run it. Striking, said Mike, was a way of making it costly.

On Friday morning, Barbara Vatter and I led a small Park Blocks teach-in on imperialism. That evening brought a memorial service for the Kent State martyrs. By now, 350 American colleges and universities had closed their doors and millions of students and sympathizers had taken to the streets. Yet the climax to the Portland State drama did not come until Monday, May 11th. As protesters began to dismantle barricades along the Park Blocks cross-streets, city officials extended the permit for the strikers' medical tent. At 4 p.m. that day, however, Commissioner of Parks Frank Ivancie rescinded the extension and ordered 170 members of the Tactical Operation Patrol (TAC) Squad to campus to dismantle the symbolic heart of the protest.

Ivancie may have hoped to win political favor by making an example of PSU. Possibly misreading the situation, strike leaders called for a non-violent sit-in. Instead of preparing for civil disobedience, however, the helmeted police formed a V-wedge, readied their forty-two-inch batons, and slowly advanced on the two hundred activists gathered in front of the medical tent.

I was in the middle of the assembly. Hearing the order to disperse, we hissed the uniformed phalanx surrounding us. Suddenly, the formation surged forward. Finding myself before swinging clubs, I sought to save face by retreating in as dignified and deliberate a fashion as I could. Yet just as an officer's baton grazed my uplifted thigh, the stranger alongside me lunged at the perpetrator, who calmly raised his club and bounced it off the top of the protester's head. The young man instantly crumbled to the ground. It had all the feel of a Saturday morning cartoon. Nevertheless, I decided to save the dazed man from serious injury by grabbing his shoulders and dragging him through the side door of the student union to the backup first-aid center.

When I returned to the street, the confrontation was over: thirty-two protesters had been clubbed or beaten; twenty-seven would be hospitalized with head injuries or lacerations. Fifteen of the TAC Squad had been slightly hurt. A *Vanguard* photo of the aftermath shows me at the front of an angry crowd taunting the police with cries of "*Sieg Heil.*"

FUGITIVE

My voice still trembling from fear and rage, I returned to the history department to describe the attack to my colleagues. This was unnecessary. Several had witnessed the event with a perfect view from the corner conference room window. When I ventured the fiasco had given new life to a strike close to its natural conclusion, my colleague Jim Heath concurred. Yet he warned that the turn of events had not displeased some people. Pressed for detail, he reported that an older historian who often complained that sociologists were taking over the discipline had chortled that the "damn anarchists in the Park Blocks got what they deserved."

Attitudes of this sort were not completely rare. During a special meeting to heal the rift in the university community, the strike committee asked me to deliver an appeal for financial assistance for injured students. When I dutifully complied, a huge round of boos echoed across the gym. I had failed to realize that many academics and their spouses saw my plea as an attempt to fuel the partisan fires they viewed as a threat to the continuing health of the university and their livelihoods.

In reality, I was not completely at ease in the role of agitator. Marching to City Hall with three thousand people the day after the Park Blocks blowup, I felt a sense of futility, a sentiment I often experienced in political demonstrations. I was more comfortable when a few evenings later I appeared on a local TV news program with strike leaders Cathy Wood and Peter Fornara. Assuming a reflective pose, I sought to place student protest in historical context and portray the idealism with which young people were assuming the burdens of democracy. I had taken to heart New Left historian Martin Duberman's work on antislavery. Rather than creatures of emotional instability, argued Duberman, activists embodied the virtues of rational adulthood because they assumed responsibility for the consequences of their actions and accepted society's challenges.

As classes resumed after the strike, I prepared for a visit from my brother. Michael had bounced back into the swing of things in the two years since I had last seen him. He now had a political science MA from the New School. In February 1969, the *New York Free Press* had published his "Birth of Techno-Technology," a pithy exploration of Marshall McLuhan's desire to link modern communications to the "retribalizing" of the planet. Two months later, *Crawdaddy* printed the profile on Jim Morrison of The Doors that *Esquire* had rejected. Now, *Playboy* was preparing to publish Michael's "Portrait of the Marxist as an Old Trouper," a breezy attempt to award pop culture status to philosopher Herbert Marcuse, one of Michael's former Brandeis mentors. With the outlines of a manuscript on "Our Hippie Heritage" in hand, my brother was on his way to San Francisco to see about hooking up with one of the city's new counterculture magazines.

"Guess what?" I announced as Michael came off the plane.

"It looks like I'm going to be arrested."

Rumors had circulated for days that the district attorney was about to press charges for my involvement in the classroom incident after the student who objected to my presence had registered a complaint. I filled Michael in on the details as we hoofed over to meet Penny Allen at Reuben's Five, the tavern serving as the prime gathering spot for antiwar activists. There we talked to bartender Mike McCusker, a former Vietnam Marine sergeant who had organized the Park Blocks medical tent. On the way back, we ran into Walt Curtis, Portland's reigning street poet. The next afternoon, Penny and I completed Michael's initiation by whisking him away to the North Coast, where we settled in at Picture Window Cottages, a funky group of rentals on an ocean bluff between Cannon Beach and Arch Cape.

Several days after we returned to town, the *Oregon Journal* ran a front-page blurb that the police were about to serve me with a disorderly conduct warrant. A radio news bulletin even described me as a fugitive professor. When nothing materialized by the next afternoon, Joe Uris, now a *Vanguard* columnist, decided to investigate.

Disguising his voice, Joe called police headquarters and inquired if the authorities were "lookin' for this guy Horowitz 'cause I think I saw him around here a couple of times."

The officer on the other end explained that the police expected me to accept the warrant at downtown headquarters.

By 2:30 p.m. the next day, I had filled out the requisite forms, been fingerprinted, posted one hundred dollars' bail, been assigned a plea appearance in municipal court, and been freed on my own recognizance. Curiously, a page-one insert in the following day's newspaper carried the headline, "Complaint Catches Up With Professor." One report even had police coming to my room to arrest me at 2:30 *a.m.*

"I'm already tired of being a celebrity after two days," I told *Vanguard* reporter and strike leader Cathy Wood, "but if the press wants to make a folk hero out of me, that's all right."

On June 1st, my attorney, Nick Chaivoe, for whom Rita now worked as a legal assistant, submitted a not guilty plea. Eight days later, the *Vanguard* reported that PSU Vice President Robert Low had authored a memo exploring grounds for my termination. Yet history chair Jesse Gilmore insisted that the offense was not serious enough to warrant dismissal. Seeking to ascertain any political pressure for my firing, Michael drove to the state capital in Salem to test the waters. Nobody wanted my head, he learned; their main interest was John Froines, the University of Oregon chemist indicted as a member of the Chicago Eight.

Just as Michael returned from Salem, a movement lawyer informed me that the district attorney had issued a subpoena for my appearance before a grand jury investigating the PSU strike. Prosecutors were intent on tying the protest to the Radical Social Science Union. Aware that grand jury witnesses risked contempt if they refused to answer questions or withheld information, I was not anxious to testify. Several days after the end of spring term, I received a gesture of support from summer school coordinator and history department colleague Charlie White, who hired me for a one-day workshop on social change. As the session was about to close, I spotted a man in a dark suit standing in the outer hallway. I was sure he had my subpoena in his hands. Accepting a final student query, I noticed the room had a second exit. Slowly making my way to the side door, I told the questioner that the issue he raised was most interesting but right now, I had to be going.

It was the only time in my academic career that I cut off a student's curiosity.

JAMBOREE

In a flash, I was out the door, racing down a back stairway to the street. I never stopped running until I reached a pay telephone eight blocks away, where I asked Penny to pick me up by car. During the following week, I only returned to Montgomery Street under cover of darkness to retrieve fresh clothes and mail. By now, Penny and I were preparing a trip to Paris, where she was going to lead a PSU summer school workshop on French theater. I had agreed to accompany her because I was ready to type my dissertation, a task as easily accomplished in a French hotel room as anywhere. Earlier that spring, history colleague Whitney Bates had delivered a friendly word of advice.

There were several people who would be delighted if I never finished the thesis, Bates warned.

"Do me a favor," he pleaded. "Get the damned thing done."

Penny had arranged for Bob Williams, a PSU philosophy instructor who had just completed a federal prison sentence as a Vietnam War draft resister, to house-sit for the summer. Michael was to ride with us to our charter flight in Vancouver, B.C., before driving my car to San Francisco to check out job leads. As we crossed the freeway bridge across the Columbia River to Washington State, my brother bore witness to the escape from the grand jury's clutches.

"They are closing in on the border!" Michael exclaimed in an announcer's voice.

"They are only yards away – so close they can taste it!"

"Here it comes! Yes, they have made it across the state line!"

Once in Paris, Penny and I settled into a hotel on Rue Jacob rumored to have been poet Allen Ginsberg's Left Bank headquarters. As she spent each day exploring the city she loved, I repaired to the desk beneath the front window to transfer the contents of the yellow legal pads containing longhand drafts of my dissertation to a rented typewriter. By summer's end, I had completed a functional typescript of four hundred pages. Yet even in distant Paris, the legacy of the Portland State Park Blocks remained. As Penny and I emerged from the Metro subway onto a large square in search of an anarchist festival on Bastille Day, we found ourselves surrounded by a circle of club-wielding and helmeted police, a frequent event two years after the abortive French student revolt of 1968.

"Uh-oh," I cracked without missing a beat. "I've seen this movie before!"

We never did find the anarchists. Yet the fires of protest beckoned once again following the return to Portland in August. Rumor had it that the American Legion, scheduled to hold its national convention in the city that month, had invited President Nixon to lead a "Victory in Vietnam" parade down Broadway. In response, Mike McCusker, Kevin Mulligan, and other former PSU strike activists had organized a People's Army Jamboree to fuse counterculture and antiwar energies into the festival of life that had been disrupted by the Chicago police two years earlier. Underground press outlets on the West Coast now predicted that thousands of long-hairs and street fighters would descend on Portland. The White House even used the anticipated protest to justify consideration of the secret Huston Plan to coordinate covert domestic intelligence operations.

To prevent a confrontation, local officials insisted that the Jamboree locate its activities several miles away in North Portland's Delta Park. Nevertheless, the People's Army assembled its own security force to preclude any pretext for police intervention. I was one of a number of NUC faculty invited to Hugo Maynard's attic to learn to use walkie-talkies. In the end, there was little need for our services. In a brilliant stroke of co-optation, Oregon Governor Tom McCall worked with a group of Portland's "hip" merchants to organize a free rock festival, called Vortex, at Clackamas County's MacIver State Park, the site of the previous summer's Bullfrog II. By attracting potential protesters outside Portland, McCall hoped to avoid any violence between Legionnaires and protesters. In a further gesture, Nixon's people ruled out a presidential visit.

The Jamboree came down to a dispirited gathering of some two hundred souls. Beyond a demonstration of self-defense techniques and a moving explanation of the humanistic principles behind gay liberation, most of the conclave's predictable rhetoric appeared to be preaching to the choir. For me, the highlight of the week occurred when an easily identifiable middle-aged Legion veteran stumbled out of a taxi toward the door of our security trailer.

Getting There

"I just wanted to see what all the fuss was about," he stammered.

"They told me I was crazy to come out here, but hell, I had to see what you all were up to."

When we invited the obviously inebriated but curious visitor into the camper for a stale cup of coffee, the dreaded face-off was over. The next day, the People's Army mounted a small march outside the Portland Coliseum, where Vice President Spiro Agnew addressed the Legion in Nixon's place. As Jamboree press officer, meanwhile, my brother had the task of convincing visiting media that Portland had taken the lead in the national antiwar movement. This did not fool *Washington Post* columnist Nicholas van Hoffman.

"The mood here is wrong for massive manifestations," wrote van Hoffman. "The country is too beautiful, the Oregonians too polite and civilized."

FIREWEED

(1970-1972)

Nobody's right/if everybody's wrong
— S. Stills

The radical aspirations of the People's Army Jamboree had been successfully diverted by state officials and dismissed by the media. Curiously, however, Portland State University still faced reverberations from the student strike. At the suggestion of Social Science Dean George Hoffman, President Wolfe asked the faculty advisory council to create an ad hoc committee to determine if my classroom disruption presented "probable cause" for a formal dismissal hearing. By insisting on due process, Hoffman may well have sought to protect me from pressures within and outside the institution. In the end, at any rate, the panel declined to press the case. At the same time, the Division of Continuing Education (DCE) announced it had hired an instructor from a nearby college to replace me in the supplemental night school position the history department had assigned me. In the administrator's professional judgment, I was not the right person to teach adults.

DIVIDED LOYALTIES

History Chair Jesse Gilmore strenuously objected to the withdrawal of my appointment, as did my department colleagues, who voted not to teach night classes until DCE reversed the decision. Barbara Vatter also came to the rescue. A DCE economics instructor, she initiated a widely publicized campaign to reinstate me and reverse what some activists described as the first political firing to come out of the strike. Barbara's petition also demanded equal pay rates between night school and day faculty and addressed evening student concerns with calls for a childcare center, expanded evening library hours, and other reforms. Yet DCE claimed it had the right of veto over department appointments, deemed it professionally inappropriate to provide reasons for its decision in my situation, and refused to consider reinstating me since I never had been "hired" in the first place.

Choosing to overlook the fact that the history faculty had backed me to the hilt, I now placed myself in the middle of another department controversy. An NUC colleague, a Hungarian-born scholar who taught Eastern European history, had been denied tenure and faced termination at the end of the academic year. Taken by surprise, I begged for an explanation at a private meeting with a liberal-minded historian I admired. Yet as a member of the department tenure committee, my colleague told me, he had to maintain total confidentiality. I could only conclude that the radical professor's rather brusque demeanor and uncompromising politics had offended the accepted expectations for a tenured academic.

My comrade's case was not helped by his mercurial wife, a quick-tempered Puerto Rican nationalist who sported spiked heels, openly cursed PSU President Gregory Wolfe, issued threats against the CIA, and had been suspended from student status for disrupting Marine recruiting on campus. At the same time, I learned that the department previously had declined an interest in William Appleman Williams, who wound up leaving Wisconsin for Oregon State University (PSU hired two historians instead, I subsequently discovered). Seeing the tenure denial as part of a pattern, I authored an unsigned Radical Social Science Union broadside that focused on the senior professor of Russian history, a Ukrainian anticommunist with World War II service as both an anti-Nazi and anti-Soviet partisan.

By posing the motivation for the decision as a series of questions, a ploy I have repeatedly used, I hoped to dramatize the problematic status of radicals in the university. To my consternation, however, a recently hired historian sent me a note stating that if she were a member of the committee overseeing my own tenure, she would not support me for showing public disrespect toward a colleague. As the case continued to fester, in fact, I felt torn between loyalty to my dissident faculty friends and to fellow historians. Not surprisingly, I experienced a sense of relief when the radical instructor left that June. Years later, I learned the controversy had originated in a complaint involving the exchange of a female student's grade for personal considerations.

ECOLA

It was perhaps ironic that my departing NUC colleague had been the friend who had told me about the vacancy on Montgomery Street. Returning from campus one evening during the fall of 1970, I stopped for a light bite at Lydia's, a dimly lit cocktail lounge a block away. The establishment's black vinyl booths provided the perfect setting for a jukebox pulsating with soulful country hits that included Kris Kristofferson's "For the Good Times" and "Help Me Make It Through the Night." In the darkened space of the bar, Valerie, a student in my Social Change seminar, waved hello and invited me to join her table. She was seated with a wide-eyed blonde about five-foot-two, whose bright lipstick, revealing neckline, and pink-tinted glasses caught my attention. This was Suzanne, her new roommate in the flat just below mine.

Not yet twenty-two, Sue had worked as a production assistant at a San Francisco TV station. She had been raised in the Alameda district of Northeast Portland, but her mother now had a small motel and antique shop in Cannon Beach, where Sue had been married to a garage operator. Once the couple split and she took up with a congenial hippie craftsman in a converted caboose, she decided to taste the waters of academia and enroll in PSU literature classes. Suzanne liked the fact that I was a professor. When the conversation turned to old-time music and this alluring and seemingly available woman swayed both her outstretched palms as if doing the Charleston, I reciprocated her interest.

Not long after, I attended a NUC weekend retreat at Neahkahnie Beach on the North Coast. By now, a pleasant cohesion had developed around the PSU radicals. When a movement luminary visited that year, he complimented us on how well we got along.

"But we don't do anything!" someone objected.

The visitor responded that back East, the Left never accomplished anything either but spent all its time feuding.

I had invited Sue to join the meeting, but the pretensions of radical politics merely amused her. Instead, she arranged to pick me up at the end of the session and take me to her mother's place in nearby Cannon Beach. The Elk Beach Lodge was a six-unit motel with a wooden stairway leading to the "Crow's Nest" antique shop. Situated near the marshes along Ecola Creek, it faced westward to the sands where the Native American Clatsop people had shown Lewis and Clark a beached whale. Clumps of pampas grass dotted the front lawn, a complement to the faded yellow paint on the weatherbeaten cedar shake siding.

Sue's mother, Inez, was the granddaughter of an Oregon Clatsop Plains pioneer. Her father had carried the mail by horseback along the treacherous beach and mountain trail from Astoria to Tillamook. During the 1930s, Inez had run the Tu-be Tavern in Southeast Portland. After divorcing her husband and purchasing the motel, she had adopted a distinguished-sounding French surname. Sue's uncle, Willis Eberman, an effusive gay poet given to bouts of theatricality, occasionally visited from Seaside, where he lived with his lifelong companion, an accomplished sculptor. As her eccentric brother swept through the front door with a flowing cape, Inez would announce the arrival of "His Majesty." Yet she seemed taken by my academic status.

"Will the professor be spending the night?" she liked to inquire with a twinkle of the eye.

At first when Sue and her mother mixed talk of "one-night stands" and "Saturday night specials" with doses of Thirties slang, I wondered what sort of establishment they ran. At a modest nine to twelve dollars a night, however, the motel's clean and modern units were just what they appeared to be. Inez did her own laundry, made the beds, booked reservations, kept the accounts, and ran the antique shop. On top of this, her second husband was dying of cancer.

Inez had three complaints. First, she had no tolerance of the "freeloaders," daytime coastal visitors who never rented overnight lodgings. Second, she took exception to "the Christians" who ran the nearby religious conference center and paid no property taxes. Finally, she reserved her strongest condemnation for the town fathers in the process of tearing down Cannon Beach's old businesses and replacing them with upscale boutiques. The place was fast becoming "the Carmel of the North," she complained. Accordingly, Inez loved to scandalize the locals by heralding the Legion Hall as the only place in town where "a white man" could get a drink on Sundays and shoot a decent game of pool (an uncanny confirmation of Mickey McCleery's lessons at Antioch College).

Politics at the Elk Beach Lodge were decidedly populist. Inez had no taste for the Vietnam War but had supported Hubert Humphrey in 1968 as the only candidate representing "the working man." Referring to Chicago and the Yippies, she complained that "you kids" had destroyed the Democratic Party and elected Richard Nixon, an admonition I took to heart. Although Inez had a distaste for people who used pot or drugs, she had a distinct taste for whisky. Furious that her mother had indulged when we came down for Thanksgiving, Sue demanded that we drive to San Francisco. On the way, we stopped in Davis, where my brother was taking advantage of cheap student housing and the university library to compile his "Hippie Bible" of the world's metaphysical traditions. Fittingly, the California rains approached Biblical proportions.

APRIL FOOLS

When winter term resumed in January 1971, Bob Williams, now teaching philosophy again, led a campaign to prevent Portland State's student-run housing cooperative from erecting a sixteen-story apartment building in the historic bohemian community of Goose Hollow. Located ten blocks from the University, the district featured single-story Victorian housing and an eclectic collection of artists, craftspeople, students, and hippies. In early February, several of us attended a city council meeting to register objections to the proposed development. A week later, 150 PSU faculty and students met to condemn U.S. logistical support for South Vietnam's invasion of neighboring Laos. Although President Nixon had withdrawn U.S. troops from Cambodia, lowered draft quotas, and reduced Vietnam troop commitments following Kent State, he had stepped up air strikes. In an open letter that Bob and I distributed to the faculty, we stressed that hostilities were far from over and called for continued discussion of the "morally debilitating war" amid a virtual news embargo from Laos.

Despite its best efforts, the antiwar movement seemed to be on the defensive after Kent State. Accordingly, visiting speakers played a crucial role in sustaining morale. In March, my namesake, David J. Horowitz, then an associate editor of the radical *Ramparts* magazine, addressed an overflow crowd in the PSU Ballroom on "The Fall of the American Empire." Summing up the critique of U.S. foreign policy he had presented in the widely read *Free World Colossus*, Horowitz argued that after 1945, the United States had used the Open Door Policy to dominate other countries. Washington's expansionism, he insisted, had resulted in a role as "policeman of the world." Self-determination in developing nations, he argued, posed a threat to such power.

"The only way the American Empire is going to fall," Horowitz predicted, was "for the world revolution to finally come home to this country."

Following the talk, I joined a small contingent who lunched with the speaker at the Wayfarer, a vegetarian restaurant operated by a group from the radical Storefront Theater. Eager to cultivate friends among the Left, Horowitz passed out his Berkeley address and phone number.

On April Fool's Day, 1971, I appeared in court for my classroom disruption trial. By now, my attorney, Nick Chaivoe, was representing Portland Black Panther Kent Ford in a high-profile civil case against city police. Not surprisingly, Nick had barely prepared a defense for my misdemeanor. When a witness asserted I had used profane language on the day in question, Chaivoe inquired if he was aware of the cursing prevalent in military barracks.

Moments later, the judge asked me if "they ever read the Bible up there at Portland State."

When I replied that some classes probably studied the Scriptures as literary texts, he snapped that he didn't mean that.

"Bailiff, does this man have a record?" the judge asked.

"Well, he does now," he declared from the bench. "One year probation and a hundred-dollar fine."

EARTH RED

Minutes after the proceeding, I met my probation officer. Aware of the judge's reputation, he laughed when I recounted the courtroom exchange. Then he asked about prospects for a teaching position in PSU's school of social work. Handing me some forms, he explained that if I mailed one in every month I would satisfy the terms of my sentence.

Nick Chaivoe also handled my divorce. Since Rita completed all the paperwork as his legal assistant, there was no charge for the service.

Later that month, I drove up to Longview, Washington, where the president of Lower Columbia College had hired my brother for a series of lectures on American youth culture. Michael invited me to join him for a dialogue on the counterculture. He even talked a drive-time radio host into putting us on the air at 7:30 in the morning. I was to present a critique of alternative culture from a conservative perspective, a task that had to be accomplished in fifteen-or twenty-second sound bites. I enjoyed reducing ideas to spare phrasing. Playing devil's advocate, I spoke for the work and family values associated with the white ethnic working class while

Michael addressed the cultural revolution. The exchange of perspectives would continue to be one of our favorite topics of discussion.

In June, I flew to Minneapolis to defend my dissertation, which a professional typist had put into final form. The friendly exam committee of Allan Spear, Clarke Chambers, and Dave Noble urged me to get the work published. Yet I never followed through, partly because its string of long quotations required substantial revision, and partly because the same distractions that had delayed completion of the manuscript continued to preoccupy me.

With the resolution of my legal case, divorce, and PhD, the future seemed promising. Yet I still felt conflicted between the expectations of radical cohorts and loyalty to professional colleagues. Like Thomas Jefferson, I wielded a sharp pen but shied away from direct confrontation. When the history department moved to the other end of our building, therefore, I cheerfully accepted an office assignment in the outer hall. I also felt relieved that my noon class prevented lunching with fellow faculty in the department conference room. Enclosed in my own mindset, I failed to acknowledge that most of the historians shared my antiwar views and had defended me during the DCE scrape. Instead, I blithely assumed that "liberals" had reasons for whatever they did.

Partly out of the need to infuse humanistic qualities into politics, I signed on to a new men's liberation group that included philosophy professors Bob Williams and Mike Phillips. The idea was to free men from sexist behavior through feminist-styled consciousness-raising. Each participant was to present an autobiographical narrative for group comment. When it was my turn, I explained how during the 1950s my mother had convinced my father that she could build up the college fund for my brother and me by attending night school and preparing for a teaching certificate. Years later, I recalled, she told me that these aspirations for a career had left some of her Bronx neighbors clucking that her husband's paycheck "wasn't good enough for her."

I enjoyed everyone's stories. Yet the constant quest for ideological rectitude and selfless purity made me somewhat uneasy. At the same time, when an old college friend of Bob Williams attended one of our sessions and published a piece about us in *Life* magazine entitled "You've Come a Long Way, Buddy," I came across even more self-consciously sensitive than anyone else.

Suzanne never took the men's liberation group seriously. Enamored of her curiosity about the universe and working-class grit, I saw our relationship as a way of getting beyond my protected upbringing and predictable identity as an academic intellectual and radical. I now had a full beard and sported a tiny, red-ruby opal earring in my left ear once Sue pierced it. Virtually moving upstairs to my flat, she painted the walls earth red, providing the place with a hippie ambience. Then she redid the kitchen in a cheerful blue, decorated the room's outer wall with a painting of a window looking out to flowers and trees, and framed the image with real curtains. Not long after, Sue brought home a huge waterbed, beaded doorway curtains, and an ample supply of incense.

By 1971, the understated lyrics and acoustic instrumentation of folk rock had become a counterculture fixture. We grooved to the exotic Cajun fiddles and mandolins of Doug Kershaw and Rod Stewart and took to the winsome tales of James Taylor, Jackson Browne, Randy Newman, Bonnie Raitt, The Band, and Bob Dylan. My favorite, "Our House," Crosby, Stills, Nash, and Young's country-style tribute to domestic intimacy, reminded me of the home-cooked dinners Sue occasionally served on a linen-covered table in the flat's back room. Living right in town, we easily accessed city nightlife. The eastside waterfront's Euphoria Tavern provided a venue for Paul deLay's Brown Sugar and other hot blues bands. Additional haunts included the historic bar at the old Hoyt Hotel near Union Station, the twenty-four-hour Quality Pie eatery in Northwest Portland, and occasionally, the Carriage Room, a downtown lounge featuring exotic dancers.

These excursions often included Bob Williams, who lived three doors down the hill in a daylight basement apartment. More often, we entertained overnight visits from Billie, an older friend of Sue's from Cannon Beach whose interests included politics, baseball, vintage movies, 7 a.m. high-rise cement pours, the metaphysics of the *I Ching*, and the *National Enquirer*. Between the *Enquirer*'s scare headlines about space aliens and insidious conspiracies, Billie insisted, one could find pithy summations of "trippy" academic papers charting new directions in medicine, astrophysics, astrology, and parapsychology. Billie's taste for popular culture prompted Sue's purchase of a black and white portable TV. We now caught late-night 1940s and '50s movies on the local independent channel and regularly tuned into Saturday night roller derby, during which we all cheered on the brazen women skaters with the fervor of recent converts.

SMOKE

As I began teaching summer school, Sue borrowed my newly purchased 1963 VW bus for a trip to California. When she returned, she presented me with a huge, curly-haired black Hungarian sheep dog, a Puli she named Buddha. Two weeks later, Bob Williams and Sue pursued our fixation on roller derby by organizing a group excursion to a roller rink on the city's east side. Returning in exhaustion on that hot and dry mid-July night, we mellowed out and watched a TV screening of *On the Waterfront*. As the movie ended, I thought I smelled something burning and consulted my housemate Fred, a physics student whose interest in theoretical cosmology made him a household favorite. Yet when the two of us circled the building, we lost track of the scent. Fred said we had probably picked up the residue of ash from the apartment complex trash incinerator across the street.

This proved to be an unfortunate misjudgment.

After falling into a deep sleep that night, I awoke in a horrifying instant around 3:30 a.m. Simultaneously, I heard Buddha's insistent bark, shrill screams from the street, violent shattering of glass, and a howling roar outside the window that seemed about to consume all existence.

An instant later, I felt my nostrils inundated by the pungent order of burning paint.

"There *is* a fire!" I shouted, my heart racing so fast I could not utter another word.

As I leaped out of the waterbed with nothing on but my red underwear, I instinctively put on my glasses and grabbed my favorite red plaid jacket. When Sue screamed for her spectacles, I clutched them in my hand as we headed for the front stairs. As we passed the kitchen, however, flames lapped at the bottom of the curtains Sue had attached to the outer wall. The stairway to the front entrance was now impassable. Turning around, we saw our house guest Peter stroll out of an adjoining room and light a cigarette.

"What's happening?" he asked as if he had slept through an appointment.

In panic, we rushed to the window leading to the rear balcony. As we frantically climbed through the last escape route out of the developing inferno, I inadvertently crushed Sue's glasses in my hands. Once on the porch, we raced for our lives through the roiling smoke enveloping the rickety stairway leading to the front sidewalk. I was moving so fast, in fact, that I stumbled, fell, and scraped my leg in the pitch dark. Yet the rush of adrenalin was enough to ensure an instant recovery, and we emerged on the street relatively unharmed.

Just as we reached safety amid the flashing lights and sirens of the rescue squads, the incredible heat of the holocaust exploded the front windows of our bedroom. Not yet noticing our deliverance and having just evacuated his building three doors down, Bob Williams assumed we had been trapped.

Relieved to be out of harm's way, I casually watched the canvas roof of my VW bus go up in flames. Then, in a state of shock, I suggested we go down to Bob's for a cup of coffee.

"Get me out of here!" my seemingly flaky girlfriend shouted.

Just about this time, we realized Buddha had not made it out the back window.

By now, twenty-six units and a hundred firefighters had arrrived on the scene. Yet the hot July winds had whipped the blaze into an intense firestorm that made it difficult to approach. Even the palatial homes of the West Hills seeemed threatened by clouds of burning embers. It felt as though the entire city was in jeopardy. Ironically, the three houses to our east and our own were involved in a tenant strike over alleged safety violations. Only two days earlier, a California bank had taken over the properties in an estate settlement. Nevertheless, investigators concluded that although unused dry timbers beneath the rear balconies no doubt fueled the flames, the fire had started in the basement of the structure to the *west* and probably resulted from faulty wiring.

The building where the fire began hosted a charismatic Christian commune. Its leader had sustained cuts and bruises while rescuing his seven-year old son, the victim of second and third-degree burns. Several of us had been curious about our neighbors. On one occasion, I peered through our stairway window into an anteroom where a group holding lit candles had surrounded a beautiful young blonde woman lying on a red velvet platform in a white gown. One day, another woman from the house asked to use the telephone in our flat.

"They took my baby!" she exclaimed through the line, a cry that brought to mind the satanic conspiracies of *Rosemary's Baby.*

Then the conversation abruptly shifted to Governor McCall's Vortex Rock Festival.

"You sold your soul for a f-----g Chevrolet!" the agitated woman screamed.

Our unsettling suspicions about the adjoining house remained shrouded in mystery.

Wearing nothing but underpants, my wool jacket, and my glasses, I accompanied Sue to my friend Alex's house around the bend of the Montgomery Street hill. The next morning, we returned to the scene to see if there was any chance Buddha had turned up or if there were any possessions to salvage. Neither proved to be the case. The five-alarm blaze had completely destroyed five structures, damaged or obliterated a dozen vehicles, and left sixty-five people homeless. Nothing remained of the VW but a burnt-out hulk, and all but one of the devastated buildings was now rubble. As the fire smoldered, we approached the remains of our building where the only survivors were several of my records, melted out of shape but still recognizable by the labels. Fortunately, I had turned in the completed copy of my dissertation six weeks earlier. Yet as we surveyed the burnt-out site, the realization hit that Buddha was gone.

The fire took all the lecture notes for two of my courses, my entire record collection, my two-volume fake book of sheet music, the writing clipboard my father had bestowed upon me, and nearly all my clothing. Yet regret over losing these things paled in comparison to the anguish I felt over the life of the sweet and undemanding being whose barking may have saved our lives.

HEGEMONY

With new I.D., fifty dollars' worth of clothes courtesy of the Red Cross, a generous check from my parents, and temporary housing with Barbara Vatter, now separated from Harold, I prepared to proceed with my life. Once I found a virtual replica of the VW bus, I began to look for a place to live. Sue soon spotted a rental in the Sunday newspaper that seemed the perfect set-up – a two-bedroom, *rock-sided* house in Bridal Veil, a tiny enclave near a lumber mill some thirty miles east of Portland in the Columbia River Gorge.

"You'll never have to worry about a fire again!" she exulted.

An excursion to the site revealed a neat-looking structure with a cluster of funky "hippie" houses to the rear. Set along the old river highway between an abandoned gas station and a functioning tavern, the place featured a back room whose dramatic view of the river offered promise as a study. Once we filled the house with a few of Inez's antiques, including an old piano, some Goodwill furnishings, and several Maxfield Parrish prints, Suzanne introduced me to Beulah, a scruffy-looking, mid-sized female Hungarian Puli who shared her name with a Plymouth sedan Sue once owned.

Just before Halloween we decided to combine a holiday costume party with a Bridal Veil housewarming. The ingredients of a successful gathering, I had come to believe, included great dance music, a healthy quota of mysterious strangers, ample supplies of dandelion wine, and most of all, subtle lighting. Yet even I was unprepared for the entrance Suzanne made. Sporting a "baby doll" outfit highlighted by Shirley Temple curls, bright red lipstick, and floppy high heels, she cruised into the house sucking an infant's plastic milk bottle full of gin.

Part of my attraction to Suzanne involved her mix of outright decadence and conventionality. On Thanksgiving, for example, the only holiday for which I ever have felt real enthusiasm, Sue prepared a traditional turkey dinner with all the trimmings. Sometime that afternoon we heard a radio report that someone identified as D.B. Cooper had taken over a plane at the Portland airport, demanded a huge cash payment, and parachuted with the loot somewhere along the Columbia River. Anticipating the mythic status Cooper would achieve, we exulted that the daring feat had been accomplished so close to home. In fact, as I subsequently discovered, Bridal Veil itself had a colorful history of outlawry as a nineteenth-century hideout for river bandits and highway men.

Living in the Gorge required a forty-minute commute to Portland State, a ritual that had its moments. As mop-haired Beulah lay in the VW passenger seat with her head in my lap, it seemed that every trip back home included an airing of Rod Stewart's eight-minute "Maggie Mae." Each time I heard "it's late September and I really should be back at school," I was hooked by the tune's plaintive fusion of independence and wistful regret. Whatever the allures of the counterculture, however, I maintained a loyal commitment to my classes at the university and the critical approach to history I sought to convey.

Renamed Social Change and Ideology, my fall term seminar in 1971 explored the development of racial attitudes under slavery. I was particularly interested in Eugene Genovese's interpretation of planter-class paternalism. By offering an analysis of the slaveowning ethos, Genovese went beyond purely moralistic condemnations of the South's "peculiar institution." Winter brought an examination of historian Aileen Kraditor's discussion of the tensions between moderate and radical strategies of antislavery activism. Kraditor pointed to the discrepancy between those who saw chattel slavery as the single blot on an otherwise perfectable America and those who viewed slavery as sympomatic of capitalism's commodification of all human beings. In turn, the spring seminar, now called Corporate Hegemony, built upon New Left scholarship to address the dominance of market-oriented American values and policies.

Charles Reich's *The Greening of America* (1970) was one of the main texts of the corporate hegemony class. Often seen as an excessive celebration of the counterculture, Reich's book presented a credible account of the transition from mid-nineteenth-century individualist and entrepeneurial values ("Consciousness I") to the contemporary corporate ethic ("Consciousness II"). I liked the book because it described America's mix of technology, expertise, and bureaucracy as one in which middle-class identity and status were defined by institutional ties.

Just as the seminar moved toward a conclusion, my parents made their first visit to Oregon. My father's status as his company's number one salesman had led to his publishing a monthly motivational column in the firm's national newsletter. For her part, my mother had served as a public school guidance counselor in working-class Corona, Queens, before taking on the additional task of teaching guidance principles as an adjunct professor of graduate education at Long Island University.

Uncle Mickey had warned that my parents had turned quite conservative. My mother had been active in the New York teachers' strike of 1968 that pitted predominantly Jewish union members aginst Black Power activists seeking control of curricula and hiring in minority school districts. Mickey also reported that both parents were now strong defenders of Israel, which they had visited on two occasions. Although my mother was a life-long religious agnostic, the young Israeli nation embodied the dream of idealistic rebirth she once had associated with the socialist and civil rights movements. For my father, a regular attendee at Friday evening services, Israel offered a connection with the Jewish people and a bond with the traditions of childhood.

Following his sixty-third birthday in 1971, my father had confided that the "bearded hairy picture" I had sent was hard to reconcile with the suburban Jewish boy he once knew. Despite my uncle's foreboding, however, the visit proved a great success, particularly on a trip to the Oregon Coast, where we feasted on a fresh salmon dinner and lit the fireplace in a spacious ocean-view motel room. I even brought my parents to one of my classes, where my father chortled at the ease with which I dismissed American heroes of the past.

A HELPING HAND

Not long after the 1971-72 academic year ended, my brother invited me to Del Mar, a southern California beach community where he had rented a house with a friend, Frank Beyerle. Michael had finally completed his hippie bible. The selections in *A Freak's Anthology: Golden Hits from Buddha to Kubrick* spanned the world's spiritual traditions from the *I Ching*, *The Tibetan Book of the Dead*, and *The Upanishads* to the works of Marshall McLuhan, Herbert Marcuse, and Arthur C. Clarke. My brother had created a counterculture canon of alternative metaphysics. I was in Del Mar to help proofread. When we stopped at Sherbourne Press in West L.A., the first thing Michael's publisher told me was that "your brother is going to be famous."

In free time, we drove the VW bus to La Jolla's all-nude Black's Beach or simply spent time on the Del Mar sands. The sun-bleached hair of the blithe young creatures around two sons of the jittery East only accented their god-like appearance. Yet there seemed to be a vacant and self-absorbed quality to these people, a sentiment no doubt sustained by their apparent lack of interest in our existence. One day, Michael, Frank, and I wound up in a volleyball game with a pair of muscular characters who seemed to view our presence as a minor nuisance. I wanted nothing more than to vanguish these arrogant and condescending foes. Yet the more the three of us struggled to return a series of ferocious serves, the further behind we fell. In the end, we quietly succumbed to a humiliating shutout.

At Michael's initiative, we drove up to Isla Vista and Santa Barbara, ventured out to the desert to view the Palomar Observatory, spent a day at Disneyland, and embarked upon a jaunt to Rosario on Mexico's Baja Peninsula, where we stayed in a decaying hotel that once served as a hideaway for Hollywood celebrities of the 1920s. At the end of August, Beulah and I finally headed north. Our first destination was Mike Kaye's ranch in the Los Altos Hills north of San Jose. My father had been steered to the country club houses in Roslyn Heights when on a routine errand to Macy's department store he had run into Mike's dad Julie, a boyhood pal. At Wheatley High, I had known Mike Kaye as a cigarette-smoking "bad boy." Yet my brother now informed me that our former schoolmate had become a major counterculture figure.

Having inherited a fortune after his wife was killed in a horse riding accident, Mike had established a riding academy and alternative school incorporating non-directive approaches to education. He had been drawn to experimental education, he told me, in reaction to the excessive and gratuitous discipline he had experienced at our high school. After dinner, Mike took me to a camper to mellow out with Wavvy Gravy, a legendary Haight-Ashbury fixture who now lived on the property. Yet my men's group training had emphasized the sharing of household chores, and I insisted upon retreating to the kitchen to help "the women" clean up.

As I returned to Cannon Beach to reunite with Suzanne during the late summer of 1972 and took long walks along the sands, I contemplated my future. Michael had just produced a book dedicated to invigorating the counterculture's philosophic coherence. Mike Kaye was at the forefront of educational reform. Meanwhile, many of my radical friends were leaving the university. What was in store for me? Was I merely destined to popularize the work of William Appleman Williams, Eugene Genovese, David W. Noble, and other scholars?

I was also aware that reform-minded Democrats had just nominated George McGovern as the antiwar candidate for president. Yet New Left political resistance appeared to be on the wane. Where would the movement for change direct its focus, I wondered, if Richard Nixon actually ended the Vietnam War? Was there any energy left among activists? Most important, was there a way to combine analytic tools with a vibrant approach to society and politics that incorporated a counterculture form of spontaneity and sense of play?

After some time, my heady ruminations led to the idea of writing an opinion column for the Portland State University student paper, the *Vanguard*. What better way to grapple with prospects for change than to compile a weekly diary of observations expressed in a disciplined and concise manner? By fulfilling the role of "people's" intellectual, perhaps I could succeed in demonstrating that rigorous cultural analysis could be fun and even enlightening. Sensing that prospects for expanded consciousness and social justice faced a long haul, that the "revolution," if at all plausible, was far in the distance, I aspired to taking on a minor role in the ensuing dialogue.

After all, no one else seemed to have any idea of the way forward.

Perhaps I could help.

FERMENT

(1972-1974)

I may not have the answer but I believe I got a plan
– J. Browne

THE FIRST INSTALLMENT OF *FREEWAY*, MY NEW *VANGUARD* column, welcomed "the steel-eyed 1970s, a time of reckoning for the troubled campus and for a weary and unhappy nation."

"Changing Times," PSU President Gregory Wolfe's September 1972 address to the faculty, I noted, pointed to a sagging economy, taxpayer revolt, and a 12 percent drop in enrollment. Wolfe took particular note of "the low utility of undergraduate education for the younger generation." At issue, I wrote, was the requirement that universities lead the way to capitalizing on human resources to increase the demands for goods. This meant advanced training in fields such as urban studies and media communications, programs at the heart of Wolfe's institutional blueprint. Technique, not critical questioning of values, I concluded, was the relevant ingredient.

PIGS

My initial foray into opinion making humanized the president's predicament but emphasized the economic factors that radical critics saw as central to business domination. This was not surprising for a historian with a reading seminar on "Corporate Hegemony." Influenced by the New University Conference, I devoted my next column to the proposed PSU Pacific Rim Studies Center. Citing a statement by the State Board of Higher Education, I explained that the key for Asian market development was knowledge of the culture, behavior, and values of the region's people. The Center would seek to manage this population in a manner conducive to U.S. interests, I contended. I even repeated accusations that one of the principal figures in the scheme had CIA connections. The next week, I focused on economic imperialism as an expropriation of global resources that social revolutionaries wished to use to benefit their own societies.

Although a faculty senate committee subsequently questioned whether the focus of the Pacific Rim Studies Center was academics or business interests, few professors would have accepted my terms for discussing these issues. Sometime that fall, Joe Uris told me that Greg Wolfe had joked that I wrote like an "old lady." Indeed, by repeating boilerplate radical rhetoric, I had opened myself up to this sort of critique. In search of a fresh approach, I switched tactics with a column reflective of language itself. Citing terms such as "model cities," "preventive retaliation," "body count," "administrative justice," and "economic opportunity," I wrote that corporate culture's depersonalized discourse had so distorted words that nobody trusted them anymore.

"Enigmatic lovers drag heavily on dangling cigarettes and coolly blow smoke in each other's eyes," I noted, "but nobody talks."

It was no wonder, I ruminated, that the popularity of political candidates had an inverse relationship to their public exposure. Yet the piece saw academic jargon and truisms about race, sex, and homeland as sharing the blame. When people did not communicate, I warned, they had little patience for problems without simple resolutions. Political activists, like others, had to abandon hasty moral judgments and clichés and learn to adopt complex modes of analysis.

Having asked dissenters to understand the subtleties of motivation, I now turned the tables on myself. Like Puritans in Babylon, I observed in the next column, radical professors were in constant fear of taking on the colors of the Philistines. The irony was that they served the institutions they sought to subvert. Academic dissidents were like court jesters whose presence legitimized their patrons. They knew that an overly assertive stance could elicit dismissal but also that an excessively conciliatory posture reduced threats to the status quo. The social system, moreover, easily absorbed ideas about alternative lifestyles and cooperative economics with no resulting change. It may be, I acknowledged, that radicals did more to uphold the market apparatus by staying within the university than by leaving. After all, their continuing presence suggested that ideas were more important than social structures. Yet I concluded it never hurt to help people think critically, deal reasonably with limitations, and proceed from there.

Perhaps the way out of the bind, I ventured, was a creative cynicism open to surprise.

Days before the 1972 presidential election, *freeway* profiled George McGovern, a peace crusader for whom I had great affection. Yet I complained that the Democratic candidate filled passionless speeches with stilted pieties and had failed to win hearts and minds. McGovern, I wrote, seemed to come across as a lofty moralist out of touch with an electorate that wanted a president ruthless enough to protect its interests in a harsh world. Voters could not afford the illusion of believing in promises to bring America home to old-fashioned government morality, I surmised, when they knew in their hearts it could never be and preferred to forget it was not.

Nevertheless, when I walked down the hill to cast a ballot at the tiny shed that served as the Bridal Veil post office, a chill raced through my spine: Americans were going through the same ritual of democracy all across the country. Still, my unease with McGovern's campaign scarcely prepared me for the scale of Richard Nixon's 60+ percent landslide. When my brother called on Election Night as I sat silently before the TV in the darkened living room of the Bridal Veil house, as he subsequently recalled, he sensed a level of despair that made him wonder if I was going to survive the night.

Desperate to make sense of it all before attempting another column, I sought the counsel of Mike Passi. During the spring of 1971, the history department had found funds to hire a social historian on a non-tenure basis. Asked for a recommendation, I contacted Bruce Goldstein, who knew of a brilliant Minnesota graduate student who had just completed his PhD in immigration and ethnic history. Arriving at PSU that fall, Passi came to exert a major influence. A tall and gangly Finn from the Minnesota Iron Range with an aquiline nose and a mop of straight dark hair hanging over his peering eyes, my new colleague had a gruff and brooding air about him not the least abated by a taste for undiluted black coffee, unfiltered cigarettes, and rounds of straight-up Scotch. The first of his family to make it to college, never mind graduate school, Passi left behind a host of cousins and uncles still serving on the county road crews. Little wonder his passion was working-class history and the social values and experience of ordinary people.

Set amid the cushioned complacencies of academia, Passi's populist credentials opened up new worlds. Where else could I have learned that you could tell a person's social class from the state of their teeth, since only the affluent could afford dental care? Beyond these insights, Mike introduced me to Michael Novak's *Rise of the Unmeltable Ethnics* (1971). A critique from a Polish-American Catholic, the book called for historians, journalists, and progressives to accept the cultural legitimacy of blue-collar and lower-middle-class Euro-Americans. In the eyes of many Poles, Italians, Greeks, and Slavs (whom Novak humorously referred to as "PIGS"), as well as Orthodox Jews, countercultural inroads into the media and condescension toward white ethnics made the alternative culture a class-privileged extension of the Establishment.

Passi was a far more diligent scholar and teacher than I was. He already had taken advantage of Portland State's university status to assume directorship of several history MA theses. Could my colleague's fusion of experience and theory offer the chance to explain the election? For three anguished weeks, no *freeway* appeared. When it finally did, I presented a distillation of an extended interview with the department's new social historian.

Although McGovern's defeat did not spell fascism for America or a victory of racism, bigotry, or reactionary hysteria, Passi suggested, the results should prompt those seeking social change to take a good look at the millions of Americans who had repudiated their vision of the future. Nixon had pointed to the limits of moralistic liberalism and the danger of an arrogant government telling ordinary people how to run their lives. Indeed, many voters resented paying taxes to support social services for those who did not work or for those perceived as failing to practice personal discipline. By courting favored minorities at the expense of other Americans facing similar struggles, said Passi, McGovern and the liberals had sealed their fate.

Passi pictured the quest for alternative values and lifestyles as a form of middle-class missionary idealism. Ordinary Americans, he said, took exception to media and youth-culture depictions of their lives as empty and meaningless. Embittered by the manner in which their dedication to hard work and family morality seemed belittled, working people did not as much object to marijuana, homosexuality, abortion, and draft evasion, Passi suggested, as to efforts to legitimize and universalize these practices. In effect, they refused to tell followers of alternative lifestyles how liberated and free they were. Accordingly, the nation had witnessed an upsurge of conservative populism against a seemingly arrogant liberal Establishment.

WORKING THE SYSTEM

The conversation with Passi provided a paradigm-altering experience that meshed with the populist predispositions I had explored in the Longview debate with my brother, and indeed, with some of my own family's roots. Building off these insights, I concluded the column by noting that progressive social change would materialize only when the dreams, hopes, and fears of working people received serious treatment by those who should be their allies, not their adversaries. It probably was not a coincidence, then, that I turned to the world of commercial television for the term's final *freeway*.

Rejecting the puritan and academic convention that pleasure and knowledge could not co-exist, I produced an effusive treatment of the popular *Mary Tyler Moore Show*. Scriptwriter Rob Reiner, I suggested, had a perverse genius for zeroing in on those moments when middle-class niceties became total absurdities. The best intentions of pert, pretty, and peppy television news producer Mary, I marveled, seemed to generate complications beyond her control when well-meaning clichés stuck in her throat. I pictured the series as a tragicomic look at the inner fears, anxieties, and absurdities of American social life. Yet although the dialogue captured the inanity of middle-class convention, I wrote, the ensemble's exquisitely drawn characters gave the drama real vitality when they engaged in genuine communication at unexpected moments.

At Christmas, Bruce Goldstein visited and we split for the Coast. Having left academia for commercial photography, Bruce loved shooting images along the rocky Pacific beaches, drinking wine amid hazy smoke half the night, and staring up at the stars to theorize about the mystery of the great Mayan pyramids or the imponderables of the universe. In the spirit of countercultural play, we carried on intense discussions that seemed highly significant at the time but often escaped subsequent recollection. Our concerns, nevertheless, usually centered on the spiritual essence of existence and the apparent superficiality of conventional social morality.

Just after the turn of 1973, a response to one of my letters from former Antioch classmate Lucy Gilbert offered a distinct counterpoint to these speculations. A dedicated feminist, Lucy was completing a PhD in psychology. She said I sounded angry at women trying to liberate themselves *from* men instead of *with* them. It seemed as if I wanted them to go off and work out their rage without dumping on me, she wrote. If my privileged position left me without the desire to break down inequality and injustice, she scolded, I was ultimately engaging in a self-defeating strategy. The truth, she said, was that my life was as incomplete as anyone else's because of the very system I had become so good at manipulating.

I *was* skilled at working the system. With my dissertation complete in 1971, I had looked forward to academic tenure and an associate professorship. Yet my classroom disruption and public criticism of the department prompted the opposition of several older historians. As a result, only a bare majority of tenured members voted in my favor. Following the counsel of Jesse Gilmore, I visited Social Science Dean George Hoffman, who said he had no problem supporting my promotion but wanted to wait another year. Hoffman assured me that no one in the administration had pressured him. Against the advice of several friends, I took the dean at his word. When the department produced a more favorable vote in the fall of 1972, then, Hoffman sent his approval up the chain of command. Convinced that my antiwar activities were sincerely rooted, he stated that he was sure I would pursue further dissent within proper bounds.

I discontinued *freeway* during the winter of 1973. By now, the Bridal Veil commute had become a burden, requiring overnight stays in town during bad weather, and the search for a more convenient rental seemed to consume all spare energy. Finally, I discovered a vacant 1920s-era house with a garbled roof and lush laurel shrubbery in front at the edge of the Ladd's Addition neighborhood of Southeast Portland. Tracking down the owner in city records, I learned the property was for sale for fourteen thousand dollars. Since I dismissed home ownership as a "bourgeois" responsibility, I struck a deal to rent the place at $140 a month, 1 percent of market value, if I took care of minor repairs. With a fireplace, hardwood floors, and mullioned windows in the living room; a sunny dining area with a bay window seat; a cheerful kitchen; and two spacious upstairs bedrooms, this was all I possibly desired.

Relocation to Portland coincided with increased involvement at the university. Based on a reading of my columns, Liberal Arts Dean Bill Hamilton asked me to participate in a symposium on "America 1984." Joining film studies professor Andries Deinum and an urban studies graduate student, I provided a synopsis of William Irwin Thompson's *At the Edge of History* (1971), a wide-ranging work of cultural criticism that ostracized planners for resorting to one-dimensional models of human behavior. Following the panel, Suzanne and I joined a small reception at the dean's apartment. Thrilled to mingle with the academic crowd, Sue engaged Greg

Wolfe's wife, Marianne, an expert in Latin American literature, in an extended conversation on Colombian novelist Gabriel Garcia Marquez. Then she moved on to President Wolfe himself, whom she easily charmed.

"You won't have any trouble getting your tenure now," she giggled as we left.

We had a hearty laugh when, by coincidence or not, Wolfe signed the papers weeks later.

WITNESS

Increasingly confident about my place in the profession, I asked Bill Williams to talk to slavery historian Eugene Genovese about delivering a lecture at Portland State. The plan worked beautifully until a scheduling conflict forced Genovese to cancel. Mike Passi then suggested that I contact Dave Noble. Noble was now exploring how pre-modern people had defined Nature as Place, and Time as cyclical. In contrast, modern civilization saw Nature in terms of Space and viewed Time as a linear road to perfection. Noble used Thomas Kuhn's model of evolving worldviews or paradigms to suggest that modern cultural identity was on the verge of a breakdown. Promoting the lecture as "The End of the Myth of Progress," I prepared a *Vanguard* article around the speaker's contention that Americans no longer could escape history.

By the time Noble arrived in May 1973, developments in Washington, D.C. were on the front page. After mounting a publicity campaign back East for *A Freak's Anthology*, my brother had returned to Portland in January to rent my spare bedroom. On the day Michael arrived, news reports revealed that James McCord, the former security head of Richard Nixon's presidential campaign, had informed federal prosecutors of White House involvement in a burglary designed to extract political intelligence at Democratic Party headquarters at Washington's Watergate complex the previous June.

"Nixon's in trouble," Michael declared.

Ferment

"No way," I responded. "None of the higher-ups will ever talk."

This cautious reading of Watergate lasted for about seven weeks. Then news emerged that Presidential Counsel John Dean had begun to cooperate with Justice Department attorneys and that he suspected the White House of setting him up to take the fall for the burglary.

"Some may hope or think that I will become a scapegoat in the Watergate case," Dean announced to the press. "Anyone who believes this does not know me."

Suddenly, everything had changed. Had Michael been right after all? Was the Nixon presidency really in jeopardy? Did Dean's warning suggest the sort of ruthlessness that could bring down a sitting president, even one who had made a life's work of the political game? As Congress voted for a Watergate special prosecutor and the Senate organized a select investigating committee, I felt an excitement about politics I had not experienced since the Bobby Kennedy campaign. Here was a perfect laboratory for testing notions about power and the political system. Besides, the thought of pushing Nixon into history was utterly intriguing.

The televised Watergate Senate hearings began on a low key in May with testimony from former secretaries and underlings at CREEP – the Committee to Re-Elect the President. Yet as the questioning worked its way up the chain of command, the tension accelerated. With teaching responsibilities over by mid-June, I devoted all day to the spectacle, a ritual that spanned the start of morning sessions at 7 a.m. Pacific Time to the re-runs of the proceedings twelve hours later. I rapidly became adept at distinguishing hard-hitting questioners such as Hawaii senator Daniel Inouye from less-focused colleagues, and truthful witnesses from pretentious frauds. As the Watergate Committee grilled Nixon's two closest aides, H. R. Haldeman and John Ehrlichman, the mix of memory lapses, evasive language, blind loyalty, and personal arrogance became too much to bear, particularly when Ehrlichman insisted that the illegal

151

search and seizures clause of the Fourth Amendment did not cover break-ins deemed to serve national security.

The climax to the hearings came with the appearance of John Dean. For two weeks, the former White House counselor rattled off the details of one after another face-to-face meeting with the president. The gist of his testimony was that Nixon had personally managed the cover-up of the Watergate break-in and even authorized hush money payments to the original burglars. Dean's veracity was so obvious that I bristled when the media cautioned about a lack of corroboration. Even Bruce wrote to say that no one would back up the star witness. Then in July, the committee received testimony about an audio taping system in the Oval Office.

NOMAD

Weeks after Michael's arrival, Ladd's Addition served as the venue of an all-night housewarming party for some hundred guests. As the weather brightened, Sue had me dig up a garden in the tiny backyard. Having shed my beard, I now sported a drooping moustache that matched my contorted curly hair, subsequently grown out into a full-blown Afro. As I leaned on a hoe resting on two bags of fertilizer and scratched Beulah's mane in my faded work shirt and jeans, Goodwill vest, and worn leather boots, a snapshot recorded the scene in detail.

"Well, well, Dandelion Dave!" my brother exclaimed when he saw the photo.

The coming months witnessed a good deal of household discussion on the unity of physical and spiritual realms. Anthropologist Gregory Bateson's meta-dialogues on consciousness in *Toward an Ecology of Mind* and Carlos Castaneda's trilogy on Yaqui Indian mysticism were prime texts. Although a rationalist, I cherished the possibility of cosmic realities beyond the grasp of the empirical mind. These interests prompted an investment in a bulky atlas of the universe and rapt attention to *Star Trek* TV reruns and the weekly *Kung Fu* series. As stifling desert winds assaulted the Willamette Valley during the summer of 1973, I identified with the musical balladry of poet Leonard Cohen, whose trancelike mystical odes seemed to replicate the ethereal scene in Ladd's Addition.

"Nancy wore green stockings and slept with everyone," Cohen sang, "but none of us would meet her in the House of Mystery."

This was the season of *Worthy Advisor*. After I introduced Suzanne to Marjorie, a self-styled street poet and free-spirited adventurer who supported herself as a Goodwill "rag picker," the two agreed to collaborate on a biographical treatment of Marjorie's life and verse. The volume's original contribution would be a series of exchanges between the two authors reflecting their past and present adventures and struggles for survival.

"I've got a hell to buy for someone and I'd kind of like to go to Jupiter," Sue wrote in one aside.

Beyond the text, *Worthy Advisor* featured a collection of photographs from Marjorie's family history and several staged images. I agreed to pose for one as a New Delhi dentist who had treated Marjorie to East Indian food while the two sat unclothed in the lotus position. Published by "Crow" under a Cannon Beach address, the pamphlet sold for two dollars. Its dedication addressed "Nomad," a misdirected spaceship once featured in a *Star Trek* episode. Following a promotion campaign that I led at Portland State that fall, two English and psychology colleagues assigned the book to their classes.

INVISIBLE MAN

Invigorated by Watergate and counterculture influences, I returned to *freeway*. I had named the series for the interstate beltway that passed by Portland State and the freedom of inquiry I hoped to incorporate. Pursuant to my instructions, the title now appeared between two divergent lines branching toward infinity. Convinced that *Worthy Advisor* offered a fresh approach in what I described as the waning season of the American Century, I devoted my first column to the book. While the Promise of the Sixties had withered into played-out warriors trudging off to Survival, Inc., I wrote,

Worthy Advisor offered a quest for faith. Marjorie's story, I insisted, taught the timely lesson that the toughness of the hustle need not destroy the tenderness of the spirit. If we were to persevere with any energy in the severity of the 1970s, I pleaded, Sixties innocence had to go somewhere beside self-hatred and cynicism.

In the search for a spirit that might transcend the times, I turned to the musical motion-picture extravaganza *Jesus Christ Superstar*. In intellectual circles, the movie had a reputation for glorifying unthinking devotion to organized religion. In contrast, I saw it as a pioneering, even revolutionary, effort to fuse rock music, dance, visual imagery, humor, and metaphysics into an inspiring work of art. Its unconventional portrait of Christianity's central figure, I suggested, spoke to the innate spirituality and vulnerability inherent in the human condition.

After devoting the first two columns to works of the imagination, I used the third to explore my primary preoccupation of the fall. I called it "The Invisible Man." Richard Nixon had only four months left to his presidency, I declared in a bold stab at historical prophecy. Catching the outlines of the drama in Washington was like plotting the orbits of unnamed planets, I acknowledged. Yet I insisted that events ultimately would assume a life of their own. The illusion that no one was above the law, I asserted, was more important than any individual's fate.

Although friends and colleagues saw me as either naïve or deluded, I continued, I was certain the Supreme Court would support the special prosecutor's subpoena for the Nixon tapes, because it had to ensure a legal defense for White House subordinates. If the president turned over the recordings, he would be accountable for the Watergate cover-up; if he defied the Court's orders, the House Judiciary Committee would start impeachment. Either way, I predicted with no hesitancy, there would be a new president by the winter of 1974.

"The Invisible Man" marked the first of a number of Watergate meditations allowing me to test my political acumen. Curiously, less than a week after the column appeared, Vice-President Spiro Agnew resigned over a kickback scheme involving government contractors. In "Sweepstakes," I cited an exchange from a Mae West film of the 1930s.

"Goodness!" a hat-checker exclaims as she admires Mae's diamond ring.

"Honey," the irreverent West responds, "goodness had nothing to do with it."

Two weeks after Agnew's demise, Nixon sought to quash the subpoena for the White House tapes by firing the special prosecutor. Commenting on "the Saturday Night Massacre," I wrote that the president thrived on battle and was playing his kind of ball game:

"Only it's the last inning, and his advisors are running in panic to keep up with him. His back is against the wall. There's no way out."

When Nixon responded to a firestorm of public disapproval by appointing a second special prosecutor, the official announced that some of the tapes were missing. I responded with a column entitled "Credibility." American capitalism depended upon people's faith that things were fair and that everyone got what they deserved, I wrote. For destroying that illusion, I declared, Richard Nixon had become a liability for the ruling class. My brother disagreed. In "Richard Nixon, Futurist," a piece that appeared in the University of California at San Diego student newspaper the same month, Michael portrayed the beleaguered president as an innovator. Nixon's actions, he wrote, anticipated corporate interests in scaling back the welfare state in the face of America's declining position in the world.

TOOLS

Prompted by Bill Hamilton, Systems Science Director Hal Linstone asked me to participate in a second symposium, called "Beyond Reality and into Experience: Alternative Forms to Historical Explanation." I was to extend my assessment of Thompson's *At the Edge of History*, a task I pursued with a graduate school routine. First, I noted significant passages with a mark at the margins of relevant pages. Then I listed the page numbers at the back of the volume with a one-or-two-word key. At that point, I could prepare a summary of the book's main points.

Although Bill Williams said he found *At the Edge* too passive, I took inspiration from the work's systemic scope. Thompson divided human history into tribal, agricultural, industrial, and scientific stages. In turn, he argued that contemporary society incorporated roles derived from four elemental archetypes: the headman (administration), hunter (military), shaman (religion), and joker (information and the arts). He then equated these functions with the spheres of government, labor, media, and education, respectively.

By replacing a linear model of political behavior with a circular one, Thompson showed how reactionaries could be courageous opponents of bureaucratic expertise but irrational defenders of pre-industrial traditions. In turn, liberals might lean toward human rights yet act as spineless bureaucrats. On the other hand, radicals could promote social change but entertain violent fantasies of destroying all structures. Finally, conservatives might keep society from breaking down into anarchy but simultaneously exhibit a devotion to profitable economic arrangements such as the military-industrial complex.

Thompson's model demonstrated why some working-class followers of George Wallace favored the military, despised the corporate state, and feared liberal race-mixing at the same time. It also explained how radicals moderated their position through alignments with Establishment liberals but leaned toward revolutionary postures in a similar fashion to those reactionaries who negated compromise and veered toward extremist violence. Picturing the political universe as a dial, *At the Edge* suggested it was impossible to focus on all attributes at once, so that strength in one direction often accompanied weakness in its opposite.

The notion that opposing traits contributed to a greater whole proved useful in dealing with cultural process without relying on theoretical jargon. In a *freeway* piece called "Tools," I addressed gender roles, partly in response to a growing feminist presence in academia. I already had devoted one of my seminars to women's history and had helped teaching assistant Amy Kessleman construct a non-credit survey of the subject. Custom held that men used rational tools while women relied on intuition, I began, a belief that now led some women to discount non-rational tools as a legacy of oppression. Yet intuitive techniques were valuable, I insisted, because they enable us to see beyond superficial content and become more empathetic. In contrast, excessive rationalism could close off the experience of other people and the mysteries of existence. I pleaded that if the past relegated women to the intuitive sphere and men to rationality, there was no reason to discard either.

Two halves were better than one, I concluded.

The final *freeway* of the fall of 1973 responded to the fact that the Organization of Petroleum Exporting Countries (OPEC) had cut off sales to countries supporting Israel in its recent war with its Arab neighbors. Borrowing Dave Noble's language, the column suggested that the 1970s might be the time when history ultimately caught up with the United States. After all, an energy crisis marked by oil shortages, inflated prices, and long lines at the pump had just about put an end to illusions about unlimited growth and frontiers of opportunity.

As the nights got longer and colder and the last Middle East tankers neared their hungry ports, I noted, "all but ten gallons a week" of the American Dream were over.

"Surely this is the winter of our discontent," I ventured.

Unknowingly, I had put my finger on the eclipse of the Golden Age of American working-class prosperity that economic historians subsequently attributed to the period between 1945 and 1973. Yet *freeway* pleaded for a spirit of transcendence. It described NASA's Pioneer 10, which soon would break away from Jupiter's gravity field into outer space, as containing a plaque depicting human comprehension of lens theory and binary logic.

While Nixon was in the White House counting the days, I noted, the birthdate of a martyred Jewish holy man approached, a reminder that "occasional visionaries bless our days and soften our nights."

If the human species was to survive, I concluded, we had to commit to deploying our rational tools to get our house together and our spiritual ones to free our souls.

It was, after all, the season of Faith.

WINDOW DRESSING

Following a winter break stay in Roslyn Heights, I flew to visit Suzanne in Los Angeles. In an effort to see if *Worthy Advisor* would open doors, Sue had arranged to share a modest rental in the Hollywood hills. The day after my arrival, the gang received an invite to a boating outing on Santa Monica Bay. Once we set out, supplies of tequila and vodka quickly appeared, and the jovial crowd soon engaged in lighthearted banter about their projects and activities.

"And what's your thing, David?" the slightly debauched owner of the vessel asked.

When I replied I was a college history professor who compiled a weekly column for the student newspaper, everyone responded with an indulgent smile.

As we moved into choppy waters and I started feeling seasick, my discomfort grew. I now lost all patience with the shallow, half-drunk people who seemed to think they were so clever. Besides, the yachtsman seemed particularly focused on Suzanne. Feeling like a fifth wheel, I wondered what I was doing in L.A. The next night, which happened to be New Year's Eve, never one of my favorite times, I caught the midnight Amtrak for Portland.

Once home, I circumvented Portland's long gas lines by finding an out-of-the-way service station to fill the VW tank and proceeded to organize the new term's classes. The plan was to center the Corporate Hegemony seminar on an abridged collection of the Pentagon Papers – the secret analysis of U.S. decision making in Vietnam that defense secretary Robert McNamara had commissioned in 1966. A good deal of the course content, however, originated with American Studies scholar Gene Wise's *American Historical Explanations* (1973), a book Mike Passi had recommended. Wise applied Thomas Kuhn's notion of conceptual paradigms to the creation of historical arguments. Just as communities of scientists shared criteria for making sense of reality and evaluating fresh discoveries, he suggested, historians related new interpretations to accepted conclusions and world-views.

Wise placed particular emphasis on anomalies – findings opposed to conventional wisdom that initially met dismissal as ill-conceived or faulty. Yet he argued that the fault lines generated by contrary evidence could produce earthquakes in dominant explanations and result in the acceptance of new paradigms.

This meant that historians provided *perspectives* on objective reality, not absolute truth.

The seminar sought to apply Wise's approach to a study of Vietnam War policymaking. Beyond treatments of the conflict's origins by critics such as Daniel Ellsberg and analyses of corporate culture by radical sociologist C. Wright Mills and others, the class addressed the relationship of documents to history, the ability of individuals to assess contemporary historical situations, and the connections between ideas and strategies. Through this lens, it became clear that Washington's security managers had viewed Vietnam primarily as a test case of U.S. will to lead the Free World coalition against communism, not as a challenge to core national interests.

The work of Dave Noble, William A. Williams, Eugene Genovese, and Gene Wise helped emphasize the importance of paradox and nuance in my thinking and teaching, especially when it came to fusing ideological and economic concerns. Steering away from sterile formulations and conventional wisdom, these scholars conveyed a dynamic quality to the world of ideas that fired my imagination.

Meanwhile, I continued to see *freeway* as a laboratory for the free-rein vitality that I envisioned as a prerequisite for the reconstruction of American life.

Was it possible, I wondered, to combine the strengths of the counterculture and movement for radical change with a plausible and intellectually accessible approach to life, one that incorporated working-class toughness with a touch of magic and feel for beauty? Was there a way to envision a fusion of politics and culture, tradition and innovation, and reason and intuition? Did the sorry state of American society preclude a consideration of more hopeful prospects, or was die-hard cynicism the only thoughtful response for an honest person? With no blueprint at my disposal, I still believed that as civilization entered the telling era of its ability to survive with grace, virtues such as humor and a sense of mystery were essential.

Aware of the element of surprise in sustaining interest in any piece of writing, I dedicated my first column of 1974 to a tribute to "Junk People."

Portland had a long history of independent enterprise marked by a variety of used-goods dealers. These unheralded merchants were true heroes, I proposed, because their vision and persistence transformed discarded refuse into objects of beauty and utility. To appreciate these recyclers of physical treasures, I urged readers to check out the pages of *Nickel Ads*, the Sunday flea market at the North Portland Sports Arena, and my favorite second-hand furniture outlet on the east side of town.

In February, the topic turned to the Dream of the Sixties. As Suzanne returned from L.A., we drove up to the Tacoma Dome for a Bob Dylan concert. As usual, I wrote of Dylan's appearance before fourteen thousand loyalists, he let his music convey the message: he was nobody's guru and never had been. The review described a performer who moved with total irreverence through the diversity of styles and postures spanning his career with no introduction or side patter. Then he delivered the pay-off.

"You said you'd never compromise," Dylan sang as the spotlights panned across the hooting, stomping throng.

"How does it feel, how does it feel?" he screamed, "To be on your own, with no direction home, a complete unknown, like a rolling stone?"

Bob Dylan seemed to be taunting an audience that knew as much as he did that the hustles of the 1970s had come to shape the life of a generation that once thought it had it made. Yet the crowd seemed liberated by the new twist to the old standard. Unwavering in artistic honesty, Dylan ended the single curtain call with "you go your way and I go mine."

Dylan's performance left me wondering if there was a place for utopian thinking and even rationality in hard times. The query resurfaced when I saw *The Exorcist*, a motion picture that seemed to speak to the loss of faith in reason. As I wrote in *freeway*, the film suggested that beneath the veneer of modern science, technology, and logic there were no ultimate explanations. Beyond that, *The Exorcist* insisted on humans' complete impotence before evil. Modern approaches through drugs, psychotherapy, hypnotism, or reason all failed to remove the alien force. In the end, evil defies eradication it merely assumes another form.

The Exorcist advanced the possibility that centuries of human optimism and progress had been mere window-dressing. It was hard to deal with the limitations of both human spiritual will and modern rationalism. Did evil come out of the human imagination, or did it have a separate existence? Either way, how could we reconcile the vulnerability of love, faith, and truth to the forces of guilt, hatred, and falsity? At the same time, it was still somewhat liberating to realize that so many crucial elements of human culture and behavior remained stubbornly inexplicable.

PRIMROSE

(1974-1975)

teachers, learners, incense burners
– L. Russell

Just as *freeway* contemplated the possibility of combining reason and imagination in a socially responsive life, San Francisco Bay's Symbionese Liberation Army (SLA) stormed onto the scene. In February 1974, the self-styled band of urban guerrillas staged a dramatic kidnapping of college student Patricia Hearst and demanded that the captive's wealthy family deliver free food to the poor as ransom. The SLA revolutionaries outraged conservatives and disturbed liberals. For those remnants of the New Left and counterculture still sharing visions of radical social change, however, the gang presented an even more onerous challenge.

BITTER FRUIT

At first, the Hearst kidnapping generated a mixed response in *freeway*. The column offered reservations about ideologues who pretended to speak for the deprived and tactics that frightened working people away from social causes. Yet it also acknowledged the group's skill at symbolic politics. These activists sought to feed poor people to show it was possible, I marveled, and had compelled officials to admit that nearly one-third the population of the most glamorous state in the nation was needy. Anyone who had driven through the cotton fields of southern California's agribusiness complexes knew what the abductors were talking about when they asserted that wealth came "over the backs and bodies of human fodder," I noted.

"When you come down to it," I continued in tribute to nineteenth century French socialist-anarchist Pierre Proudhon, "property is theft."

Although I received no direct criticism of the piece, one of my students let me know that his father objected to the column's characterization of *all* property without taking into account the modest holdings of ordinary people. This well-taken critique reinforced the peril of overly glib phrasing in opinion writing. Six weeks later, the plot thickened when Patty Hearst claimed to have defected to the SLA, changed her name to "Comrade Tania," and brandished an automatic weapon during a bank robbery. Like everything else in American life since 1963, I suggested, the kidnapping refused to follow a predictable script. Instead of the innocent terrorist victim, the public had to contend with a revolutionary sister denouncing her own class. What affluent family could go to sleep, I asked, confident they would never see their son or daughter sporting a sub-machine gun and crying out for revenge against the oppression of the rich?

After several SLA members precipitated a shootout at a Los Angeles variety store in mid-May, the mood darkened. The news from L.A. was discouraging, I wrote my parents. The group's gratuitous violence and fanatical agenda made me doubt their sanity. Not long after, in fact, a house fire consumed most of Tania's comrades following an all-out police assault. *freeway* never responded to the virtual suicide. Yet the obvious deterioration of prospects for constructive political and cultural change generated a broader commentary later in the month.

It was ironic that as Vietnam and Watergate had taught the American people about the duplicity and venom of their leaders, I observed, we had only come to lose faith in ourselves. We were emerging into a culture of alienation and despair that crushed the faintest stirrings of social imagination. The Left understood how alienation had roots in capitalism's substitution of market requirements for human needs, I admitted. Yet progressives sought to replace the enveloping culture of death with hopes of collective liberation and self-denial. This evaded any response to Oscar Wilde's quip that socialism would be fine but would make for terribly boring evenings.

Virtuous revolutionaries lacked soul and a sense of play, I admonished. That was why sensualists rejected the deadening rationalism of the politicos and sought out the rush of trashy nostalgia for the 1940s, cocaine highs, "f--k me" heels, and a good boogie band. Yet the sleazes often fell victim to their own cynicism and mocked the slightest glint of aspiration.

Nowhere did prospects for cultural vitality seem more problematic than in academia. A few years ago, I reflected in a column entitled "Hire Education," radical literature outlined the role of the university in molding students to the rigors of corporate discipline. Yet I suggested that business leaders and state legislatures seemed to have given up on the utilitarian purposes of advanced education, viewing college graduates as too independent, demanding, and hostile to follow orders. A social system might not survive if it failed to produce theorists and innovators, I pointed out, but systems did not always operate in the long range. Although economic activity sustained the university, the market appeared to reject tools of critical inquiry.

As recession and energy crisis budget cuts loomed for the coming year amid increased public hostility to state spending, a *freeway* piece entitled "Bitter Fruit" compared the halls of academia to a cold morgue. If the vibrant counterculture of the 1960s amounted to "a dance of prosperity," I concluded, the Seventies were a time of crumbling illusions. This seemed to be the case when the Oregon State Board of Higher Education demanded the inclusion of some fifty PSU instructors on a contingency list of those subject to layoff with a year's notice. Each department now received a quota of potential cuts based on enrollment declines. The history department faced the loss of three positions. Waiting for the axe to fall subject to directives from above, I confessed in *freeway*, left one's fate bouncing along the walls of an unseen corridor.

Once again, Mike Passi stepped into the breach. Passi's two-year contingency contract was about to expire. Yet this did not prevent him from arguing that the young tenure-track instructors were an indispensable part of the history department. As a June column explained, the historians responded by voting to include summer school as part of the regular teaching load, a sacrifice of potential extra income designed to avoid any layoffs. Ironically, a spike in fall enrollment would erase the case for financial exigency and preserve everyone's position.

THE LAST YIPPIE

Although the vulnerabilities of the progressive movement and the troubled state of academia continued to provoke the pithy colloquial writing style that had come to characterize *freeway* installments, Watergate remained the column's primary focus. Richard Nixon had gambled that the political system lacked the courage to impeach him, I wrote in January. Like classical Marxists, he saw adversaries as motivated by narrow goals of self-interest and power. Accordingly, Nixon believed that contrived public relations would pacify public concerns over his presidency. Such an approach, I concluded, embodied the height of self-deception.

"All the White House front groups and newspaper ads in the kingdom can't put Humpty-Dumpty together again," I warned.

Nixon was falling, I explained, because his view of human behavior had failed him. He did not understand that self-interest sometimes drove people to uphold self-images they cherished. If those who ruled the country had any belief in their capacity to lead, I insisted, they would ensure the president's removal. Nobody with anything to protect wanted to see the personification of the national way of life in a lying, double-dealing scoundrel who sold out his friends as quickly as he invented his enemies. A ruling class without the capacity to lead only invited anarchy or revolution.

"Nixon, you're not that important, sweetheart," I concluded.

During the winter of 1974, polls revealed overriding public belief in Nixon's guilt for obstruction of evidence but equally strong opposition to forcing him from office. The president believed that he, not his prosecutors, summed up the country's mood of stark realism and disdain for lofty ideals, I suggested in a subsequent column. Yet I thought that Congress might press impeachment even if it defied majority will. The Watergate cover-up grand jury, I noted, already intended to indict Nixon for criminal conspiracy. I read the president's strategy as delaying as long as he could, releasing as little evidence as possible, and hoping for unseen surprises or the possibility that thirty-four senators would see an impeachment conviction as too disruptive. Yet as Nixon campaigned in Michigan for a Republican candidate for the House, I thought he looked like a poor relation making a last-ditch appeal for a family loan. By October, I joked, his main concerns would be those of any smalltime hustler – paying bills and staying out of jail.

When the White House released tape transcripts in May detailing conversations between the president and John Dean, there no longer appeared any doubt that Nixon had been party to a conspiracy to obstruct justice by silencing the seven convicted Watergate defendants. Nobody could figure out where in the hierarchy to draw the line for taking the blame, I wrote. What was shocking about the transcripts, I insisted, was not merely the Machiavellian image of the chief executive, but the tone of incompetence and irresolution that permeated his ruthlessness. I wondered if the president's inability to handle the crisis had driven Dean to the prosecutors. Had Nixon's dependence on his closest aides and yes-men discouraged him from selling them out even to save his own skin? Once the House voted to hold impeachment hearings, I predicted, a 75-25 Senate conviction would result if the president did not resign by the end of July. If he resisted, I wrote home, Republican leaders would march up to the White House and tell him that the jig was up.

Given the uncertain outcome of Nixon's plight and the continual publication of fresh evidence, the spring term seminar I devoted to Watergate crackled with energy. Readings included an abridged paperback account of the Senate Watergate Hearings, a *New York Times* summary of the scandal, several essays on the politics of the corporate state, and mimeographed handouts of White House and CIA tape transcripts. As we systematically worked our way through an account of the Senate hearings and the published excerpts of

White House and CIA documents, class discussion inevitably centered on whether Richard Nixon's presidency would survive. I found it interesting that most of the students, like nearly all my history colleagues and my father, remained skeptical that the most powerful leader in the world lacked the ability to ensure the continuation of his political life

Just as I began preparing for a fall Watergate lecture class designed to coincide with a Senate impeachment trial, the drama came to a sudden climax. As I had anticipated, the Supreme Court ordered Nixon to relinquish the White House tapes. Then the House Judiciary Committee reported three impeachment charges to the full House. Days later, the special prosecutor released the "smoking gun" – three tapes containing Nixon's orders to engineer a cover-up. Late in the afternoon of August 8th, I returned home just as the president began a televised farewell speech to White House staff.

"Always remember," he admonished. "Others may hate you. Those who hate you don't win unless you hate them. And then you destroy yourself."

I was ready for Nixon's resignation, I wrote my parents, but watching him as he crumbled was almost a religious experience. To my surprise, my former nemesis came across as a human being. You pursue an enemy for years and when you get him, I explained, he turns out to be a pathetic, helpless, sentimental creature crying for his mother. The emotional twists of Watergate inspired an article that the liberal *Oregon Times* accepted as my first magazine piece.

"It became clear in the closing days of the Nixon Era," the feature began, that "the emperor had no ideological clothes."

The White House had sketched the first outlines of managerial fascism, I contended, "but unintentionally and haphazardly, with no transcendent goal except minding the store."

Taking off from Nixon's impromptu farewell to his staff, I pictured him as an outsider.

"This was a man of mean breeding," I explained, "out of the rootless and cold world of cheap southern California hustles ... a man who'd come up from the underside, struggling and kicking all the way, the objects of taunts and disdain all his life, a man who knew the costs of success and defeat ...."

Nixon's world collapsed when he crossed the line between national security and partisan paranoia, I argued. The president's men had extorted campaign funds from corporate elites, compiled an "enemies list" of Democratic donors for Internal Revenue Service audits, and managed a cover-up that subverted the credibility of the presidency and the government itself.

"The Chairman of the Board became the Last Yippie," I concluded.

FRIENDS

After a year of ridicule from friends and colleagues, not to mention my own episodes of self-doubt, I finally could celebrate Nixon's demise. If I had been mistaken on this one, I had speculated, I would have no right to consider myself a serious student of public affairs. Now at least, Watergate had validated my understanding of the non-materialist ingredients of political culture and I could pursue my calling in good conscience. Just at that point, however, my personal life raised troubling questions.

Beholden to the lessons of the life teacher Suzanne was for me – someone whose sense of cosmic play had helped open me to direct experience and adventure – I had chosen to minimize the fact that she carried a great deal of baggage. Much of her time in San Francisco had been spent among the street people of the Tenderloin. Her closest friend had climaxed an acid trip by leaping off an apartment house roof, paralyzing her lower body for life. Whether rooted in poor self-esteem, in an attempt to escape the banalities of existence, or in communion with other spiritual seekers, Suzanne was inevitably drawn to drugs, alcohol, and the "don't give a damn" people who surrounded them. Despite a genuine affection for me, she had a long history of personal and psychedelic adventures involving both sexes. Fixated on the pitfalls of male possessiveness, to which I certainly was prone, I clung to the hope that things would work out in time.

By the summer of 1974, it had been some time since the two of us had lived together as a couple. Just a few nights after Nixon's resignation, however, things spiraled terribly out of control when Suzanne invited a girlfriend to spend the night at Ladd's Addition and a series of misread signals, for which I shared some responsibility, precipitated a near-calamity.

No longer able to ignore my partner's volatility, I finally realized that although we might remain friends, an intimate relationship was no longer in the cards. In this wizened state, I actually welcomed the start of a new academic year and the resumption of *freeway*.

MISSION BLUES

"Mission Blues," fall term's initial column, described the convocation speech of Joseph Blumel, a PSU economics professor the State Board of Higher Education recently had appointed to the university presidency after orchestrating Gregory Wolfe's resignation. The piece compared Blumel to Nixon successor Gerald Ford. Both, I explained, had risen from the ranks to replace more dramatic but less-than-successful predecessors and had inherited economic catastrophes requiring budget retrenchment and curtailment. While Ford elicited cheers for an optimistic economic prognosis during his first address to Congress, the faculty afforded Blumel a standing ovation when he foresaw the imminent end of the academic recession.

Like President Ford, who offered clemency to recent draft evaders and deserters, President Blumel had to deal with the legacy of the Vietnam War. The fall of 1974 brought the federal conspiracy trial of former Portland State graduate student Jim Cronin and Foreign Languages Professor Frank Giese, a New University Conference colleague. The government accused the pair of participating in an effort to bomb two Portland military recruiting stations following the "Christmas Bombing" of North Vietnam's two largest cities in December 1972, weeks before Richard Nixon signed off on a peace treaty with the Communists.

Supporters of Cronin and Giese insisted that the government had framed the defendants for antiwar activity. Yet the case came down to two witnesses. Robert McSherry had spent the initial two months of a fifty-five-year sentence in solitary confinement after pleading guilty to the conspiracy and three other felonies. Lynn Myer faced seven and a half years for several state and federal charges, including a dynamite conspiracy rap. Both testified they had met the defendants during discussion sessions Cronin and Giese led at the Oregon Correctional Institute. After leaving OCI on work release, testified Myer, he had visited Giese at his radical bookstore and been treated to a steak and vodka dinner at the professor's residence. He claimed that Giese had driven the getaway car for the second bombing and celebrated the feat by treating the group to rounds of Bloody Mary cocktails.

In preparation for the trial, I had devoted a *freeway* feature to a sympathetic profile of Giese. As the proceedings got underway at the Federal Building only blocks from Portland State, a second column made a point of noting how the unfolding Watergate cover-up trial of Nixon subordinates centered on government abuses in treating political dissidents. Yet in a letter to my parents, I confided that the strenuous defense cross-examination I anticipated had not materialized. Facing a deadline the following week, I sat at my typewriter from 9 p.m. to 3:30 a.m. lacking any way to proceed. In the end, I excerpted a piece on the brutality of the U.S. air war in Vietnam from sociologist Philip Slater's *Pursuit of Loneliness,* an implicit confession of my inability to frame a plausible case for the defense.

When Giese took the stand and seemed to contradict much of the prosecution, I regained some confidence. Then, two former students of mine who lived at the professor's farm east of town testified they had been there with him the weekend of the bombings. Yet my sense of relief proved temporary. When the lead prosecutor opened his summation by insisting that the case had nothing

Getting There

in common with government civil liberties abuses during Watergate, I had the uncanny impression he was looking directly at me. Pushing these doubts out of my mind a week later when I received a telephone message that the jury had come in, I rushed down to the courthouse.

As Judge James M. Burns read the verdicts in a measured tone, I wrote, "the sound of 'guilty' judgments shattered the hushed courtroom like rounds of machine-gun fire."

The jury had found Cronin and two others guilty on all counts, requiring ten-year sentences; Giese had received a five-year maximum on a single conspiracy rap.

In something of a daze, I spied a few members of the defense team outside the building.

"What happened?" I asked.

They turned out to be Cronin's attorneys, stung by the disparity in sentencing between the two principal defendants. Inviting me for a drink, the lawyers hesitated when I recounted my difficulty in reconciling Giese's verdict with the two witnesses who claimed to have been at the professor's rural property the weekend of the bombing.

Then, one of them looked right at me.

"Did you ever think that maybe there never was a weekend at the farm?" he asked.

VIRTUE

My final column on the trial summarized the judge's instructions to the jury, the verdict, and details of the sentencing with barely any commentary. Anxious to move into a more comfortable terrain, I turned a Portland State appearance by African-American activist Angela Davis into a profile of lifestyle and culture for the *Oregon Times*. Describing Davis as young, beautiful, and revolutionary, I painted a portrait of a political figure whose blue denim jacket and jeans suggested a stylistic emphasis that left many progressive uneasy. Yet this advocate for black liberation, I noted, spoke to people in lucid terms and conveyed the impression that the social struggle need not ignore sensuality, humor, and personality.

Having achieved an enhanced sense of my emotional vulnerabilities, I used a *freeway* column entitled "Virtue" to describe the "greening" of Wilbur Mills of Arkansas, the powerful Democratic chair of the House Ways and Means Committee. At the age of sixty-five, Mills had grown his hair long, lost interest in work, began joking about marijuana, and been discovered drunk and bruised in a car with a thirty-eight-year-old striptease dancer named Fanne Foxe, whom he promised to make a movie star. I connected the Mills saga with Philip Slater's contention in the recently published *Earthwalk* that traditional traits such as courage, perseverance, and individual achievement cut people off from another and no longer had survival value. In contrast, Slater argued, cowardice, sensuality, inconsistency, dependency, and corruptibility were "humble virtues" that expressed human participation in a greater whole.

Mills finally had checked himself into Bethesda Naval Hospital for alcoholism.

"Pray for Wilbur Mills," I wrote in a plea for empathy and understanding, "and the brotherhood and sisterhood of collective human sin."

Unfortunately, I pushed the argument too far, suggesting that while Democrats drank and gave vent to their sexual passions, cold-hearted and emotionally repressed Republicans only gave their love-starved wives breast cancer. This may have been the only time that German history colleague Frank West gently scolded me for bad taste, and the criticism hit the mark.

A subsequent column, "Breakfast at the Hilton," sought to apply Slater's views to a gathering designed to solicit local business help in offsetting PSU football's continuing financial deficit. Several speakers claimed that football could be a source of pride and an economic stimulus for the university and the city. Others emphasized the sport's character-building benefits, such as courage, competitive spirit, persistence, and discipline. Yet the old values applauded by the coaches and business leaders, I noted, were the very ones the culture was learning to re-evaluate. Why must we reinforce tired male stereotypes of ruggedness and determination without bothering to wonder why we were fighting? I asked.

Pleased that President Blumel, a strong football supporter himself, saw the piece as a serious discussion of a subject that concerned many people, I used the inaugural column of 1975 to link athletics to the complex issue of gender politics.

"Remember when sex was dirty and the air was clean?" the opening quote inquired, a sample of folk wisdom I had spotted behind the bar of a Northwest Portland tavern.

"Super Sunday" described an afternoon viewing the most celebrated event of American sports at Sun and Rosie's tavern in Southeast Portland, the area I habitually referred to as "the working side of town." While technology and consumer capitalism reduced the importance of the family, weakened traditional sex roles, and encouraged the integration of women into the market, I marveled, working-class men seemed to cling to old stereotypes. Yet where was the "privilege" in having to support the wife and family on a weekly paycheck? I then told the tale of the fan who said he had just bet his wife, kids, and the electric bill on the defeated Minnesota Vikings.

"He laughed and went back to shooting pool," I reported.

The column then turned to a benefit dance for the pro-feminist Men's Resource Center. These women's rights advocates and allies, I stated, saw a positive ideal of sexual relations flowing from consciousness-raising and open communication. Yet where was passion and spontaneity? Prospects for getting beyond sexism, I ventured, might not come as much by *working* to overcome it as by *playing* with new possibilities with a sense of humor and mystery.

Two weeks later, I explored another aspect of ideological rigidity in the debate between capitalism and socialism. The conflict, I suggested, had changed very little over more than a century and drew only tiresome yawns. Socialists insisted that *work* and *production* were the essence of life while proclaiming the virtue of the oppressed and devotion to collective will. Yet political radicals needed to make clear, I argued, that cooperation for survival did not have to mean loss of personal identity or subscription to "the forces of history." Socialist ideology, I warned, could not afford to regulate or collectivize the inner and psychic side of human activity.

Midway through winter term, I flew to see my parents in southern California, where they were renting a condominium in Orange County's Leisure World. After my father underwent surgery to replace an arthritic hip and passed his sixty-fifth birthday in 1973, West Chemical had pushed the twenty-eight-year sales veteran to the sidelines. To ease his adjustment, my mother closed out her career as a guidance counselor the following spring. This enabled the couple to take a trip out west to explore retirement possibilities and visit my father's cousins, Mo and Lil Golub, at Leisure World. Upon returning home, he chronicled the entire experience in a typescript entitled "I Tripped Over the West." Following the visit to California, I devoted the next *freeway* to a moving excerpt from the manuscript on the traumas of forced retirement.

DIRTY WORK

Influenced by my father's next project – an autobiography spanning his childhood and youth – I moved toward incorporating personal elements in my own writing. One result was a column called "Conspiracy." The piece began with a reference to graduate school history professors who stressed the complexity of human behavior and warned about the follies of a conspiratorial view of the past. Then I introduced Bruce Goldstein.

"I still believe in conspiracy, man. Look at the CIA," I remembered Bruce saying with a shake of his head.

Skeptics who once scoffed at the simplistic notions of the Left, I suggested, now had to account for Watergate and revelations that the CIA had engaged in illegal surveillance of dissidents, kept files on thousands of domestic dissenters, penetrated antiwar groups, and plotted the assassination of foreign leaders. Once the thread of rationality in human events was gone, I speculated, anything became possible. Conscientious historians might have to send their students to the tabloids to re-tool to learn how conspiracies work.

"Bruce Goldstein, where are you now that we need you?" I concluded.

When the communists captured the Marines' original South Vietnam outpost in Da Nang early in April 1975, I stumbled upon another framework for first-person storytelling. As I heard the news on the radio of my new car, a four-year-old Datsun wagon, I was on the way to visit Mike McCusker. Having served in Vietnam as a Marine photographer and reporter in the mid-Sixties, McCusker had become a founding member of Vietnam Veterans Against the War and been a central figure in the Portland State strike and People's Army Jamboree. He now managed Picture Window Cottages, the rustic and well-worn coastal motel where I had introduced my brother to the Pacific.

A bottle of Jim Beam in hand, I greeted Mac and two former jarheads. They had heard the news and, abetted by refreshments, had begun to rehash old times. Over the next several hours, I sat riveted as I listened to an inside version of the Vietnam War that would work itself into a *freeway* piece I called "Da Nang Saturday Night."

"You wouldn't believe how quickly you can dig a hole when you're in the line of mortar," the bearded McCusker recalled in a monotone that disguised the narrative's edge.

"You can do it like a dog, with your bare hands, if you have to.... You spend half the night worrying that you're not in deep enough, and every hour start digging to get down further."

The Viet Cong were a perpetual presence, even watching the movies shown to grunts in base camp. Mac swore the facility absorbed intensive shelling after every John Wayne flick. As the evening progressed, he recalled the day the gunnery sergeant stopped the war. The exhausted company had been moving through waist-high jungle mud in a futile search-and-destroy mission when the noncommissioned officer sat down on the trail and refused to move until he rested.

"Davis just stopped the war," the word went down the column.

"Right on, Davis," the response came back.

Four hours later, the sergeant got up and the operation moved on.

Later that evening, the stories got grimmer. One day during a patrol in the rice paddies, a Viet Cong sniper took out Mac's partner, leading the commanding officer to call for an air strike against the nearby village. When the platoon went to mop up, Mac and a fellow soldier stopped in their tracks. In the center of the settlement, they found a three-foot-high pile of charred bodies of village children, burned into oblivion by napalm. In their last moments before fleeing to certain death in the paddies, the survivors had collected the remains to confront their tormentors.

McCusker's partner just stared into the pile.

"Mac, I can't take this s--t anymore. It's no good, Mac."

McCusker had to be dragged away. The company lieutenant, freshly arrived from district headquarters, tried to say the Viet Cong had murdered the victims.

The grunts just stared at him.

"We did your dirty work," McCusker concluded with scarcely a hint of emotion.

"And you hated us for it."

CABARET

Not long after returning from the coast, I redirected my attention to the plight of the university. Through the initiative of Hal Linstone, I had cross-listed my corporate culture seminar with a systems science course focused on the future as history. Citing William Irwin Thompson, I now took on higher education in a column called "State of the Cathedral." Like the medieval church, Thompson argued, universities bestowed blessings upon the converted and lent approval to select social practices. Now academia had become as hierarchical and ossified as the church, an example of the tendency of institutions to convert the charisma of founding visionaries into routine forms. A second column, "Sixty-Nine," used a crude figure of speech to depict PSU's Vital Partners Conference, an event hosting planners and administrators from the university and the downtown community who believed they could plan the future.

Although I suspected that periods of economic contraction such as the 1970s promoted cultural stagnation, I soon came to question the notion. Having left the university, Penny Allen had gravitated to her passion for theater. The result was *Mirage*, a musical farce about the contemporary Middle East. Staged at the Euphoria Tavern in the warehouse district along the Southeast Portland waterfront, the production took on the traditions of cabaret-theater by merging popular music, raucous comedy, and biting social satire. Its song-and-dance portraits of corrupt political leaders, arms dealers, terrorists, and post-Sixties depression victims, gushed an *Oregonian* newspaper review, presented the oil crisis through the lens of the Marx Brothers.

My appraisal in an April *freeway* was even more enthusiastic. Nobody escaped in this fast-spaced, off-the-wall approach to the absurdity of war and the insanity of world politics, I wrote. Highlighting performers such as comic actor Cork Hubbert and the glamorous Lola Desmond, I suggested, *Mirage* offered some of the most exciting and freewheeling political and musical satire Portland had ever seen.

Not long after seeing the production, I stopped for a beer at a favorite downtown haunt and ran into Susan Sweeny, a friend and leading mainstay of the Storefront Theater. Storefront was the brainchild of Tom Hill and Anne Garety, who formed the troupe in 1970 after leaving the directorship of PSU's American Theater Company. Experimenting with radical political pieces at the time of the student strike, the ensemble moved on to the work of Jean Genet and a modern version of the Greek antiwar classic *Lysistrata*.

Primrose

Within a year, Hill and Garety had secured a run-down storefront near the North Portland industrial waterfront.

By 1975, when the theater received a three thousand dollar grant from the state arts commission, its roster included costume designer Ric Young, set creator Henk Pander, directors Sweeny and John Zagone, and a host of highly energized and talented actors and stage crew that included radical feminists, gays, and lesbians as well as so-called "straights."

Storefront's pianist was the classically trained Terri Risley. After having prepared for the coming summer production, however, Terri had suffered a slipped disc.

"David!" Sweeny cried out as we bumped into each other in a crowded passageway.

"David," she repeated, most likely recalling my stints at the old upright in her Northwest Portland living room, "would you be interested in playing piano for a vaudeville show?"

Inspired by the example of *Mirage*, I instantly said yes.

Caught off guard by the immediacy of the response, Sweeny cautioned that the show involved a great deal of work.

I was aware of that, I responded. It would do me good.

"You're kidding!" she replied, throwing her arms around me.

The next night I met with John Zagone. There was hardly any money in this, John warned. Undeterred, I committed to joining the house band for *Vaudeville II* to the end of June, when I would reassess my plans. As Terri Risley and music director Teddy Deane, former horn player for the Holy Modal Rounders, guided me through the show's numbers and helped locate incidental music, honky-tonk pianist and Storefront veteran Richard Tyler let me photocopy his fake book. Meanwhile, my parents sent on the remaining portions of my sheet music collection.

The reconnection with old-time music inspired a *freeway* commentary. It began by referencing critics who denounced musical nostalgia for furthering a decadent resurrection of antiquated and sexist values. In contrast, I insisted, the recycling of discarded forms enlarged creative vision and provided models to build upon. Exploration of diverse styles by Bob Dylan and the Beatles, I suggested, showed that subtlety and intensity of expression were far more important to art than philosophic assumptions or moral judgments. Great music, like the Tin Pan Alley gems of the 1930s and '40s, I said, operated outside the boundaries of rational discourse.

"If I could tell you what it means," I quoted modern choreography pioneer Isadora Duncan, "there would be no need to dance it."

During the midst of rehearsals for *Vaudeville II*, I came out of class one morning to find a desperate Penny Allen. The piano player for *Mirage*, a brilliant musician with a drug habit, had left the show. When Penny begged me to take his place, I panicked. Teaching three classes, writing a weekly column, rehearsing for a major production, and making plans for a coming sabbatical, I was in no position to take on anything else. After a day or two of frantic phone calls, however, all potential replacements turned out to have weekend bookings. As Penny pleaded that *Mirage* would close without a piano player, I signed on, overcoming my discomfort over having published a highly favorable review of the show in which I now would appear. As I rehearsed for two openings with complicated cues and stage directions, I vowed that if I got through the next several weeks, no challenge would ever intimidate me.

TEACHERS

Just as things could not get more intense, a long-brewing crisis at the *Vanguard* came to a head. The controversy centered on an Eastern Europe specialist who served as a faculty representative on the PSU publications board. In a previous column, I had reported that the professor had complained that the "negative" quality of *Vanguard* news coverage and editorial commentary did little to foster university spirit and provided a poor institutional image. Specifically, he condemned domination of the paper by a "left wing social club" and objected to compensation for faculty who used the publication as a "sounding board." With all the world's political and economic problems, I commented, it seemed like a peculiar time to be turning away from what we could not avoid. Besides, as I wrote home, I failed to see why I could not receive seven dollars a column (little more than a dollar an hour) when the *Vanguard* customarily paid far more for syndicated feature writers such as San Francisco's Arthur Hoppe.

In late April, the crisis escalated when the professor objected to *Vanguard* coverage of Vital Partners Week.

"And then you run Horowitz," he berated the editor, "and he's against everything."

Like the student government leaders who tried to de-fund the newspaper and now sought to take over the publications board, I wrote, the complainant hoped to reshape the campus press. When a *Vanguard* staffer signed an affidavit claiming the professor had used backdoor methods to rescind the appointment of a gay transfer student as the coming year's editor, therefore, I jumped at the chance to discuss what I saw as an attempt to control and strangulate one of the most precious institutions on campus.

After restating the allegations in painstaking detail, I said that those who worked to close down free expression and shut off critical opinion came "very close to a fascism of the spirit."

Infuriated at the charge, the target of my censure took to the faculty senate floor to insist that he would not permit anyone to call him a fascist and stated that he intended to sue for slander. Nevertheless, the campaign against the new editor never materialized. Since I had carefully characterized the case against my colleague as *accusations* and had not actually called him a fascist, moreover, nothing came of his threats.

I saved my concluding thoughts on the subject for a "Last Freeway."

As I described the divergent personalities of my iconoclastic family, I noted that I had delighted in dialogue all my conscious life while finding teachers everywhere. Learning was a dialectical process, I insisted, requiring people to clarify what they believed by testing it against something else. *freeway* was not the product of a rigid political philosophy, I pleaded, but an attempt to deal with an ever-evasive cultural universe through irony, contradiction, and paradox. Politics might be a necessary tool in an imperfect universe, I suggested. Yet the real mark of a civilization was the allocation of creative space for imaginative play.

It was now time to close shop, I concluded. After more than six years in the PSU wilderness, an ancient privilege entitled me to a sabbatical year off with half pay. I intended to explore other ways of preserving and extending vitality. Readers now could find me weekend nights supporting *Mirage* and *Vaudeville II* at the piano.

Playing for two shows was easier than I thought, particularly when *Mirage* moved to midnight performances at the Storefront. Indeed, the experience could be inspiring. At one *Vaudeville* rehearsal, clarinetist Gary Guenther and I got into an easy blues in which the interplay was so intimate I thought it would never end. Storefront production numbers included a Depression-era chorus line tap dance, a ragtime soft shoe, and a classic Ric Young extravaganza featuring glamorous showgirls descending a circular stairway. My favorite was a languidly paced and sultry "Makin' Whoopee!" delivered in Marlene Dietrich fashion by Linda, a PSU education student. Without doubt, however, the most challenging task was accompanying Anne Garety's "Sunny," an introspective and halting ballad whose timing Anne altered with every rendition.

Over two thousand people saw *Vaudeville II*. A blending of diverse energies, Storefront printed no programs and shunned individual curtain calls. Only once do I remember a performer receiving special attention. As the ensemble bowed in appreciation to the audience one early July evening, John Zagone stepped to front stage and announced it was my final night at the piano.

After saluting my enthusiasm and good cheer, Zagone said I now was off to investigate the CIA.

The entire audience had a hearty laugh at that one.

HABITAT

(1975-1976)

no political solution, to our troubled evolution
  – Sting

A WEEK AFTER JOHN ZAGONE'S SALUTE AT STOREFRONT THEATER, I found myself sprinting across the U.S. Capitol green in the company of a congressional staffer and the official press liaison of the Church Committee, the select Senate panel charged with investigating abuses in the American intelligence community. Zagone was perfectly serious when he told the crowd I was on the way to Washington, D.C., to take on the CIA. Plans for my first sabbatical had taken shape earlier in the year when newspaper exposés of improper FBI and CIA activities had prompted the Senate to choose Frank Church, an Idaho Democrat and former historian, to chair an inquiry. Having missed out on a firsthand view of the Watergate hearings, I vowed to bear witness to the capital's new political drama.

PRESS CORPS

I was to serve as "national correspondent" for the *Oregon Times* at thirty-five dollars a feature. Meanwhile, I would earn considerably less than that for weekly contributions to the *Scribe,* Portland's latest underground weekly. After former *Vanguard* news editor Steve Farris and I raced the Datsun across the country in three days, I settled in at a trailer park outside Alexandria, Virginia, and received accreditation at the Senate Periodical Press Gallery. Next, I visited the Center for National Security Studies, a dissenting think-tank that monitored U.S. intelligence and military abuses.

After interviewing director Robert Borosage, who explained how the organization distinguished legitimate information gathering from covert actions, I sat down with star fellow Mort Halperin. A former senior staff member of Richard Nixon's National Security Council, Halperin had initiated a highly publicized civil suit against

Henry Kissinger for authorizing wiretaps on his phone conversations. I did not expect to hear any details of the case but thought a human-interest piece on the figure whose treatment anticipated Watergate would make a great story. Given the circumstances, however, Halperin was overly cautious about personal inquiries and abruptly cut off the interview.

As the Church Committee met behind closed doors to look into assassination plots against foreign leaders, Robert Maheu, one-time manager of the Howard Hughes interests, former CIA asset, and a key witness, held a press conference. Acting in behalf of the agency in 1960, Maheu acknowledged, he had negotiated a voluntary commitment from organized crime figures to take out Cuban President Fidel Castro. Sitting next to *Washington Star* reporter Norm Kempster, I wondered aloud if syndicate leaders expected return favors.

"Go ahead and ask him," Norm prompted.

To my surprise, Maheu called upon me. Yes, such accords may have existed, he said.

"Friends of the agency prosper and are free to pursue their vital interests," I concluded in "Murder in the Cathedral," my initial dispatch to the *Scribe*.

A week later, I provided Portland readers with a synopsis of CIA Director William E. Colby's appearance before the House Select Committee on Intelligence Activities. I described Colby as a quiet, bespectacled man who parted his hair straight as an arrow and never moved his upper lip when his studied monotone referred to "intelligence products" and allocation of resources. The director had provided congressional testimony on forty occasions since January. Yet the CIA insisted upon the importance of secrecy to protect "sources and methods," even extending such reticence to the total agency budget, some seven to seventeen billion dollars a year. All Colby would say was that CIA efforts reflected the *capabilities* of foreign powers, not their current intentions. In the company of three dark-suited assistants carrying three-foot attaché cases, the director treated the hearing as a simple appropriations exercise.

While the panel merely shadow boxed with him, I noted, Mr. Colby never even perspired. The fatal punch never came.

My background reading had included Colby's admission of his role in Operation Phoenix, a U.S. program to identify and turn over suspect Viet Cong cadre and collaborators to the South Vietnamese Army that led, according to the director's own testimony, to the torture and execution of twenty thousand civilians. As electronic experts swept the room to prepare for a closed session, Colby stood idly in the hall of the Rayburn House Office Building. Ignored by the press corps, who had heard everything he had to say, he remained alone except for a longhair pressing him about CIA complicity in the Kennedy assassination. Seeing my chance, I asked the top intelligence official of the United States to clarify his position on covert activity.

It was a definitional problem, Colby answered. If we supplied certain parties with technical assistance, he responded with a smile, were we responsible for ensuing acts of violence? Switching subjects, I wondered if the agency ever considered the possibility that Fidel Castro had turned to Moscow in response to U.S. plots on his life.

Castro was "in knee-deep with the Soviets all along," Colby assured me.

As the summer progressed, I often joined the Capitol press crew at the journalists' table at the Senate café. On several occasions, CBS correspondent Dan Schorr detailed how the Nixon administration had investigated him under the false pretense of establishing clearance for a White House appointment. My most significant press contact was David Beckwith, the lead correspondent of *Time* magazine's Washington bureau. Beckwith had come to Portland in June to visit an Urban Studies graduate student. Taking him to see *Vaudeville II,* she introduced me to her guest, after which Beckwith handed me a business card and urged me to contact him when I got to Washington.

Getting There

As advertised, Beckwith knew everyone in Washington. As we walked along 16th Street near the White House one day, a black limousine rushed by just as a waving hand emerged from the barely opened passenger window and the occupant called out Dave's name.

"Hi, Jerry!" Beckwith laughed as he returned the greeting to President Ford.

"He likes to kid me," Dave explained.

A few weeks later, the two of us lunched at the National Press Club, where we sat by the oversized wall photographs of the principals of Watergate, one of the seminal episodes in the history of American journalism. When I spied a portrait of E. Howard Hunt, the former CIA official who had teamed up with ex-FBI agent Gordon Liddy to direct the Watergate burglars, I remarked that it certainly would be interesting to talk to him.

Pulling a letter out of his pocket, Beckwith said he had just heard from Hunt.

The Watergate defendant was serving a thirty-month to eight-year prison sentence at a federal correctional facility at Eglin Air Force Base in the Florida Panhandle. Convinced that *Time* had run a sympathetic profile of him during his early period of incarceration, he now sought additional coverage to facilitate an appearance before the Church Committee and the chance of early parole. Hunt wanted him to do another interview, said Beckwith, but despite his reluctance to alienate a source, the reporter had no interest in holding the inmate's hand. As a historian interested in the CIA, he proposed, I should go to see him.

HUNT

Once Hunt received assurances that Watergate issues were off the table, a requirement mandated by federal Judge John Sirica, he approved the visit. Stopping at a tobacco store in Alexandria, I scored some Cuban-leaf cigars and set out for Florida in mid-September. After sleeping on the Datsun's foam rubber mattress somewhere in South Carolina, I arrived late on a Friday afternoon.

Reacting to a wave of unfavorable publicity over press relations, prison officials were completely cooperative. A twenty-one year CIA veteran and political action officer during agency operations in Guatemala (1954) and Cuba's Bay of Pigs (1961), Hunt had published forty-seven novels, eight of them spy stories cleared at headquarters. Several took place in Old Havana. Building on this premise, I concocted a startling lead for my article:

"E. Howard Hunt and I sat smoking pre-embargo Cuban cigars in the visitor's lounge of the Federal Prison Camp at Eglin Air Force Base."

My first question concerned Hunt's response to Frank Church's speculation that the CIA sometimes acted as a "rogue elephant." Dissenting, he said he always believed that techniques such as covert entry, wiretapping, and the falsification of documents, standard procedures in overseas missions, were in the national interest as long as they received approval from higher authorities. Foreign assassination attempts, he believed, presumably benefited from similar authorization. Hunt attributed recent disclosures of CIA domestic spying to leaks from operatives who never received promised promotions or transfers during tough duty assignments in Vietnam. He claimed the war had vitiated the agency by asking it to do too much in a conflict the nation was unprepared to win. Nevertheless, he warned that publicity about CIA abuses would result in a loss of American prestige, economic deprivations on a scale not presently imaginable, and reduction of the United States "to a dismembered octopus that flaps feebly now and then."

As visiting hours expired, Hunt volunteered that he had enjoyed our conversation and said he was free the next day. Then he added that inmates could have meals brought in from the outside on Saturdays.

"Why don't you order two well-done steaks from the Americana Motel?" he instructed.

The following morning, our conversation returned to domestic spying in the late 1960s, which Hunt defended because of wide-

Getting There

spread radical violence and pressure from President Johnson. When I noted that as a participant in campus protests, I saw little threat to social order, he replied he sometimes felt that way about Watergate targets. Nevertheless, in either case, he added, it was not his judgment or mine that counted.

Hunt was a reflective man with a sense of history who enjoyed political dialogue. My profile presented him as an unreconstructed conservative who believed the West had been enervated by war, pleasure seeking, and pervasive consumerism. Yet I saw Hunt as perceptive enough to realize events had overtaken him. Although animated and barbed, I observed, much of his talk involved a sense of loss.

As the Saturday session extended into the afternoon, I asked if prison had changed his mind about anything. Yes, he answered, two things. First, he had learned there was little harm in marijuana, which mellowed out the institution's population and kept the peace. Second, he did not believe people should do time because of a financial dispute with the Internal Revenue Service. As I ran out of questions late in the day, the conversation assumed a decidedly father-and-son tone. Referring to me as a "nice Jewish boy," Hunt said he respected my intellectual pursuits. He confided that his wife, who had gone down in a plane crash while carrying funds to the families of the Watergate burglars, had talked of converting from Roman Catholicism to Judaism. As it came time to leave, he slipped me an envelope.

"It's a note to a lady friend," he said in a lowered voice. "I'd rather not have it read by the guards. Would you drop it off in a mailbox?"

As we shook hands, Hunt promised a "real" interview upon his release.

"Sirica's my rabbi," he explained.

Holding to the promise as a matter of honor, I dispatched the unopened letter.

As I prepared the story, I was intent on letting Hunt speak for himself, an approach I had learned in describing anti-New Deal business conservatives, the latter-day John Dos Passos, Thomas Carlyle, and Henry James, to working-class opponents of the counterculture. I was pleased, then, that upon receiving the article, Hunt wrote Beckwith that the Horowitz piece was "not bad," although he could not resist adding "that sure is a liberal rag he writes for."

CAPITOL CITY

Shortly after my return from Florida, the congressional hearings got underway.

"You sit in velvet-draped and richly carpeted hearing rooms," I explained in an *Oregon Times* feature, "and hear of CIA biological poisons and dart guns, post office cooperation in opening mail, NSA monitoring of overseas phone calls, illegal FBI burglaries hidden in 'do not file' files, and IRS audits of troublesome taxpayers."

Talk in the halls, I continued, then "shifts to cabalistic Mafia-CIA plots to kill Fidel Castro" or to transcripts of CIA debates about the "disposing of nuisances" in the Dominican Republic or the Congo. Indeed, when the Church Committee subsequently published a report on U.S. elimination of foreign leaders, it would confirm the existence of a process by which intelligence chiefs protected the commander-in-chief from responsibility for plots the White House set in motion. It felt strange to use a desk in the decorous press chambers of the Senate, I reported, and leaf through subpoenas of White House documents outlining the use of bribery, gunrunning, kidnapping plots, propaganda, and economic pressure to disrupt the elected socialist government of Chile's President Salvador Allende, assassinated in a military coup in 1973.

Occasionally, the hearings produced lighter moments. As Henry Kissinger testified about foreign assassination plots in closed-door sessions in the top-secret quarters of the Joint Committee on Atomic Energy, the press held extended vigils to catch departing comments from the star witness. ABC television reporter Sam

Donaldson often entertained these gatherings with mock salutes to the Free World press. One day, Susan Ford, the striking daughter of the president, hung with us on a photographic assignment for a New York magazine. I even thought we exchanged a friendly glance. Another time I shared a cordial elevator ride with Tennessee Senator Howard Baker, a key Church panel member. Interviews with Oregon senators Mark Hatfield and Bob Packwood proved amiable but hardly more enlightening. Lacking hard news, I published a self-parody in a *Scribe* piece I called "Sleuthing the CIA in Capitol City."

ROOTS

As the Church Committee completed open sessions in December, I returned to New York for the American Historical Association convention and a meeting with Peter Carroll. Our association dated back to the spring of 1974 when a family illness had forced labor historian Herbert Gutman to withdraw from a guest lecture at Portland State and Mike Passi recommended Peter to take his place. Born in Queens, Peter had taught at the University of Minnesota, where he and Dave Noble coauthored *The Free and the Unfree*, an innovative radical U.S. history textbook. His talk in Portland centered on the pitfalls and consequences of graduate school life in the mid-1960s. To my delight, this straight-shooting, witty New Yorker shared my passion for radical politics, countercultural values, and the ferment of ideas. Peter demonstrated that you could fuse historical thinking with an unconventional outlook and have a great time doing it.

After resigning from Minnesota and starting a freelance writing career in California, Peter had approached a publisher about doing a twentieth-century U.S. history textbook with Dave Noble. The idea was to integrate the new social history about ordinary Americans with a narrative covering political history and international relations. Yet the duo needed someone to cover the 1920s, 1930s, and 1960s. Would I be interested, Peter asked over a beer?

I never hesitated.

It was about time I did something useful, I said.

Habitat

As Peter prepared to solicit a contract, I headed back to Portland in early 1976 to file taxes and organize finances. I planned a route through the South because I wanted to explore the home of blues and country music. My first stop was a traditional folk festival in Chapel Hill, North Carolina, where I wound up jamming on the piano with some locals in a converted country barn. One of them, a longhaired street corner guitarist, invited me to sleep on his trailer floor. The next evening, he asked me to dinner at his parents' house. His father, it turned out, was the dean of the University of North Carolina law school and used the occasion to pump me for a full report on the Church hearings and prospects for intelligence agency reform.

After a brief taste of Atlanta nightlife, where a music promoter told me former Georgia governor Jimmy Carter was going to be the next president, I headed for New Orleans. My destination was a children's circus run by several Antioch graduates in nearby Algiers, a free ferryboat ride across the Mississippi. After helping the crew erect their tent in return for sleeping space on their house floor, I proceeded to Mobile. There I came across a Victorian mansion run by the Daughters of the Confederacy. Thrilled to learn I was a historian, the elderly docents took me under their wing, gave me a personal tour of the premises, and told me I simply *had* to visit the old Mississippi plantations up near Natchez.

Following their instructions, I descended upon a deserted white clapboard structure surrounded by trees and greenery. The rustic feel of the place did not correspond to the image I had of a slaveholder's mansion. Climbing onto the porch, I creaked back and forth in a wooden rocker. Except for the lack of human beings, it felt as if time had frozen these hundred-plus years. My odyssey through the Old Confederacy continued that evening when I stumbled upon a nightspot on the Mississippi River near the old slave auction dock. There, a distinguished elderly African-American entertainer at the piano ran the gamut from blues to rag to pop standards with the grace of a well-seasoned professional. Noticing my interest, a white

Getting There

couple in their late-thirties invited me to their table, where they plied me with mixed drinks and amiable chatter.

The portly male of the duo let me know I was in the company of a real southern belle.

"Dyvid, forget that," his partner slurred with a wave of her hand.

"Dyvid," she repeated as she gathered her thoughts and nodded toward the piano player.

"Dyvid," she said, "this man is the soul of the South – the soul of the South."

As my friends retreated into the night, I pulled the Datsun into a vacant space along the riverbank to sleep off the evening. Only a full day of driving succeeded in purging the hangover. I was on my way to Houston to stay at the home of Ben Golub, another of my father's cousins. With the family out of town, I had free rein of the palatial residence and breakfasts of bacon and eggs that the live-in black housekeeper insisted on preparing for me. At night, I rode around the city's far-flung freeways with a young Golub family friend who was the heir to his late father's steel business. A veritable man-about-town, my guide treated me to front-row seats at a Houston Rockets basketball game, led me to several excellent jazz clubs, and at one late-night haunt miles across town, introduced me to the best beef sausage I have ever tasted.

My next stop was Austin, the nexus of the new country and western sound challenging Nashville through the music of Willie Nelson, Waylon Jennings, Guy Clarke, and company. As I drove aimlessly into town, I stopped for a hitchhiker. He turned out to be an aspiring musician who needed to retrieve his guitar at a club across town. With the errand complete, he offered to let me crash on the floor of his minimally furnished rental. After spending a few afternoons swimming at nearby Lake Travis, my host brought me to hear Willie and the band at a benefit dance for the local sheriff's re-election campaign, where I spent most of the evening standing by the piano with a first-hand view of the keyboard artistry of Willie's sister, Bobbie.

ZIHUATANEJO

Austin marked the high point of my musical journey across the South. By March, I was back in Portland. My mail included the response to a Freedom of Information query I had filed nine months earlier in preparation for the Church Committee assignment. Following my arrest as an antiwar protester in 1970, the FBI had opened a file on me, including any *Vanguard* story in which my name appeared. Curiously, one of the clippings in it described the PSU lecture on corporate control of U.S. foreign policy that my namesake David J. Horowitz of *Ramparts* had delivered in 1971. Additional *Vanguard* stories described the Radical Studies Center, the DCE controversy, and my comments on violence and social change before the PSU forum. Beyond the false report that I was a "worker" in the communist youth movement in Minneapolis, the FBI recorded an informant's disclosure that I had accompanied several "local dissidents" to a Portland city council meeting to protest the construction of student housing in Goose Hollow.

Shortly before I resumed my travels, Frank Church came to town as part of a run for the 1976 Democratic presidential nomination. When I greeted the senator, mentioned my stint in Washington, and asked what might come of the CIA investigations, he said he recognized me.

"As you know, Dave," he responded, "we're up against some very powerful forces."

I was not sure whether Church had treated me to a heartfelt confession or a stump speech.

Days later, I headed south. I was on the way to Mexico for an extended sojourn, an idea that Bruce Goldstein and others had continually promoted. In La Jolla, I stayed over with Michael's former Del Mar housemate, Frank Beyerle. Before I left, Frank's wife Lynn scribbled the name "Zihuatanejo" on a slip of paper and insisted that I check out this small Pacific fishing village and resort a hundred miles north of Acapulco.

Armed with *The People's Guide to Mexico*, a pocket dictionary, and a map, I entered Mexico south of Tucson. My first major stopover was the small coastal community of San Blas. At the near-empty seaside motel, I met an American who knew one of the locals. On Mexican Mother's Day, a near-sacred holiday in this Roman Catholic country, our host shepherded us past one street stand after another serving stiff shots of "industrial alcohol." Then he insisted we come back to his modest home, where he roused his sleeping pregnant wife to fetch us bottles of beer as well into the night he raised weeping toasts to the saintliness of motherhood.

The situation placed my American friend and me in a cultural bind. Compassion for the silent and belabored wife of our benefactor made it difficult to participate in the evening's revelry. Yet it was impossible to tear ourselves away from the gathering without deeply insulting our friend's generosity, a violation doubly problematic for privileged visitors from the North.

Machismo offered lighter moments. Several Mexican men mentioned that I resembled Henry Kissinger, no doubt a nod to my curly hair, black frame glasses, and "Jewish" nose. When I objected to the association with someone whose politics I condemned, people assured me that since Kissinger was a powerful figure, they had paid me a supreme compliment. I kept these cultural idiosyncrasies in mind as I moved down the coast. In Puerto Vallarta, I learned about a launch to a nearby island where bamboo huts rented for pennies a day. All you needed was a beach mat and a change of clothes. Here, protocol dictated respect for each person's privacy and maintenance of a low profile. The more I penetrated the tropics, in fact, the more my metabolism decelerated and the more I learned to "go with the flow."

The morning after my arrival in Zihuatanejo, I stepped outside my run-down hotel into the bright sunlight of the main square. Having been a smoker for ten years, I lit a Camel and contemplated my next move. Within seconds, a trim fellow in his early twenties approached and in casual English asked for a cigarette. He introduced himself as Roberto and said he lived in L.A. but was in Zihuatanejo to help repair his uncle's fishing boat. When he learned that I was looking for a place to rent, he said if I gave him and his wife a ride home with the groceries, he could show me an "American" beach with plenty of inexpensive places.

As promised, Roberto brought me to a quiet enclave a couple miles south and pointed to an unoccupied three-room stucco hut a few hundred yards from the ocean. Renting for a dollar a day, it offered the perfect setup. In return for the favor, Roberto said I could give his wife and her cousin occasional rides to town. Life soon settled into a routine that included morning coffee and sweet rolls, Spanish language study, body surfing, lounging on the beach, and evening rides into town for red snapper dinners and an occasional disco.

My supply of apple soda, my favorite drink, and other sundries came from a small market. Each time I entered, I noticed that a pale, ailing elderly woman, most likely the family matriarch, lay in a bed to the rear of the store in full sight of customers. Assuming she was on her deathbed, I stifled my discomfort. To my surprise, however, the woman improved within days and reassumed a place behind the counter. Keeping her in contact with family members and regular patrons, it seemed, had served as perfect therapy.

RAILROAD BILL

As part of the international beach culture, Zihuatanejo attracted young European adventurers, Latin American tourists, and a number of American women living on trust funds, alimony, or child support. June, a tall, rangy, dark beauty from Austin, was in the last category. A perennial presence on the beach, she liked to tease me about my romantic interests while I enjoyed playing with the musical sound of *Junia*, her Spanish name. June was a registered pharmacist raising three young children in a primitive hut in the hills, to which she hauled fresh water every day. As we lay in her front porch hammock on languid nights or explored deserted beaches, she recounted several experiences with Latin patriarchy.

"Don't ever trust a Mexican," she warned.

"Things are never what they seem. There's always a dark reality beneath the surface."

Sometime before I arrived, June had ended a relationship with a local who owned a villa in partnership with a well-to-do American. Curious, perhaps, about Junia's new beau, he asked us to an evening's get-together. After everyone enjoyed an array of local fruits and desserts, we all gathered in a circle on the floor. The host then asked each person to perform something from his own culture. I felt some apprehension because of my difficulty in carrying a tune. I also suspected my friend's "ex" wanted to have some fun at the expense of the American academic. Nevertheless, as I realized June counted on my rising to the challenge, I steeled my nerve.

When my turn arrived, I looked the master of ceremonies straight in the eye. Summoning all the force I could muster, I proceeded to belt out the lines from a gritty folk ditty I had learned as a boy off my ten-inch Cisco Houston LP.

"Railroad Bill! Railroad Bill!" I nearly shouted.

"He never worked and he never will! I'm gonna ride old Railroad Bill!"

As our host rose to his feet amid a rousing ovation and shook my hand, I knew I had passed the challenge.

June laughed all the way home.

MADISON SQUARE

By August, both June and I had business back in the States. She had to return to Austin to renew her pharmacy license and contemplate a return to work. I had received credentials from the Senate Periodical Press Gallery to cover the Democratic National Convention for the *Oregon Times* and the *San Francisco Bay Guardian,* whose literary supplement Peter Carroll now edited. At June's initiative, we packed the kids and our belongings into the Datsun to drive to her parents' in the Dallas suburbs. As we proceeded through a stretch of the marijuana region of Guerrero on that first day, I passed several vehicles only to have to screech to a halt before an outpost of *Federales* blocking the road with drawn automatic weapons. Fortunately, June talked our way past the sentries and we moved on to Guadalajara and Monterrey.

Once in Texas, I met June's seventeen-year-old brother. A brilliant electric bass player in an up-and-coming country group, he invited me to observe a new rhythm guitarist's tryout at a friend's garage. I marveled how every one of these musicians traced his roots to Chuck Berry. The only downside of the experience came when I had to convince the auditioning performer I was not the band's manager and had no power to get him off the Pontiac assembly line.

A few days later, the scene shifted to the farming community of Gonzales, where tens of thousands of fans had gathered to celebrate the 1976 Bicentennial at Willie Nelson's annual July 4th picnic. In truth, the gathering felt little different from the rock festival I had attended in Oregon seven years earlier. The high point of the event came late during the final night when Leon Russell mounted the stage to sing "A Song for You" with Willie sitting a few feet away.

By now, however, I had begun to feel overwhelmed by June's financial and family obligations. Besides, my brother had just returned to Roslyn Heights at loose ends and my mother looked forward to my joining him. The plan was to stay at Uncle Mickey's new apartment in Manhattan's Lincoln Center, a quick subway ride to convention headquarters at Madison Square Garden. Unfortunately, the presidential nomination presented little drama as Jimmy Carter expanded upon a southern base to leave rivals such as Frank Church and California governor Jerry Brown far behind. Since I represented two small-press outlets and had limited access to the convention floor, my only option was to adopt a human-interest slant.

Jerry Brown, I wrote for the *San Francisco Bay Guardian*, had a speaking style that mixed Buckminster Fuller planetary consciousness with tough street talk. At times, I suggested, Brown seemed to parody the rituals of political discourse and even the process itself. Turning to the Oregon story, I noted that the state's delegation was the only one at the convention to boast a majority of women members. I also reported that twenty-six Oregonians had voted in a losing effort for a rules change to facilitate the introduction of minority reports on health care, civil rights, and labor laws, while another twenty supported failed attempts to introduce debate on gay rights and Vietnam amnesty. Beyond that, I described how Brown alternate and former PSU activist Dan Wolf had unfurled a free-form American flag featuring peace symbols as stars.

At a loss for substantive news to provide readers of the *Oregon Times*, I culminated my account of the convention by telling the story of my inclusion in the delegation's excursion to Big Julie's, a discotheque around the corner from its midtown hotel. Sadly, my attempt to humanize the band of unassuming Oregonians would have unforeseen consequences.

CREVICE

(1976-1982)

there's no escape/without a scrape
— R. Ocasek

F OLLOWING THE CLOSE OF THE DEMOCRATIC CONVENTION AND the culminating episode of an eventful sabbatical, I returned to Roslyn Heights to see my family and prepare for the trip back to Portland. A week later, when Uncle Mickey paid a visit, I used the occasion to show my brother and uncle the "with it" fern bar I had discovered in the old village of Roslyn Harbor. Alienated by the growing conservatism of many of his former allies and the country itself, Mickey had come to question the integrity of the younger generation. Not surprisingly, he wasted no time in dismissing the watering hole's clientele as a collection of self-centered brats.

Somewhat defensively, I replied they were just "working people."

"Yeah," Michael retorted, "they work for their fathers."

CHARMAINE

It was clear that my brother's rapid-fire wit remained one of his most endearing features. Over the past several years, Michael had worked for bookstores, waited on tables, produced freelance articles for the local press, and served in a federally funded position at Portland's Contact Center, a downtown social agency serving counterculture street youth. Once the grant ran out, he scampered for a new gig. The result was a position as advisor to a student monthly published by Portland State's Urban Studies School. Accordingly, we decided to drive west together where we would once again share the Ladd's Addition house and prepare for fall term.

At Michael's initiative, we chose Yellow Springs as our initial destination with the idea of looking up Louis Filler. I had lost contact with Filler since 1964 but had heard that he had married one of my classmates, gone through a bitter divorce, and lost a son from his first marriage to a heroin overdose. Yet my disheveled mentor seemed delighted to see us and completely taken by the old-time standards the two of us performed around his rinky-dink piano. From Ohio, we circled our way across the Middle West, Great Plains, Rocky Mountains, Grand Canyon, and California coast before reclaiming the Ladd's Addition house.

Number one on my agenda was the *Oregon Times*. I had delivered my convention article by telephone from Roslyn Heights. Proud of gaining the confidence of the Oregon contingent, I had fashioned an empathetic piece that described how a group of well-meaning people had made the best of a process in which delegates served as mere window-dressing. When I saw the printed story in the magazine, however, it felt as if someone had stolen my breath.

Under the byline "David Horowitz and Staff," someone had sandwiched a few details from my report into a condescending parody.

"Bored Oregon Dems Boogie in N.Y.," read the headline, a course reference to my brief mention of the discotheque outing.

"Cousin Jimmy's Dream Machine just swept right on past, a-huffin' and a-puffin' and a-sprayin' out great clouds of sleepy gas," one passage described the nomination race.

"Well, it's hot down here in New York City, back of my neck getting' dirty and gritty. Guess I'll head for the country and get some sleep," the narrative concluded.

Apparently, I wrote in a mimeographed form letter sent to each delegate interviewed for the article, the editorial staff preferred its own attempts at flippant humor above the sense of the story conveyed by its correspondent. Then I expressed shame at having my name associated with the piece. After receiving a note of thanks from delegation head State Senator Betty Roberts, I learned that Roberts had delivered a copy of my letter with a protest to the *Times* editor, Tom Bates, and cancelled her subscription. Convinced that my integrity was more important than a career in journalism, I had no regrets about burning bridges. Meanwhile, Dan Wolf produced a framed blow-up of me posing on the convention floor with credentials fastened to my jacket and his peace-symbol flag unfurled in the background. It still hangs in my office.

During the fall of 1976, I began to expand my vita by publishing simultaneous book reviews of John Dean's Watergate memoir, *Blind Ambition*, in *Portland Today* and the *San Francisco Bay Guardian*. To bolster a case for promotion to associate professor, I built up a department service record by soliciting an *Oregonian* write-up and attracting two hundred people to a visiting Russian scholar's lecture on the American Revolution. Signing the textbook contract for *Twentieth Century Limited*, a title I suggested to reflect the notion of ecological limits, provided another milestone. Dave Noble, Peter Carroll, and I now agreed that each chapter would feature mini-biographies of key figures along the lines of Dos Passos's *U.S.A.*

Unlike most textbook contributors, I had no monographs to my name and no scholarly specialty. To compensate, I undertook a survey of dozens of journal articles and book-length studies on the three periods assigned to me. During Christmas, however, I took a break from textbook preparations to join my friend Steve Jenkins, who recently had moved to Maui. A Vietnam vet, Jenkins had gone completely counterculture. For my part, I appreciated engaging a non-academic in the philosophic and political discussions that continued to intrigue me.

Upon my return from Hawaii, my brother informed me of repeated telephone messages from "Charmaine," a woman I had met at a Halloween party. Taken by the red carnation playfully pinned to her striking black hair, I had engaged her in conversation. Charmaine had a tough-but-vulnerable quality that attracted me. When I invited her to walk down to my place for a session at the piano, her cautious need for trust touched me. Accordingly, when she said we could get together again sometime for coffee, I looked forward to the opportunity.

Charmaine served as a workshop leader for Portland's poet-in-the-schools program. As we spent brief periods together, I pressed for more involvement but she said she needed to know me better. I accepted this because I saw her as the kind of woman a man wanted to prove himself worthy of deserving. Teaching classes and working on the textbook during the day, I spent nearly every evening of the winter of 1977 at Charmaine's house in Sellwood, a working-class district in Southeast Portland experiencing gradual gentrification. I learned that she came from an affluent Italian-American Catholic family and had spent her childhood in the exclusive San Francisco suburb of Hillsborough. After two divorces, however, she wound up raising three children in Portland, where she supplemented her sparse earnings from the school district by pitching beers at The Long Good-bye, an alternative downtown music venue owned by friends.

By no means was this an ordinary family. Charmaine was a hemophiliac, a condition requiring frequent infusions of a clotting agent to stop internal bleeding. "Allison," at age twelve, suffered from the same malady, as did fourteen-year-old "Vittorio." "Robert," two years older than his brother, was overweight and diabetic. Curiously, however, the three teens seemed to welcome me as someone who might distract their mother's attentions.

FLESH AND BLOOD

By early summer, Charmaine and I prepared to move into larger quarters a few blocks from her home. Built in 1906, the ample five-bedroom, two-floor clapboard structure sat on a small lot next to an old church. To raise the initial costs of securing the mortgage while Charmaine sold her house, I asked my parents for a temporary loan. They, in turn, warned about buying property before selling an existing home; expressed concern that moving might distract me from completing the textbook; and cautioned against taking on the obligations of a mortgage, a house, another person, and three teenagers.

In reality, my parents despaired of ever having Jewish grandchildren.

To resolve the dilemma, they wished me good luck and forwarded an $850 gift.

Since Charmaine had a VW bus, I raised additional cash by selling the Datsun. Once the former house sold, I signed a rehabilitation loan for the new place. After weeks of sanding floors, wallpapering, painting, and other tasks, I found myself in a new home with a large family and enhanced responsibilities.

Barely settled in, however, I flew to Yellow Springs.

Earlier in the spring, Louis Filler had sent on a copy of an interview he had given to an alternative newspaper at Antioch. When I complained he had drawn a superficial picture of Bob Dylan as a mere protest singer, Filler said he enjoyed the coherence of my response and asked permission to have the letter reprinted. Several months later, my former mentor came to Portland as part of a campaign to rally Antioch alumni support and, at his request, I arranged to host the meeting in Charmaine's former house.

During the visit, Filler assessed Antioch's recent troubles. Once the Rockefeller Foundation brought a number of inner-city African-Americans to campus in the late-1960s, he said, the newcomers followed the logic of Black Nationalism to insist upon a blacks-only dormitory, a controversial position given the college's long standing as an opponent of racial segregation. According to Filler, black student leaders buttressed these demands with personal threats and talk of violence. In the end, he said, the faculty caved in, and Antioch created the first segregated dorm in its history.

Intent on restoring academic quality and involving alumni in the institution's survival, Filler had created the Distinguished Lecture Series around the theme of "Youth in America" and asked me to participate. When funding fell through, he offered to provide me airfare, lodging, and meals in return for a public presentation called "What Happened to the Youth Movement?"

Once on campus, I agreed to an interview with the *Antioch Record*. The most alive people I knew, I recalled of my undergraduate days in the early 1960s, were the political people who seemed to have boundless energy. Nevertheless, I added, I had experienced disenchantment with contemporary politicos who had lost their sense of humor, looked at everything as a moral test, and become too predictable.

Upon leaving Antioch, I explained, I could not conceive of life in the "outside" world. Since then, I had gained sufficient perspective to see that the college suffered from a strain of elitism, excessive alienation from the greater world, and difficulty in adjusting to the fact that American society had become more liberal. As for the youth culture, I thought its greatest failure was the tendency to alienate working people. Bridging the gap between ordinary Americans and affluent youth was not something you could accomplish at the snap of your fingers, I suggested. Yet my hope was that progressive country singers such as Willie Nelson might help to bring the two segments of society together.

Shortly before my lecture, I came to understand why the subject of the counterculture was so important to my mentor. Late that afternoon, I made the mistake of agreeing to share some personal stash offered by Filler's congenial teaching assistant. I had reached a mellow state when Lou burst into the room in a nervous twit. Insisting that we proceed to dinner some two hours before the presentation, he hustled me over to the student union like a mother hen. By now, I felt quite disoriented. As we stood on the noisy cafeteria line with Lou talking up a storm, a friendly young woman approached me and insisted that she knew me from Berkeley.

It took a while to convince her I was not *that* David Horowitz.

Then Filler went off.

"They try to say time heals, that you'll get over it," he suddenly exclaimed.

"Oh, Lou, you've got to get hold of yourself," Filler mimicked.

"Those bastards Hoffman and Rubin killed him!" he now shouted.

This was an unmistakable reference to 1960s radicals Abbie Hoffman and Jerry Rubin and the terrible loss Filler had suffered.

Instantly brought down, I realized that the purpose of my trip was to explain why this poor man had lost his son.

Peppering my presentation with recorded music ranging from the Stephen Stills classic, "For What It's Worth," to the shadowy L.A. odysseys of balladeer Tom Waits, I offered as best a reading of the alternative cultural legacy as I could.

Lou was delighted and never again touched on the painful association between the counterculture and his son's drug abuse.

Nevertheless, the cafeteria outburst helped to explain *Vanguards and Followers: Youth in the American Tradition*, which Filler published the next year. My review, appearing at the author's initiative in the *Journal of Popular Culture*, described Filler's contention that the worst manifestations of youth culture irreverence had surfaced in the "love generation" of the 1960s. *Vanguards and Followers* pictured the counterculture as completely deficient in compassion, loyalty, and "standards of deportment." Dismissing all aspirations toward idealism or seriousness of purpose, the book presented a litany of 1960s drug abuse and violence that led me to draw parallels to a *National Enquirer* article.

My mentor obviously insisted upon the preservation of universal standards of decency and responsibility amidst any redefinition of social values, morals, and lifestyles.

SELLWOOD

By the fall of 1977, work on the textbook had hit full stride. Preparing a special topics class on the cultural conflicts of the 1920s helped me appreciate how the modernizing influences of the Jazz Age competed with a far more resonant traditionalism defined by Prohibition, Fundamentalism, Nativist agitation, and a second Ku Klux Klan that reached up to five million followers. With Peter Carroll serving as editor of my chapter drafts, I gradually learned how to synthesize complex narratives in a concise and clear manner that excised excessive detail, utilized transitional phrasing, and livened up the prose with pithy quotes, often at the start of paragraphs or sections. Most of all, Peter's feedback brought home the lesson that descriptive material needed a logical line of development connecting one train of thought to another.

In the midst of working on the textbook, I got married.

Despite obvious disapproval from my parents, I thought it was time to grow up, be part of a giving relationship, and, at the age of thirty-six, take a final step to adulthood. I also agreed with Charmaine that the stabilizing influence of marriage would counter the challenge of raising three teenagers. Yet the decision came at a heavy price.

My father wrote that the news had left him and my mother numb, devastated that I would never experience the joy of my own children and distraught that I was abandoning Jewish identity. Seeking to placate my parents, we arranged to have a Unitarian minister conduct the ceremony in the church's study without any references to Christianity. Yet the only members of my family to witness the proceedings were Uncle Mickey, who flew to be at my side, and Michael, who had to rush from the reception in Sellwood to catch a plane for a long-awaited trip to Mexico.

I would not see my parents again for nearly three years.

Charmaine was a caring person who taught me the importance of rhythm in the creation and reading of poetry. Yet as my new family settled into the routines of domestic life, it was clear I had seriously overestimated my ability to rise to any occasion. In fact, I had stumbled into a remorseless struggle of wills between an overprotective mother and three restless teens. Allison and Vittorio now sought company among peers in Sellwood's white underclass. When the two began cutting school, I initially shrugged it off as an inevitable rebellion against the regimentation of a "middle-class" educational system. A teacher herself, Charmaine insisted that if her children ever were to amount to anything, they needed to be in school, not on the street with hoodlums. Yet her desperate clinging only drove them further away.

As Allison took to running away from home to be with her boyfriend, I found myself the subject of a nefarious form of psychological blackmail: if I intended to be emotionally supportive of the woman I had promised to love, I would help retrieve her daughter. When on several occasions I objected to this seemingly self-defeating strategy, Charmaine would remind me that these were *her* children, and that she needed my loyalty. Meanwhile, Vittorio, a good-looking boy who could turn on charm like a faucet, drifted into the local dope culture. At the same time, overweight and diabetic Robert, the oldest of the three, spent most of his time watching television or retreating to his room to devour sweets.

THE INSURGENTS

With no plans for the summer of 1978, I followed a colleague's lead and applied for a two-week, all-expenses-paid workshop for mid-level faculty at Stanford University. Enrolled in historian Bart Bernstein's symposium on Post-War America 1945-1960, I found myself particularly drawn to the subject of domestic anticommunism and the place of intellectuals in Cold War society. The removal of the security clearance of Atomic Energy Commission consultant J. Robert Oppenheimer, for example, demonstrated how the period's anticommunist sentiments could coincide with distrust of supposedly amoral scientists and knowledge elites. Bernstein also introduced sociologist Daniel Bell's *Cultural Contradictions of Capitalism* (1978), which argued that the liberating and hedonistic ethos of the consumer market defied traditional notions of social morality. By tying late capitalism to cultural innovation, Bell's analysis resonated with the way New Left scholars outlined the influence of corporate liberalism.

The following winter, Charmaine and I taught a cross-disciplinary English and history course on 1920s literature and culture. By now, preparation for the textbook had sensitized me to the Jazz Age's collision of modern and traditional social values. Yet I also saw continuities among 1920s adversaries. For example, both Lost Generation writers and leaders of the resurrected Ku Klux Klan complained of the rootless quality of modern society. One of my final essay questions asked students to use class texts to relate the concept of the "stranger" to both the period's literature and its social confrontations. Another inquired whether the creative writers of the 1920s had as much ambivalence about the future as that evidenced in public disputes over the teaching of evolution in the public schools or the presidential campaign of New York Roman Catholic and Prohibition critic Al Smith.

Spring term offered the opportunity to organize the material gathered in Washington for my first class on the CIA and the intelligence agencies. Placing the subject in a critical but balanced academic setting proved to be a major challenge. I decided the best way to do so was to require a single final essay as the only course requirement. Instead of permitting students to proceed with research papers on a chosen topic, a freedom I feared would result in excessive polemics and posturing, I followed the protocol of my cultural history classes by requiring responses to a detailed series of questions.

One query asked students to explain the difference between undercover activities at home and abroad in addition to the contrast between intelligence gathering and covert action. Another asked them to speculate whether the CIA had responded primarily to presidential demands or acted as a "rogue elephant." A subsequent question required students to determine whether the intelligence agencies had gone beyond reasonable requirements of internal security in different periods. Finally, the assignment asked for workable definitions of national and internal security as well as criteria for distinguishing between proper and improper activities. To my surprise, one of my students informed me years later that the class had inspired her to join the CIA!

As the summer of 1979 approached, I learned about an eight-week history faculty seminar sponsored by the National Endowment of the Humanities. Directed by Herbert Hoover specialist Martin Fausold, the workshop on Reform and the 1920s was to take place at the Hoover Presidential Library in West Branch, Iowa.

The program's stipend and living expenses, I reasoned, could help meet family expenses over the summer.

Following up on the readings on 1920s cultural history I had completed for the textbook, I proposed to place the second Klan and other moral traditionalists within the framework of reform. This approach owed much to a segment of *The Tragedy of American Diplomacy*, which involved a group of post-World War I Senate Republicans that included Idaho's William E. Borah, Wisconsin's Robert M. La Follette, California's Hiram W. Johnson, and Nebraska's George W. Norris. While advancing the individualistic legacy and social conservatism associated with small business and independent farm interests, wrote Bill Williams, these so-called insurgents opposed concentrations of political, diplomatic, and military power, even to the point of complaining about the threat of overseas imperialism.

As I searched through the finding aids of the Hoover Library for a topic for the seminar's required research paper, I came upon the papers of North Dakota Republican Senator Gerald W. Nye. Although Wayne S. Cole and other scholars had documented Nye's noninterventionist activities before U.S. entry into World War II, far less had surfaced on his Senate career in the 1920s. As I pursued Nye's ample paper trail, he seemed to fit the mix of conservative and progressive impulses that Williams had outlined. Seeking to assist struggling independent farmers, the North Dakotan wound up aligning himself with Republican President Herbert Hoover. Despite a reputation as an agrarian radical, Nye supported Hoover's controversial Agricultural Marketing Act of 1929 because he believed the federal government's program to purchase surplus wheat would help offset disastrous declines in farm price levels.

The experience at the Hoover Library prompted me to begin composing my first research-based essay. Beyond that, it encouraged me to look at much of twentieth-century American history as a response to concentrated forms of political, economic, and cultural power. Framing my fall term Social Change seminar as an exploration of "anti-corporate movements," I brought together material from the Republican Senate progressives, Cold War nationalists, and 1960s populist conservatives such as Barry Goldwater and George Wallace.

Was there, as historian Richard Hofstadter suggested, a "paranoid style" embedded in grassroots politics? On the other hand, were there rational grounds for the anti-statist and anti-intellectual dissidence that characterized so much of American "populist" discourse? I had come upon the questions and subject matter that would frame the next thirty years of my scholarship.

DIVIDENDS

To assist in the location of material on insurgent political figures, I asked my seminar to compile reports on a list of individuals appearing in the course syllabus. Several proved quite helpful. Yet I dreaded oral presentations from people with little interest in the subject or from those who found public speaking painful. The fall of 1979 turned out to be the last time I taught a seminar. Hereafter, I would confine myself to lecture classes. Meanwhile, my brother and I teamed up for a special winter term topics class called Recent Ethnic Ideologies. By now, Michael had entered the PSU Urban Studies PhD program and was preparing a dissertation on the tensions between the Contact Center's counterculture orientation and its ability to survive. Taking off from our debate over hippies and European ethnics at Lower Columbia College, we used the class to revisit the contrast between the alternative culture and traditional worldviews.

Soon after *Twentieth Century Limited* reached print in 1980, I received my associate professorship. The history department then asked me to serve on the organizing committee of a spring conference. Co-sponsored by the teaching committee of the American Historical Association, "The Politics of History – Textbooks and Curricula" brought together high school and university faculty. One of the guest speakers, a creative writing specialist, explained that people demonstrated their most evocative powers of description when recalling details from their experiences between ages eight and ten, a period in which skills of observation matured before the self-consciousness of adolescence. He then asked us to take a few minutes to place our own childhood memories on paper. As I typed up a single-page reminiscence of my family's West Bronx life later that evening, I found the prediction to be amazingly prescient.

That spring, Storefront Theater's John Zagone called. The troupe was about to inaugurate a move to the New Paris Theater, a former burlesque house off Portland's Burnside Street, by staging a modern-day variety show with original tunes by Teddy Deane. Did I want to join the house band for the summer run? I jumped at the chance to work again with Zagone and Ric Young, the brilliant choreographer and costume designer who brought a unique aesthetic sensibility to Storefront productions. The decisions paid dividends. When Ric asked for a piece to accompany a parade of showgirls down a stairway for the first act finale, I was delighted when he approved my choice of the Rodgers and Hart classic, "You Are Too Beautiful."

Backed by the five-piece Fine Jazz Band, "A Storefront Burlesque" used a rotating set to dramatize the backstage tale of its fictional troupe. Although the feisty production numbers and intimate ballads required intensive interplay among the musicians, the piano had the task of following cues and setting the tempo. As I carefully monitored audience response to each piece, I learned to introduce the next act just at the instant the applause began to wane so the production never lost energy or pace.

The show's high point came with veteran L.A. performer Wendy Westerwelle's poignant rendition of a Teddy Deane torch ballad, "Don't Worry 'bout Me." As a piano player, I was adequate. My strength came from the feeling I put into the music, consistency in showing up on time, and a studied diligence. Staying clear of internal politics, I was everybody's friend and did whatever the show required. Besides, I relished the connection to my parents' burlesque days.

TRUST

In contrast to the experience at Storefront, tensions at home got to the point where Charmaine brought in a family mediator. When everyone spoke their piece, Robert, Vittorio, and Allison sympathized with my peacemaker efforts and lashed out at their mother for refusing to trust them and let them grow up. The counselor then proposed that Charmaine take a trial "vacation" away from home, to which she agreed. This left me as the sole parent of three teenagers. Since Charmaine had taken the VW bus, I reverted to public transportation while teaching two summer school classes and putting in three nights a week and Sunday matinees at the theater. Pressed for funds, I applied for food stamps and took each day in stride.

It did not take long for Charmaine to return. Nobody was going to keep her from her children, she said. Demands for unconditional loyalty now intensified. If I could not be supportive and stop undermining her, Charmaine warned, I might as well leave. I soon realized I had given up all vestiges of an independent identity in a bleak marriage in which I had lost my partner's trust. No longer able to provide a bottomless well of emotional security for someone who seemed to have insatiable needs, I decided to call Charmaine on the ultimatum.

In October, I moved into the basement of my former Ladd's Addition home, since my brother had spread his dissertation notes across the floor of the second bedroom. A few weeks later, Michael discovered a vacant two and a half room unit in a single-story duplex on nearby Ladd's Circle. Retrieving my piano, desk, and some personal items, I settled into my own place for the first time in years and filed for divorce with financial assistance from my relieved parents.

THE MASTERS

With no car and more than half my income devoted to temporary spousal support, I pursued an austere existence just as Ronald Reagan swept the 1980 presidential election. I had sought to make sense of the campaign in a book review solicited by David Milholland, co-editor of Portland's *Clinton Street Quarterly*. The work in question sought to link finance capitalism to revolutionary communism. It suggested that American bankers had extended private loans to the Russians to keep them on the Allied side in World War I and then lobbied for recognition of the new Soviet Union in 1917 to cultivate future market opportunities for U.S. corporations.

Familiar with New Left historiography, I responded that coordination between political progressives and capitalist interests was no anomaly. Tracing the record of twentieth-century corporate liberalism, I explained how reformers in both parties often had leaned on the state to manage the market economy. This arrangement included a social welfare safety net, tolerance of trade unions, deficit spending, and government regulations and subsidies. Statist activity at home, I wrote, had counterparts in free trade internationalism and a multilateral foreign policy.

In contrast to corporate liberals, I maintained, Ronald Reagan drew support from small business, independent farmers, domestic entrepreneurs, and local elites beyond eastern and urban power centers. I argued that Reagan represented a populist conservatism opposed to cooperation between big business and the centralized state. Instead, his views had their origin in the pre-World War II America First Committee, anti-union activity, and Cold War era anti-collectivists such as Joe McCarthy, Barry Goldwater, and George Wallace. The Republican nominee, I asserted, sought to broaden the conservative coalition by using the traumas of inflation to convert working people to an agenda of economic freedom for Sunbelt industries and energy interests.

Reagan most likely would accommodate the financial sector if elected, I suggested. Yet I wondered whether corporate and banking leaders still believed the struggling economy could afford the corporate state's social and economic services. Economic and geo-political challenges in the Middle East and elsewhere, I added, might prod liberal internationalists toward more militant assertions of strategic power. In that case, I concluded, a Reagan presidency could incorporate the worst of both possible worlds of American politics.

The *Clinton Street Quarterly* piece afforded the opportunity to integrate historical description with a heightened level of analysis. By the spring of 1981, however, as Charmaine continued to drag out divorce proceedings, my focus once again shifted. Concerned about his client's ability to sustain support payments, my lawyer asked if I had given any thought to a second job to supplement the modest income I expected at summer school. At that point, Debra, a Portland State communications major who played flute and tambourine in a women's rock band, suggested approaching the owners of Bogart's Joint, a 1940s nostalgia tavern in Northwest Portland where she waited on tables several evenings a week.

By the early Eighties, Portland had become a nexus of swing and jazz. Groups such as the Wholly Cats, fronted by singer Rebecca Kilgore, and the Ron Steen Trio, featuring vocalist Shirley Nannette, were among several acts sustaining local clubs. Given my love of 1930s and '40s classics, Debra said I could be the house piano player at Bogart's. The proprietors agreed if we could locate a reasonably priced upright. Fortunately, I knew a Storefront Theater regular who wanted to extricate an old piano from his third-floor apartment in a nearby walk-up. Once a crew of volunteers wrestled the bulky instrument down the stairs and eased it into the bed of a friend's pickup, I pounded out an up-tempo tune as we made our way through the city streets.

As a small establishment, the tavern had no advertising budget. This required me to mount my own publicity campaign. Using the lead, "Professor David Horowitz at the Piano," Debra put together a flier that I mailed to friends, distributed to record shops, posted on utility poles, and sent out to local print media and appropriate radio outlets.

"It's a whole new experience being a PR person," I told a reporter for the *Downtowner* weekly, "I just have to swallow my ego and sell the act."

In an interview with the *Vanguard*, I called attention to the lyrical melodies and artful chord changes of the urbane composers I admired, a list highlighted by George Gershwin, Richard Rodgers, Cole Porter, Duke Ellington, Vernon Duke, and Jimmy Van Heusen. Although I opened and closed every set with *Casablanca's* "As Time Goes By," these tunesmiths provided the mainstay of my repertoire. At the piano Thursday through Saturday evenings from May through October, I earned a nominal sum each night, whatever tips I could make, and a free meal. Patrons often asked if music was my true passion. Despite the modest pay-off, I liked to tell them that I needed to play piano to support my devotion to history.

Meanwhile, the publicity campaign quickly accrued dividends. A profile in the *Northwest Neighbor* by Dan Lissy, an old friend, praised my bluesy version of wartime jazz and balladry as a fitting fusion of body, soul, and emotion.

Not long after, *The Oregonian's* John Wendeborn offered his own appraisal.

"Horowitz plays a sort of living room-smoky dive piano," he wrote, and "tickles the ivories with the sure hands and fingers of a lad who's studied the masters with delight."

On the weekend following the Wendeborn piece, standing-room crowds cheered my every move, even when the execution was not at its best. Only the week before, I recalled, the same tunes had brought a scattering of polite applause, if any. A single newspaper story had made me a minor celebrity on the local scene. As much as I appreciated the hard-won results of my publicity efforts, it was somewhat unsettling to realize that it no longer mattered how I played a particular piece. As the season progressed and crowds gradually returned to their normal size, I felt a sense of relief at the freedom to improvise without undue self-consciousness.

Still without access to a car, I boarded a Greyhound bus in August for a two-day refresher with Bart Bernstein's Stanford seminar. When I outlined my interest in an overview of political history focused on opponents of concentrated power, Bernstein said it sounded as if I had turned Richard Hofstadter upside-down. He was right. Building from my interest in Gerald Nye and the slant of the *Clinton Street Quarterly* piece, I contemplated a synthesis that ignored the conventional labels of liberalism and conservatism. Instead, I saw American political culture divided between corporate and cosmopolitan modernizers on one hand and anti-corporate traditionalists who distrusted experts, centralized institutions, and urbane values on the other.

I had begun to build the foundation of an ambitious work of scholarship.

When I returned from California, I started work on an account of the anti-chain store campaign. Initiated by independent merchants, the movement had accelerated in the Great Depression with accusations that Wall Street had reduced retailers to hired clerks, introduced uniformity to the life of commerce, and milked local communities of capital. My essay followed the crusade to Portland, which in 1932 became the first American city to tax chain store outlets, a reflection of Oregon's small business tradition.

In August, I met up with Oregon State University historian and Hoover seminar colleague Bill Robbins. Through Bill's efforts, William Appleman Williams had agreed to chair the panel featuring my chain story paper at the Eugene meeting of the Pacific Coast Branch of the American Historical Association. A former jazz drummer, Williams introduced me as a hot piano player. Following the session, which came on my fortieth birthday, Bill insisted that Robbins and I join him at his favorite watering hole for a friendly game of pool, where my performance, to be direct, left a great deal to be desired.

Crevice

By March of 1982, my second marriage was history and I was free of all financial entanglements. To celebrate the divorce and the imminent award of Michael's PhD, we staged a rites-of-spring party at Ladd's Addition that attracted three hundred guests. A cocktail server I knew even invited jazz drummer Mel Brown, who arrived with his crew around 3 a.m. and gigged until nearly dawn. As the school year ended, I looked forward to a second sabbatical and the chance to sample the archival collections and papers of the tradition-minded political and cultural insurgents I found so compelling. Emerging from a failed marriage with a new sense of personal limitations, I nevertheless had hopes of initiating a new phase of my life and fashioning a historical interpretation that might have a modicum of influence among my peers.

FOLIAGE

(1982-1983)

what you say, is what you do
  – P. Fishman

On a hot and humid afternoon in June of 1982, a taxi ride from the airport brought me to a dormitory at the University of Texas at Austin. I was there to join a second National Endowment of the Humanities workshop. Led by Eisenhower-era specialist Robert Divine, the seminar would cover the Cold War era spanning the presidencies of Harry Truman and Richard Nixon. The campus also housed the Lyndon Baines Johnson Presidential Library, where I hoped to study political and social behavior defying normal "liberal" and "conservative" labels.

ANTI-CORPORATE CONSERVATIVES

I wanted to learn more about "anti-modernists" who expressed hostility to bureaucratic government, financial consolidation, cosmopolitan social values, and internationalist policies. Did such animosity relate to local, regional, and social class constituencies? Was it possible to contextualize the politics of small business interests, social conservatives, anticommunists, and noninterventionists without necessarily defending their positions? Could the perspectives of these groups fit into models of progressivism, populism, or insurgency? To pursue these questions, I planned to use the LBJ Library holdings to determine whether the viewpoints of Cold War anticommunists, social conservatives, and civil rights opponents contained an inherent logic and suggested a broader criticism of a corporate and bureaucratic society.

Stints at the library soon led me to the civil rights public opinion correspondence files. Despite long-held sympathies for the racial justice cause, I began to sense that resistance to government intervention on these matters stemmed from more than white supremacy. Indeed, the feelings of powerlessness and betrayal revealed by the archives seemed quite startling. White southerners often conveyed a distrust of federal power and resentment that Washington had intruded into the private realm of human relations. Many complained that the use of compulsion through federal court orders, civil rights laws, and the dispatch of federal troops amounted to an invasion of the rights of private association reminiscent of a communist tyranny. For that reason, one writer described Supreme Court Chief Justice Earl Warren as a "socio-communist." Forceful erasure of racial differences and the distinctive features of the human personality, warned others, promised a future of mass depersonalization and conformity.

Given the series of terrorist atrocities that preceded and followed passage of civil and voting rights legislation between 1957 and 1965, I obviously had stumbled upon a minefield of controversy. Yet seminar leader Bob Divine remained a steadying influence. He praised my use of constituent mail to show that patterns of distrust and alienation in the white South could transcend issues of race. As Divine guided me toward preparing an article for publication, he drew my attention to a key memo from White House Advisor George Reedy. White southerners saw racial justice as a zero-sum game, Reedy cautioned President Johnson, in contrast to liberal optimists, who believed that an inclusive and expanding economy would lift all boats. Bob also endorsed my intention to mine the Kennedy and Johnson archives for evidence that civil rights progress bridged the goals of the federal government and the national corporate community.

After eight weeks in Austin, I returned to Portland to organize my sabbatical research trip. On August 9th, the eighth anniversary of Nixon's resignation, I took possession of the 1979 Datsun wagon I would drive for the next twelve years. My first destination was the Bancroft Library at the University of California at Berkeley, where I surveyed the papers of Republican progressive Hiram W. Johnson. A dominant presence in the U.S. Senate from 1917 through 1946, Johnson espoused a traditional morality of middle-class virtue and economic independence opposed to financial privilege, political corruption, and international entanglements.

The next stop was Mission Viejo. Reacting to Long Island's cold winters and the loss of friends to warmer climes, my parents had relocated to a self-standing condominium in Casta del Sol, a gated community in southern California's Orange County. Once there, I began organizing my typewritten notes from the Bancroft Library. Instead of photocopying documents at the site, I had taken notes on a portable typewriter and filed them in appropriate folders. I reasoned that as new information came in, I could divide the material into sub-categories and place it in additional folders. Moving on to the LBJ Library, I examined the Johnson administration's use of civil rights allies in corporations, labor unions, civic groups, and the media in what amounted to an informal alliance between corporate modernizers and an activist federal government.

The Western Historical Manuscripts collection at the University of Missouri, in turn, allowed me to explore the papers of Senator Peter Norbeck, a South Dakota well driller and landowner who publicized the plight of Plains farmers in the 1920s and '30s. As small growers faced rising costs and declining income, Norbeck raged at subsidies and tariffs benefiting manufacturers and railroads. Simultaneously deriding eastern ignorance of western economic problems and impractical radicals, he called for a government "new deal" to bring about reduced freight rates, improved farm marketing arrangements, and low-interest credit.

I then drove to the Harry S. Truman Presidential Library in Independence, Missouri. Having mined Lyndon Johnson's correspondence for grassroots attitudes toward civil rights, I now pored through cartons of mail to see how ordinary citizens responded to the controversies of the early Cold War and the perceived threat of domestic and international communism.

Like race, communism was an issue that reached deep into my childhood. As former followers of the anti-Stalinist Socialist Workers Party, my mother and uncle never tired of denouncing Soviet repression or apologists for the communist cause at home. Yet both objected to the indiscriminate witch-hunts of Senator Joseph R. McCarthy and others in the early 1950s. I learned this after a sixth-grade substitute teacher noted that it would be informative to read Hitler's *Mein Kampf,* an innocent remark that precipitated rumors that the instructor was a "nazi or a communist or something." When my mother asked me about the matter, I repeated exactly what the teacher had said.

Shaking her head, she muttered, "I thought so," adding that the neighbor who had branded the instructor a communist was "a crackpot."

In junior high school, our crotchety and elderly music appreciation teacher liked to mix a repertoire of patriotic odes and religious selections with seething references to "traitors-like-Alger-Hissssssss," the former State Department official convicted of perjury for misleading a federal grand jury about his communist background. Meanwhile, my seventh grade social studies instructor engaged in endless debates with one of my punch ball teammates about the Federal Bureau of Investigation, which she accused of purging the country of meaningful dissent. Years later, my mother would inform me without passing judgment that my favorite teacher had been a loyal Communist Party member. She also confided that in the midst of the McCarthy furor, she had purged her Marx, Engels, and Lenin collections from the household.

I already knew from existing scholarship that conservative political leaders and opinion makers saw communism as a coercive threat to democracy advanced in the interests of a hostile Soviet Union. Nevertheless, I experienced a degree of surprise in detecting the populist nature of this antipathy among a variety of sources.

"If you and the rest of your bunch don't quit pampering those Red rats and clean 'em out of our government," a Truman Democrat with an Irish surname warned the White House on one occasion, "there's going to be some changes made!"

Similar strands of anti-elitism characterized a comic book appearing in the Truman public opinion files. Published by a conservative religious organization in Minnesota, it set forth the nightmare scenario of a successful communist takeover of the United States. In the end, a goateed Lenin-like figure in dinner jacket and ascot lifts a champagne glass to toast the victory with a group of well-dressed comrades. Examples like this enabled me to understand that opponents did not as much portray communism as a radical anti-establishment force so much as a manipulative and dishonest conspiracy that threatened to overthrow rules of democratic fair play and create a new, self-interested elite.

NORTHERN LIGHTS

Bruce Goldstein's comfortable old house in St. Paul served as my Midwest base. Bruce had been married to a professional woman and now had sole custody of the couple's infant daughter. His commercial photography business had thrived but left him dissatisfied.

"I am winding up more and more in the guts of corporate capitalists," he confided.

Instead of doing promotions for microwaves, computers, retail giants, and egotistical rock bands, Goldstein fantasized about photographing the lifestyles of the elderly and poor. Providing for his daughter, paying studio rent, and meeting the mortgages on his home and a rental unit, he nevertheless offered me an attic mattress and a share of breakfast and dinner provisions. Bruce even scored two tickets to see my new cultural hero, National Public Radio's Garrison Keillor, host his *Prairie Home Companion* show at St. Paul's World Theater.

A short drive from Bruce's house, the Minnesota Historical Society housed the papers of Magnus Johnson and Henrik Shipstead, two Farmer-Labor U.S. senators elected in the 1920s. Each combined opposition to financial centralization with a noninterventionist foreign policy. Shipstead also showed how economic radicals could be social conservatives. His public opinion files brimmed with resentment at Depression relief recipients accused of driving cars, going to dances, and consuming beer while ordinary taxpayers lacked essentials.

Critical of government bureaucracy during World War II, the Minnesota dentist blamed "long-haired men and short-haired women," the self-styled "brainy people" who presumed to think for all Americans.

Anxious to move on to the University of North Dakota Library before the autumn snows arrived, I set out for Grand Forks at the end of October. Once there, I settled in at a cheap motel by the railroad yards. Early each morning, I caught breakfast at a trackside café before driving to the archives. Over the next five weeks, I filled a half-dozen bankers' boxes with folders containing notes on three North Dakota Republicans whose careers spanned the period between World War I and the Cold War – Nonpartisan League activist and U.S. House member William Lemke, Representative Usher L. Burdick, and Senator "Wild Bill" Langer.

All three politicians spoke for the interests of small farmers and independent producers while railing against overseas financial, diplomatic, and military entanglements. As I devoured their speeches and letters, it was clear that their views had roots in agrarian distrust of bankers, middlemen, and Wall Street power brokers – symbols of unseen and remote centers of power associated with Old World colonialism and East Coast aristocracy. Lemke campaigned for farm-bankruptcy relief in the 1930s. Langer mocked "appeasement-minded cookie pushers" in the Cold War State Department and joined Burdick in opposing Marshall Plan aid to Western Europe, the North Atlantic Treaty Organization (NATO), and universal military training.

On the morning the first snowstorm approached, I packed the Datsun for the trip to Minnesota's Marshall College, where graduate school pal Mike Kopp served as a professor after years outside academia. Mike and I were to share a bachelor's Thanksgiving dinner with Bruce Goldstein. Sometime that weekend, one of

Bruce's tenants came by to pay the rent. At twenty-seven, Susan was an aspiring photographer and university art student who favored any item of clothing, including the subsequent paint job on her old Plymouth, with leopard-spot decor. A tall, almost gangly woman with short, sandy hair, Bruce's soft-spoken renter seemed somewhat enigmatic and a bit sardonic but not standoffish. When she mentioned a few of the local alternative music clubs, I asked if we could make a night of it sometime. Over the next month, Susan introduced me to the underground band The Wallets, who mixed hard rock with accordion polkas, as well as to cutting-edge groups such as the Replacements and Hüsker Dü.

THE PARADOX OF DISSIDENCE

As Christmas approached, I headed for Chicago to stay with former PSU sociologist Gary Waller. Frustrated with the intellectual games of academia, Gary had refused to complete his PhD, forcing his department to deny him tenure and terminate his contract. Moving to the Midwest, he served as a union organizer at the auto parts factory where he found work. After marrying a like-minded Jewish activist from suburban New York, Gary began raising a family with his wife in a small frame house on the North Side. By coincidence, Joe Uris was in town. After checking out a Maxwell Street blues club, the three of us spent most of the evening arguing politics and the direction of my research. I insisted that American populism transcended liberal and conservative creeds by rejecting all forms of consolidated power, including social planning. Joe, in turn, accused me of giving credence to reactionary and even racist ideologies.

Following a brief stop at the Ohio Historical Society in Columbus, I headed for the cooperative apartment complex on Manhattan's Lower East Side that Uncle Mickey now called home. Offering views of Wall Street, the World Trade Center, the East River, and the Manhattan Bridge, the flat would function as my weekend base of operations for the next several weeks. Like Joe Uris, however, Mickey was not on board with my research plan. Having resigned

Getting There

from the Federation of Jewish Philanthropies, taken a part-time bookkeeping job, and gone on to do volunteer work in the labor and peace movement, he viewed my interest in "fascist" populists and conservatives as just another symptom of the misplaced priorities of the Reagan era.

"Professors shouldn't be allowed to write, they do enough damage in the classroom," he vented in one particularly vitriolic letter.

Undeterred by criticism, I devoted the first several weeks of 1983 to the Franklin D. Roosevelt Presidential Library in Hyde Park. I wanted to see how New Deal officials in the 1930s had responded to the anti-chain store movement, to William Lemke's agrarian relief measures, to Father Charles Coughlin's campaign against the World Court, and to Democratic House member Louis Ludlow's constitutional amendment to enact a public referendum before declarations of war. Then I looked at small business criticism of the New Deal, public opinion concerning Roosevelt's attempt to expand the size of the Supreme Court, and pre-Pearl Harbor views of the war in Europe. One day, I ran into an elderly Henry Morgenthau, Jr., at work on his memoirs. When I explained that my research concerned several leading New Deal opponents, Roosevelt's former Treasury secretary responded with a gracious smile.

Following Hyde Park, I moved on to Boston's John F. Kennedy Presidential Library. Making use of the Oral History Program and the civil rights files of White House assistant Burke Marshall, I studied how the administration employed corporate and civic leaders to push the South toward a degree of racial harmony. Marshall's collection included the transcript of a notorious conversation between Alabama governor George Wallace and President Kennedy in which Kennedy warned that racial tension in Birmingham threatened to destroy the state's business climate. The collection also included an early 1960s advertisement from a Birmingham newspaper that boasted that its progressive and educated "Negro" readership offered the perfect target for retail marketers. Certainly, this kind of evidence supported the argument that the South's long-term health depended upon a resolution of racial issues and that white extremists endangered the region's chances for integration into the U.S. economy.

I arrived in Washington, D.C., in time to witness the parade celebrating the city's professional football championship. Following the cleanup of a twenty-inch snowstorm a few days later, I boarded the Metro for the Library of Congress. My first task was Senator Robert La Follette's extensive correspondence. Opposing overseas military activity as an extension of finance capitalism, the armaments industry, and presidential autocracy, La Follette tried to halt the drive toward U.S. involvement in World War I. Once Congress declared hostilities, he campaigned for a war profits tax on the wealthy instead of burdening ordinary citizens with the expense of government bonds. After the Armistice, La Follette opposed the Versailles Peace Treaty and U.S. membership in the League of Nations. Up to his death in 1925, the Wisconsin insurgent led the fight against suspension of Allied war debts and U.S. membership in the World Court, both of which he equated with the interests of the international banking community.

Nebraska Senator George W. Norris offered another instance of Republican political insurgence. Like La Follette, Norris adamantly opposed U.S. involvement in World War I. As war became inevitable, the senator defied advisors and rented an auditorium back in Lincoln to warn constituents that Congress was about to put the dollar sign upon the American flag. Idaho's William E. Borah provided still another example of a Republican senator whose combination of traditional morality and economic individualism could place him at odds with the establishment. An opponent of U.S. involvement in the League of Nations and the World Court, Borah became a leading critic of the New Deal's National Recovery Administration. Unlike conservative members of his party, however, the senator criticized NRA codes for exempting privileged corporations from antitrust restrictions on price-fixing and other practices.

Getting There

While in Washington, I made a luncheon appointment at the Smithsonian Institution to meet Wayne S. Cole, the reigning expert on World War II non-interventionism. Cole had published defining works on Gerald Nye and the America First Committee and had just released a new book on Roosevelt and the Isolationists. I was comforted when he pointed out that his Nye study had emphasized the importance of agrarian radicalism to the noninterventionist posture. Still, I needed to demonstrate the survival of the insurgent impulse during the Cold War. Robert Taft's papers at the Library of Congress offered important help for this task. Elected to the Senate as an Ohio Republican in 1938, Taft positioned himself as an advocate for small business, an opponent of coercive bureaucracy and executive power, and a foe of internationalism. Seeing the Cold War as a struggle over ideas, he opposed the Marshall Plan, NATO, and universal military training for placing too much emphasis on foreign aid and militarism.

THE NATIONALIST CREED

After completing my work at the Library of Congress, I headed for Yellow Springs. By coincidence, progressive Antioch College had figured in the attempt to discredit the managerial techniques of a leading New Dealer. Robert Taft's papers at the Library of Congress had included correspondence with former Antioch President Arthur E. Morgan over the confirmation in 1947 of David E. Lilienthal as first head of the Atomic Energy Commission (AEC). Franklin Roosevelt had replaced Morgan with Lilienthal as chair of the Tennessee Valley Authority in 1938 over a dispute over the relationship of public and private utilities in the agency's power-pooling arrangements. Nine years later, modern Antioch's founder joined forces with the conservative Taft to question Lilienthal's character.

Morgan insisted that his successor had colluded with aluminum monopolies, slighted small business concerns, and relied on coercive management techniques. His correspondence with Taft and his pronouncements in *Antioch Notes* and the *Yellow Springs News*, all filed with his papers at the college library, completed the story. Lilienthal lacked ethical principle, he charged, was intellectually dishonest, appeared as an actor who could play any part to perfection, and was not sufficiently trustworthy to run a sensitive agency.

Normally no friend of Antioch, Taft used Morgan's testimony to castigate Lilienthal as an embodiment of the amoral modern bureaucrat.

"He is a man who does not care what means he uses to reach the end which he thinks happens to be desirable," the senator asserted.

Former Detroit reform judge Senate Republican Homer Ferguson pursued a similar line. Lilienthal resembled those New Deal administrators who followed the doctrine that the end justified the means, declared Ferguson. He described the nominee as a social aristocrat who believed experts should rule in a benevolent despotism. As questions persisted over Lilienthal's past political affiliations, communist activity inside TVA, the internationalization of atomic energy, and public power, the debate tested the relative influence of Harry Truman's White House and the newly elected Republican Congress. In the end, the nomination passed the Senate, but the confrontation signaled another blow in the fight against government planning.

Sixty miles north of Yellow Springs, I returned to the Ohio State Historical Society to focus on the papers of John W. Bricker. Elected to the U.S. Senate in 1946 as a Republican opponent of New Deal bureaucracy and taxation, Bricker pegged conservative fiscal policies to the beleaguered middle class. Rather than portraying himself as an extremist, he insisted he wanted to restore liberalism to its nineteenth-century emphasis on individual rights. Bricker argued that high taxes led to rising interest rates, inflation, and public debt, placing a burden on those with fixed incomes or few resources.

Seeking to tie the senator's suspicion of federal power and social planners to Cold War anticommunism, I delved into his constituent mail. One sample stuck with me.

237

"Congress must realize," one correspondent insisted in 1952, "that this atheistic communism is not a working class movement ... and never has been. It is a movement of frustrated intellectuals who are out to seize power."

The Ohio archives also contained dozens of files on the Bricker Constitutional Amendment. First introduced in 1951, the measure mandated congressional approval for executive agreements with international agencies and other nations. Beyond that, it sought to endow all overseas accords with the status of U.S. law. An embodiment of nationalist, noninterventionist, and socially conservative politics, the amendment attempted to reassert congressional control over presidential diplomacy and military policy and ensure that no international agreement could overrule the authority of American jurisprudence. The proposal also outlawed endorsement of United Nations' human rights covenants regarding racial equality and public health. Denounced by President Eisenhower, the measure nevertheless came within a single vote of the two-thirds Senate majority needed for referral to the House in 1954.

Indiana Senator Homer E. Capehart, a former farm implements dealer and appliance manufacturer, was another nationalist who made a career denouncing New Deal regulation, Wall Street finance, and foreign aid. Capehart's papers at the Indiana State Library demonstrated how his campaign against the Marshall Plan represented the interests of independent business and agricultural interests who feared that assistance to Europe would reduce supplies and inflate prices at home. Capehart proposed to extend credit to continental manufacturers through a public corporation funded equally by the United States and participating nations. Although Congress easily ratified the Marshall Plan, the controversy revealed how the economic interests of small producers resonated with the political ideology of nationalists and noninterventionists.

I now moved on to Philip La Follette's papers at the Wisconsin State Historical Society. One of two sons of the state's most illustrious senator, La Follette attempted to forge an independent reform movement that rejected New Deal emphasis on relief and collectivist solutions. His New Progressives of America (NPA), launched in 1938, called for government-controlled banks and monetary policy to accelerate investment and market growth without federally sanctioned production cuts, huge relief rolls, or deference to organized labor. Wedding advocacy of personal initiative with a noninterventionist foreign policy, La Follette encountered intense opposition from New Deal interest groups, and the movement quickly dissipated. Nevertheless, the iconoclastic governor had fashioned a brand of producer-oriented populism that would continue to influence national politics.

TWO GREAT ISSUES

By the time I returned to the Minnesota Historical Society, the relationship between economic individualism, social conservatism, and insurgent politics had become a major theme of my inquiries. Poring through the papers of social worker Catheryne Cooke Gilman, I learned that independent theater owners had joined the motion-picture reform movement of the 1920s and '30s because they believed the Hollywood studio practices of block booking and blind booking gave them little choice in screening films for their localities. As a result, exhibitors worked with purity activists concerned about the impact of sex and violence on children to push for a federal regulatory agency to address trade practices and the moral tone of motion pictures. Although market freedoms and First Amendment rights doomed such efforts, the Supreme Court would end theater ownership by the five largest studios in 1949 and outlaw block booking.

Leaving St. Paul, I headed for Iowa City, where the Hoover Library had awarded me a modest grant to complete a survey of the noninterventionist movement. Although Wayne Cole and others had pretty much covered the story, the Robert E. Wood Papers offered occasional surprises. One was the identity of the author of an unsigned memo I had come across in the Bricker Archives.

Written in 1942 as a proposal for Republican wartime strategy, the document laid out a choice between conservative economic nationalism and liberal internationalism.

"The two great issues of the twentieth century," it proclaimed, "have been internationalism versus isolation and individualism versus collectivism."

The author, it turned out, was Lawrence Dennis, a theoretical fascist who believed in one-party rule but wanted to nationalize banks and monopolies, subsidize small enterprises and farms, and use progressive taxation to redistribute wealth.

After my brother joined me in Iowa City, we drove to Madison, South Dakota, where I explored the papers of former high school and college speech teacher Karl Mundt. Elected as an anti-New Deal House Republican in 1938, Mundt argued that liberalism should stand for the protection of the common people against the monopoly of political overlords. After 1945, he became a fervent anticommunist. Soviet ideology, he insisted, did not represent a legitimate political movement but the left flank of tyrannical fascism. As chair of the subcommittee of the House Committee on Un-American Activities that investigated Alger Hiss, Mundt celebrated the New Dealer's perjury conviction by marveling that liberal elites found it so difficult to believe that someone with a refined Harvard accent could be guilty of disloyalty.

Democrat Burton K. Wheeler shared many of these same sentiments. A Montana senator between 1923 and 1947, Wheeler had opposed U.S. intervention in Nicaragua, helped to expose the Teapot Dome scandal, and served as Robert La Follette's Progressive party running mate in 1924. During the 1930s, Wheeler campaigned against chain stores and branch banking, pushed for an inflationary monetary policy to help small producers, and opposed Franklin Roosevelt's "court-packing" and executive reorganization plans. Once the Second World War broke out in Europe, the Montanan became a leading noninterventionist. Accused of changing political colors, Wheeler insisted he was consistent. Like Mundt, he equated liberalism with opposition to concentrated economic and political power and a guarantee of equal opportunity.

Wheeler had kept most of his papers out of the public domain. Yet some speeches and correspondence remained at Helena's Montana Historical Society. This was the last stop of a cross-country research trip that had consumed thousands of miles, two summers, and a full year's sabbatical. Now, as we made our way back to Portland, two major challenges confronted me:

First, could I work my disparate findings into a credible narrative?

Second, could I find a publisher for a book halfway between a monograph and a general synthesis?

CLEARING

(1983-1986)

half the distance takes you twice as long
– D. Henley/G. Frey

On the drive across the country during the summer of 1983, Michael briefed me about new developments in information technologies. On a recent trip to southern California, he had experimented with an early version of email through "The Source," an electronic social network of twenty thousand subscribers. Once we reclaimed the Ladd's Addition house, he alerted me to a promotion waiving the installation fee for a cable-TV hook-up. During a visit to the Richmond home of Bob Williams's parents over the winter, young Katy and Cody had introduced me to the rock videos of Music Television (MTV).

It took very little, consequently, to convince me of the desirability of converting to cable.

THE MINUTES

As it turned out, cable TV became my salvation when I finally stopped smoking, a habit dating back to 1966. Suffering a severe case of nicotine withdrawal, I distracted myself with MTV's constant feed of New-Wave pop and WGN's broadcasts of Chicago Cubs baseball. It was not until August that I was ready to re-enter the world. The beneficiary of a $2,000 summer stipend from the Oregon Council for the Humanities (OCH), I made my way to the Oregon Historical Society in hopes of studying Ku Klux Klan activities in the Pacific Northwest during the 1920s.

Extensive reading for the textbook had convinced me that the Jazz Age provided a key transition to an urban, secular, and heterogeneous society endowed with consumerist values and cultural innovation. At the same time, pioneering works such as Kenneth Jackson's *The Ku Klux Klan in the City* (1967) highlighted profound resistance to such change, even among urban populations. Beyond racial and religious bigotry, insisted Jackson, the "second" Klan appealed to millions of lower-middle-class native white Protestants with hostile views of modern culture and the new morality. Since both Jackson and historian David Chalmers listed Oregon as a significant center of KKK activity after World War I, I intended to discover the extent to which regional Klansmen acted as populist conservatives opposed to big-city cosmopolitanism.

My starting point was the Historical Society's manuscripts room, which contained an old-fashioned, handwritten card catalog. Under "Ku Klux Klan," I found a citation to a sparse collection of KKK pamphlets and paraphernalia, including a few issues of *The Western American*, a Klan newspaper published in Oregon. The archive also held the papers of George Estes, an attorney and writer who self-published a tract in support of the Klan-endorsed state ballot initiative of 1922 requiring all children to attend public schools. Beyond several pamphlets on the school controversy, the catalog pointed to a newspaper exposé by a former Klansman and correspondence by former Governor Ben Olcott, a key KKK critic. Other entries included sympathetic assessments of the order by conservative activists Eva Emery Dye and Grace Wick.

None of these materials turned out to have the importance of the final source I consulted. To my surprise, one of the index cards listed the proceedings and minutes of a Klan chapter operating between 1922 and 1924 in the eastern Oregon town of La Grande. After fifteen years in the state, I was not even sure where La Grande was. When the archivist brought out a huge folder with some two hundred pages of typed notes, therefore, I tentatively began making my way through the contents. It took days before the cursory references and elliptic language of the manuscript made any sense, particularly when so much of the text seemed focused upon lodge matters such as dues, membership drives, and organizational loyalty. Gradually, however, I began to piece together anecdotal bits of information that pointed to the La Grande klavern's place within the larger perspective of 1920s social change.

The preservation of a traditional American culture in a period of emerging ethnic diversity was a sincere concern of many native-born Protestants, I told an interviewer for the PSU *Vanguard*. Such a focus, I explained, captured a fixation over moral character amid the perceived relaxed standards and secular values of the Jazz Age. When I submitted my research report to the OCH, I stressed the need to cultivate a nuanced treatment of the 1920s Ku Klux Klan. I cited Oregon historian William Toll's insight that Knights in coastal Tillamook had welcomed commercial growth after World War I but felt intimidated by the social and moral consequences of modernization. By emphasizing fraternal solidarity, creating business support networks, and undertaking civic improvement projects, I suggested, eastern Oregon "Invisible Empire" offered a taste of identity politics for middle-class, white, Protestant, native-born men.

The Klan's role in purity reform provided one of the features of "The Two Cultures of the 1920s," a lecture for a series entitled "The Rituals of Modernity" I delivered that fall at the request of Mike Passi and his wife, Diana, a professor of Hispanic literature at the University of Nevada. Using audiocassette excerpts from the period's popular music, I opened with a chronicle of the consumer attractions and self-indulgent pastimes of the cosmopolitan Jazz Age. Then I contrasted that side of 1920s culture with the traditional social morality and producer values associated with Klansmen and Klanswomen, the period's anti-evolution campaigns, motion-picture reformers, and efforts to restrict immigration.

The temptations of the new way of life, I asserted, often led traditionalists to ignore their own acceptance of metropolitan practices and mores. As I took over the three-term twentieth-century U.S. history survey lecture class in the fall of 1983, the idea of seeing culture as a dialogue between opposing forces became a central feature of my teaching. Yet a new course, The Anticommunist Crusade, 1945-60, provoked my greatest interest. Instead of focusing exclusively on the notorious threat to civil liberties during the early Cold War, I chose a different path. This included consideration of Victor Navasky's *Naming Names* (1981), a critical view of the House Committee on Un-American Activities that nevertheless included accounts by former Hollywood communists of the party's undemocratic methods and suppression of its members' free speech.

URBAN NOIZE

Paradoxically, my academic interest in traditional values coincided with re-immersion in Portland's popular culture. Following my return to town, I had run into Michael Hornburg, a former student who played rhythm guitar in a band called The Usual Suspects. Michael initiated me into the local musical underground that had been thriving since the late 1970s. Not long after, a Storefront Theater acquaintance brought me to a performance of Jon Newton's *D'Anse Combeau*. I watched in amazement as a full orchestra laid down a tight Latin beat for faux folk protest songs delivered in fractured French by the androgynous Jim Baldwin, who shared the same name as the ensemble. Subsequent shows included "Woodstock Goes Hawaiian" and a series of Newton original scores for Halloween silent film showings at the Portland Art Museum.

Exposed to the alternative bands of the Twin Cities and MTV's New Wave Pop, I felt inspired by Portland's mix of musical genres. During the winter of 1984, I agreed to provide piano accompaniment for a solo recital by interpretive dancer Josie Moseley. I also experimented with interpretations of David Bowie's "China Girl" and other pop favorites for three modern jazz dancers who occasionally performed between sets for The Usual Suspects. Just as I moved into a two-story carriage house behind a Victorian Gothic mansion in late spring, I took up a diet and brisk walking to offset the weight gained after kicking cigarettes. At this point, I began offering piano versions of New Wave Music at the Metro on Broadway, a subterranean downtown café.

Doing cultural history and playing popular music, I told a *Vanguard* interviewer, shared similarities. As a historian, I wove raw information into interpretive patterns, while my stints at the keyboard involved improvisation from written notes and chord names.

Besides, I said, playing piano let me make sense of the culture I studied and taught.

My thoughts on these matters stemmed in part from a lunch with *Oregonian* opinion-page editor David Sarasohn, who asked if I ever thought about combining pop music and history in a newspaper feature. The result, appearing in the daily's Sunday Forum in August 1984, described the British New Wave's keyboard synthesizers and repetitive rhythms as representations of modern alienation and detachment. It then traced the mix of vernacular expression and technological innovation in pop music history from ragtime to heavy metal.

Musical and cultural forms continued to separate themselves from predecessors and serve the needs of each generation, I concluded.

I had hoped to devote an unpaid leave of absence during 1984-85 to work on scholarly projects. Yet my passion for popular culture was hard to cast aside. Having referenced MTV in the *Oregonian* piece, I decided to devote an entire article to the cultural significance of rock video. "The 30-Year War – a Reconstructed Diary of an MTV Fanatic" recounted my extended love affair with rock 'n' roll from Jo-Jeans in the Catskills and Alan Freed through the first British invasion of the 1960s to the contemporary scene. At each stage, I reported, emerging forms attracted negative criticism. Now rock video, the new art form of television, sought to synthesize music, visual imagery, and dance. Contemporary artists such as the Police and the Eurythmics, I wrote, embodied a dark humor and abstract sense of absurdity that generated a psychological impact instead of a political or sentimental agenda.

The idea was to place the MTV feature in the *Clinton Street Quarterly*. Yet David Milholland could not convince filmmaker and co-editor Jim Blashfield that a treatment of rock video belonged in a literary arts publication. Ironically, Blashfield subsequently directed video productions for the Talking Heads, Joni Mitchell, Michael

Jackson, and others, permitting the two of us to share a good laugh about the whole thing. Meanwhile, I published "The 30-Year War" in the fashion-oriented *Multnomah Monthly*, which ran it with a drawing from alternative comic book illustrators Arnold and Jacob Pander, to whom I turned over the modest author's fee.

I saw New Wave Pop as a rebellion against the burnt-out mentality of counterculture remnants. In this spirit, I agreed to join a Portland television station's Sunday evening Town Hall on the local punk scene. No expert on the subject, I urged the producers to include Ronnie Noize and Fred Seegmuller, former managers of the underground Urban Noize club. Ronnie had been the source for the brief segment on punk in my *Oregonian* piece and Fred, a former student, was now *Vanguard* editor.

When I arrived at the studio as one of 160 participants, someone passed on a "corrected" version of the official program notice with the title "Down Fall" instead of "Town Hall." Each time the station handout generalized about punk behavior and values, a clever editor had substituted language that turned the piece into a mirror image of *mainstream* habits and fixations.

The "executive tendency" of middle-class conformists, ran the spoof, illustrated "how easily the overbearing and flaccid can prevail in these days of unsure aesthetic standards."

As it turned out, the parody brilliantly anticipated the show's difficulty in describing a subculture on its own terms. First, the moderator questioned the political activists in the crowd about antinuclear protests and Central American issues. When he asked me to comment on whether punk fit into earlier political and social movements, I responded that this sort of cultural dissidence had very little in common with those sorts of causes and more to do with the process by which each generation separates itself from its elders. Then he moved on to the testimony of a contingent of ministers, social workers, school counselors, law enforcement personnel, and parents regarding punk's problematic status. These expressions of concern neared the point of absurdity when a counselor from Los

Angeles admitted that adherents of the punk lifestyle often wound up in mental institutions *because their parents freaked out* at their refashioned identity.

Invited to respond, a Portland court official said his only issue with punk culture lay with the rare cases of people who might hurt themselves or break the law. Likewise, a downtown police officer reported few problems of any kind with the punk community.

After much of Town Hall struck a conciliatory tone, the publisher of an independent street 'zine finally blurted out that punk was "about sex and violence." This led to a discussion of slam dancing in the "mosh pits," defended by proponents as a masculine ritual of solidarity. Yet there was a dark sign to the discussion. On my way out, the leader of an underground band complained about the mindlessness of apparent poseurs. He had seen the casualties of punk culture in L.A., he said – dead people in creepy hotel rooms and wasted lives going nowhere.

Incorporating his warning in a feature about the show I compiled for the *Vanguard*, I nevertheless focused on the media's tendency to concentrate on social pathology rather than cultural creativity. With this in mind, I approached *Multnomah Monthly* about an article on Satyricon, which I described as the city's leading experimental nightspot and showcase for innovative live music. Located in the Old Town waterfront district, the club had opened in March 1984 as the brainchild of Greek immigrant George Touhouliotis, a friend of poet Walt Curtis and a one-time student of mine. Sharing a bottle of Johnny Walker and filling three audiocassettes with oral interviews conducted on my living room couch, I recorded George's personal history and the story behind Satyricon.

"I cater to the most civilized population in Portland," I quoted the proprietor as saying, "by far the most sophisticated, the most artistically inclined."

Featuring upcoming Northwest bands such as Poison Idea and Nirvana and iconic performances by Billy Kennedy and others, Satyricon attracted a regular clientele of musicians, artists, and entertainment industry employees. Touhouliotis described the place as a "hard-core" establishment whose most important ingredient was guts. The club was not the sort of drinking spot where people searched for someone to go home with. Indeed, its dimly lit and low-key ambience offered privacy from unwanted intrusions. Like a classic jazz venue, however, it provided the opportunity to maintain contact with friends and transact business: "a nexus from which to conduct one's life," I wrote. Touhouliotis even provided the opportunity for Walt Curtis to host weekly poetry nights and on one occasion, a midnight amateur theatrical farce.

STRANGERS

When "The Passion Behind Satyricon" appeared in December 1984, it marked the first treatment of the club in a commercial print outlet. By then, I had become a denizen of Portland's noir culture and the watering holes, jazz haunts, dance establishments, and cafés that enlivened the city after dark. As powdered cocaine permeated the indulgences, distractions, and pitfalls of the period's nightlife and art scene, however, academics continued calling me.

After delivering a paper on North Dakota noninterventionists in Grand Forks a year earlier, I had agreed to publish an extended version of the piece in *Heritage of the Plains*, a small journal out of Emporia State University in Kansas. The essay developed the concept of "political culture," which I described as a merger of rational political and economic motives with longstanding ideological and emotional affinities. Taking off from historian Alan Brinkley's work on 1930s demagogues Huey Long and Father Charles Coughlin, I suggested that dissident perspectives could have an internal consistency and dominate particular communities.

Published in the summer of 1984, the article marked my entry into the world of research publication. A second milestone came later in the year when Iowa seminar colleagues Karl Krogg and Bill Tanner published an anthology of our Herbert Hoover papers with the University Press of America. A referee assessing a previous submission had failed to see how my essay on the "solitary and eccentric" Gerald Nye related to the Hoover presidency. More troubling, he assumed I was the author of the "other" David Horowitz's *Free World Colossus* and wondered why I had not explored foreign policy. I thought my contribution described an unusual collaboration between a conservative president and an insurgent progressive in enacting government control of commodity distribution in Depression agriculture. It was rewarding, therefore, when the *North Dakota Quarterly* reprinted the article in 1985 and when a review of the Hoover anthology by historian Ellis Hawley depicted my work as a commentary on the tension between managerial and anti-corporate values.

Freed of teaching responsibilities in the fall of 1984, I revised my essay on southern resistance to civil rights and prepared two journal submissions on Oregon's anti-chain store movement and 1920s Klan activity. Comprised of forty-five pages of scattered narrative with an extra fifteen pages of notes, far beyond the limit set by most journals, the KKK article proved particularly problematic. It seemed easier to synthesize my work into oral form. As part of a stipulation that scholars share the fruits of their research, the Oregon Council for the Humanities required two free public lectures. Upon fulfilling the obligation at the PSU Campus Ministry Center and Portland's First Unitarian Church, I qualified to enroll in OCH's Chautauqua Program. Between February 1985 and 1990, I delivered sixteen lectures in virtually every corner of the state on the Oregon Klan's mixed record of anti-Catholicism, hostility to European immigrants, civic improvement efforts, and social purity concerns.

Beyond the difficulty of narrowing the focus of journal submissions, I discovered a good deal of resistance to placing the 1920s Klan and its followers in historical context. As a scholar, I wanted to avoid arbitrarily demonizing the movement while shunning any attempt to excuse its prejudices. The problem became obvious when I published an article on KKK activities in Astoria in former anti-Vietnam War activist Mike McCusker's *North Coast*

253

Times Eagle. Weeks later, the paper ran a response from Sailor John McGarrity, a veteran turned peace advocate living in New York. McGarrity accused me of apologizing for the Klan by placing too much credence in rhetoric and failing to acknowledge that KKK terror campaigns against Astoria's Finnish workers, Roman Catholics, blacks, labor radicals, and others served to protect privilege.

My rejoinder noted that despite puerile Klan rhetoric against Rome, support for public schooling meant that Catholic children would share the same classrooms as others. I read this as an attempt by white, native-born Protestants to bolster a sense of security by bringing European ethnics into the American fold. Conceding that these efforts defined national unity in the narrowest of terms, I nevertheless insisted that 1920s Klansmen saw themselves as outsiders. Instead of aligning themselves with privilege, I wrote, lodge members pictured themselves as powerless in the face of immigrant political and economic networks.

To buttress the argument, I pointed out that the Oregon Alien Land Law of 1923 prohibiting foreign-born property ownership had garnered the signature of Governor Walter Pierce, a Democrat, former dirt farmer, and tax reformer. Populist rhetoric about private academies for the rich also underlay Klan support for the Oregon ballot initiative of 1922 that proposed compulsory attendance in public grade and high schools. In a period in which the "Invisible Empire" focused on Catholics and allegations of moral iniquity, I noted, rare instances of vigilante violence, mostly in the South, mainly targeted fellow white Anglo-Protestants. Lynching rates in southern states actually declined after 1922 when the KKK sought to refashion itself as a mass political movement and lobby.

Citing the La Grande minutes, I noted how Oregon Klan leaders had rejected candidates for admission to the group on moral grounds, joined law officials in enforcing Prohibition, reported instances of child neglect to county officials, and contributed generously to Protestant churches and other charities. Klansmen of the 1920s acted to garrison their own personalities from the rampages of secular modernism, I suggested, and sought to defend themselves against the powerlessness they experienced as perceived strangers in their own land. In other words, they feared that modern society prompted a loss of personal control.

In a state of anger and confusion, I observed, Knights struck out at people who had even less power than themselves. I described a great deal of what they did as atrocious, some simply as stupid, and a tiny faction as admirable. Yet I insisted that one of the tragic lessons of history lay in the realization that those who perpetuated various degrees of horrors against others may nevertheless have been victims themselves. In the end, I concluded, history was not a cookbook available to the most adamant bidder. Instead, the discipline offered parables of compassion, understanding, and empathy – contributions to an appreciation of the dilemmas humans confront, even when they did not always respond in ways we could admire.

Much of what I ever would say about the 1920s Ku Klux Klan flavored the response to Sailor John.

Learning to deal with criticism helped prepare me for a lecture at the Oregon Historical Society. By the spring of 1985, I fully appreciated how attitudes about the Klan of the 1920s stemmed from its violent and racist conduct in the post-Civil War and post-World War II South. The lesson came home when I asked Luis, a Nicaraguan art student and friend, to prepare a poster for the talk. True to form, Luis proposed a blood-soaked portrait of nightriders attacking traumatized blacks. We finally compromised by keeping the red and black motif but confining the image to a single Knight on horseback.

"The Ethical Dilemmas of Tracking Down the Klan" attracted an overflow crowd of 125 and coverage by *The Oregonian*. Although the staff and I may have catered to the sensationalism surrounding the Jazz Age KKK by placing a mannequin by the door in full Klan regalia, the lecture dealt as much with prevailing misconceptions about the subject as anything else.

FAMILY TIES

My appearance at the Historical Society came during a time in which family commitments repeatedly intervened. Shortly after I had left New York two years earlier, Uncle Mickey began to complain of intense angina. His discomfort did not improve his political outlook. Warning that Reagan America was on the road to fascism, he wondered if I would finish my book before World War III. In 1984, he lost his bookkeeping job. His defenses punctured, he agreed to relocate to Leisure World, a few miles distance from my parents' home in Mission Viejo. Yet the move quickly turned into a disaster.

"I hate California," Mickey wrote days after arriving – "the young and the old, the surfers and fanatics and all the bastard Reaganites – mostly Democrats."

"I warn you," he added, "if you bury me in California I'll haunt you in all your classes." The following April, my uncle relocated to Florida's North Miami Beach.

By all accounts, in contrast, my parents flourished in California. Taken by the region's dramatic mountains and seascapes, my father produced a number of new poems. His continuing interest in Jewish themes led him to publish several older verses and brief excerpts from his autobiography in the English-language edition of the *Forward*. Meanwhile, my mother accompanied her husband to Hebrew and Bible classes, created skits on female empowerment for the local B'nai B'rith Jewish women's organization, and continued her own creative writing.

Dealing with Mickey's mood swings and irascible outbursts, nevertheless, left my mother with a great deal of anguish. Whether this had anything to do with the periodic abdominal cramps and diarrhea she experienced is not clear. Whatever the case, diagnostic testing in early 1985 revealed she had a malignant intestinal tumor, prompting a surgeon to remove twelve inches of her colon. At Michael's prodding, I learned that the cancer had penetrated the abdominal walls and entered the lymph nodes, a serious prognosis my father seemed incapable of absorbing. Dorothy Horowitz now became a patient at UCLA's John Wayne Clinic.

When I returned to Mission Viejo for a month-long visit in June, my mother had inaugurated a low-fat diet, taken up a routine of rigorous daily walking, and begun reading the works of holistic cancer surgeon Dr. Bernie Segal. In excellent spirits, she insisted that I keep up my work, serving me daily lunches on the backyard patio as I struggled through drafts of the early chapters of my book and revised journal article submissions. Yet the idyllic interlude did not last. In August 1985, she learned that her cancer had spread to the liver. Back at UCLA the next month, she had a lengthy operation to remove another tumor. With a temporary sense of relief, I pushed the future out of my consciousness and returned to Portland to resume teaching.

RESPECT

It did not take long, however, for politics to interrupt the routines of academia. As a New Leftist, I had not shared the euphoria over Israel's takeover and occupation of Arab territories following the Six Day War of 1967. Still, a *freeway* column on anti-Semitism had strongly endorsed Israel's status as a legitimate nation-state deserving security as well as Palestinian rights to independent statehood in the West Bank and Gaza. These efforts failed to impress my parents, whose fervent support of the Jewish state accounted for their rage at the Palestine Liberation Organization's (PLO) record of terrorism against Israeli civilians. As many American Jews expressed concerns about Democrat Jimmy Carter's sympathies during the 1976 presidential campaign, my parents informed me that a United Jewish Appeal official from Portland had told Uncle Mickey I had a reputation as a "radical pro-Arab."

Seeing myself as even-handed when it came to the Middle East, I was angered by the attribution. At the same time, I had a deep desire to reconcile on the issue with my aging parents. These concerns framed my response when in October 1985 an armed PLO team took over an Italian cruise ship and tossed an elderly wheelchair-bound Jewish passenger into the sea. The realization that my father's arthritic ailments promised to leave him similarly immobilized enhanced my identification with the victim. Accordingly, a *Vanguard* opinion piece by Palestinian student Mazen Malik that reacted to the atrocity by denouncing "Zionist" ideology prompted a sharp response.

The tragedy of the Palestinian movement, I asserted, lay in its use of indiscriminate terrorism against innocents, coupled with a denial of Israel's sovereignty as a nation. Diplomacy and political negotiation were substitutes for murder, not supplements to it, I insisted. Palestinians would have to abandon charismatic fantasies of dismantling the Israeli nation, I argued, and practice timeworn acts of politics and diplomacy instead.

"It's time to cut a deal," I commented in a second *Vanguard* piece in January 1986.

These calls for an Israeli-Palestinian dialogue stemmed in part from *Tikkun*, a progressive Jewish bi-monthly. Editor Michael Lerner, a former New Left activist, had taken the magazine's title from the Hebrew Scripture's exhortation to mend, repair, and transform the world in a spirit of social justice. Seeking to build a local context for peace, I proposed that Portland State could provide the perfect venue for Arabs and Jews to engage each other. Following weeks of wrangling between the concerned parties, the student government agreed to host a debate between the General Union of Palestinian Students (GUPS) and the Jewish Student Union (JSU).

Realizing the need for allies, I joined the Portland chapter of New Jewish Agenda (NJA), a group recently revitalized by former Berkeley radicals Stew and Judy Albert. Like *Tikkun*, NJA sought to be the progressive voice in the Jewish community and the Jewish voice among progressives. Influenced by this confluence of goals and seeking to align our position with democratic values, I convinced JSU President Levi Taylor to allow his organization to be the signatory of a full-page ad in the *Vanguard*. Underwritten by several PSU faculty and NJA supporters, the text equated President Reagan's aid to the violent Contra uprising against Nicaragua's socialist government with murderous attacks on Israeli civilian life. The statement's provocative heading reinforced the call for negotiations on both fronts:

"HOW CAN WE COMBAT TERRORISM IN THE MIDDLE EAST WHEN WE SPONSOR IT IN CENTRAL AMERICA?"

Moderated by Black Studies professor Candice Goucher, the debate took place before an audience of 450 people in June 1986. The line-up pitted a local Palestinian leader and a secular San Francisco Jew in favor of a bicultural Israel against Lev and me. Our side believed that the only way to make an impression among a crowd of international students and others was to transcend the usual Israeli-Palestinian exchange of grievances with a constructive model for engagement. Concern for the dignity of human life dictated the creation of a just peace in the Middle East, I asserted in my opening statement: the depressing cycle of violence and reprisal had to be broken.

The main obstacle to negotiations, I suggested, was one of timing. Palestinians wanted the right to self-determination recognized *before* talks ensued just as Israelis demanded *a priori* acknowledgement of their legitimate existence as a Jewish nation. The trick was to conceive a formula by which both sides obtained mutual guarantees *at the same time*.

Our answer was the "Portland Pledge," a summary of four principles long advocated by Middle East peace activists: Palestinian rights of self-determination in the West Bank and Gaza, Israeli rights of territorial sovereignty and security, the right of return and equal citizenship for all people in the region, and bilateral negotiations on the future of Jerusalem.

The unique aspect of the plan consisted of its call for delegates from Israel and the Palestinian people who subscribed to its principles to join a peace conference in Jordan. In this way, we bypassed the question of whether the PLO would recognize Israel before talks began. To dramatize the need to advance past the current deadlock, Lev and I issued a statement that referred to Israel's permanent stage of siege and the destructive cycle of violence enveloping both parties.

Although critics on all sides saw the Pledge as a naïve oversimplification of a complex issue, it received coverage in the *Vanguard*, *The Oregonian*, and the *Portland Observer*, the main outlet of the African-American community. We never pretended the plan was a literal model for negotiations. Instead, we saw it as a potential inspiration to opening communication channels. Despite skepticism from many of the Arab and other international students, I sensed a growing degree of goodwill because we treated the grievances and aspirations of Israel's perceived adversaries with respect. At this point, the quest for acceptance of Palestinians as a people with legitimate goals seemed more important than the details of any peace plan.

RECOMPENSE

Several positive developments came out of the debate. As Mazen Malik and I became friends and allies, other members of the Arab community extended themselves. A particularly poignant moment occurred when I accepted an invitation to attend a lecture by a former Arab-American diplomat who had served as U.S. ambassador to Syria. When the speaker delivered a one-sided rant castigating the Israelis for the region's problems, the wife of an Arab-American economist at Portland State sought me out to apologize. As much as I appreciated the gesture, I was used to hearing far more anti-Israeli vitriol, much of it from Jewish friends.

Shortly before publication of my second opinion piece on the Middle East, graduate school pal Mike Kopp called from Minneapolis with devastating news: Bruce Goldstein had suffered a fatal stroke. Wary of depersonalized funeral ceremonies, I hesitated about making the trip. Yet my brother and Bob Williams convinced me to go to St. Paul. They were right. A woman attending the reception told Mike and me that we were Bruce's real family.

"I wanted some more time with my good friend," I subsequently wrote in the memory book compiled for Bruce's daughter, "so that we could drink wine, laugh, and stand up to the stars and face them down."

The next several months brought little relief from emotional distress. During spring break, my father had a second hip replacement at UCLA. Weeks after I flew to California, he fell and knocked the joint ball loose. Then in May, he suffered a cardiac arrest, leading doctors to prepare bypass surgery. The series of maladies continued when I returned to Mission Viejo during the summer and learned Uncle Mickey had experienced a severe stroke. The move to North Miami Beach had blunted my uncle's fury but not his alienation. He had foresworn politics, he said, but continued to rage at the surviving Ku Klux Klan, racist Florida Democrats, "Stalinist" peace activists, and a "mindless" youth culture of drugs and rock 'n' roll. My mother now asked me to go to Florida.

Little of Uncle Mickey's fire remained when I walked into his room at Hollywood Memorial Hospital, where my maternal grandfather, Nat Levine, had died thirteen years earlier. Unshaven and disheveled, Mickey sat despondently, his left hand and several fingers paralyzed. His progress with a walker was extremely shaky and hesitant. He hated the nurses and doctors for putting him through hell. Worst of all, he hardly had a response to anything I said. It was clear my uncle seemed to think he had nothing to live for and was ready to die.

Finally, I put it to him.

No one could convince anyone else of a reason for living, I said.

It was his choice, but I was there if he wanted help.

That did the trick. The first thing I did was to buy an electric shaver and teach my uncle to use and clean it. Then we worked on mastering the walker, starting the shower, and getting dressed. By the time the week ended, he was a new man.

Getting There

His first letter when I got home recalled that I had been the apple of his eye from the very beginning.

"One doesn't give love and devotion to be repaid," he wrote, but my visit had more than compensated for the gift.

Following a trip to Honolulu to present a conference paper on the Klan, more bad news awaited. On a hot night in August, I awoke around 3 a.m. to a terrible crash on the nearby through street. Later that morning, the phone interrupted me again. It was the mother of Allison's old Sellwood friends. They were trying to find Robert so they could locate Charmaine. Allison had been in a car wreck on the fringes of Southeast Portland.

Although I had lost contact with my former wife, I knew she had not only converted to Judaism but had convinced herself that her biological father had been Native American. Accordingly, she had relocated to the Lakota Sioux reservation at Pine Ridge, South Dakota, taken the name "Whispering Colt," and received state arts backing to conduct poetry workshops under the rubric, "Journey Home: A Native American Voice." I now learned that Allison was on life support and that Charmaine, not yet fully aware of the circumstances, was due to fly into Portland that day. Could I take Vittorio to the airport to pick her up?

Charmaine's younger son broke the terrible news as his anguished mother raced off the plane. Finding it impossible to walk away from the situation, I spent the following week at the hospital. As Allison's condition showed no improvement, Charmaine received permission to bring in an Indian medicine man to expel the malevolent spirits. With the ritual completed, she consented to discontinue life support for her twenty-one-year-old brain-dead daughter, a single mother about to leave behind a four-year-old boy, a two-year-old girl, and an infant son barely four months old. Allison's children had not suffered a scratch in the low-impact collision. As a hemophiliac subject to internal bleeding, however, their mother had sustained fatal injuries when her head hit the dashboard of the flat-nosed VW bus.

Following a Native American memorial service that Charmaine's mother and Vittorio refused to attend, the spiritual elder and I had a conversation about the historical plight of Native people. Suddenly, he peered at me with an intent look.

"You see through things," he said after a pause.

Months later, Charmaine hosted a potlatch at a Portland Catholic Church and presented me with a blanket as a token of appreciation and a sign that the rifts of the divorce were over.

SLOW DANCING

While personal and political issues seemed to cloud the agenda, scholarship remained a key part of my life. At the suggestion of Texas seminar leader Bob Divine, I had revised my article on southern resistance to civil rights by cutting examples, paraphrasing quotes, and assuming a more analytic bent. After the article was rejected by a political science journal, referees for the *Journal of Southern History* called for more emphasis on the way race and caste framed white southern approaches to politics and social relations. They also requested polling data to support assertions about public opinion. With the suggested changes in place, the journal subsequently published the piece as "White Southerners' Alienation and Civil Rights: The Response to Corporate Liberalism, 1956-1965."

Meanwhile, *Pacific Northwest Quarterly* agreed to print my essay on the anti-elitist aspects of the Oregon Klan of the 1920s. This time, critics in the field asked me to distinguish between the rhetoric of leaders and the motivations of members, an understandable point. I was less enthusiastic about removing the term "populism" to describe Klan views but made a strategic decision to accommodate the editor despite my concerns.

A second Klan article generated interest from Rick Harmon, the new editor of the *Oregon Historical Quarterly*. Yet Rick balked at associating 1920s Klansmen with moral regeneration and wondered if I took public relations efforts too seriously. By now, I had come to realize that at least 90 percent of critical comments expressed valid points and that it was easy to incorporate them without sacrificing the main burdens of an argument. While noting that the Klan reflected the belief that only white, native-born Protestants shared traditional American virtues, I explained that the essay employed terms such as "idealism" and "morality" in the way Klansmen of the Jazz Age would have understood them. Rick then agreed to publish the piece and accepted my article on the Oregon anti-chain store crusade as well.

Responding to this surge of productivity, the history department pushed through my promotion to full professor. Meanwhile, I completed a draft of the first seven chapters of the proposed study of political insurgency. Over the past year, I had struggled with the proper title, an indispensable aid when trying to convert a massive project into a cohesive undertaking. At one point, my brother suggested calling the work, "The Populist Left."

"It's not about the Left!" I screamed. "This is *beyond* left and right!"

"That's your title," Michael shot back.

Just as work on the manuscript gathered momentum during the fall of 1986, I returned for a stint at the Storefront Theater. A year earlier, I had taught a new PSU class on the roots of American popular culture. It was easy, then, to accept John Zagone's invitation to serve as the backstage piano player for August Wilson's *Ma Rainey's Black Bottom* (1984), an award-winning drama about the racial and psychological tensions plaguing the 1920s African-American blues vocalist and her band. As a Jewish academic, I loved the idea of providing the instrumentation for Tony Armstrong, a former PSU athlete and history student who played the band's piano player.

One evening, a special guest showed up. Raised on a Connecticut dairy farm by a hard-working Polish-American family of Roman Catholics, Gloria had eloped to Reno after high school, supported herself and an infant daughter as a San Francisco accounts clerk following a divorce, and relocated to the Portland suburbs during a second marriage. When she enrolled in Portland State's U.S. History

Clearing

Survey several years later, my colleague David Johnson recognized Gloria's abilities and encouraged her to complete a degree in the field.

Weeks before attending the Storefront production, Gloria had run into me at a graduate student's Halloween party.

Once the two of us slow danced, neither of our lives would ever be the same.

CONIFERS

(1987-1988)

blind man looking for a shadow of doubt
– Sting

THROUGH THE TAPED WINDSHIELD OF THE BATTERED EARLY 1970s Chevy Caprice taxi on the drive from the Managua airport, it was impossible to avoid noticing the endless rows of primitive shacks of cardboard, scrap metal, and discarded planks cluttering the landscape. It was spring break, 1987. I was in Nicaragua as part of an eight-day educators' trip organized by Portland State communication professors Steve Kosokoff and Larry Steward. Since I always had avoided guided tours, I initially hesitated at the offer. Yet as an opponent of CIA aid to the Contra insurgency against the Sandinista government, I agreed, after some urging from Gloria, to pay $1150 to join the official delegation of the Portland-Corinto Sister City Association, experience Central America, and submit to another test of my narrative skills.

EIGHT DAYS

The devastation surrounding us had its origins in the severe earthquake of 1972, U.S. sanctions, and the displacement of refugees from the Contra war. Yet our digs at the Intercontinental Hotel, the gathering spot for visiting business officials, diplomats, intelligence operatives, aid workers, filmmakers, writers, and political tourists, offered a dramatic contrast. The hotel provided running water only during limited hours. Yet this plush earthquake survivor offered its upscale clientele sumptuous dinners graced by fresh fruits and vegetables.

On our first evening, fellow tour member Dick Campbell introduced me to three Nicaraguan professional women – a dentist from Grenada, an accountant, and a poultry production manager – at the hotel to dance to the Mexican house band. The women complained of Sandinista incompetence and commodity shortages and rejected

269

Cuban-styled communism as a model. Yet they insisted the Contra War would only guarantee U.S. control of Nicaragua's resources. The next morning, Sunday, our tour bus took us to Pochomil Beach on the Pacific Coast, once part of the former dictator Somoza's enormous holdings. The radio carried the deciding game of the Nicaraguan World Series of baseball, a sport to which the people of the country had been devoted since U.S. Marines introduced it during the 1920s. Everyone was rooting for Managua against the Army, our driver explained, a curious development in a country Washington accused of monolithic submission to military dictatorship.

That evening, roommate Larry Steward left the door halfway ajar while out to make a phone call. Leaning against the entry while waiting for the elevator minutes later, an attractive woman in her thirties inadvertently stumbled backward into our room. Introducing herself and two friends, she asked if they could come in for a drink while they waited to meet George, a Danish United Nations food administrator. Just as George showed up, Larry returned to find two of our guests laughing, smoking, and lounging about the room and a third passed out on my bed.

"What the hell is going on?" he seemed to ask as he stole me a glance.

Adela, the most forward, implored us to order a bottle of "extra-dry" rum from room service. Love is the only thing that counted in life, she explained as George translated, but the revolution had obsessed people with money. A boutique owner who imported Panamanian fashion wear, she lamented that the country's poor investment climate discouraged business. Lucy, a dairy distribution manager, bemoaned the fact that Nicaraguans had to rely on UN donations of powdered milk. She believed in Scandinavian social democracy, she said, but not the communism she feared the Sandinistas favored. Having sent her oldest son to Miami to avoid the draft, she nevertheless opposed U.S. intervention in the Contra war.

Our tour spent most of the week visiting government ministries of culture and education as well as far-flung schools, hospitals, a cooperative dairy farm, and mountain villages. When we delivered pencils and notebooks to a sparsely equipped rural school, we learned that the students had to carry their desk chairs from home each day. Touring a nineteenth-century hospital where we contributed medical supplies and received a briefing from a volunteer UCLA medical student, we came across a captured Contra soldier about fourteen years old.

The staff told us that the insurgents had kidnapped the boy and told him to fight or see his family killed. Sandinista forces often appeared no older. During our stay at an old German mountain resort, Larry and I took a brief evening's walk into the jungle only to startle a military patrol of two teenagers. At Corinto, we turned over additional supplies to city officials, who directed us to the burnt-out and dented oil storage tanks CIA commandos had hit in 1984. Although the port had prospered under the Somoza dictatorship, the assault apparently had unified the town behind the Sandinistas. Yet sensitivities remained. When two Cuban workers at a café boasted about local prostitutes, our hosts dismissed the duo as unreliable Puerto Ricans.

Nicaragua offered its share of ironies and contradictions. When our tour group joined a hundred other demonstrators outside the U.S. Embassy for the brief weekly protest against Reagan's support for the Contras, we observed Nicaraguan troops protecting the embassy by closing off the street. At the same time, we could not help noticing that the number of ordinary Nicaraguans lining up for U.S. visas to *leave* the country far outnumbered our modest ranks.

Additional complexities surfaced during a two and a half hour visit with Omar Cabezas, one of the Revolution's military heroes and the aspiring mayor of Managua. A physically imposing, charming, and even charismatic figure, Cabezas attracted a fair share of young European female admirers, lending the scene a distinct aura of revolutionary chic. As the Sandinista leader worked the room, setting up a lesson on the injustices of imperialism by playing off the relative innocence of Kosokoff's two sons, I had to concede the effectiveness of the performance. Yet I began to chafe at the manipulative nature of the encounter and wondered how to get past the patronizing quality of the discussion.

I already had presented the National University Library with a copy of *Twentieth Century Limited*, which featured a passage on the anti-imperialist politics of Montana's Burton Wheeler and other U.S. Senate insurgents of the 1920s. I now informed Cabezas that a photo at the Museum of the History of the Revolution documenting Wheeler's participation in a delegation to Nicaragua mistakenly contained the caption, "agents of American imperialism." Acknowledging the importance of recognizing the legacy of opposition to imperialism *within* the United States, Cabezas promised to correct the error.

Politics, I volunteered, was a way of organizing to change what may initially seem inevitable.

I am not sure if I had bested the skillful Cabezas at his own game, but at least I had tried.

On our next-to-last evening in Managua, I asked tour member Barrie, a Spanish-speaking California Legal Aid lawyer, to accompany me to affluent Carmen Park to deliver some sketches to the parents of Luis, my Nicaraguan artist friend. Luis's father, a prominent attorney, said that the Sandinistas had confiscated most of his law books. He and his family were fine, he insisted, but the poor had gone through suffering, and the government used the Contra War as an excuse for its own ineptness. It was easy to make a scapegoat of the United States, another member of the dinner party volunteered.

These middle-class professionals seemed convinced that the Sandinistas had no idea how to run an economy. Later in the evening, things lightened up when I knocked out a version of "Begin the Beguine" on the living room grand. Yet our Nicaraguan hosts, who claimed they originally supported the Revolution, conveyed a distinct pathos. When Luis's father drove us back to the Intercontinental, he had to detach the door-handle on the driver's side of his aging European sedan and insert it on the passenger's side to let us out.

I found the uncomplaining dignity with which he accomplished this menial task profoundly moving.

CONSERVATIVE MINDS

As our plane took off from Managua, I tried to put the journey into perspective. Was my country truly afraid of an army of teenagers and a military that encouraged the mothers of its young soldiers to visit their sons on active duty? Wasn't it possible that a people who loved baseball, Coca-Cola, and American pop music could achieve a nationalist political identity without becoming militaristic or totalitarian? If the Soviet and Cuban governments won friends by donating trucks, petroleum, sugar mills, and even helicopters for military defense, why could not the United States do the same? Did U.S. leaders realize that the Contra War was a slap at national pride and the best unifying force the Sandinistas had?

The one thing that infuriated Nicaraguans of all persuasions, I recalled, was the perception that Washington trivialized them as proxies for Havana and Moscow instead of a legitimate political force of their own. Why couldn't the Reagan administration let this poor Central American country find its own way? After all, the most ambitious Sandinista social program was a massive literacy campaign. Even if the government often failed to provide efficient services and fulfill its promises, was it really a threat to U.S. national security interests?

Equipped with extended notes as I returned home, I completed a report called "An Eight-Day Week in Nicaragua." The manuscript ran twenty-four pages of single-spaced typescript, equivalent to a hefty pamphlet. Since the text was too long for most publications and too short for a book, I photocopied its contents, sent it out to an extensive mailing list, and gave a copy to Mike McCusker, who later ran it as a two-part series in the *North Coast Times Eagle*.

273

"Congratulations! You are your grandmother's boy after all," enthused Uncle Mickey.

"Great work – I'm proud of you. Take back all the insults."

Mickey sent duplicates to all of South Florida's congressional representatives. Less than a month later, news broke that the Contras had used CIA-delivered weapons in an attack that killed Ben Linder, a twenty-seven-year-old volunteer engineer from Portland surveying the site of a future hydroelectric plant in northern Nicaragua. Linder had met his fate with a gunshot to the head at close range, one of thirty-six thousand people to die at the hands of anti-Sandinista forces. Joining fifteen hundred protesters in an emotional vigil at the Portland Federal Building, I worked with a group on a resolution to demand an investigation of the murder and a halt to aid to the Contras that Commissioner Mike Lindberg ushered through the city council.

The loss of the gentle and idealistic Ben Linder, a young man who loved to juggle, ride a unicycle, and do what he could to serve others, put a human face on the costs of the Reagan administration's attempt to bully an impoverished nation into political submission for no reason other than it had the power to do so. Ironically, a week after Linder's death, the PSU Faculty Senate received a proposal to create a military science department so that the university's Reserve Officer Training Corps (ROTC) program no longer would be an extension of Oregon State University's.

As a member of the faculty senate, I circulated a statement about academia's relationship to military objectives dedicated to Linder, who had spent time as a PSU student. The independent pursuit of truth and the exploration of theoretical knowledge were at the heart of university life, I noted. No faculty with intellectual integrity could sanction the creation of a department of learning that compromised those standards. The management of techniques and technologies integral to the violent exercise of government power simply had no place at an institution of higher learning. As a center of independent and critical thought, I insisted, the university could not become a servant of the military.

Portland State's ROTC instructors presented a strong case for integrating analytic tools into the study of military tactics and meeting the needs of students interested in national service. Yet the emerging Iran-Contra scandal over the Reagan administration's diversion of funds to the war in Nicaragua and the Linder assassination worked against them. In a letter to the *Vanguard* acknowledging victory, I pointed to two statements that helped carry the day. First, Hugo Maynard of the psychology department argued that warfare violated the two most essential taboos of academic life – violence and the intentional use of deceit. Second, literature professor Marjorie Burns asserted that military discipline encouraged obedience as a substitute for thought, an inappropriate virtue in a university setting.

In the end, the faculty senate defeated the proposal, 26-20, although an eventual arrangement between the campus ROTC and the University of Portland rendered the act largely symbolic.

Not by coincidence, the military science debate occurred just as I began co-teaching a new course on Vietnam. My partner was diplomatic historian Barney Burke, who took on political and military issues while I covered antiwar protest and the counterculture. We alternated lectures and offered brief responses to each other's remarks. Barney was a strapping Irish-American from Worcester, Massachusetts, who had worked his way to a history degree and PhD at the University of Washington following Navy service. A passionate and committed teacher with a biting wit, he opposed U.S. involvement in Vietnam, which he blamed on the purge of State Department Asia specialists during the anticommunist 1950s. Nevertheless, Barney's working-class roots left him with little patience for elements of the antiwar movement that appeared to discard reason, civility, and respect for others.

In response to the kind of criticism that Mike Passi and Louis Filler had offered, I struggled to present radical activism as best I could. Yet I found myself continually losing ground to my amiable but sharp-tongued colleague. Barney always said he learned a great deal from me. In truth, things probably worked the other way around.

Burke's critique of Vietnam era activism came as I composed a review of Filler's *Dictionary of American Conservatism* (1987), at Lou's initiative, for the journal of the Ohio Library Association. By now, my former mentor's rants had led most historians to dismiss him as a right-wing ideologue. Yet I saw the work's fifteen hundred entries as a useful guidepost to conservative political philosophy and moral sensibility. Tracing such thinking to a belief in free market capitalism and freedom from government restraint, Filler detailed the way the permanent welfare bureaucracy and New Deal subsidies had prompted modern conservatives to criticize public agencies as self-serving and wasteful.

By the late 1960s, Filler explained, populist anticommunists such as George Wallace and Ronald Reagan had succeeded in portraying liberals as "elitists" who manipulated the poor for their own political ends and contributed to the loss of individual initiative, the decline of the cities, and the decay of patriotism and other moral values.

Whatever its limitations, Filler's work had provided conservative ideology with an intellectual coherence I had never fully grasped. Yet my review raised several questions. Was devotion to familial love, organized religion, and social authority a reasoned response to the chaos of modern life, or was it simply a product of unthinking devotion to the status quo? Did conservative support for the fundamentals of civilization originate in a sincere attachment to traditional values or stem from the convenient need for a more orderly and deferential social order? Could conservative endorsement of traditional institutions and practices sometimes mask narrow self-interest and privilege? Finally, I asked whether social innovation and new cultural perspectives might redefine customary beliefs and morality instead of destroying them.

DOUG FIRS

Once the academic year ended in June 1987, I flew to Mission Viejo, where my parents had arranged two speaking engagements. In a presentation to my father's B'nai B'rith lodge, I noted that although the 1920s Ku Klux Klan viewed Jews as excessively insular, it did not picture them as the threat to American institutions supposedly represented by Roman Catholics. "American Jews and the Progressive World Challenge," a talk delivered at the temple, suggested that between the 1910s and the 1970s a working-class Jewish population had experienced social mobility through trade unions, government benefits, opportunities in education and professional life, an expanding popular culture, and a consumerist ethic stressing achievement instead of family origins. This foundation, I argued, reinforced liberal values such as social justice, concern for the oppressed, individual rights, and the defense of human dignity.

My point was that present circumstances compelled an extension of Jewish traditions of compassion. Since Jews had been subject to the same intolerance that oppressed other minorities, I suggested, it seemed fitting that we identify with marginalized people. This brought me to Israel, which I described as a nation whose prospects for peace and security ultimately rested with its Middle Eastern neighbors. Only a two-state solution to the Palestinian conflict could accomplish this, I insisted. In spiritual and survival terms, I asserted, Jews did not belong with those who wielded power without concern for its consequences. For Jewish identity to persevere, Jewish people had to do more than protect their most narrow interests.

Like the Palestinians at Portland State, the Mission Viejo audience seemed to appreciate an effort to engage them on a sensitive issue without condescension or undue pandering. Even my parents appeared proud of the performance and asked me to return in August for a joint dinner of their B'nai B'rith lodges. Later that summer, they even drove up to Portland to attend the revival of

Ma Rainey at the Winningstad Theater in Portland's new performing arts center.

Although my full professorship was due to take effect in the fall of 1987, I had applied for another unpaid leave of absence to clear the decks for my writing projects. As I prepared to proceed with "Beyond Left and Right," however, Oregon Klan scholar and Bart Bernstein seminar colleague Eckard Toy connected me with Shawn Lay. Just emerging from graduate school, Shawn planned to publish a collection of research essays on the western Ku Klux Klan of the 1920s and asked if I would contribute a chapter on La Grande. When I agreed, he sent me a detailed set of questions about the religious and occupational background of the membership as well as the surrounding economic, cultural, social, and political environment.

Upon completing a Chautauqua talk on the Klan at La Grande's Eastern Oregon College a year earlier, I had met Circuit Court Judge R. Thomas Gooding. Gooding had been one of the probate attorneys who had found the La Grande minutes in the files of a former Klansman and donated them to the Oregon Historical Society. Months after my talk, the judge sent me a photocopy of the documents. Since the chapter secretary had recorded the occupation of most recruits, and a copy of a local business directory provided by the librarian at Eastern Oregon College contained added data, I could compile the vocational information Lay requested. It turned out that most La Grande Klansmen came from the same skilled working-class and lower-middle-class strata as counterparts across the nation. The *La Grande Observer*, available on microfilm at the Historical Society, filled in the details on local political and social affairs.

As I pursued my study of the Klan, I received a call from former *Clinton Street Quarterly* editor David Milholland. The book I had reviewed for the journal in 1980 had touched on Portland-born John Reed's ties to the Bolshevik Revolution. To celebrate the centennial of the journalist and creative writer's birth, Milholland, Walt Curtis, and attorney and literary arts activist Brian Booth had organized a "Pantheon Celebration" for downtown's Pioneer Square. Asked to participate, I volunteered to recite several passages from John Dos Passos's poetic tribute to Reed in the *U.S.A.* trilogy. A photo of the event by Ilka Kuznik shows me reading from a script stapled to a file folder while several protesters hoist an American flag in the background to counter the honoring of a communist revolutionary on "Portland's Red Square."

"Reed was a westerner, and words meant what they said," I shouted.

A week after the event, I flew to visit Uncle Mickey, fully recovered from his stroke, now settled in a North Miami Beach condominium apartment. When Gloria picked me up upon my return, she had a promising report. Earlier that fall, the owners of my carriage house had sold the entire parcel to a couple who intended to build a garage alongside my rental. This prompted me to take up a long-standing offer from my parents to help me buy my own place. I told real estate agent and former history graduate student Karen Reyes I was looking for something with a "rustic" feel. By coincidence, an agent in Karen's office was about to list her ex-husband's log-sided, single-story Frontier Revival home in Northeast Portland. Situated on the backside of a double lot amid a grove of mature Douglas firs, the three-bedroom layout featured a cozy living room with crafted cedar paneling and a corner woodstove placed in a river rock setting.

Gloria promised to check it out while I was in Florida.

"As soon as I walked inside the door, I told Karen, 'This is David's house,'" she announced.

With a family loan covering half the purchase price, I overcame my longstanding aversion to "bourgeois" attachments and prepared to take title to my own home.

DESERVING CHARGES

By January 1988, when Gloria and I set up housekeeping in Northeast Portland, I was in the middle of a simmering controversy at Portland State. The saga had begun nearly a year earlier when my graduate assistant Michael Brewin relayed a story about his stint as coordinator for Student Government's Popular Music Board. As plans for the university's first homecoming dance in twenty years proceeded in the fall of 1986, Brewin said, he recommended a racially mixed funk band. According to Brewin, Student Body President Mike Erickson shook his head and made a face while Vice President Dan Swift replied this was a dance for *white* students.

Brewin claimed that witnesses later overheard Swift ask him to remain silent about the incident in a conversation broadcast on an office speakerphone. He also insisted that several mid-level administrators summarily dismissed his version of events. Since football place-kicker Erickson enjoyed a special relationship with Portland State President Natale Sicuro, Brewin predicted, nothing would come of the matter.

A former college football athlete and Ohio high school coach with a PhD in educational psychology, Sicuro had administered Kent State University's continuing education program and served as president of Southern Oregon College before taking the helm at Portland State in 1986. Although insiders claimed that higher education chancellor William E. ("Bud") Davis had pushed the Sicuro candidacy upon a reluctant selection committee, the new president dismissed faculty "inferiority complexes" and vowed to provide the university national exposure with a "Plan for the '90s" and upgraded sports program.

When PSU hosted the opening round of the nationally televised Division II collegiate football playoffs in the fall of 1987, Sicuro appeared before the cameras at halftime.

Viewers may not have not have heard of Portland State, he proclaimed with a flourish, but they soon would.

Brewin's story challenged me. Whatever views I had in the past, I still liked to believe that public universities promoted opportunity for all students and offered a relatively uncorrupted arena for reasoned dialogue. Yet the alleged refusal of administrators to deal with accusations of improper behavior by favored protégés amounted, if true, to a level of cronyism and abuse of power that tainted the institution and higher education itself. Convinced that public expression of even casual racism by campus leaders warranted at least an inquiry, and anxious to show Brewin and others that universities held everyone to the same standards, I agreed to compose a summary of the allegations for publication in the *Vanguard.*

In the middle of my preparations, Mike Erickson called me into his office to assure me that President Sicuro was completely aware of the accusations and totally supported him. If this was supposed to intimidate me, the ploy failed. My extended feature, "Charges deserving of serious investigation," reached print in March 1987. Ironically, the same issue of the newspaper reported that Portland State's president had recommended Erickson for a seat on the State Board of Higher Education as an outstanding student leader deserving promotion to public service.

When the State Board convened its next meeting on the PSU campus and thirty minority and international student activists protested Sicuro's endorsement, the president asked to meet with the group. According to participants, he insisted there was insufficient evidence to pursue the accusations against Erickson and told the students that their demonstration had embarrassed him. Staffers under Vice-Provost for Student Affairs Orcilia Forbes subsequently leaked Sicuro's complaint that she needed to do more to contain the minority students.

Erickson's State Board nomination never materialized. In fact, *Vanguard* coverage of irregularities in the student body president's re-election campaign led to his disqualification from the race. Student Affairs insiders now revealed that Erickson told Sicuro that the newspaper was out of control. It was no surprise, therefore, when during the summer of 1987 the president ordered Forbes to conduct a review of publication board guidelines and its advisor, Jerry Penk, former chair of the journalism department before its elimination in the early 1980s.

Portland State's student newspaper dated back to the Vanport campus era. Under faculty pressure in the 1960s, the administration had empowered the publications board to ensure "a free and responsible student press." Sensing that Sicuro sought more of a hold over the *Vanguard*, I asked to testify before the Forbes panel and submitted my statement for publication.

"Why review publications guidelines that ensure campus freedom of expression?" I asked. I speculated that the president wanted to convert the student press into a house organ to push athletics, a violation of higher education's mission to provide an open forum of ideas. Democratic societies treated those in authority with no special deference, I insisted. This included the ability to distinguish grandiose public-relations schemes from the self-importance of those who engineered them.

Portland State would never submit to servile dependence on personal dictatorship, I warned.

CIVIL WAR

President Sicuro may not have appreciated the important role students and faculty had played in the institution's history. During the 1950s, PSU professors had taken the lead in devising the expanded liberal arts curriculum, ratified an academic constitution, and created an elected senate and advisory council. In 1959, the faculty voted to oppose Cold War loyalty oaths. Three years later, President Branford P. Millar publicly defended academic rights of free speech and supported student discretion in choosing visiting speakers. Portland State student government would win its own constitution in 1966. Nine years after that, the faculty senate passed a constitutional amendment calling for shared responsibilities and cooperative action in university governance. In 1978, a vote of the faculty designated the American Association of University Professors (AAUP) as its collective bargaining agent in contract negotiations.

Whatever Sicuro knew of the past, the controversy over the publication board review intensified later in the summer when the *Vanguard* used public records to document $92,000 worth of renovations, twice the original estimate, at the presidential mansion in exclusive Dunthorpe in Southwest Portland. As fall term began in 1987, the Vice President for Finance and Administration responded with a memo requiring all *Vanguard* information requests to come through his office in writing. *The Chronicle of Higher Education* trade weekly later revealed that Sicuro had been the sole source of the gag order. The second shoe fell in October when the president used a special edition of the administration newsletter to announce Jerry Penk's termination.

Freedom of expression, declared Sicuro, was not a license for misrepresentation.

Portland State's confrontation over the freedom of the student newspaper now received coverage in several local press outlets. An internal publication board review subsequently noted that Professor Penk had performed his job in an exemplary fashion and that the *Vanguard* had received the highest ratings. The panel's chair could only conclude that the administration had been unhappy with the content of the paper.

However contentious the administration's dealings with the *Vanguard* appeared to be, plans for upgrading the sports program quickly supplanted the controversy. As deficits continued to plague PSU football in the mid-1970s, the faculty senate had created a university athletics board to monitor the program. The administration also set up a student-faculty arbitration board to provide partial control over the student incidental fees that supported intercollegiate sports. Facing a shortfall of nearly $600,000 for 1987, with estimates for the following year approaching a million dollars, Sicuro acknowledged that previous presidents had regularly diverted surplus student fees to offset sports imbalances. He now asked local marketing consultant Fred Delkin to head a panel of business figures and team boosters to chart the future of PSU athletics.

I had questioned the place of intercollegiate football in a *freeway* column in 1974. Now that the Sicuro administration appeared to be usurping student autonomy, faculty governance, and control over the direction of the university, Michael Brewin and I concluded that the best way to counter the president's ambitions was to confront his effort to make Portland State a major power on the gridiron.

No one doubted that the Delkin committee would recommend upgrading PSU football from Division II to Division I-AA. Accordingly, I worked with psychology professor Hugo Maynard to gain unanimous faculty senate approval of a resolution labeling the move a misapplication of university priorities and opposing the use of student fees to pay off the athletics debt. A week after the senate's action, I took the case against intercollegiate competition to the *Vanguard* in an opinion piece entitled "Big-Time Sports Stifles Academics." The column cited an estimate by the Carnegie Foundation for the Advancement of Teaching that college athletics ranked as one of the most corrupting and destructive influences in higher education.

Citing one survey, I noted that one-third of Division I university presidents acknowledged the presence of athletes in their programs who did not belong in college. I also passed on a report that only 30 percent of competitors in college revenue sports ever received degrees, a disturbing figure made more concerning considering that only one out of 183 student athletes made it to the professional ranks. Originally designed to teach teamwork and sportsmanship, I concluded, university sports departments had deteriorated into athletic factories obsessed with churning out victories and scoring lucrative media contracts. Fair play, I suggested, long ago fell victim to winning at any cost in a billion-dollar industry that exploited athletes and mocked academic standards.

Portland State was "not for sale. Division I football is not our game," I insisted.

Days after my article appeared, the Delkin Committee voted to support the move to Division I. Yet the panel acknowledged that its own survey indicated that 55 percent of PSU faculty wanted to *de-emphasize* intercollegiate sports. Revenue-producing football at PSU was an unrealistic fantasy that would not serve the University, I asserted in a special *Vanguard* supplement devoted to the issue.

Seeking to expose the PSU administration to national scrutiny, I had approached the *Chronicle of Higher Education* about submitting another opinion piece. Instead, the editors chose to cover the story as a news feature. When reporter Doug Lederman appeared on campus, I turned over a detailed outline of the controversy as well as contact information for relevant parties on both sides of the issue. Following my framing of the debate, Lederman noted that the proposal to upgrade PSU's football program had elicited vehement disagreement among many faculty and students and was a symptom of a deeper rift.

"This is not about sports," it quoted me as saying.

"This is a civil war over the soul of this institution."

One day after the *Chronicle* published its report in December, I testified against the upgraded football proposal at a special meeting of the State Board of Higher Education. When the panel approved the move the next day, my first response was to tell *The Oregonian* that the decision amounted to a great victory for mediocrity and reflected a state-wide tradition of not facing up to real issues. Yet the board imposed a set of financial guidelines for the program and ordered PSU athletics to refrain from soliciting student funding. Accordingly, when Sicuro subsequently announced his intention to divert a hundred thousand dollars of surplus student fees to help offset the sports deficit, the faculty senate unanimously demanded he abandon the plan.

Yet Sicuro was not someone used to backing down.

Two days after the faculty senate meeting, the president told a public forum he was saving the students time by making the decision himself.

"You may not like the way I'm doing it," the *Vanguard* quoted him as saying, "but I'm sorry – that's the way it's going to be."

MEADOWS

(1988-1990)

days of miracle and wonder
– P. Simon

Just as anti-Sicuro stickers began appearing across campus in February 1988, *The Oregonian* ran a major profile entitled "A Man with a Mission."

At first glance, the story seemed to be a "fluff" piece in which Oregon business and professional figures offered the highest praise for PSU's president. Yet the article gave voice to critics concerned about the use of corporate models of top-down rule in university governance. My contention that Sicuro's management style offended faculty because of its reliance on imagery and coziness with the business community fell into this category. At the same time, Sicuro's response to student discontent demonstrated an autocratic mindset that came off poorly.

"They're going to get used to me; they're going to enjoy it," he told *The Oregonian*.

THE COLOR PURPLE

Despite the kinks in Natale Sicuro's armor, the state board's qualified endorsement of the sports upgrade left Michael Brewin and me believing that the case against the president had gone as far as it could go. Four days before publication of "Man with a Mission," however, a local TV station had revealed the existence of a near hundred thousand dollar deficit in the presidential account at the Portland State Foundation, the university's non-profit fundraising arm. After Sicuro had used up his annual expense stipend, the report explained, the foundation had replenished the deficit with funds borrowed from accounts designated for student scholarships, research, and other purposes.

Leaked documents revealed that Sicuro's fundraising expenses included a trip to Italy in the company of his wife, four season tickets to the Symphony, and membership in several private clubs. The president also had slashed the library budget to meet a state board requirement that $500,000 for the renovation of his office come from other accounts.

Following these revelations, Sicuro compounded his difficulties by barring access to foundation records, refusing to respond to press inquiries, and declining to come before the academic senate. In response, historian Charles M. White and a group of senior professors formed their own Faculty Trust Fund and appointed senate presiding officer and English professor Marjorie Burns as its president. In the months that followed, Oregon's Department of Justice and the Secretary of State mounted official inquiries into the foundation's potential breach of fiduciary trust. A state report would absolve PSU of illegal activity but conclude that President Sicuro had improperly controlled the foundation and presided over the co-mingling of the non-profit's staff, accounts, and activities with those of the university. In the end, the deficit in the presidential account reached $165,000.

The foundation disclosures provided new life to the anti-Sicuro campaign. In March, a campus group designating itself as the Student Coalition for Responsible Administrative Policies (SCRAP) put together a forum attracting 250 people. As the last to address the crowd, I punched out a detailed timeline of each Sicuro episode. Then I paraphrased a plea Populist agitator Mary Lou Lease had directed to Kansas corn farmers in the 1890s.

PSU students, I declared, "may have to raise a few less grades and a lot more hell."

"Whose university is this?" I thundered.

Administrators were mere *facilitators* of teaching and learning, I insisted. PSU did not require a coach, a father figure, an empire-builder, or a Napoleon.

I concluded with a reference to recently disposed Haitian dictator Jean-Claude Duvalier.

"We need no Papa Doc for PSU!" I nearly shouted.

As demands for Sicuro's resignation mounted within and outside the university, I received a phone call from an attorney and part-time business school instructor who often dispensed free legal advice to PSU staffers and service employees. He thought I might be interested in what he had learned. His sources told him that Sicuro had issued orders that only the president could sign memos in purple ink. On another occasion, the president had ordered the grounds crew to plant purple cabbage in the campus shrubbery beds in *three days' time* or risk mass firings. When a food service worker delivered the president's breakfast thirty minutes late one morning, another story indicated, Sicuro lost his temper and had the employee transferred.

The most revealing tales concerned the expenses involved in sprucing up the publicly supported presidential mansion. These included the removal of a microwave oven to replace the door handle for the left-handed Mrs. Sicuro and touch-up paint on hundreds of spots on a completed wall and the *underside* of the bathroom cabinet drawers.

Repeatedly, faculty, staff, and even administrators privately told me of cases of presidential bullying, bluster, and intimidation. The intensity of the Sicuro outbursts seemed inversely related to the victim's power status. By this time, I knew that the president dismissed me as a half-cocked gadfly. Yet I felt confident that my concerns channeled the pervasive and reasonable discontent brewing across the university. Still, I was not sure the faculty would be willing to engage in a *public* confrontation with the institution's prime disperser of funds. Accordingly, I took it upon myself to show the emperor had no clothes.

Protected by academic tenure and my full professorship, I sought to demonstrate that even the power-driven Sicuro had no ability to prevent even the most capricious attacks. If the president failed to see the campus-wide sentiment behind such shenanigans, he would merely contribute to his own isolation. Meanwhile, I wanted to

Getting There

provide a latter-day example of Abbie Hoffman's and Jerry Rubin's point that you could work for change and have a good time doing it.

When my business school informant disclosed that the swing standard "Chattanooga Choo Choo" was a presidential favorite, I could not resist the temptation to devise a parody with help from Gloria. After all, playful tampering with lyrics was a time-honored tradition in my family.

"Pardon me, Judge/I'm from the PSU Foundation," the spoof began. "We'd like to state/That our financing's just great!"

"When we receive/A very generous donation," it continued, "We place the amount/In the president's account."

The lyric then described the president leaving Dunthorpe in a "leased Oldsmobile," heading down to the Athletic Club "to cut his next deal."

It went on to reference timely breakfast deliveries, orders to screen out reporters' phone calls, "state grants for cabbage plants," paid trips to Italy, and confidential requests for a microwave door replacement and touch-up painting at the presidential mansion.

"Faculty are just nosy and just get in the way," the parody declared.

"Library books/Are only there for looks."

"Students may cry/But they can find a banker's loan," the final verse concluded.

"The Portland State Foundation/We take care of our own!"

HUMPTY DUMPTY

The complete text of the Sicuro parody appeared in the *Vanguard* in early May, after which I distributed copies to a large mailing list of friends, community leaders, officeholders, and members of the PSU alumni board. When one alumnus complained to Liberal Arts College Dean William Paudler that a "silly professor" had distributed a sophomoric, vindictive, and ridiculous song demeaning to the school, I published a *Vanguard* reply. The day before the parody found its way into print, I reported, President Sicuro had met with his faculty advisory council and warned that professors and administrators who served on the board of the recently organized counter-foundation ultimately would hear from him.

"We will not allow the use of gangster-like intimidation or bullying," I wrote, "to destroy a university in which individuals are dedicated to enriching their lives through the pursuit of knowledge and critical perspective."

My letter then invited everyone to attend a "Cavalcade of American Popular Music," an informal outdoor stint at the piano I would present the next day nearly under Sicuro's window. Appropriately, I would save a raucous version of the foundation spoof for the finale.

By the time I gave my recital, the administration had released a public relations packet blaming the entire controversy on a small but vocal group of faculty dissidents fearing change.

"I think we're being taken for a ride by a street hustler," I stated in an *Oregonian* story appearing the next day. "This guy is out in Disneyland; he's out of touch."

The State Board was not "going to baby sit him with his soaring deficit," I warned.

Not long after, physics professor John Dash assured *Vanguard* readers that a majority of faculty, students, and staff viewed the president as a tyrant who had paralyzed the university. Meanwhile, a spokesperson for College of Liberal Arts department heads and program directors publicly decried the breakdown of governance at Portland State and the perception that a mean and vindictive leader was governing the institution through intimidation. Twenty-one academic chairs subsequently signed a personal letter to Sicuro stating that widespread dissatisfaction across the campus did not come from fear of change. The president no longer could regain the necessary support to serve Portland State's welfare, they insisted.

In June, a faculty senate task force reported that the PSU Foundation was in serious financial difficulty. The senate now called for an early state board presidential performance review and prepared to poll the faculty on their views. Sicuro responded with a news

293

conference in which he proposed a "blue-ribbon" panel of distinguished senior professors and the retention of a public relations firm to repair the administration's rift with the faculty and improve communication with the public, news media, and university personnel. Yet the president faced a daunting task. Among the three-quarters of eligible professors who participated in the faculty poll, 62 percent expressed dissatisfaction with the administration.

As the state board agreed to the senate's call for an early review, Gloria and I took to the *Vanguard* to publish another parody. This one accompanied the melody to "Frere Jacques."

"Nat's pretending, that we're mending," it read, "we say 'nope,' to such hope."

At a party that summer, I asked Liberal Arts Dean Paudler about loyalist administrators.

"What loyalists?" he retorted.

I was not surprised, therefore, when in early September, thirty tenured department chairs submitted a letter to the performance review board calling for the president's termination. Sicuro's demand for personal rather than institutional loyalty lay at the heart of the problem, Paudler told the press. My own testimony cited the president for managerial arrogance, sterile public relations, and a conscious disregard for truth. In a democratic society, I argued, teachers had a responsibility to encourage students to develop the full potential of their critical minds and creative capabilities. To function properly, I stated, institutions of higher learning had to provide open arenas of uninhibited dialogue and free expression. People who made material sacrifices to become academics, I asserted, would not permit anyone to demean their choice through the imposition of imperial fantasies or the erection of edifices of sand.

PSU had no need for self-inflated rhetoric and posturing, I concluded.

Two weeks after the start of the hearings, Michael Brewin and student leaders organized a PSU Solidarity Day to initiate a period of healing. I, in turn, saw the rally as an opportunity for the university community to close ranks on Sicuro's fate. Some people thought Portland State's reputation had deteriorated, I told the *Vanguard*, but we should be proud how we stood up under destructive tendencies. As one of the final speakers at the gathering, I congratulated the crowd on their promotion from a small vocal minority.

Public institutions were not banks for a few self-styled elites and their cronies, I declared.

"All the resources of top PR men," I taunted, "couldn't put Humpty together again."

DANCING IN THE DARK

By the time the state board convened a public meeting in October to announce the results of the performance review, I had inside information that Oregon's political establishment wanted to push Sicuro out the door. As the session opened, therefore, Gloria and I distributed fliers for a "Good-Bye Sicuro Celebration" at our home that evening. I fully understood that once the foundation improprieties entered the picture, the case against the president had fallen to more-potent forces than the few souls who had initiated the campaign. Yet I thought it important to demonstrate that you did not need to be a well-placed power broker to effect change or bring salient issues to the table. By pre-empting the announcement of Sicuro's fate, we hoped to dramatize the relevance of those of us who had come to the issue early in the game. After all, it was important to celebrate a rare collective victory when it occurred.

Stocking the house with a case of champagne, we invited the local TV media to the party.

Up to this point, I had great success in framing treatments of the Sicuro saga. Yet it is impossible to anticipate how the media will process a given story. In this case, the single feature on the local news drew a moral distinction between the gleeful sipping of champagne at a raucous celebration in our living room and somber reflections on Sicuro's demise by presumably more thoughtful members of the PSU community. In truth, our event attracted several of the same faculty and student leaders who publicly insisted they had no joy in seeing the president resign. The story took on an added dimension when *The Oregonian* printed a letter by a former state board president and Sicuro review panel member who characterized the victory party as a sad sight. In contrast to the sober individuals who had testified concerning the gut-wrenching situation at Portland State, he claimed, the sight of Horowitz and friends "dancing on Sicuro's grave" only belittled them in the eyes of those who really cared about the university.

My "year-long Romper Room antics and accompanying doggerel poetry," the letter concluded, were unbecoming of a man with a professor's title.

Taking a page from Saul Alinsky, I used the public scolding as the pretext for a response, in this case an abbreviated version of a letter previously published in the *Vanguard*. Our celebration, I explained to *Oregonian* readers, commemorated the triumph of a broad coalition that succeeded against overwhelming odds in toppling an autocratic and dictatorial university administration. Sicuro's fall, I stated, showed that normally powerless people were capable of great accomplishments when they were organized and unified.

"You bet we claim victory, and we're proud to celebrate our triumph," I declared.

When the *Chronicle of Higher Education* reported that PSU faculty had not rejoiced over the resignation, I sent the journal a shorter version of my *Oregonian* letter.

"Not quite true," I admonished, "the campus mood actually approached elation."

Whatever sense of triumph many of us shared, I was fully aware that the Portland State controversy transcended Sicuro's idiosyncrasies. The president was the symptom, not the underpinning, of growing corporate influence in the university. The problem was that business leaders and campus boosters tended to see public institutions of higher learning as agents of market growth and stimulants of economic opportunity. In contrast, most academics viewed access to the life of the mind as a democratic right available to those committed to reason and open dialogue. Aware that my confrontational theatricality disturbed some allies, I nevertheless had taken pains to relate the *substance* of my protests to mainstream academic values.

THE SOUNDS OF SILENCE

As the Sicuro episode resolved, people liked to tease me by asking about my next project.

"Israeli-Palestinian peace," I replied without hesitation.

I was only half-joking – the debate in 1986 had left a good deal of unfinished business.

When in November 1988 the Palestinian National Council issued a declaration of independence that rejected terror in all forms, I told a *Vanguard* interviewer that the time for argument was over and it was now time to negotiate. Sending out a press release in the name of a CIA-styled "Friends of Israel for a Palestinian State" (FIPS), I invited Conservative Rabbi Joshua Stampfer, a long-time adjunct instructor at PSU, to address a university gathering on the topic of "American Jews, Israel, and the New Palestinian State."

Born in Jerusalem and a veteran of the 1948 War of Independence, Stampfer had concluded that the hatred surrounding Israel's occupation of the West Bank and Gaza ultimately could wreak irreparable damage upon Israel. Pursuing a similar line of analysis, my press release asserted that current developments in the Middle East posed the gravest threats to the integrity and morale of world Jewry because Israel represented the Jewish people on the global stage. FIPS operated on the premise that a just and peaceful settlement of the Israeli-Palestinian conflict was essential for the preservation of a stable and democratic Israel, it stated.

Over the years, I had learned that Arab and Palestinian violence left a great majority of American Jews and members of Congress incapable of mounting direct criticism of Israel. Any appeal for peace had to rest upon enlightened self-interest, a strategy that New Jewish Agenda had pursued. Speaking before 150 people, Rabbi

Stampfer argued that we could not afford to abandon the arena to the gladiators. The Palestinian people, he insisted, had to have freedom to exercise self-determination. I summarized the rabbi's remarks and my own views in a *Vanguard* opinion piece in January 1989. The United States, I pleaded, had to help Israel replace expansionism and military repression with reason and vision.

Of no surprise to anyone, progress on the Middle East peace front remained elusive. Meanwhile, as classes ended in June, Gloria and I prepared for our first cross-country auto trip. Just before we left, however, Joe and Charlotte Uris alerted us to a pending threat a half-mile from home. A Korean firm sought to retrieve copper components by burning off electrical transformer residues in an incinerator they planned to build along the nearby Columbia Slough. Providing initial approval of an air discharge permit, the Oregon Department of Environmental Quality (DEQ) claimed the operators would process transformer parts already drained of oil, producing minimal emissions and insignificant levels of toxicity. Yet several citizen groups insisted on an additional round of hearings.

Once I alerted our Concordia Neighborhood Association, the meeting attracted a large crowd. Among twenty-five witnesses, state legislators Ron and Jane Cease stated that the PCB compounds and dioxin residues were some of the most toxic substances known to man and that no safe level of exposure existed for these potentially carcinogenic materials. Given my mother's ongoing battle with cancer, any reference to the disease struck at my gut. As tensions escalated with additional testimony, the crowd broke out in a raucous demonstration, which my brother and I assisted by loudly banging a rear table. At that point, DEQ scheduled another session.

Days later, Ed Washington, a local African-American activist with an eye on a potential legislative seat, invited Gloria and me to attend a televised press conference on the controversy. To dramatize the presentation, the two of us dressed in stark black and white clothing and donned shades. As we stood behind Ed with our legs spread and anti-PCB placards in our hands, we stared intently at the camera. Sometimes, silence can be more intimidating than speech.

Days after Gloria and I had taken to the road, Michael read the statement I had prepared for the next hearing.

"We will not allow ourselves to become guinea pigs at the risk of our health and safety," it stated. The DEQ was "in danger of making potential serial killers and mass murderers" of plant operators.

No amount of corporate puffery, I warned, could protect outside financial interests preparing to poison our community.

As one of thirty-nine testimonials presented before a crowd of two hundred, my veiled threats presumably had no special impact. Whether in reaction to the cumulative effect of public furor over the issue or a result of mere bureaucratic shuffling, however, DEQ turned the matter over to the Portland Planning Bureau, which subsequently ruled that the site's proximity to the Columbia Slough disqualified it from a land-use permit.

FIELDS OF DREAMS

Driving east with Gloria's thirteen-year-old son David, we planned to take in a series of major league baseball games on the way to visiting Gloria's family in New England. David had prepared himself for the trip with a collection of *Wolverine* comics and a Walkman cassette unit supplied with the sounds of rappers Tone Loc and Living Colour. Up front, Gloria and I played Paul Simon's *Graceland* and dozens of samples from my eclectic tape collection.

Following a Chicago White Sox baseball game and a twenty-fifth class reunion at Antioch, we spent the Fourth of July tracing my family history in Honesdale, Pennsylvania, and the Catskills. After searching in vain for the site of my grandparents' Lake Huntington cabaret, we drove through the town of Bethel toward White Lake, the location of the former Horowitz family bungalow colony and of Jo-Jeans, the ice-cream stand where I had first heard Bill Haley and the Comets. On the way, Gloria spotted a sign that directed us to the site of Bethel's legendary 1969 Woodstock Rock Festival. After explaining to David what Woodstock meant to a distant generation, we continued to the bungalows, now a Hassidic Russian Jewish compound surrounded by barbed wire. Finding a way into the grounds through the parking lot, David and I tossed a rubber ball on the weed-infested softball field.

Ironically, our destination was Woodstock, Connecticut, in the northeast or "quiet corner" of the state where Gloria's mother Mary Kowal lived in a modular home on a corner of the family's former dairy farm. Inspired by the recently released *Field of Dreams,* a film that reincarnated a team of 1919 baseball legends on an Iowa cornfield, we snapped photographs of each other among the acres of towering stalks that Gloria's brother Tony now leased. As we explored the unheated attic bedroom Gloria had shared with younger sister Paula in the abandoned farmhouse, we nearly stepped on a dusty framed photo. It was a picture of Gloria's father in his World War II Army uniform juxtaposed between portraits of President Roosevelt and General MacArthur. At Mary's urging, we packed the historical treasure into the Datsun. With the benefit of new matting and protective glass, it still hangs on our bedroom wall.

One of our excursions led us to Roger Williams College in nearby Rhode Island, where Natale Sicuro had assumed the presidency. After we briefly summarized our former connection to Sicuro, both a student affairs administrator and the student newspaper editor informed us that the board of trustees had dismissed the PSU controversy as misleading. Just in case, we dropped off a file of old news clippings at the *Providence Journal.* Three and a half years later, a reporter would call to say that Roger Williams's new president had resigned over philosophical differences with the board, faculty problems, and fundraising issues.

After several stops at major league parks, we returned to Portland, where I prepared an account of the trip to the Catskills for the *North Coast Times Eagle.* "The Road to Woodstock Went Through Jo-Jeans: A Dialogue on Pop Music" explained that the ice-cream stand where I first heard "Shake, Rattle, and Roll" had been halfway between

Lake Huntington, where my parents had first met, and the site of the most acclaimed rock festival in U.S. history. Yet young David had little interest in our generation's cultural odyssey.

"Your music is boring," I quoted him as saying: "it's lame."

Forced to reflect on the generational divide, I suggested that the dissident 1960s embraced the revolutionary notion that if Woodstock Nation could create its own culture, it might also work toward political and economic vitality. Yet succeeding years had tarnished these hopes. Did every generation simply have to discover its own form of puberty ritual and rebellion? I concluded that rock music involved a tribal culture of the young and a transition to adulthood. No one should feign surprise, then, that Woodstock Nation was only a historic quirk to a thirteen-year-old straddled on his own crossroads of life. Veterans of rock 'n' roll wars needed to open themselves to new musical forms, I ventured.

Preparation of "The Road to Woodstock" proceeded on a new Smith Corona word processor, a compromise with computer technology that facilitated easy editing and document saving. I soon returned to "Beyond Left and Right." Following the appearance of my civil rights article in the *Journal of Southern History*, the editor of a prominent university press had inquired if the essay was part of a book. Several months after I sent him drafts of the first seven chapters, however, he forwarded two devastating referee reports. The first castigated the manuscript for false dichotomies, factual inaccuracies, and a lack of context. I had confused anti-corporate claims with history, the critic asserted, and produced nothing more than a jeremiad. The second reviewer maintained I had taken simplistic propositions about the corporate economy at face value. Seeing U.S. entry into World War I solely through the eyes of Robert La Follette did not do the topic full justice, the critic scolded. A list of accusations was not history.

It took months for the criticism to percolate before I could return to the manuscript. When I regained my bearings, I modeled the work on the analyses of historians Alan Brinkley, Justus Doenecke, and Wayne Cole and took a far more critical approach to the antiinstitutional and noninterventionist sentiment the work outlined. With a degree of confidence restored by the end of 1989, I looked up University of Illinois Press editor Richard Wentworth at the American Historical Association conference in San Francisco. Illinois was about to publish Shawn Lay's Klan anthology, for which I had just submitted my chapter. When I sent Wentworth a twenty-chapter outline, however, he replied I might be trying to do too much.

Interested in clarifying the ideas embedded in "Beyond Left and Right," I accepted an invitation from Mike McCusker to contribute a *Times Eagle* essay on the state of the discipline of history at decade's end. "The Loneliness of the Synthetic Historian: A Plea for the Nineties" argued that professional historians needed to go beyond the outright flattery of entrenched interests or treatments of minorities and the powerless that lacked sufficient context. Borrowing again from Alan Brinkley and historian Leo Ribuffo, I called for scholars to address ordinary Americans who rejected scientific rationalism, liberal religion, and reformed capitalism without castigating them as backward-looking. The article emphasized the extensive political and cultural legacy of populism and the need to dispel the exclusive association of radicalism with the left or working class. The most insistent critics of society, I suggested, were those rejecting the established order, no matter their political orientation.

I concluded the essay with a call for a new synthetic history based upon the experiences and perceptions of non-elites, whether liberal or conservative.

THE PACT

The Popular Culture Association conference, held in Toronto during March 1990, provided another opportunity to test my formulations when I delivered a paper on the coalition between movie-purity crusaders of the 1920s and '30s and independent exhibitors. Yet the most lasting legacy of the meeting was its introduction to the growing literature on discourse theory and the deconstruction of texts.

Several sessions sampled "post-modern" modes of analysis that prioritized the interpretation of material above the stated intentions of authors. Inspired and amused at the same time, Gloria and I created a parody of the new catch phrases.

"Amid the simulacra of hyper-reality and semiotic discourse," we wrote, "a signifying culture witnesses deconstruction and recoding of its reified inscriptions and fetishes."

Days after returning to Portland, we had the opportunity to deliver a performance art rendering of our creation. After working as a journalist for a health industry weekly and putting in a stint with a Bay Area library automation project, my brother had returned to Portland to complete a novel. Rebuffed by New York publishers, he worked with Mike McCusker to establish Times Eagle Books and release the work under the pseudonym V .O. Blum. Billed as a work of New Age fiction, *Equator* (1989) followed a Greek-American agricultural specialist to West Africa, where he enters an intricate web of relationships with a Norwegian male adventurer and an older Dutch woman whose grounding in advanced mathematics and metaphysics co-exists with a penchant for bodily pleasure.

Michael hosted a celebration of the novel's publication at Cassidy's, a downtown eatery and watering hole catering to an eclectic mix of writers, artists, and hospitality industry employees. The establishment provided a perfect venue for Gloria and me to perform our sampling of advanced semiotics, which, in the post-modern spirit, hovered ambiguously between parody and flattery. Before Penny Allen, my brother, and a crowd of rather bewildered friends, we culminated the reading with speculation that the simmering "cultural bricolage" of *Equator* pointed toward the "post-novel" and even "the deconstruction of the author."

By the spring of 1990, both Michael and I were spending a good deal of time in Mission Viejo. Just a week after moving into the house in Northeast Portland, I had driven to California when my father required surgery to repair severe degeneration of a lower-back disc. Suffering from lumbar stenosis, rheumatoid arthritis, and painful circulatory problems, he continued to rely on a walker for mobility. Despite these obstacles, he managed to produce a rousing Yiddish Club version of his mock marriage as a temple fundraiser during the summer of 1988.

My mother had served as narrator of the comic farce before resuming chemotherapy the next day. In September, the *Times Eagle* published her play, *The Survivor*, an account of a conversation between a cancer patient, her brain, and her surgeon that included a poem entitled "Reprieve." The following month, the paper ran "A Baseball Fan Fights Cancer," her summary of the diamond's mythic role in Horowitz family life from Babe Ruth to Bobby Thomson to the therapeutic value of Vince Scully's L.A. Dodger radio broadcasts.

When Gloria and I visited in August 1989, however, my mother was facing anemia, high blood pressure, heart problems, and other complications from the cancerous cells in her body and the chemotherapy seeking to eradicate them. We managed to take her to a California Angels baseball game, an outing that thrilled her even when the opposing team scored seven runs in the top of the first inning. Nevertheless, her condition continued to deteriorate over the following year. Following several weekend flights to see her in the spring of 1990, I returned with Gloria when the school year ended. My mother already had arranged to pay off the remaining half of my home mortgage and urged me to prepare the paperwork for a family financial trust. As I took my dad for rides in the surrounding hill country, meanwhile, she confided in Gloria.

She was ready for whatever came next, she said. Her main concern was my father, who had never dealt with the seriousness of her illness and panicked at any hint of abandonment.

When I returned in August to fill in for the vacationing home aide, I found my mother even weaker, partly a result of an ample supply of morphine painkillers at her disposal.

One morning she told me of a dream in which her deceased father waved to her as if in welcome. Then she nodded when she asked if I intended to marry Gloria and I said yes.

Finally, she made a point of asking me to look out after Uncle Mickey.

For some time, the two of us had shared an unstated pact that I would do everything to enable her to see through the inevitable outcome at home. Yet I had not fully prepared myself for the pace of events when a visiting nurse advised that not much time remained.

I needed to make necessary arrangements, she said.

Indeed, every day seemed to bring a new crisis. The turning point may have come on the morning my dad called me to my parents' bathroom, where my mother had taken a bad fall. As I lifted her off the floor, her nightgown opened. Thinking I was embarrassed, she apologized.

That evening, she asked the visiting nurse for a bath, only to learn that the caregiver was behind schedule.

Five minutes later, the doorbell rang. The aide had reconsidered. My mother called her a guardian angel.

Sometime after midnight, I awoke to my father's insistent calling. When I came into the fully lit bedroom, my mother's head rested upright against the bed pillow. Her eyes closed, she exhaled heavily with a mechanical monotony. There was no response when my father tried to arouse her. Finally, she took one last rattled breath and a dark mass of blood oozed out of the corner of her mouth.

Instinctively, I cleansed it with a tissue.

As my father began to call wildly for his wife, I realized that at last, he no longer was in denial. Desperate for official confirmation, he asked me to contact my mother's surgeon, who responded to the answering service message with instructions to alert the cemetery.

With that accomplished, I said I needed to inform Uncle Mickey.

Instantly, my father sprung from his seated position on the bed.

As he lifted his walker over his head as if to crash it down on me and screamed wildly, it took all my strength to subdue him before he went limp and fell back on the bed.

From that moment on, I knew our relationship had forever changed.

Getting There

Although I might try to placate his desires as much as possible and continue to seek his counsel, the fate of my eighty-two-year-old father rested solely in my hands.

LEADING EDGE

(1990-1993)

some metal-tempered engine on an alien, distant shore
– B. Springsteen

Late on a Wednesday afternoon in October 1990, Gloria and I jumped into the cab of a twenty-four-foot rental van to begin the two-day, 1,050-mile trek to southern California. Days earlier, we had hosted a memorial reading of my mother's poetry on the front patio of our house. Now we were on the way to Mission Viejo to transfer my parents' household, place their 1989 Chrysler sedan on a towing rig, and put my widowed father on a plane to Portland, where my brother would see to his needs until our return.

POOR VS. WORSE

I had secured an airy two-room corner suite for my father on the lower level of the semi-autonomous wing of southwest Portland's Robison Jewish Home. After using funds from the family trust to convert the inaccessible bathtub into a shower and negotiating with Medicare for a power wheelchair for access to the dining room, we moved my father's possessions into the unit a few days after returning to Portland. The idea was to personalize the setting with a few pieces of the Mission Viejo furniture, several paintings, and the entire inventory of my parents' photographs, classical music cassettes, and writings.

Once my father settled in, I made a habit of swinging by the Robison Home on Tuesday and Thursday afternoons and once or twice on weekends. Parked in full view of the cafeteria, the Chrysler proved handy for lunch dates at Portland's best Jewish deli and a Lebanese restaurant in the city center where the *falafel* recalled my father's memories of Jerusalem's Arab quarter. We also drove around town to find his brand of cereal, locate typing supplies, or visit the public library. To sustain his interest in the world, I used these occasions to pass on the details of my teaching, political interests, and professional activity, including hopes of exerting influence in my scholarly field.

Curiously, the time spent with my father hardly interfered with my personal agenda. First, I met the deadline for a review of a book for the *Journal of American Ethnic History* that emphasized the role of moral reform in 1920s' Klan activity in industrial Ohio. Then I agreed to join David Milholland's Pantheon group for a second reading of John Dos Passos's tribute to John Reed. In collaboration with Walt Curtis and Brian Booth, Milholland had prevailed upon Mayor Bud Clark to issue a proclamation christening our motley crew of literati and activists as the Oregon Cultural Heritage Commission. With a grant from Reed's fellow Harvard graduate Corliss Lamont, the OCHC initiated plans to erect the nation's first memorial to the author of *Ten Days That Shook the World*.

Just about the time my father settled in at the Robison Home, the furor over Iraq's invasion of its oil-rich neighbor Kuwait reached fever pitch. As I struggled to come to terms with the situation, I realized how my mother's battle with cancer and the necessity of placing my father in a care facility had influenced my political sensibilities. Having compromised expectations and dealt in a realistic fashion with my parents' needs, I found myself increasingly inclined toward the anti-utopian impulse that often lingered in my thinking. This involved the realization that not all problems were capable of completely positive outcomes. In fact, choices between "good" and "bad" seemed to occur far more rarely than those pitting "poor" options versus "worse" ones.

Disturbed by the antiwar movement's reflexive opposition to *any* use of force, I published an opinion piece in the *Vanguard* called "No 'Good' Choices in Gulf." Saddam Hussein's Iraq, I said, had challenged principles of international order and standards of civility that kept the world from sinking into barbarism and chaos. Dictators who saw no legitimacy in national boundaries, I warned, gave little respect to anything else.

"Saddam merges cries for holy war and social revolution with a pat on the head and a taste for genocide," I wrote in reference to Hussein's use of lethal chemical weapons against Iraqi Shiites and Kurds in the 1980s and his rhetorical espousal of Arab nationalism.

Contesting the Left's view of the crisis, I insisted that U.S. imperialism was not the issue.

"There are no 'good' choices ahead in the Middle East," I pleaded, "but choices must be made."

PARRICIDE RECONSIDERED

As the United States moved toward confrontation with Iraq early in 1991, I returned to the pages of the *Vanguard* with "An Open Letter to Chairman Arafat."

Since Saddam had stated that talks for withdrawal from Kuwait must embrace the future of the Palestinians, I declared, PLO Chair Yasir Arafat should ask the United States and the European community for an understanding in support of a Palestinian state. In return, Arafat would convince the Iraqi leader to bring his troops home and the Arab states would extend formal recognition to Israel. The Palestinian cause might give Saddam the reason he needed to extricate himself from a difficult situation. If not, Arafat could remind him that the Arab masses looked to Palestine as a symbol of regional aspiration and expected their leaders to be of help.

One of the few lessons of history, I reasoned, was that "those who cling to sterile ideology and rhetoric rarely survive to become players of substance."

Palestinians would achieve their state, I argued, only when the international community became convinced it was essential to the stability of the world and Israel saw it as no threat.

A week after the article appeared, I was one of only two voices defending military action against Iraq when I served on a University of Portland panel organized by the Catholic Archdiocese on the moral dimensions of the Persian Gulf crisis. Days later, U.S. forces began bombing Baghdad, prompting Saddam to unleash a flurry of

Scud missiles into Israeli territory. Although the attacks did minor damage, they terrorized Israel's population and reinforced the notion among people like my father that radical Arabs sought the destruction of the Jewish state.

As press accounts indicated substantial Palestinian support for the Iraqi cause, I expanded upon the themes of the *Vanguard* piece at a session of PSU's International Studies Colloquium, sending copies, as usual, to an extensive mailing list. My talk compared the sterile rigidity of anti-Zionism to Cold War anticommunism. The Arab masses, I contended, had undermined their own interests by buying into "the blank rhetoric" of a militaristic Saddam. I blamed Arafat for dragging legitimate Palestinian aspirations for self-determination into global power politics instead of making direct appeals for peace to the Israeli people.

The failure of the Palestinian movement, I argued, lay in its inability to comprehend that the average Israeli wanted security, not conflict. Palestinians had turned to Saddam out of despair and powerlessness, I acknowledged, but in the end, he would leave them even more desperate and powerless.

On February 24, 1991, the same day a consortium of U.S., Saudi, Egyptian, Syrian, and other ground forces moved into Iraq, I appeared at an outdoor teach-in at Portland's Lewis and Clark College. Exasperated by the antiwar movement's refusal to acknowledge there could be legitimate grounds for *any* U.S. military action, even in a coalition with Arab states, I castigated Vietnam-era peace crusaders for recycling old rhetoric without regard to present circumstances.

This proved to be too much for an old friend in the audience, a Vietnam veteran, peace activist, and fellow musician who interrupted my remarks by yelling that "professors" like me had no idea "what they were talking about."

Incensed at this brand of anti-intellectualism, I shouted back that it was time "to get over" Vietnam.

Then I lunged forward from the microphone with a colorfully articulated assertion that nobody would intimidate me from saying what I thought.

Taken aback, my fellow panelist, the gentle and cerebral Lebanese-born PSU political scientist and Middle East specialist John Damis, looked on in complete amazement.

Three nights later, the atmosphere seemed more relaxed when I made a guest appearance on the commercial radio talk show that Joe Uris now hosted. Joe and I engaged in animated but friendly banter about whether the war concerned control of Persian Gulf oil and about the potential threat of U.S. fascism. Then a bulletin came over the wire that President George H. W. Bush had issued a coalition cease-fire as the Iraqis retreated from Kuwait and would not order troops to Baghdad with prospects of an extended occupation and bloody conflict. To my surprise, Joe characterized Bush's offer as a generous one, and we no longer had much to discuss.

A few days later, I synthesized my thoughts on the matter in a *Vanguard* opinion piece entitled "Why We Fought." The war was not about freedom or democracy, resources, or hegemony, I argued. It concerned the need to prevent naked force from becoming the arbiter of nations and political loyalties, and the necessity of discouraging regional despots from harnessing ideological fanaticism and weapons of mass destruction to their own ends.

"Parricide, the murder of a nation-state," I insisted, was not negotiable.

Pointing to Saddam Hussein's dictatorship not as a guidepost to liberation of the poor but as a symptom of the repressive pathologies of post-colonial trauma, I contended that Arab peoples once again were the victims of a ruthless tyrant who constructed illusions of grandeur upon the dead bodies of their young.

Revolution had become the opiate of the intelligentsia, I asserted.

The article took particular exception to antiwar activists who confused U.S. desires for Middle East stability with conspiratorial goals of regional military superiority or mastery of resources. The United States *serviced* the international economy but did not dominate it, I suggested. American progressives needed to abandon tired scripts of "compulsive Ameriphobia," I pleaded. Citing Iraq's record of human rights abuses, I asked critics to consider the possibility that U.S. national interests might coincide with doing the right thing in particular instances.

"This was not Vietnam and it is not 1969," I scolded.

HOME

Having offended many friends by supporting the Gulf War, I felt some validation in the fall of 1991 when the Bush administration orchestrated an international conference in Madrid to encourage negotiations between Israel and its Arab neighbors. Ever since my father's arrival in Portland, I had taken a renewed interest in Jewish themes. Not long after the war ended, I addressed a conference on East European Jewry at Portland's Reed College organized by Rabbi Stampfer's Institute for Judaic Studies. "Radun: The Life of a Polish Jewish Village between the Wars" offered a historical view of the Horowitz family's ancestral home. As president of the women's auxiliary of Radun's mutual-aid society in New York in the late-1920s, my grandmother Becky had arranged for a photographer to record images of the village's Jewish homes, businesses, social institutions, religious facilities, and residents. The organization then sold the prints to New York relatives as a fundraiser for Radun's religious schools.

After my father had turned over custody of the pictures to me a few years earlier, the Texas branch of the Golub family forwarded a slightly different set of images. Their research pointed to the Radun photographs as the most extensive existing documentation of Jewish life in interwar Poland, if not all Europe. After having the pictures converted into state-of-the art slides and duplicating both sets of prints, I donated a copy of the collection to New York's YIVO Institute for Jewish Research. Meanwhile, I combined the slides with notes from an interview I had conducted with my grandmother in 1968 to present an account of the life of Radun less than a dozen years before Nazi storm troopers obliterated the village and executed nearly all its remaining 1,175 Jewish inhabitants.

My father was in the audience for the Reed College presentation. A month later, Gloria and I escorted him on a flight to Orange County. According to Jewish custom, it was time for the unveiling of my mother's gravestone at the Newport Beach cemetery plot she and my father had selected with a view of the Pacific. With Michael and a few of our parents' friends in attendance, the rabbi from the Mission Viejo temple led a brief ceremony to dedicate the simple bronze plaque marking the grave.

Appearing beneath the name of Dorothy Horowitz and the years of her lifespan, the tablet featured the inscription "MOTHER WIFE TEACHER."

Family memories easily rekindled thoughts of the Bronx. It had been eleven years since the creative writing expert at Portland State had asked us to record details of our childhood. I recalled this exercise when former Popham Avenue pal Tom Schumacher forwarded a copy of *Back in the Bronx*, a newsletter devoted to reminiscences of the 1940s, '50s, and '60s with a subscription list of sixty thousand readers. Expanding my original paragraph, I sent in a story called "Faith of a Bronx Dreamer," which the editors ran on the cover of the next issue.

My selection described several of the adult characters of our West Bronx apartment building and the street games and diversions of city life in the years after World War II.

"Thirty-five years and three thousand miles from the Bronx," I wrote, "I dream of it as if it still was my home."

"When I dream of home," the piece concluded, "I'm back in the Bronx."

Getting There

THE CROSS OF CULTURE

I found it amusing that each of my visits to the Robison Home ended with a similar ritual. First, my father would insist he did not want to take away time from my writing duties. Then he would ask when he would see me next. In truth, my professional career was taking shape. During spring break of 1991, Gloria and I flew to San Antonio to join New York social historian Ed Pessen for a session at the Popular Cultural Association on 1930s and early '40s popular music. Gloria delivered a paper on Dorothy Fields, one of the few women lyricists of the period. My presentation on Tin Pan Alley songwriters noted that romantic fantasies held particular relevance for young women leaving families and closely knit communities for clerical and retail jobs in the city. Yet the romantic marketplace could generate fears of abandonment, rejection, isolation, and loneliness. The point was that superb lyricists such as Lorenz Hart, Cole Porter, and Ira Gershwin had a particular feel for the pitfalls of emotional dependence and self-abnegation.

To illustrate a number of songs in our presentations, Ed was to deliver vocal renditions to my piano accompaniment. To our dismay, however, we discovered that the PCA provided presenters with only audiovisual aids, not musical equipment. At that point, Gloria noticed there was an unlocked grand piano in the lobby by the hotel ballroom. After wheeling the huge instrument into a gathering space, we concocted a change-of-venue sign with magic marker and the backside of a discarded poster. As conference attendees crowded the halls just before the start of the session, I sat at the grand performing a medley of tunes. We estimated the ploy doubled attendance and certainly did wonders for audience enthusiasm.

After returning from Texas, Gloria and I drove to Walla Walla, Washington, where I presented a paper on 1920s La Grande at the Pacific Northwest History meeting. Incorporating details excluded from my essay for the Shawn Lay anthology, I examined the impact of New Era market practices and consumerism on eastern Oregon's Grande Ronde Valley. By heralding its natural beauty, simple living, and economic opportunity, the region embodied the dream that moral striving and material reward could find a receptive home in the West's natural landscape. Yet ethnic diversity, economic consolidation, and consumer values threatened community stability. The contradiction surfaced in labor tensions surrounding the railroad strike of 1922, in pervasive complaints about the perceived decline of moral duty and family decorum, and in heightened anxieties about the spread of juvenile crime and liquor, gambling, and opium abuse.

Caught in the "cross of culture," La Grande's civic leaders sought material benefits for the community while trying to preserve the valley's cultural isolation and autonomy.

Lay's anthology, *The Invisible Empire in the West: Toward a New Historical Appraisal of the Ku Klux Klan of the 1920s*, finally reached print in 1992. Falling within the revisionist school of Klan scholarship, the volume pictured the Jazz Age KKK as a fraternal order and patronage machine that sought organizational respectability and political power by aligning itself with law enforcement, civic improvement, and social reform. With its emphasis on community activity and standards of personal decorum, my chapter on La Grande portrayed the way cruelty and ethnic divisiveness could co-exist with social accomplishments. I concluded that historians needed to approach the culture wars in a fair-minded fashion that enabled them to serve as forces of healing rather than as ideological partisans.

CHAIN REACTIONS

On sabbatical leave in 1991-92, I sought to apply these lessons by revising "Beyond Left and Right" to create greater distance from the work's insurgent activists. A New Jewish Agenda workshop on racism at a Northeast Portland church provided another opportunity to work out the approach I had in mind. Conducted by two telephone company employees, the meeting lent itself to statements that whites practiced vertical or hierarchical racism, while people of color exhibited a horizontal ethnocentrism among relative equals. One of the leaders explained that black people frequently felt intimidated from speaking out in gatherings of whites, an assertion that appeared to test the patience of Stew Albert, a former Yippie radical and Black Panther ally. When it came time to volunteer personal testimony on the impact of race in our lives, I asked everyone to close their eyes as I tiptoed to the piano in the corner of the social hall.

Without saying a word, I broke into a bluesy version of "Summertime." Then I explained that a Jew, George Gershwin, had written the music. African-American vocalist Billie Holiday had made the first recording of the piece, I pointed out, followed by versions by a host of black artists including Louis Armstrong, Ella Fitzgerald, Miles Davis, and Ray Charles. Acknowledging the existence of racism in popular music, I nevertheless emphasized the profound history of cultural exchange and collaboration between Jews and African-Americans.

"All the rest is talk," I concluded.

Thomas Edsall's *Chain Reaction: The Impact of Race, Rights, and Taxes on American Politics* (1991) offered further prospects for overcoming social divisions. Like the perspective advanced by Mike Passi and the early work of Michael Novak, Edsall's book offered a context for the culture war between traditionalists and progressives. The author began by tying the effectiveness of the Republican Party to a top-down coalition that fused the interests of economic elites and the less affluent. Singling out European ethnics in the urban Northeast and Middle West and poor and working-class white Southerners, Edsall outlined a mindset that saw government taking more than it gave. The Republican Party had convinced these Americans, he suggested, that welfare amounted to a protectionist system that rewarded failure by extracting wealth from those who worked to benefit those who did not.

As a result, asserted Edsall, the American political system seemed tilted toward entitlement recipients over taxpayers, social preferences over meritocracy, the public sector over private activity, jobless Americans over working people, and the needs of beneficiaries over the costs of federal intervention. The tragedy was that liberals had failed to realize that social programs required a distribution of resources among the non-affluent, Edsall contended. Defending minority rights against the majority fed a form of antidemocratic elitism, he warned, that threatened the Democratic Party's fifty-year bond with the working class.

As the presidential candidacy of independent H. Ross Perot accelerated in the spring of 1992, I mailed out a two-page synopsis of *Chain Reaction* to a list of friends. Edsall offered a way of explaining tax revolts, the rise of "Reagan Democrats," Republican electoral majorities among youth, anti-incumbency, the fervor for term limits, and growing distaste for government budget deficits. An *inside* critic of liberal strategy, Edsall wanted progressives to unite behind a refashioned insurgency based on common values of equal opportunity. Political parties that did not relate to the needs of working Americans and the lower middle class, he warned, would find themselves permanently marginalized. In a state such as Oregon with a tradition of independent enterprise and anti-institutional values, these lessons seemed particularly apt.

VILLAINS AND VICTIMS

Given my reading of the 1920s Ku Klux Klan and the serious consideration I gave to critics of liberal social programs, it was not easy to maintain legitimacy within the progressive community. My namesake, David J. Horowitz, whom Stew and Judy Albert liked to call my "evil twin," made this even more problematic. During the spring of 1991, *Oregonian* columnist Steve Duin reported that Horowitz had appeared in Portland to decry affirmative action and declare that white racism no longer remained an American problem. Enraged by the Bay Area Left's refusal to come to terms with several atrocities he attributed to the Oakland Black Panthers in the 1970s, Horowitz, the former activist and editor of radical *Ramparts*, had drifted to the conservative cause and Ronald Reagan Republicanism. By the 1990s, he had become a vociferous critic of anti-

Vietnam War dissent, civil rights campaigns, government threats to the free market, and academic liberalism.

Following Duin's column, I learned that PSU Black Studies Chair Darrell Millner had told his students I was the source of Horowitz's comments on affirmative action, a mistake he quickly corrected along with a personal apology. I also prevailed upon Duin to set the record straight, although he could not help noting I had "taken a little heat in the local theater of the politically correct." Then Portland State's Conservative Alliance brought Horowitz to campus in the fall of 1992 to support Measure 9, a ballot measure advanced by the evangelical Oregon Citizens Alliance (OCA) that limited antidiscrimination laws protecting gays and lesbians and denounced the gay lifestyle. In a preemptive strike, I sent a disclaimer to the *Vanguard*.

"I would be terribly saddened," I stated, "to have my name associated with the desecration of Oregon's tradition of individual liberty that is embodied in Measure 9's requirement that the state adopt an official standard of 'Christian' morality and family life."

Horowitz did tell the PSU audience he did not approve of statutory language denouncing anyone's way of life. Nevertheless, he persisted in opposing "special rights" for gays, allowing me to feel justified for my letter's description of his "hysterical attacks" as the work of a "born-again" reactionary.

During the spring of 1993, I had an opportunity to expand my thoughts on the Oregon Citizens Alliance. As a commentator on a paper Eckard Toy presented to the Pacific Northwest History Conference on the use of sexual imagery in conservative movements, I stressed the populist subtext to campaigns against Freemasons, Roman Catholics, Asian immigrants, and urban cosmopolitans. When it came to the OCA, I acknowledged the importance Toy placed on economic dislocations in Oregon's timber and agriculture industries. Yet I noted that the organization's real targets – homosexual and abortion rights, sex education, and relativist social mores – seemed more concerned with cultural politics.

Conservative Christian evangelicals, I suggested, seemed to tie homosexuality to the perceived decadence of urban elites. In this sense, gay "promiscuity" was a convenient scapegoat for those who feared losing control over the erosion of life-defining values and personal discipline. Coining what seemed to be a new term, I referred to the OCA's moralistic orientation as "value-centric": an approach focused more on family cohesion and traditional social values than the racist and sexist goals liberals normally attributed to the group.

Emotional debates over sexual politics, I contended, actually represented philosophic fissures over the boundaries of life, death, social obligation, and meaning and involved disputes as to who had the power to set them. I stressed that the polarizing nature of the dialogue made it almost impossible to resolve. Nevertheless, I thought that critics of traditionalist views should appreciate that those resorting to sexual imagery were probably more powerless than powerful. Social theorists and progressives, I concluded, needed to cease talking about villains and victims and adopt a more empathetic approach to perceived adversaries.

BEHIND CLOSED DOORS

The challenge of dealing with controversial groups such as the 1920s Klan, World War II noninterventionists, civil rights opponents, and evangelical Christians influenced my view of professional history. After publishing "The Loneliness of the Synthetic Historian," I had agreed to resume teaching Historiography, later renamed Historical Imagination, for a term every two years. Assigning Peter Novick's *That Noble Dream: The "Objectivity Question" and the American Historical Profession* (1988), I became so enthusiastic about the author's account of the discipline's checkered search for scientific prestige and legitimacy that I urged PSU's Friends of History support group to bring him to campus for its endowed lecture in 1992.

Novick was one of many scholars to call attention to the emerging fields of discourse theory and deconstruction of texts. Although initially taken with these approaches at the Toronto Popular Culture Conference, I had a good deal of sympathy for traditionalists who insisted that by de-emphasizing the use of evidence, the new intellectual history seemed to be at war with reason itself. Certainly, the jargon-filled methodologies and treatises associated with textual analysis seemed better at condemning existing historical practices than creating lasting work of their own. Beyond that, multicultural orientations seemed to privilege the perspectives of racial, gender, and sexual minorities with little reference to social class or a fuller context.

When I expressed concern over these issues in a private conversation, Novick seemed sympathetic but had no answers. Part of my discomfort with the political correctness less-generous critics attributed to academia had to do with developments at Portland State. After meeting newly appointed President Judith Ramaley at a faculty breakfast in 1990, I had suggested that university researchers should explore the economic consequences of diverse state tax scenarios for potential impact on higher education budgets. A year later, I received such a proposal from a public policy group and forwarded it to Ramaley with a note suggesting that the survival of our institution conceivably rested on speaking to the needs of ordinary taxpayers. Yet such an approach appeared to be far from the focus of the new PSU administration.

By 1993, Ramaley was calling for a new University Studies program to replace the general education elective system. As state-imposed cuts threatened Portland State at the same time, I produced a *Vanguard* opinion piece adopting a populist critique of higher education trends. I began by complaining of the bloated salaries and cronyism of university administrators who seemed "to metastasize like condominiums on a California hillside." Then I noted how buzzwords including "process," "multidisciplinary dialogue," and "cultural diversity" were filling the halls as desperate faculty sought to find the mantra to save their programs and jobs. I compared higher education's articulation of grand organizational missions with a contemporary management pathology that substituted rhetorical compulsions for substantive thinking.

"We may be faced with educational institutions that produce smug illiterates merely capable of aping socially approved prattle and postures," I protested.

Programs such as University Studies, I argued, seemed only to validate the widely held perception that universities sought to impose the social fixes and values of the professional elite. The legislature needed to hear from faculty and staff in the educational trenches instead of those who spent their time in conference rooms, I stressed, and hold administrators accountable for their productivity. I pleaded for political leaders to provide support for public education and other services by enacting a genuine graduated income tax.

True to form, I sent copies of the piece to the local media. Seizing on my reference to administrative salaries, one of the television stations put me at the top of the five o'clock evening news. Without the full context of the critique, however, my remarks may have seemed mean-spirited: two or three colleagues who served as part-time administrators did not talk to me for months. Yet I received several notes of support, including a handwritten note from author Ursula Le Guin, whose husband Charles had recently retired from our department.

Everything "needed saying," exclaimed Ursula, and was "what so many professors say – to each other – behind closed doors."

SALAL

(1993-1999)

and I think it's going to rain
– R. Newman

A BRIGHT SATURDAY MORNING IN MAY 1993 FOUND GLORIA AND me heading for the Coast. The day before, Peter Carroll had delivered a Portland State guest lecture on his new book on the Abraham Lincoln Battalion – the three thousand American volunteers who had fought a losing battle against the fascist uprising led by General Francisco Franco in the Spanish Civil War of the late 1930s. At the request of Peter's partner, Jeanette Ferrary, the biographer of food writer and essayist M. F. K. Fisher, we were on the way to the coastal town of Bay City to see one of Fisher's daughters. When we found the appointed address, a cryptic note on the front door led us to the other end of the business strip and Art Space, a storefront gallery and café.

A SPLASH OF RED

Settling in for lunch, we met the proprietors, Trisha and Craig Kauffman, who had converted the former meat market into its present form four years earlier. When I mentioned Peter's book, Trisha nodded and said she had something that might interest us. Moving to the next room, she pulled out a drawer from a huge wooden cabinet and gestured toward a pile of unframed watercolors and gouache paintings. The artists were Arthur and Albert Runquist, she explained – two brothers from the Pacific Northwest whose work spanned the period between the 1930s and late-'60s. Immediately, our eyes focused on a picture that at first glance seemed to depict a mature woman entering a sedan as a man stood by with an infant in his arms.

That was no baby, interrupted Gloria.

It was a sailor holding an American flag for a World War II Gold Star Mother.

Getting There

Trisha revealed that Arthur Runquist, the artist responsible for the image, was a communist and labor movement supporter who had served as a welder and crew supervisor in Vancouver, Washington's wartime shipyards. As we sifted our way through scores of modestly sized representations of dry dock workers, the Portland waterfront, logging operations, and coastal scenes, we marveled at the richness of these once hidden treasures. Accordingly, when Gloria and I returned to Art Space for a fall exhibit, I placed a down payment on the Gold Star painting as well as one of shipyard welders and another of Portland's Broadway Bridge, each accented with frivolous splashes of red.

GOOD-FAITH EFFORT

Amid my newly discovered enthusiasm for "people's art," the Middle East returned to the center of events. Back in January 1990, New Jewish Agenda's Stew Albert and I had placed an ad in Portland's *Jewish Review* co-signed by seventeen local Jewish professional, academic, and business figures. The statement reiterated the relevance of a two-state solution to the Israeli-Palestinian conflict to both Israel's moral legitimacy and long-range interests.

"AMIDST GLOBAL UPHEAVAL AND RISK WHO WILL SPEAK FOR ISRAEL?" we asked.

In November 1992, I published an *Oregonian* opinion piece pleading for U.S. leadership in the peace process.

Less than a year later, PLO Leader Yasir Arafat, Israeli Prime Minister Yitzhak Rabin, and President Bill Clinton appeared on the White House lawn to shake hands in anticipation of a comprehensive settlement within five years. Moved by the historic gesture, Stew and I placed a second ad in the *Jewish Review* supporting the far-sighted approach of the Rabin government. Well-aware of my father's skepticism about peace between the two peoples, I clung to the hope that the future would prove him wrong, if only to complete the reconciliation with my sole surviving parent. Besides, if I were to honor his wish that I never be ashamed of being a Jew, I needed to see a good-faith effort at a Middle East accord.

CHOOSING LIFE

Although my father had little faith in politics, he managed to turn his life around.

Several months after arriving at Robison, he had suffered a bad fall, prompting transfer to a room off the main foyer of the nursing wing. Suffering from chronic arthritis, painful vascular and circulatory problems, swollen ankles, skin lesions, and bouts of melancholy, he nevertheless responded to the efforts of Laura Engle, a young volunteer who ran the Robison poetry group. Within months, he composed a short story for a contest run by New York's Jewish Association for Services for the Aged. His fourth place entry, "Choose Life," described a depressed elderly widower who turns the page of a prayer book for a palsied fellow worshipper and discovers he is still of use to another being. The story ultimately elicited a write-up in the *Jewish Review* and publication in a HarperCollins anthology of contest winners. Laura and I even arranged for my father to read the selection at an event at Portland's Broadway Books.

A second entry – a description of my parents' first meeting and my mother's fight with cancer – garnered another fourth-place finish in 1994. Meanwhile, "The Party," a sardonic poem about a cocktail reception for seniors, was a Judges' Choice Winner at a writing festival for the aged held at Eugene, Oregon's Performing Arts Center. My father's essay on the importance of autonomy to the elderly, moreover, received recognition at a statewide conference of long-term care professionals and became the focus of another *Jewish Review* feature.

"If I didn't have writing to do, I don't know what I would do," my father told the reporter. "What else is there?"

Getting There

TRIBUTE

When Gloria and I returned from a second cross-country baseball and family reunion trip in August 1994, I discovered that the University of Illinois Press had forwarded a contract for "Beyond Left and Right." My father and Laura Engle had a second surprise: they were well on their way to assembling a collection of the poetry of Robison's star writer for sale as a fundraiser for the facility. Days after returning from a week's hospitalization due to another fall, my father reviewed the galleys. From there, he moved on to hosting a series of organizational meetings to coordinate a book-release party and an appropriate marketing strategy.

Final plans, however, soon took a backseat to the increasing toll of my father's physical ailments. As the pain and discomfort intensified during October, the Robison physician increased morphine allotments, precipitating further bodily deterioration. By the last week of the month, my father was bed-ridden, no longer eating, and gradually shutting down.

As Michael, Gloria, and I kept a bedside vigil one afternoon, I sought to ensure my father's comfort by applying a wet rag to moisten his dry mouth. Under the impression that I was forcing him to take nourishment, he lashed out.

"What do you think is going on here?" he sputtered with unmistakable annoyance.

That was the last thing my father ever said to me.

At the burial service in Newport Beach three days later, I read two of his poems.

"Final Sleep" celebrated liberation from pain.

"Two on the Aisle" recalled the day my father had selected twin cemetery plots as if they were choice seats for a Broadway opening.

The facility's staffers and I now scheduled a combined memorial service and book release party for late November. To ensure Robison the full benefit of sales, Michael and I agreed to underwrite the anthology's entire production costs. More than a hundred people showed up for the Sunday afternoon event. A printed program included family photographs, a brief biography, and the list of selected poems, readers, and speakers. For the finale, Michael offered a spirited vocal rendition of "Chicken Dinnah!" to my piano accompaniment.

"There's nothin' better than the good things!" – the signature line of the song – appeared beneath the author's biography.

The Newport Beach gravestone would feature the tribute "FATHER HUSBAND LYRICIST."

MEMORY

Using a portion of our inheritance, Michael and I paid homage to our parents with a five thousand dollar contribution to the Oregon Cultural Heritage Commission. At the behest of Walt Curtis, OCHC had postponed plans for a John Reed memorial in favor of honoring 1920s poet Hazel Hall. Confined to a wheelchair after a childhood bout with scarlet fever, Hall had lived with her mother and librarian sister in Northwest Portland. To supplement their income, Hazel did embroidery and needlework for the matrons of the West Hills, a task she often referenced in tightly constructed and unsentimental verse. Hall died at age thirty-eight on Mother's Day, 1924. When Walt discovered that a Florida couple had bought her former home, OCHC began making plans for a Hazel Hall Poetry Garden on an adjoining strip of vacant property.

To build support for the effort, the organization assembled a reading by local literary and media personalities under the title, "The Stars Come Out for Hazel," as well as a symposium that included scenes from *Monograms*, a new play about the poet by Portland dramatist Sue Mach. Nevertheless, modest donations from Oregon's literati could not begin to meet the project's estimated twelve thousand dollar price tag. Once my brother and I made our pledge, Brian Booth agreed to supplement the amount from his family foundation, and OCHC President David Milholland solicited a stipend from the Collins Foundation to put us over the top.

Milholland now commissioned graphic designer John Laursen to install three granite tablets inscribed with samples of Hazel's poetry and a biographical plaque with a portrait rendered by graphic artist Stephen Leflar. When we dedicated the garden in a Mother's Day ceremony in 1995, I told the crowd my brother and I saw the project as a way to acknowledge our parents' aspirations as lifetime writers. Beyond that, the installation represented a connection to Portland's past and the significance of creative expression to shared cultural memory.

BOTH SIDES NOW

During the same month, I joined a political commemoration. Jazz vocalist Dory Hylton recently had completed a University of Oregon communications dissertation on the Portland State strike of 1970. With the twenty-fifth anniversary of the protest at hand, Dory gathered a committee to plan a retrospective. Familiar with academic conferences, I expedited the process by setting up a series of discussion panels. Assigning myself the task of providing a historical perspective, I looked forward to reconciling my personal experiences with the growing body of work on populist political culture. To clarify my thinking, I cobbled together an opinion piece.

Published in *The Oregonian* as "Vietnam War Tore Nation Along Lines Still Unhealed," the article described the way the conflict had produced a paralyzing triangular gridlock among protesters, the American public, and the federal government. Although antiwar dissidents like me stood for moral condemnation of a pointless war that targeted innocent civilians, I argued, our toleration of disruptive tactics and disrespect for authority led many Americans to dismiss us as self-indulgent and privileged children symptomatic of the country's decline.

My attempt to create some distance from antiwar and counterculture radicalism had something to do with Gloria's teasing about becoming a 1960s "leftover." Anxious that my students not dismiss me as a living dinosaur, I long ago had discarded long hair for a buzz cut. My slant on protest heroics certainly did not please many friends. At the same time, several Vietnam veterans in attendance were eager to establish ties with former adversaries in the antiwar movement. Approached by Jack Estes of the Fallen Warriors Foundation, a veterans' support organization with no position on the merits of the war, I agreed to participate in the group's annual reading of the names of Oregonians killed or missing in Vietnam, the first time the Fallen Warriors had asked a war opponent to participate in the ritual.

Two days after publication of my opinion piece, I mounted a makeshift Park Blocks stage. Aware of the poignancy of the moment, I managed to gather my wits by reminding myself this was not about me and proceeded to recite my portion of the list without a hitch.

That Friday evening, Dory, former student strike leader Cathy (Wood) Wyrick, Gloria, and I represented the protest contingent at an on-campus presentation of Vietnam War stories and memories staged by the Fallen Warriors. The program included a heartfelt reminiscence by *Oregonian* columnist Margie Boulé, who, as a teenager, had sung the national anthem at military funerals in her hometown. It was a complete shock, then, to read Margie's column contrast the solemn gathering of veterans in the auditorium with revelers in the outer hall she described as eating, drinking, and reminiscing about the violent anti-Vietnam demonstrations of 1970.

Cathy Wyrick immediately sent a protest to the paper's ombudsman. The party Margie described had been a reception for the PSU Alumni Association. Our conference was not a celebration, Cathy emphasized, but a retrospective designed to begin a dialogue in the interests of reconciliation. It had included personal testimonials from former soldiers, cooperative endeavors such as a Feast for Peace, and the reading of names from the Oregon war memorial. Finally, Cathy could not resist calling attention to the fact that the Park Blocks incident of 1970 involved the police beating up peaceful protesters, not the other way around.

The Oregonian ultimately elicited a lukewarm apology from its columnist, whose emotional identification with the story had led her to mistake a high-powered cocktail party of fundraisers and patrons with an effort to make sense of a troubled past. Having struggled with the burden of presenting a balanced assessment of the Vietnam era and having reached moments of solidarity with a few of its former soldiers, I felt genuinely deflated at becoming the target of a grievous misrepresentation, no matter how heartfelt its origin. The incident certainly illustrated the limitations of personal journalism. It also reiterated the historian's mandate that all interpretations of experience relate to established fact.

PAYBACK

Although I was co-author of a textbook, whose revised edition I had renamed *On the Edge,* and was well on the way to preparing "Beyond Left and Right" for publication, my brother and Gloria were making more news on the publishing front than I was. After editing a Bay Area media placement newsletter for public relations operatives, Michael had ushered a second novel into print. Published in 1994 by Times Eagle Books with illustrations by Henk Pander, V. O. Blum's *Sunbelt Stories* offered three narratives. One described a female cancer victim's discovery of an Albanian sex cure; a second depicted a Florida baby farm; and a third presented a Pacific humpback whale's plea for accommodation with the predatory human species.

One year later, Gloria succeeded in having a historical monograph printed. With David Johnson's encouragement, she had entered the PSU history graduate program and earned a master's degree. Her thesis described Portland's Lola Greene Baldwin. Certified as a detective in 1908, Baldwin became the nation's first municipally appointed female police officer and a pioneering advocate of women's protective work, juvenile courts, and community policing. Gloria's scholarship demonstrated the tension between Baldwin's Victorian morality and her role as a Progressive-era professional.

At David's initiative, Oregon State University Press published an expanded version of the thesis under the title *Municipal Mother*. To celebrate the event, I organized an outdoor book signing at our house. Several weeks later, Gloria presented a reading of some of Baldwin's police reports at Broadway Books.

Gloria liked to remind me it was hard to be a populist among the people. The taunt came back to haunt me as the televised trial of O. J. Simpson concluded in October 1995. In an opinion piece in the *Vanguard* earlier in the year, I had criticized the defense for making no distinction between the former athlete and media personality's public image and his private persona shaped by a record of spousal abuse. Was the justice system capable of holding people accountable for crimes when they could hire the best defenders money could buy? I asked. Would the predominantly African-American jury render a decision on a reasonable reading of the evidence?

When the vote for acquittal ignored DNA findings, the blood rushed to my head amid a wave of nausea. As a historian well-aware of the racial parameters of American criminal justice, I nevertheless clung to the ideal of applying intelligence and empirical evidence to matters of dispute. After all, the Israeli-Palestinian conflict suggested that those with less power needed a degree of moral legitimacy to level the playing field. If, as my brother suggested, the jury's decision represented "payback" for aggrieved African-Americans, where was the moral center in this sad affair? Moments after the trial ended, I told Gloria we needed to get to the Coast.

HEMLOCK RIDGE

As my Bronx family had devoted each weekend of the early 1950s to the search for a suburban home, I took to designing my own floor plans. I continued to have an interest in architecture when, seeking to maintain a vestige of morale during my mother's illness, I sat at the Mission Viejo kitchen table during Christmas break of 1989 and sketched out the plan for a fantasy beach getaway. Several months later, Gloria and I found ourselves meandering around the

Oregon Coast and spotted a real estate agent's sign on a picturesque lot. The broker at the Cannon Beach office turned out to be a former hippie acquaintance from my time at the Coast in the early 1970s. Dave urged us to check out two parcels in Arch Cape, four miles south.

"David, you could own this!" Gloria exclaimed as we eyed the old growth timber set among wild underbrush and an imposing array of full-grown cedar, hemlock, and spruce.

It took me well over a year to process the idea of purchasing coastal property. After arranging for a five thousand dollar grant from the family trust, nevertheless, I felt comfortable in making an offer of $22,500. Fortunately, the feuding cousins who had inherited the parcel in question were eager to dispose of the lot and quickly accepted. In October 1991, I took title to an acre-plus of undeveloped hillside with a glimpse of the Pacific Ocean a quarter-mile away.

Gloria always said I got the last bargain on the Coast.

My father had not been so sure. He worried that as an academic with no experience in business, I had no idea how construction and development costs could multiply.

"Do me a favor," he begged. "Wait 'til I'm gone before you start building."

Since I would have to rely on my share of the family inheritance to finance any project, I had no problem honoring the request. Two months after my father died, I gave a revised plan of the two-bedroom house I had designed in Mission Viejo to Bob Cerelli, an Arch Cape contractor highly recommended by a Portland State colleague with a second home two doors from Cerelli's residence. Once Bob's wife Sandy created a professional blueprint, Cerelli and partner John Mersereau arranged to clear the site, extend the existing road to the property, and lay down a serpentine rock-base access way past two huge spruces.

The main obstacle to proceeding was a temporary Arch Cape moratorium on hookups to the city's water supply system. When

Cerelli recommended taking a chance on a well, Gloria chose a site at the rear of the property along a crevice where moisture-dependent alder trees grew – a potential indication, she said, of underground springs. After less than an hour of drilling, the well produced a fifty-five gallon a minute flow a mere forty-five feet below the surface. At Gloria's initiative, we positioned the footprint of the house at the highest point of the property. Construction began in April. Over the next six months, I covered the project's expenses, including the costs of extending sewer and utility lines, on a "time and materials" basis. By Halloween of 1995, the house was ready for occupation.

The exterior of the finely crafted twelve hundred square foot structure was marked by board-and-batten cedar siding, a red metal roof, ample wood-framed windows with matching red trim, and a wraparound deck facing the forest below. The interior featured tongue-and-groove cedar paneling, larch flooring, a corner wood-stove set in river rock, and an insulated half-wall between the kitchen and living room to accommodate my childhood piano. With two bedrooms, one and a half baths, and a dining alcove looking out to the forest, the layout met all our needs.

Gloria and I would spend nearly every weekend, most holidays, and a good portion of each summer at Arch Cape. Weather permitting, we devoted an hour a day to walks on the beach, an eight-minute stroll from "Hemlock Ridge." Gloria often volunteered lessons on the ancient basalt formations produced by eastern Oregon lava flows and the sandstone cliffs and preserved tree roots surviving the last shift of the Pacific tectonic plates some three hundred years earlier. Striding on the sands, glancing inland at the three thousand foot peaks of the Coast Range, and taking in the sea's expanse, we loved to engage in a shared ritual.

"It's gorgeous here," one of us would exclaim.

"How did they ever let us in?" the other would reply.

Getting There

AS TIME GOES BY

Walt Curtis liked to avoid awkward allusions to "partners" and "significant others" by referring to live-in couples as "co-vivants." Whatever the romantic quality of the term, Gloria continued to hint at an interest in marriage. Reluctant to rehash the drama of an interfaith union while my father was alive, I usually responded with the euphemistic assurance that we could consider our future once the Arch Cape house was complete. Following a Christmas visit back East, where Gloria had to sleep on her mother's couch, however, the subject took on new intensity. Not long after our return, we began planning for a June 1996 wedding at the Coast.

"On the deck, in the forest, by the sea," the invitation read.

At 3 p.m. on the appointed Sunday, Michael Brewin marked the start of the ceremony with an acoustic guitar rendering of George Harrison's "Here Comes the Sun." With former mayor of Cannon Beach Herb Schwab officiating and poet Tim Barnes serving as facilitator, the proceedings moved on to an even ten readings and recitations by family and friends. The event concluded with Dory Hylton leading the crowd of 170 people in a boisterous version of "As Time Goes By" and a solo sax belting out "The Beer Barrel Polka," a favorite of Gloria's mother. The crew at Art Space catered the salmon and salad repast that followed.

TESTAMENT

As requested, Tim Barnes honored the memory of Gloria's father and my parents while noting that neither Gloria's mother nor my Uncle Mickey were able to make the trip. Since his move to Miami, Mickey had visited Portland on two occasions. His antiwar and farm worker sympathies completely delighted the New Jewish Agenda crowd. Back in Florida, he served brief stints as president of the Friends of the North Miami Beach Library, whose reluctance to offer sufficient support for a graduated state income tax to ensure funding for public institutions frustrated him. Despite vitriolic contempt for conservatives and a pattern of joining and leaving peace groups and organizations at whim, Mickey sustained the remnants of a political faith.

"Even if doomed to failure," he wrote, "we must keep up the fight or there is no purpose to living."

Mickey was particularly proud of helping Democrat Bill Clinton win Florida in 1996 in the race for his second term as president. Less than three weeks after the election and only days after my brother arrived in the South Pacific Kingdom of Tonga as a Peace Corps volunteer, however, I received a telephone call from the North Miami Beach Police. Fixing a late-night snack to satiate a craving for sugar, a result of chronic diabetes, Mickey left a sweet roll in the toaster, where it caught fire. Medics found him unconscious on the foyer floor and could not revive him. His instructions ruled out a religious ceremony. Instead, he wanted his ashes dispersed at sea.

As Mickey's attorneys began processing his modest estate, I sought for a way to create a fitting legacy. During the late 1970s, my uncle had composed a handwritten memoir on legal-size yellow tablets that covered the years between his childhood and 1945, with a postscript on his recent peace activities. The manuscript would remain in the back of my study closet until, following his death, I hired a graduate student to decipher the text, enter it on computer discs, and reproduce the contents on a laser printer. Complete with copies of *New York Times* obituaries, clippings about Mickey's latter-day activism, tributes from my brother and me, an editor's introduction, and a cover photograph of my uncle in his military uniform, "What Made Mickey Run? Episodes from the Memoirs of Milton David Levine" appeared in 1998. When former AVC colleague Bernie Bellush discovered another portion of the reminiscences the following year, I published an expanded version of the work.

My uncle had taught me everything I knew about politics in the first two decades of my life, and half of what I had learned since, I acknowledged in the editor's tribute. He had shown me that humor was the greatest form of wisdom, communication, and persuasion and that politics was the art of dealing with people. From his example, I noted, I came to appreciate that you had to like and trust human beings before you could do anything for humanity. Positive change came in small steps, but it sometimes took real courage to take them. Mickey Levine had helped me see that most people wanted the same things no matter where they came from or whoever they were. Then I recalled the contradiction of the Trotskyist-at-heart who wore fine suits, smoked expensive cigars, hailed New York cabs with abandon, lunched at trendy mid-town cafés, loved opera and theater, and preferred rye on the rocks.

After distributing copies to the State Historical Society of Wisconsin and the American Jewish Historical Society at Brandeis University, I offered the collection to anyone willing to donate to one of four labor, peace, and cultural organizations in Mickey's memory. When the campaign raised $1,500, I sent an additional two thousand dollars to PCUN (Pineros y Campesinos Unidos del Noroeste), the Oregon farm workers' movement, as a testament to my uncle's life of political struggle.

INSIDE THE KLAVERN

Two months after Mickey died,, the University of Illinois Press published *Beyond Left and Right: Insurgency and the Establishment*. Dedicating the book to the memory of my mother and father, I used the "two nations" quote from Dos Passos's *U.S.A.* for the frontispiece. By chronicling persistent unease with changing forms of corporate capitalism, the modern state, and hedonistic values, *Beyond Left and Right* sought to recapture a near-forgotten history. The most-central American political debates of the last one hundred years, it concluded, were not contests between liberals and conservatives but struggles over diverse forms of concentrated power. To publicize the work, Gloria and I presented a dramatized reading of excerpts from relevant correspondence, speeches, and documents before 140 people at Portland's Powell's Books.

With *Beyond Left and Right* complete, I turned to a project I had envisioned since working on the Shawn Lay anthology. I felt sure that an annotated version of the La Grande minutes would make a useful addition to the historical literature on the 1920s Ku Klux Klan. Yet efforts to interest regional presses attracted little interest. I sensed that publishers hesitated to deal with the KKK in terms that might appear morally ambiguous, arguably a case in which political correctness intimidated exploration of sensitive territory. After organizing a new class surrounding the La Grande documents, therefore, I welcomed an intervention by Louis Filler.

Given Filler's reputation as a cantankerous presence at professional conferences, I remained one of the few historians who bothered to keep up or talk with my elderly mentor. Gloria and I even detoured from one of our cross-country trips for an overnight stay in the basement of a converted Congregational church in Ovid, Michigan, that Filler shared with his third wife, two young children, several cats, and a library of thirty thousand volumes. Sometime in 1997, Filler prevailed upon Irving Louis Horowitz (no relation), editor of the sociology journal *Society*, to solicit an article from me on the 1920s Klan.

Like Filler, Horowitz had become a conservative with an "antiutopian" approach to the past. On these grounds, my work seemed to him promising. Published in the fall of 1998, "The Normality of Extremism: The Ku Klux Klan Revisited" traced the disputed history of Klan scholarship and summarized my treatment of the La Grande chapter. The essay pleaded for academics to place historical actors in the complex context their lives deserved instead of relying on stale predispositions, unsubstantiated theories, or pat stereotypes. To honor the drift of the new social history, I stressed, scholars needed to permit *all* ordinary historical actors to speak for themselves. Constructive and dysfunctional behavior often overlapped, I concluded.

By the time the *Society* article appeared, Louis Filler had died in Austin, where, after separating from his wife, he had reconciled with his progressive daughter, a community organizer. Meanwhile, I had a contract for the Klan book through a Peter Carroll connection at Southern Illinois University Press. I had rejected my department chair's offer of a free office computer because I wanted to be beyond the administration's reach, maintain my privacy, and be free of the "white noise" of distracting email. In response to publishers' demands and my brother's pleas, however, I replaced the Smith Corona with a Toshiba laptop. Although its Claris Works 1.0 format elicited widespread ridicule, computerized word processing made it incredibly easy to edit and revise. With the addition of two supplemental keyboards and monitors, I could work both in Portland and at the Coast, and I quickly completed the book project.

Dedicated to Mickey Levine, *Inside the Klavern: The Secret History of a 1920s Ku Klux Klan* (1999) included an introduction, annotated excerpts from the La Grande minutes, a conclusion, and extensive endnotes. To accent the element of secrecy, the front cover displayed a black and red image of two slightly ajar Gothic doors barely revealing a mysterious inner sanctum. The frontispiece consisted of a letter typed on Klan stationary to Oregon Governor Walter M. Pierce from chapter secretary Harold R. Fosner, a postal clerk whose commentaries provided a unique flavor to the minutes. After describing subsequent permutations of the Ku Klux Klan, the conclusion questioned attempts to see 1920s Knights as mere defenders of racial, ethnic, or gendered power. Yet it also noted how a movement espousing Christian, civic, and democratic values could polarize local communities with divisiveness and exclusivity.

When a producer for cable TV's History Channel happened to come across the galley proofs at a conference, the station flew me to New York. I was to provide brief historical background for a Sunday morning feature on the contemporary Klan. After my long struggle to publish the minutes, even the momentary spotlight amounted to a minor triumph. Later that summer, the *Chronicle of Higher Education* interviewed me by phone. Once again, I reiterated my insistence that historians had a responsibility to humanize those they studied and place their achievements as well as their deficiencies in full social and cultural context.

AS HARD AS IT'S GOING TO

Gloria and I spent the entire 1998-99 academic year on sabbatical at Arch Cape. As we confronted one fierce storm and power outage after the other, our faith that there was no such thing as a bad day at the beach received its greatest challenge. Oregon even garnered national news coverage when the lumber vessel *New Carissa* washed up on the sands of the state's southern coast, only to drift out to sea and beach itself again miles to the north.

Anxious to engage the Cannon Beach scene, we had become regular readers of Rev. Billy Hults's counterculture monthly rag, the *Upper Left Edge*. Billy and feature columnist Michael Burgess loved to portray the perennial war between distressed tourists wondering how long the wind-swept downpours of sideways rain would last and crusty locals reconciled to eternities of darkness. The front page of the *Upper Left Edge* customarily featured a pithy axiom from the wide range of literary and philosophic texts in Billy's library.

In February 1999, the month of the *New Carissa*, I received credit for the latest addition.

Drawn from observations of repeated coastal deluges and the vagaries of human existence, I had fashioned my own advice to coastal neophytes and stab at universal wisdom:

"IT'S NEVER RAINING AS HARD AS IT'S GOING TO"

PRECIPICE

(2000-2004)

all the news just repeats itself/like some forgotten dream
– J. Prine

The ninety-minute drive from the Coast seemed to take forever.

It was Monday, September 24th, 2001.

I was on my way to meet the first class of the new academic year.

Thirteen mornings earlier, the phone call had come from Bob Williams just in time for Gloria and me to scramble out of bed, turn on the television, and watch the second plane crash into the remaining tower of the New York World Trade Center.

September 11th was my father's birthday, I remembered. Then I felt a surge of anger as I thought about the city of my birth and nurture.

For days, everything seemed frozen in time.

How could I possibly lead a class? I wondered as we made our way to town. How could my students be in a place to delve into the intricacies of U.S. history?

Gradually, I got my head straight. I knew it might be hard to concentrate in a world that was out of control, I would tell them. Yet we had to continue trying to use reason to make sense of things, even when reason did not always explain what we were trying to understand.

This is what we do here, I would plead.

DECONSTRUCTING JIHAD

Using reason to come to terms with reality proved exceedingly difficult in the days after 9/11. Some progressives, I realized, were reluctant to grasp the significance or even existence of groups such as the Afghan Taliban, whose takeover of Afghanistan had facilitated Al Qaeda's attack on the United States. A telling moment came when I offered a defense of President George W. Bush's military campaign against the regime at a teach-in at Portland's Lincoln High School. To my amazement, my debating partner, a social historian from a nearby university, devoted her entire presentation to a recitation of the sins of twentieth century U.S. foreign policy. I countered that pacifist sermons on the sanctity of life or evils of imperialism did not erase the need to respond to killers who would continue slaughtering innocents until stopped.

Those who committed mayhem on a mass scale, I said, were enemies of life and reason who had greater interest in the destruction of others than their own earthly welfare.

As videotape and samples of Al Qaeda communications surfaced, I became convinced that 9/11 was not as much a prelude to a series of assaults on the United States as a single-shot recruiting poster. Its purpose, I believed, was to impress Muslims across the Middle East with the power of Al Qaeda as a force that ultimately would convert the region into a bastion of Islamic rule. Although I did not foresee further threats to U.S. territory, I had no illusions about the danger posed by fundamentalist radicals. Accordingly, I regretted the self-indulgent tendency I detected among friends and others who placed nonviolence, antimilitarism, and anti-Bush sentiment above any consideration of strategic options in an objectively dangerous world.

Partly to organize my own thoughts on these matters and partly because I believed academics needed to reach beyond the classroom, as the 2002 winter term began I organized a history department forum on the war against terrorism. To maximize give-and-take between speakers and the audience, I requested that panelists limit their presentations to six or seven minutes. Eager to capture the spontaneous feel of a teach-in and convinced that public gatherings in relatively confined spaces enhanced the dramatic effect, I arranged to bring in folding chairs so we could hold the meeting in the confined quarters of the history department lounge.

Drawing on his expertise in Constitutional history, Tim Garrison addressed the potential violations of civil liberties in the newly signed Patriot Act. In turn, North African specialist Karen Carr pointed to skepticism about U.S. motivations in the Muslim world. My comments focused on Al Qaeda as a militarized and politicized form of Islam that misused the defensive concept of *Jihad* to mount an aggressive war against all infidels. Did U.S. "crimes" such as stationing troops in Saudi Arabia, neutrality in the Muslim-Hindu dispute over Kashmir, or defense of Israel justify the anti-American hatred of some Middle Eastern governments and radicals? I inquired. Could militant Islam live in peace with the West? I wondered. Then I asked if any group of believers could inspire respect if it could not tolerate the existence of others.

From there I moved on to political theorist Noam Chomsky's description of 9/11 as a response to the moral decadence of U.S. imperialism. Chomsky's line of reasoning, I argued, resembled the desire of Al Qaeda and Christian Right fanatics in the United States to root the attack in questions of religious morality. Although the military, financial, and political targets of the atrocity comprised the institutional foundations of the West, I suggested, most Americans saw 9/11 as an attack on "the people." Beyond martyred firefighters, police, and rescue teams, I explained, World Trade Center victims included members of working-class families who served as secretaries, janitors, and food service employees, as well as stockbrokers. Indeed, many white-collar financial service personnel came from the same neighborhoods as first responders.

I now defended George Bush's war in Afghanistan as an effort to eradicate a Taliban regime fostering a global terrorist network. Military action could not solve long-range political matters, I acknowledged, but could address short-range problems and lead to eventual resolution of broader issues. Following this logic, I encouraged a strategic approach to international affairs that involved tough choices, even at the expense of cherished ideals.

At the same time, my presentation involved a caveat. Victory over the Afghan Taliban, I insisted, would not assist the struggle against terrorism if the United States did not address its foreign

Getting There

policy vulnerabilities. Prime among them was the Israeli-Palestinian conflict. U.S. support for Israel did not *create* 9/11, I conceded. Yet the perception that Americans held a bias against Arabs and Muslims made it difficult to take on Middle Eastern extremism. Following a panel I helped organize on regional peace prospects in May, I authored an *Oregonian* opinion piece on the subject. The present climate, I argued, made it impossible for Palestinians to afford any association with terrorism. Only a movement rejecting suicide bombings against Israeli citizens could compel Tel Aviv's allies in the United States to distinguish the Palestinian cause from Al Qaeda and support the creation of an independent state in the West Bank and Gaza.

THE USUAL SUSPECTS

In a world subject to terrorist atrocities, academic pursuits could appear remarkably gratuitous. To my dismay, developments within higher education did not always encourage an appreciation of our utility. By the start of the new century, I had solidified an approach to classroom teaching. Centering my courses on informal lectures, I used the "cut-and-paste" tools of glue-stick, scissors, and the department photocopier to piece together handwritten and typed presentations. Instead of assigning detailed research papers, even at the upper-division and graduate level, I preferred to solicit written essays addressed to specific questions covering lectures and required reading. I composed course outlines, assignment sheets, and exams in jargon-free and accessible prose, which I encouraged with a history style guide.

Good writing, I emphasized, was a form of personal empowerment.

Over the years, my upper-division history classes had addressed topics such as the culture conflicts of the 1920s, the anticommunist purges of the early Cold War, and the dissident social values and lifestyles of the 1960s and '70s. Aware of the significance of multicultural perspectives and recognizing the importance of human diversity, I nevertheless had acquired a sharp eye for so-called political correctness, the academic convention that placed issues of race, ethnicity, gender, and personal identity at the heart of scholarly endeavor. In fact, academia's ritualistic deference to "the usual suspects" often tested my patience.

Affirmative action was a case in point. Tom Edsall's *Chain Reaction* described resentment among white working-class families toward a race-based preferential hiring system designed to compensate for past patterns of discrimination. Dealing with the issue while preparing *Beyond Left and Right*, I had told a *Vanguard* interviewer that I supported affirmative action in academic hiring as a way of enhancing student learning through a diverse faculty. Yet I preferred to base admissions preferences on economic standing instead of ethnicity.

Similar concerns framed my views about educational content. When graduate student Tom Luby proposed to do a master's thesis on the political correctness issue, I steered him to the dispute over Portland Public Schools' adoption of a multicultural curriculum in the 1980s. At the time, Black Studies head Darrell Millner had solicited my feedback on an early outline of the plan. Acknowledging the effort's importance, I nevertheless questioned items such as the portrait of Socrates as a conveyor of pre-existing "alien" ideas. Why not stick with the assertion that African and Asian influences mixed in with European thinking to form "Western civilization," I suggested. The implication that white scholars had consciously demeaned African-American culture also concerned me. I believed the proposed guidelines had overstated their case.

Darrell thanked me for the input and agreed to make some changes. Yet I soon learned he had filed suit against the history department's Reformation specialist, Susan Karant-Nunn, who had responded to two *Oregonian* articles about curriculum proposals by Millner and Asa Hilliard, chief desegregation consultant to Portland Public Schools, with a letter to the editor. As a scholar in the humanist tradition, Susan took particular exception to Hilliard's view of history as a weapon. Given that inaccuracies and comfortable stereotypes about the past needed correction, she wrote, the District nevertheless should adopt a healthy skepticism toward the team's recommendations. History was a means of understanding other people and ourselves, she insisted. Warning against attempts to bolster the self-esteem of any individual or group by falsifying the past, Susan urged Portland administrators to follow the advice of people in a position to know whether curriculum changes brought us closer to or further from the truth.

As a historian, I knew that Karant-Nunn had repeated the discipline's credo that PhD specialists were the most reliable sources for balanced interpretations of the past and that professionally trained experts were less likely to espouse propaganda. I also sensed that while Susan had no quarrel with an education PhD such as Darrell evaluating shortcomings in teaching methods, such a background did not provide expertise in actual subject matter. At the same time, I understood the sensitivity of an African-American scholar regarding the long history of racial discrimination in academic life. I could see why Millner claimed the wording of Karant-Nunn's letter damaged his professional reputation. Discomfited over a principled dispute between two colleagues, I joined Steve Kosokoff in a futile appeal to both sides. It would take an effort by another group of PSU faculty to facilitate an out-of-court settlement during the summer of 1984.

Eight years later, racial politics re-emerged at PSU when Darrell Millner announced his retirement as Black Studies chair and replacement by Candice Goucher, the white Afro-Caribbean specialist who had moderated the Middle East debate. Threatening a boycott, a coalition of activist students insisted that the background of an ethnic studies department head should match the program's focus. In response, Steve Kosokoff and I composed a private letter to Millner in which we stated our objections to making appointments solely on grounds of group identity. In the end, Black Studies rejected the premise of the student demands, but when Candice declined the chair, Darrell agreed to a temporary term pending a national search. A year later, Candice's husband Joe Lambert, a black man from Guyana, invited Gloria and me to witness his installation as the world's first African-American Master of a racially integrated Masonic lodge.

THE NAKED EMPEROR

Once Tom Luby agreed to eliminate the editorializing that graduate students occasionally produced in early drafts, he completed a pointed account of how identity politics could distort the educational mission. The relationship between multicultural pedagogy and academic integrity soon struck closer to home. The issue concerned the University Studies program that Judith Ramaley had instituted in 1994. The reforms replaced the general education elective system by enrolling first- and second-year students in year-long inquiry courses that emphasized multicultural and multidisciplinary endeavors, group discussion, oral communication and writing skills, and awareness of ethical issues. After taking a cluster of specialized courses as juniors, students would complete a compulsory Capstone community service experience in their final year.

Having criticized University Studies in the *Vanguard* years earlier, I listened as PSU biology professor Larry Crawshaw, our new Arch Cape neighbor, passed on reports of student dissatisfaction early in 2000. Although sympathetic, I warned of the difficulty of eradicating bureaucracies once they took shape. Pleas to administrators would go nowhere, I predicted. As a scientist, however, Larry maintained faith in reasoned discourse. After conferring with faculty across the curriculum, he met with the provost (dean of faculty), who referred him to the University Studies director. Dissatisfied with the process, social scientists Barry Anderson and Lee Haggerty designed a questionnaire to gauge student reaction to the program. Yet administrators viewed the survey as biased, dismissed efforts to replace in-house evaluations as divisive, and insisted that professors lacked the management experience to take on such tasks.

The only way to make an impact, I told my enraged neighbor, was to proceed with the survey of student opinion *without* the administration and subject Portland State to outside scrutiny. Volunteering to help coordinate strategy and serve as an informal media liaison, I inaugurated the campaign with a press release. An ad hoc committee of fifteen professors with an average service to the institution of twenty-six years, it declared, had pooled $912 of their own funds to pay for two full-page notices in the campus newspaper. Beneath a headline asking students if anyone had solicited *their* opinion of University Studies, the ad reproduced the questionnaire the administration had rejected and directed students to an on-line response.

In a story entitled "University Studies Under Fire," the *Vanguard* cited my contention that Portland State's internal curriculum assessments involved questions that administrators, not students, saw as important. In reality, I contended, undergraduates repeatedly had confided to individual faculty complaints over the program's poor standards, a situation warranting fuller evaluation. Reaction soon materialized. An opinion piece by a University Studies professor claimed that members of the ad hoc committee had made defamatory comments about other instructors. The critique even characterized my statement about students sharing frustrations with sympathetic faculty as one suggesting they had expressed anger *at* University Studies professors.

Seeking to contextualize the controversy, I authored a *Vanguard* opinion piece. "University Studies: The Emperor Has No Clothes," published in May 2000, noted that each member of the ad hoc faculty committee had a strong commitment to liberal arts education and merely wanted to make the program more accountable. I had been disturbed for many years, I explained, by a nationwide trend in which university curricula institutionalized the faddish rhetoric and goals of educational administrators at the expense of undergraduate learning and common sense. I focused on the sacrifice of content and analytic ability on the altar of self-expression and emotional self-esteem, a process I saw as encouraging a therapeutic, instead of an intellectual, approach to education. These tendencies,

I asserted, infantilized students, trivialized learning, and defeated the broadening purposes of general education.

Cross-disciplinary endeavors made no sense when students lacked grounding in the scholarly fields in play, I asserted. The mantra of learning through speaking, in turn, ignored the fact that academic discourse demanded the sustained dedication of written work. I cited the vast difference between spontaneous spouting of personal opinion and the use of available evidence in reasoned interpretations and analysis. Disciplined writing, I argued, required the integration of information into thoughtful formulations that transcended the immediate preoccupations of either students or instructors. Along these lines, I contended that an obsessive emphasis on group tasking disregarded the reality that even collaborative projects in the workplace required completion of discrete assignments.

The goal of self-discovery, I continued, took no heed of the fact that high-quality general education required immersion in cultures, creative works, and modes of thought that provided potential alternatives to, not confirmations of, one's own way of life.

My commentary came down hardest on multiculturalism and social ethics. The focus on ethno-cultural entities, gender, and personal lifestyles, I argued, seemed symptomatic of an upper-middle-class and professional monoculture that ignored working-class perspectives and the values associated with tradition-minded people. If the university became a socializing agent advancing the specific agenda and worldview of one party to social conflict, I suggested, it would defeat the purpose of its mission to seek truth, no matter how contingent and subjective the quest might be. No public institution could impose the needs of the state or any class of elites and remain part of a free society. University Studies, I argued, deprived students of a broadly focused general education and threatened to convert skilled faculty into social workers, therapists, and glorified babysitters.

Portland State was in danger of becoming a finishing school for intellectually complacent, socially appropriate, political mannered ignoramuses, I concluded.

REASONED EMPATHY

When anthropology professor Tom Biolsi highlighted the importance of diversity in a *Vanguard* rebuttal, I responded by distributing a piece through the campus mail. "Inquiry Yes, Indoctrination No!" acknowledged the importance of diversity but criticized the tendency to focus on multicultural issues of race or gender at the expense of social class. The need to incorporate the perspectives of marginalized people, I suggested, did not mean soliciting personal viewpoints from individuals solely due to their membership in those groups.

It was essential, I wrote, for academics to observe the rigorous methods of their disciplines, no matter how open to challenge and revision they might be. I also agreed that an educated person should be familiar with society's ethical problems and appreciate the relationship between the privileges of some and marginalization of others. Yet I distinguished between *learning* about such conflicts and feeling pressure to *align* with any single position. Our responsibility was not to socialize people with a specific ethic, I argued, but to expose them to a diversity of perspectives and challenge them to see the way their lives linked to others. If we taught tools of reasoned empathy, I said, students could make their own informed choices.

The ad hoc committee's questionnaire ultimately elicited 286 student responses. Two-thirds indicated a preference for a general education alternative. Of the one hundred respondents who had taken courses in the program, 63 percent reported improved writing skills but only 3 percent felt they had bettered their math abilities. Meanwhile, well less than half thought they had received a sound liberal arts background or learned as much as they had in other courses.

When I compiled the survey's open-ended questions, I discovered seven negative responses for every five positive comments. Although some students found the program rewarding, a substantial number expressed a distinct sense of alienation from general education reform. Enough disaffection existed, I concluded, to begin a dialogue over converting University Studies to an optional program or reducing its impact on the undergraduate curriculum.

While the pages of the *Vanguard* continued to sizzle with new developments, my efforts as the campaign's virtual press officer began to attract off-campus coverage. At the end of May, Portland's *Willamette Week* ran a story with the observation that going public was the only way concerned faculty believed they could get the administration's attention. In a feature the following week devoted mainly to a positive profile of the capstone experience, *The Oregonian* placed the dispute in the headline and reported that critics accused University Studies of a deficiency of intellectual vigor and a politically correct agenda.

In response to my prompting, the *Chronicle of Higher Education* published a lengthy piece about Portland State in July. University Studies had come under heavy attack from dozens of top professors, it reported. Focusing on Larry Crawshaw, the story detailed faculty discontent with a watered-down curriculum that sacrificed content to process and depicted widespread impatience with the administration's unwillingness to confront the problem. Early in 2001, the forty-nine member ad hoc committee solicited a survey of faculty views that elicited ninety-nine responses. Two-thirds of the sample wanted an optional path to general education requirements. Eighty-three percent indicated that faculty should teach within their own disciplines instead of participating in inquiry courses outside their field.

Following the distribution of our report, the incipient rebellion seemed to stall. In response to a friendly challenge from history's David Johnson weeks later, I drafted my own general education reform plan. Its first year would include introductions to the humanities, social sciences, and physical sciences, followed by a second year of elective classes. Third-year undergraduates would take content-oriented inquiry courses incorporating University Studies goals. Senior capstones would take the form of an internship or practicum within each student's major. Not surprisingly, the proposal failed to spark further discussion. Despite some shuffling of administrators, University Studies has remained essentially unchanged.

HEALERS AND REFORMERS

Key elements of my critique of the general education experiment came out of preparations for a sequel to *Beyond Left and Right*. Back in 1993, I had drawn up the outlines of a book I called "A Trinity of Values: Cultural Conflict in the Age of Vietnam and Protest" to explore relations between the liberal establishment, the counterculture, and conservatives speaking for the working class. I was particularly concerned with the way each faction sought to align itself with the values and interests of "the people." Even while working on *Beyond Left and Right*, I realized that my main interest had come to rest on the way populist sensibilities often merged with hostility to the knowledge sector and policy elites.

I first took on the clash between the political classes and their opponents in 1995 while participating in a PSU panel on Karl Marx and history. Despite their contributions, I argued, Marxian scholars had failed to envision the socialized economy as a self-interested tool of government officials and the intelligentsia. In this respect, I suggested in a note to fellow panelist, foreign language professor Steve Fuller, some of the grass roots anticommunists I had studied had been correct in arguing that Marxism had little to do with the working class.

Two years later, I used a paper on populist anticommunism to reinforce the point. Scholarly condemnations of the Cold War red scare, I told a panel at the Organization of American Historians Conference in San Francisco, were problematic when intellectuals often were a party to the disputes in question. Instead, I said, historians needed to contextualize the adversarial relationship between liberal policy elites and their critics. Animosity toward political intellectuals, I argued, was a response to the influence of those whose work involved the dissemination of information and symbols instead of the production of commodities.

Although free-market conservatives had originated the notion that economic planners constituted a "new class," social critics such as Christopher Lasch, Daniel Bell, and Alvin W. Gouldner had legitimized the idea. Undertaking a work originally called "Strangers: The Troubled Legacy of the Socio-Political Class," I sought to explain how adversaries portrayed planners, administrators, social service providers, knowledge professionals, and academics as shadowy cultural renegades and privileged insiders. Launching the narrative with the cultural conflicts of the 1920s, I moved on to the intense controversies over New Deal regulation, World War II bureaucracy, and Cold War communism. Three final chapters described populist critiques of liberal planners and activists from the mid-1950s through the '90s.

After several revisions and a series of torturous dealings with publishers, the manuscript finally emerged in 2003 as a Routledge Press paperback. *America's Political Class under Fire: The Twentieth Century's Great Culture War* included a dedication to Louis Filler. At my suggestion, the book's cover featured a blurry image of a shadowy advisor with a briefcase in hand. In November, I organized a Friends of History book release. Seeking to provide an intimate feel to the reading, I placed ten rows of folding chairs in a wide semi-circle around the lectern. As the audience assembled, my CD boom box played a piano and violin medley of Scott Joplin rags. After outlining the work's scope, I read an excerpt about Dr. William A. Wirt, the Indiana educator who precipitated a congressional investigation in 1934 with charges that a clique of New Deal "brains trust" advisors was about to stage a socialist revolution.

I devoted the closing moments of the presentation to the book's conclusion. Even when opponents of the intelligentsia appeared unreasonable, I noted, their challenges touched on deep-seated anxieties over individual, family, and social identity. Knowledge professionals often compounded the problem with condescending attitudes toward ordinary people, I warned. The point was that if members of the political class were to retain the confidence of society, their efforts had to resonate with broad segments of the public. This meant a willingness to lend expertise to social problems without imposing their own sensibilities, needs, and special interests. Americans should not have to choose between reliance on the goodwill of narrow business interests or dependence upon reformers with their own social agendas, I insisted:

"Society cries out for disinterested healers, reformers, and authors of consent, not ideological monitors," I concluded.

WARRIORS AND ANTI-WARRIORS

The idea that knowledge professionals needed to relate to everyday Americans in commonly understood terms emerged as a major concern in the fall of 2002 when the George W. Bush administration signaled an intention to remove Iraq's Saddam Hussein by force. Three and a half years earlier, I had authored an *Oregonian* forum piece critical of Bill Clinton's campaign to bomb a degraded and poorly trained Iraqi military that no longer posed a plausible imminent threat to anyone. Fearful of appearing weak on security in the post-9/11 world, however, the Democratic Congress now gave President Bush the right to use any means to disarm Iraq of its presumed stockpile of chemical, biological, and nuclear weapons if diplomatic efforts failed.

I thought the resolution should have tied any action to United Nations approval. Yet the posture of the antiwar movement seemed equally misplaced. Invited to write an opinion piece for the *Portland Tribune*, I stated that numerous grounds existed for condemning prospective military action in Iraq but that war opponents did not seem to be focusing upon the security concerns that motivated most Americans. Instead of support for the Security Council's authorization of a new round of weapons inspections and its requirement that the United States return for deliberations before taking further action, I wrote, peace activists seemed to prefer expressing opposition to *any* war conducted by Washington, whatever its context.

Pacifism had little relevance to the dialogue, I insisted, if it merely expressed the personal preferences of those who wound up talking to themselves and putting off the public with a cloak of moral superiority. At a PSU panel of Middle East experts and historians I helped organize in February 2003, I admitted that the law of unintended consequences led me to grave misgivings about invading Iraq. I also acknowledged the opposition of groups such as Win Without War and Vets for Common Sense, who saw no imminent danger to the United States. Yet I argued that the peace movement as a whole had not engaged the American people on these vital issues.

Like many thoughtful critics of the march to war, I was not sure Iraq still had weapons of mass destruction and certainly never thought it posed an immediate threat. However, I did concede the Bush administration's point that a ruthless dictator like Saddam Hussein might *eventually* gain access to these devices and be willing to make them available to those who had no scruples about using them. The point was that if the public believed military action was essential to protecting its security from such a possibility, no spouting of pacifist sentiment, conspiracy notions about control of oil, or assessments of the war's cost to domestic programs would change its mind.

In April, the month after U.S. and British troops invaded, the *Portland Tribune* quoted my characterization of the antiwar movement as "pathetic" – "a confessional cult" engaged in self-expression instead of politics. At a PSU panel days later, I depicted activists as victims of a depressive mentality that blamed the United States for everything wrong with the world. Debates over going to war in democracies, I contended, were inherently populist ones because they focused on the security interests and values of the nation's people.

"I regret that the moral smugness, ideological rigidity, and marginalized nature of the peace lobby have left the American people without a credible opposition that can reasonably examine the strategic choices that must certainly await us down the road," I concluded.

Furious at antiwar dissidents for failing to mount a reasoned critique of the military campaign, I collected my thoughts in "Warriors and Anti-Warriors: A Historian Views Gulf War II," published in the May 2003 edition of PSU's conservative *Spectator*. Conceding that the war risked America's global goodwill and future security, I nevertheless stressed the dangers of a dictatorial state offering a potential base for international terrorists with access to lethal weapons.

BLACK HOLE

Although my public statements acknowledged ample grounds for criticizing the Iraq War, even qualified support for the Bush administration proved too much for many of those closest to me. One was my brother. After serving two years as a Peace Corps tourism advisor in Tonga, Michael had remained in the South Pacific to launch a career as a scholar, academic dean, and journalist. Following a world tour to mark the start of the year 2000, he had returned to the States to complete research for a new V. O. Blum work of fiction. Completed in 2003, *Split Creek: War Novel of the Deep West* looked beyond twentieth-century ideologies such as fascism, communism, and Christian imperialism to envision a humane social democracy.

Michael's distrust of George W. Bush's evangelical approach to the world colored his view of the war. The same held true for Bob Williams. Between April and July 2003, Bob and I engaged in a furious exchange of letters touching on every aspect of the conflict. Bob found it incredulous that I gave any benefit of doubt to an administration dominated by neoconservative ideologues. I responded that I had no problem with rational foreign policy dissent based on the peculiarities of the circumstances. Yet I remained convinced that activists had imposed the lessons of Vietnam on all time as if all situations and contexts were equivalent.

There were two paths to social change, I suggested: coercion and democratic consent. The preferred second choice required resolution of the interests of the majority and relevant elites. If the antiwar movement intended to engage the American people, I stressed, it needed to advance beyond sterile formulations and deal with the dilemmas ordinary people faced.

Bob was particularly upset about the media's role in rallying support for the war. Having frequently confronted arguments about corporate hegemony in cultural history classes, I objected to the assumption that outside Fox News, network ownership necessarily affected political ideology. As profit-making entities appealing to as large an audience as possible, I argued, television sought to make news dramatic and entertaining. The result, I contended, may have generated superficial and thinly constructed stories, but not necessarily pro-corporate ones.

I suggested that much of the news focused on the consequences of developments for ordinary Americans. In the early days of the war, I speculated, television coverage had sought to assuage public uneasiness about the operation's effectiveness and ensure viewers that the men and women in uniform had the country's support. Precisely because the military was largely working class and the media did not want to appear elitist, I argued, television reports initially hesitated to raise difficult questions. The resulting invocations of patriotism, I insisted, did not reflect a corporate agenda as much as they represented emotional bonding with a people who liked to think the American military represented the country's democratic spirit and aspirations.

During one PSU panel, Afghanistan specialist Grant Farr predicted that judgments about the war's effectiveness would await the outcome of reconstruction efforts. By the summer of 2003, however, the U.S.-led Coalition Authority faced an onslaught of problems including delays in restoring electricity and oil production, the dissolution of the Iraqi army, the ouster of Saddam loyalists from the civil bureaucracy, terrorist bombings, and the failure to find weapons of mass destruction. I now conceded to Bob Williams that Bush had overstated the weapons case by calling it an imminent threat because he lacked the confidence to sell the war as a response to *long-term* challenges. I also reiterated my belief that 9/11 had been "a Hail Mary, a one-in-a-million recruitment poster" by Al Qaeda leader Osama bin Laden that had not anticipated taking down the Twin Tower structures and was not meant as a preview of future attacks.

Sobered by the realization that war supporters, including me, had given too much credit to the Bush administration and had underplayed the occupation's potential unleashing of sectarian warfare and nationalist resistance, I joined Grant Farr in organizing a new faculty panel in October. Under the banner "Iraq and the Mideast: What Happens Now?" five participants presented six-minute talks. With American casualties rising, I noted, a creditable antiwar opposition had arisen in the same quarters some activists dismissed as servants of the power structure – former military commanders and intelligence operatives, members of Congress, and elements of the media. I also acknowledged that no credible evidence pointed to Iraqi stockpiles of sanctioned weapons or ties to Al Qaeda. The U.S. occupation, not the deposed regime, I agreed, had emerged as the focal point of attention, turning Iraq into a magnet for terrorists.

By resorting to unilateral military intervention and parading Iraq's imminent threat as a justification for war, I concluded, an administration given to arrogance, ignorance, and incompetence had seriously eroded U.S. credibility.

When we convened a sixth and final panel in May 2004 entitled "Is There a Way Out of Iraq?" I noted that the discussion now focused on whether the United States could extricate itself from a black hole. By now, Washington faced an ugly prisoner abuse scandal, the unreliability of Iraqi troops, and a domestic backlash against civilian and U.S. casualties. It was clear that the government had falsely conflated the war on terrorism with the invasion of Iraq. Beyond that, new revelations demonstrated it had failed to heed intelligence warnings about an Al Qaeda attack before 9/11; used faulty and manipulated weapons intelligence to legitimize a preventive war; insufficiently planned and allocated military resources for the postwar period; and neglected to anticipate the consequences of occupying a Muslim nation.

Did the Bush administration have the imagination and courage to reverse a disastrous course, admit its mistakes, and create the environment for a stable Iraq? I asked. Given my failure to anticipate the full scope of the war's unintended consequences, however, I could not completely escape speculation about my own standing as a historian and public intellectual.

PINNACLE

(2004-2008)

as if maybe someone could hear
— J. Taylor

'08? OBAMA!

THE SETTING WAS THE HISTORY DEPARTMENT LOUNGE EXACTLY A week after George W. Bush's victory in the 2004 presidential election. A standing room only crowd had assembled to listen to eight-minute commentaries from environmental historian Bill Lang, sociologist and social historian Joe Uris, and me. Like the forums on the Middle East and Iraq, the brief presentations were to leave ample time for audience interaction. Once again, the constricted space of the venue conveyed the intimate feel of a teach-in.

POLITICS 101

For many in the audience, the Tuesday afternoon gathering had the solemnity of a wake. Undoubtedly, the mood harkened back to Bush's victory in 2000. In a mailer sent out to friends and associates more than two years before that vote, I had predicted that the race might turn out to be the closest in U.S. history. Widespread ambivalence about the information culture boom and the virtual economy, I reasoned, in conjunction with Bill Clinton's scandalous relationship with a White House intern, even might lead voters toward a conservative candidate.

After monitoring the polls for months and noting that Democratic candidate Al Gore's fate rested in Florida, I was among many frustrated progressives as election night ended. Despite losing the national popular vote, Bush had emerged with a plurality of 537 ballots in the Sunshine State. Once the U.S. Supreme Court voted 5-4 to stop a state-ordered recount to review improperly marked ballots, a firestorm of protest emerged among Democratic loyalists, who accused the Court of stealing the election.

It was true that private contractors in Florida had purged thousands of African-American men from the rolls whose names coincided with those of convicts and that long lines and poorly functioning voting machines had discouraged balloting in black districts. It was also true that thousands of paper ballots did not appear to reflect the intentions of voters. Yet as I pointed out in notes to the *North Coast Times Eagle* and *Upper Left Edge,* Democrats on the ground had failed to monitor the use of confusing and misleading ballots. Most important, if slightly more than a *half-percent* of third party candidate Ralph Nader's 97,000 votes had gone for Gore, the Democratic nominee would have carried Florida and gone to the White House.

Assessing the implications of a second Bush victory in 2004, Bill Lang pointed to the administration's efforts to gut environmental regulation, to privatize management of national parks and forests, to encourage oil and gas drilling, to reclassify wetlands, and to dilute protection of endangered species. The Bush presidency's refusal to address the foremost issue of the new century, Bill suggested, stemmed from the loss of moderate Republicans in Congress who formerly had assumed leadership in matters of environmental sustainability.

Joe Uris attributed Bush's electoral success to the ability to play upon anti-intellectualism, the distrust of science, and the willingness to scapegoat liberal elites as the source of social problems. Concerned with the reluctance of Democrats to address the tangible interests of most voters, Uris predicted the advent of a "friendly fascism" that would exploit the sentiments of American Exceptionalism to build support for imperial adventures overseas.

I began my presentation by noting that if Democratic candidate John Kerry had mounted a slightly better showing among Hispanics in New Mexico, Nevada, and Colorado, he would have won those states and the presidency despite losing Ohio and Florida. The downside, however, involved the culture war. Exit polling revealed that one-fifth of the electorate rated social morality as the most important issue, with four-fifths of those voting Republican. Pollsters suggested that President Bush's opposition to abortion, same-sex marriage, and government support of stem-cell research conveyed the image of a forthright leader.

America's Political Class had pointed to the ties between traditional and populist mindsets. Yet I cited political commentators who saw a way out. Kansan Tom Frank argued that Democrats needed to confront the contradictions of a conservative populism that neglected to see popular culture as the creation of corporate America. Meanwhile, former speechwriter Andrei Cherny called upon liberals to articulate their own social vision and address voters' moral and spiritual yearnings. Similarly, communications specialist George Lakoff said Democrats needed to frame the political discussion by advancing a vision of the country as a caring, responsible family whose common inheritance should serve the public good.

Whether in politics or academia, I concluded, people of reason needed to reach beyond themselves and engage with an America that certainly needed their input.

The problem of viable reform and social reconstruction was the theme of "Coming to Terms with Vietnam War Protest," a panel I organized in May 2005 to commemorate the thirty-fifth anniversary of the PSU Park Blocks incident. Beyond our discussions of Iraq, Bob Williams and I had engaged in a lively exchange on the relationship between American politics and the economy. Trying to explain why ideological movements would not capture the public imagination until they spoke to its essential sensibilities, I cited the widely popular *Forrest Gump* (1994), a film that contrasted unsavory characters of different stripes who politicized events with the slow-witted protagonist, who saw the human dimension in all experience.

Forrest Gump's implicit skepticism toward politics, I suggested, helped to explain why Americans seemed to trust *economic* elites – represented by huge corporations and financial houses – but not *cultural* elites – government officials, social-service providers, information sector professionals, and the chattering classes – those that people suspected of telling them how to think, behave, and relate to others.

I thought the most significant contribution to the Vietnam-era session involved Portland author Elinor Langer's recollections of how antiwar radicals had lost faith in the American people and fantasized about exotic foreign agents of change. Building on Langer's analysis but wanting to reach out to present-day activists, I recycled the argument from *America's Political Class* that successful social movements needed to frame their appeals in terms of broadly accepted notions of national interest. Once again, I insisted that besieged minorities with a belief in their own moral superiority could not stop wars, foster democratic revolutions, or lead those they did not respect.

THE PERILS OF IDENTITY

My work on populist social values had obvious relevance to the controversy over identity politics. In a note to women's history colleague Patricia Schechter, I praised former New Left activist Todd Gitlin's *Twilight of Common Dreams: Why America Is Wracked by Culture Wars* (1995). Gitlin pleaded for progressives to transcend race and gender factionalism and adopt a broader vision resonating with the needs of the national community. The politics of victimhood, he argued, was self-defeating, ineffectual, and polarizing and needed replacement by a transformative approach that addressed social and economic justice in a way that united people instead of pulling them apart.

My sympathy with Gitlin's approach helped account for the frustrations I experienced when the history faculty made its next appointment. With news that a recent European history hire planned to return back East, the university authorized a new job search in 2001. Following several interviews, the department chose an impressive Asian-American scholar as its first choice. As a gesture to inclusiveness, particularly since the administration confined African and African-American history appointments to Black Studies, the finalists included a black applicant who specialized in racial ideology. I had attended both the job talk and question-and-answer session that followed for this candidate and had not been impressed with his grasp of broad historical themes. Assuming my colleagues would not favor a private secondary school teacher who had not yet completed a PhD and whose specialty seemed tangential to much of European history, I held back during the discussion of his case.

To my surprise, the department ranked the black candidate second. When the Asian-American bowed out, therefore, the African-American historian became our first choice.

It would take two years for the College of Liberal Arts and Sciences to learn that the new instructor had not even begun writing his dissertation. As an abrogation of written contractual guarantees, the dean had no choice but to terminate the appointment.

What had begun as a well-intentioned attempt at diversity had ended badly. Yet the history department continued coming under attack for racial exclusiveness. In December 2003, an *Oregonian* story on the move to full department status for Black Studies included a student's contention that she had taken an Oregon history class at PSU and learned nothing about African-Americans. The piece prompted a letter to university administrators from a black graduate student in education condemning the department's failure to venture outside of "white American historical teaching ideology." Even when confronted with evidence of ample treatment of Oregonians of color in the class in question, the protester insisted on the difference between a minority *presence* in content and a minority *perspective*.

Viewing the criticism as patently unfair and aware that the writer had mentioned me as one of the historians with a "white" teaching orientation, I drafted an extensive response copied to all members of the history department, to Black Studies, and to the university provost. My rebuttal noted the inclusion of racial themes in nearly every PSU history class, including my own, and in the research of nearly all department members. The protester had taken an "essentialist" view, I suggested, that distinguished between a "minority perspective" and a "white" one. In doing so, he had ignored scholarship on the tensions and contradictions *within* marginalized groups. The situation finally defused when History Chair Linda Walton and I met with the critic, who admitted he also had issues with Black Studies.

At that point, Linda offered to help him enter our MA program.

The next day, she received an email with the student's apologies.

As a cultural historian, I often confronted theoretical models that took the life out of human behavior. I particularly objected to efforts to place all creative expression within a political, economic, or racial context. At the "Marx and History" panel, I had protested that such a view could not account for the democratizing tendencies that working-class African-Americans and European ethnics brought to commercial popular culture.

I pursued these questions in 1999 at a Reed College symposium on Billie Holiday and the Political Context of African-American Art. An essay by Marxist Angela Davis accused producers of compromising Holiday's artistry by forcing her to record vacuous pop music lyrics. I disagreed. It was true, I admitted, that the communist movement of the late 1930s had adopted Holiday as a revolutionary "race woman" when she introduced the anti-lynching ode "Strange Fruit" at Café Society, New York's first racially integrated nightclub. Yet I insisted that the singer's genius came through the artistic individuality and improvised techniques she brought to the rhythmic and nuanced Tin Pan Alley standards that seemed to bring out her best.

I explored a similar path two years later when the *North Coast Times Eagle* published my reverie on the importance of American ethnic diversity in Ken Burns's public television history of jazz. At the same time, I saw a distinction between commemorating the popular arts and placing subjects in full historical context. The disparity emerged in 2002 when I organized an Oregon Cultural Heritage Commission panel on Portland's World War I era bohemians John Reed, Louise Bryant, and Charles Erskine Scott Wood.

I acknowledged how a recent book by Princeton historian Christine Stansell described the importance of these figures in fashioning new forms of cultural expression reflecting the informality and democratic irreverence of their personal lives. Yet I noted Stansell's contention that the era's male innovators found it difficult to overcome conventional Victorian gender and social class attitudes and privileges.

Not surprisingly, the OCHC crowd seemed reluctant to pursue the contradictory perspectives that cultural historians find so essential to their work.

PEOPLE'S ART

Committed to bridging the gap between academic history and the culture at large, I nurtured a growing interest in Oregon's rich tradition of realist painting. Since purchasing the three Runquist works in 1993, Gloria and I had become regulars at Art Space, where Trisha Kauffman maintained that good work sold itself when it had integrity. We eventually took title to dozens of paintings and watercolors by Arthur and Albert Runquist, Nelson Sandgren, Martina Gangle, Charles Heaney, Harry Wentz, Dan Robinson, and other regional artists. Early in 2002, I raised the possibility of creating a "people's" museum to which collectors could bequeath legacy donations or lend their art. Trisha said she had nourished the same idea for years.

With the help of a local attorney, we soon gathered a board and adopted by-laws for the Museum of People's Art: Labor, Life, and Landscape of the Pacific Northwest. Once the Kauffmans donated part of Art Space, we amassed a collection of twenty paintings and prints and received accreditation as an Oregon nonprofit corporation with federal tax-exempt status. To enhance the project, I produced an information flier placing the collection in historical context with a description of the public arts component of the New Deal's Works Progress Administration. By providing jobs for artists while bringing their murals and paintings into public view in venues such as Mt. Hood's Timberline Lodge, I wrote, the Federal Art Project had democratized the arts and encouraged popular consumption of works of visual imagery.

Besides several Runquist murals, Oregon's New Deal art program included work by Martina Gangle. A political comrade of the brothers, Gangle had contributed watercolors, engravings, and carvings to the Timberline Lodge project and produced a huge wall painting of Columbia River pioneers at Portland's Rose City Grade School. Before her death in 1994, the artist had approached Trisha about restoring a Runquist mural at a school in Pendleton, Oregon, where she had served as an assistant. Eight years later, her husband, former merchant seaman and political activist Hank Curl, turned Gangle's papers and drawings over to Trisha.

Spying several cartons of the archive dispersed across the floor of the Bay City framing shop one day, I suffered the panic attack of a historian.

"Somebody has to catalog this stuff," I pleaded.

"Why don't you just take it all and do it?" Trisha answered.

For the next few weeks, Gloria and I examined every scrap of Martina Gangle's extensive array of correspondence, notebooks, and drawings, taking particular care to extract quotations that explained her politics and approach to art. Born one of seven children into a poor Roman Catholic family of fruit pickers in southern Washington, she attended the Portland Art Museum School on partial scholarship before signing on to the WPA arts program. Joining the Communist Party during the Great Depression as an act of social conscience, she followed Arthur Runquist into the Vancouver, Washington, World War II shipyards as a welder and drafting technician. Her experience on the ways produced a collection of paintings and drawings emphasizing the individuality of sister workers. When the war ended, Gangle returned to picking fruit, married Hank Curl, and threw herself into radical political causes, including the creation of Portland's John Reed Bookstore.

"I know since I'm an artist I'm somewhat of a dreamer," she once explained.

With many of Gangle's paintings on display in Bay City or in the hands of collectors, and with her written testimony now cataloged, David Milholland and I collaborated on a biographical pamphlet. At Gloria's suggestion, we called it "Martina Gangle Curl: People's Art and the Mothering of Humanity," a reference to the artist's focus on the plight of women and children. Reproducing twenty-four color photos of her work, David designed a sixteen-page publication under the OCHC imprint. The profile emphasized the way Gangle's take on ordinary existence embraced the injustices she saw under capitalism. To my amusement, the publication generated a two-page spread in the Communist Party's *People's World*, to which Hank Curl still subscribed, which we duly photocopied and distributed to museum patrons.

Trisha, Gloria, and I now put together an illustrated overview of Gangle's life, art, and social commentary for presentation at schools and OCHC events. At the same time, Gangle's work constituted a significant portion of the museum's inaugural event on Labor Day 2004. Bringing together two hundred paintings, drawings, and prints from a dozen private collections as well as museum holdings, "Working People" highlighted the repertoire of eighteen artists, with special emphasis on shipyard and labor portraits. As Craig and Trisha hung the last pieces hours before the opening, I sat at my computer in Arch Cape frantically adding items to an ever-growing catalog. With the last entry secure, Gloria and I rushed to the nearest copy center and then doubled back thirty miles to Bay City for help in folding the programs.

One hundred visitors showed up for the opening. After dedicating Doug Lynch's drawing "Farm Wife," (1934), as the museum's official logo, independent historian Sandy Polishuk read from her recent biography of labor organizer and Gangle ally Julia Ruuttila. We also used the event to round out a "Saving Arthur" campaign that raised $3,600 to enable the museum to purchase a Runquist oil portrait of a woodcutter. Coastal writer and teacher Matt Love, a former student of mine, would include "Discovering People's Art in Oregon," my tribute to Art Space and the museum, in *Citadel of the Spirit: Oregon's Sesquicentennial Anthology* (2009), a collection of offbeat celebrations of the state's cultural legacy.

Next in line was a paper on radical painters and the New Deal prepared for the Labor Arts Forum, a conference on 1930s federally sponsored art that public historians Lois Leonard and Sarah Baker Munro organized in conjunction with OCHC and the Portland Art Museum. My talk suggested that New Deal consumerist goals coincided with the labor metaphysic of even the most radical artists. Although it seemed ironic that social critics such as the Runquists and Martina Gangle participated in federally funded efforts to reinvigorate capitalism, the link between the two lay in the desire to portray working-class dignity and the beauty of the vernacular arts. The result was an invaluable legacy of publicly sponsored visual treasures.

The *Oregon Historical Quarterly* published an extended version of my presentation along with contributions by historian Bill Robbins and other conference participants. Meanwhile, Lois Leonard worked with OCHC and Oregon State University Press to release *Waging War on the Home Front: An Illustrated History of World War II* (2004), a memoir of a pipe fitter in the Kaiser shipyards in Vancouver. Lois filled the book with color photos of Runquist paintings and other works provided by collectors that included Gloria and me.

THE PEOPLE'S VOICE

By the time *Waging War* appeared, I had produced several chapters of my own memoir, an idea that originated with student interest in the personal anecdotes I occasionally recycled. I intended to complete the work during a sabbatical starting in the fall of 2005. Yet just as I settled on these plans, I received an inquiry from Bill Webber of Sloan Publishing, a small press in upstate New York, who wondered if the rights to a new edition of *On the Edge* might be available or if I had any other ideas for a textbook. Flattered by the request, I dashed off a rough chronological chapter outline of a project I had contemplated for years.

My studies of the 1920s Klan and insurgent political culture had led me to focus on populism – a democratic faith in the wisdom and integrity of the common people. Yet my own work and that of historians such as Robert Goldberg and Michael Kazin confined the discussion to social movements or politics. Other references to "the people" normally addressed those advocating progressive social change. Asked to introduce Howard Zinn, the author of the popular *A People's History of the United States*, at a well-attended Friends of History lecture in 1998, I carefully confined my description of Zinn's work to a relatively narrow band of racial justice crusaders, labor organizers, feminists, antiwar radicals, and socialists. In contrast, I yearned for a comprehensive text to synthesize American cultural history with an emphasis on creative expression related to the daily experiences of ordinary people, not just progressives.

To my surprise, Bill Webber responded to my hastily drawn outline by requesting a formal proposal, which he sent out for external assessment early in 2005. One reviewer, whose specialty included political folk music, suggested I called the book "This Land is Your Land," after Woody Guthrie's iconic anthem. The other, presumably a conservative, complained I had not referenced the "coarsening" of life under Bill Clinton. Beyond the politics, both called for more detail and broader scope. As was my custom, I wound up adopting some 90 percent of the suggestions. Nevertheless, I held firm on two issues.

First, Woody's song would not do for a title because the text was not a survey of progressive expression.

Second, the same reviewer's displeasure that the title of one chapter borrowed the term "strenuous life" from Theodore Roosevelt ignored the fact that a Scott Joplin rag shared the same handle.

Despite outright skepticism from the conservative reviewer and only guarded approval from the progressive, Webber sent me a contract, although the agreement offered no advance and offset any royalties with half the costs of including black-and-white photos.

With school out in June 2005, Gloria and I retreated to the Coast, where I began to compile handwritten notes from a massive selection of secondary works borrowed each week from the PSU library. Following longstanding practice, I recorded information on the blank side of used typing paper and collated the individual sheets into separately marked file folders representing prospective chapters. With the help of a new computer with a reliable CD-ROM backup, I began writing in December, a year before my deadline. Dealing with an enormous amount of material, I kept the narrative under control by never letting a paragraph exceed fourteen lines and limiting sub-sections to five pages.

I had the chance to offer a summary of the project in the spring of 2006 when I delivered the University of Minnesota's Annual David W. Noble Lecture in American Studies. In "Who Speaks for the People? Coming to Terms with American Populist Culture," I suggested that history and American studies had focused inordinately on matters of social pathology while paying scant homage to the nation's legacy of expressive culture. In a period of bitter political division and sectarian loyalty, I proposed, intellectuals needed to reconnect with the American people. Portraying my book as a potential guide to a legacy shared by those of all social backgrounds and views, I held out hope that a politics acknowledging the culture of ordinary people might help lead us out of the current darkness of disunity and political stalemate.

With the advantage of a full year's sabbatical and two free summers, I sent off the manuscript two weeks before the end-of-year deadline. *The People's Voice: A Populist Cultural History of Modern America* was a descriptive synthesis. Starting with the legacy of Walt Whitman, Mark Twain, and Stephen Foster, it presented a chronological sampling of literature, painting, drama, movies, music, and other expressive forms from the age of ragtime to modern country music and hip-hop. The text characterized works as populist when they engaged a broad audience through vernacular or informal language, used unadorned and representational modes of presentation, and invoked social and spiritual values grounded in the lives of non-elites. Beyond that, most examples in the book identified with the experience of ordinary people through references to geographical place, family ties, or cultural roots.

To mark the book's release during the spring of 2007, I organized a recitation and multimedia show co-sponsored by Friends of History and the OCHC. Before a packed house, Walt Curtis, David Milholland, Joe Uris, and Dory Hylton joined me in a series of readings associated with the work's principle figures. A graduate student accompanied the presentation with a slide show of relevant paintings and photographs, while David Myers orchestrated a selection of CD musical excerpts on my boom box.

Due in part to publication of *The People's Voice,* History Chair Tom Luckett and Bill Lang nominated me for Portland State's 2007 Millar Award for teaching and scholarship. Beyond recognition at commencement, recipients had the privilege of presenting a brief set of remarks at the fall faculty convocation. Grasping at the "bully pulpit," I used the opportunity to explain my approach to cultural history. Academics, I pleaded, needed to appreciate the vitality and resourcefulness of ordinary people, an approach, I suggested, that lay beyond fashionable definitions of diversity and cultural identity.

Vernacular cultural expression had become an essential part of my persona. Using my experience in mounting public events, I assembled a Friends of History reading from Phil Metcalfe's *Whispering Wires: The Tragic Tale of an American Bootlegger* (2007). After completing a history master's thesis on Prohibition, Phil had discovered the wiretaps records of Puget Sound liquor runner Roy Olmstead and fashioned them into a riveting narrative. Sadly, a fatal bout of brain cancer prevented his seeing the book into print. With support from Phil's widow, PSU administrative assistant Amy Ross, I distributed brief selections from *Whispering Wires* for readings by several university colleagues. The event, held early in 2008, offered a fitting tribute to an author who combined meticulous research with a talent for telling a story.

Gloria delivered one of the recitations at the Metcalfe event, leading to an introduction to Friends President K.C. Piccard-Krone. As a result, the group sponsored a commemoration of the one-hundredth anniversary of Lola Baldwin's commission as a female detective. Dressed in costume, Gloria read Baldwin's speech to the Portland City Council on the day in 1922 when she announced her retirement. Through the efforts of K. C., the mayor declared April 1st Lola Greene Baldwin Centennial Day. The next month, Oregon Public Broadcasting ran a thirty-minute video biography of America's first female police officer, most of it based on *Municipal Mother* and an extended interview with the author.

THE NEXT PRESIDENT

Publication of *The People's Voice* lent itself to a two-term class on "populist expressive culture" with the help of my CD and DVD collection. To elicit further interest in the book, I published an essay entitled "Is There a Viable Populist Cultural History of the United States?" in the journal *Historically Speaking*. One of its focal points was Depression-era Hollywood. Instead of positioning the movie studios as agents of corporate hegemony or gender conformity, I described romantic comedy of the 1930s as a site of positive collaboration between men and self-assured, vibrant, and witty female characters. Films such as *My Man Godfrey* (1936) and *Mr. Smith Goes to Washington* (1939), I suggested, situated women as partners of American social and cultural reconstruction in a time of peril. Contrary to feminist convention, I viewed these portraits of romantic love as fitting metaphors of democratic choice and individual worth.

The idea of Hollywood as Depression savior served as the basis of a paper I delivered at the 2008 Popular Culture Association Conference in San Francisco, where Gloria and I spent most of the time as book exhibit agents for *The People's Voice*. The night before my presentation, however, Barack Obama appeared at a massive indoor rally in Portland.

As we watched the television coverage in our hotel room, Gloria got very quiet.

During the summer of 2006, she had caught an Obama interview on C-SPAN and marveled at the politician's reasoned demeanor and ability to transcend partisanship.

"He should be the next president!" she told me.

On her rounds at the Dollar Tree a few days later, Gloria purchased a set of alphabet decals and taped a message inside the rear window of the Escort wagon I had purchased in 1994.

"'08?" it read, "OBAMA!"

Sitting in San Francisco, she desperately wanted to be in Portland.

Gloria had anticipated Obama's run for the presidency six months before he announced it. Unlike most progressives, her interest had little to do with ethnic identity or opposition to the war in Iraq – it was a matter of temperament. Her unwavering support of the freshman senator quickly overwhelmed me. By the spring of 2008, Gloria and I were close to the "hard money" contribution federal law allowed for the primary season.

When Obama returned to Portland in May, I promised we would not miss him again.

This time, we joined eighty thousand people in the city's Waterfront Park at the largest political rally of the campaign to that point.

Obama had a magnificent triumph at the summer's Democratic National Convention in Denver. Yet interest in Senator John McCain's vice-presidential running mate Sarah Palin spiked Republican poll numbers until a series of TV interviews revealed Palin's lack of grounding on key issues. Then the financial system experienced a notorious crash in mid-September, prompting McCain to insist that the fundamentals of the economy were sound. At that point, Obama's polling inched back to positive territory.

Having waited for Democratic prospects to rebound, I sent out a carefully crafted mailer to an extensive list.

The Republicans had mounted a "Know-Nothing" campaign of bluster, denial, and tinhorn posturing, I wrote. What was at stake in the election was a choice as to whether we would have a government that addressed the complex challenges of our time with reason and deliberation. I insisted that we needed leaders able to demonstrate flexibility, open-mindedness, and adaptability instead of tone-deaf aggrandizement, denial, and posturing.

Noting that Gloria and I had donated the legal limit to the Democratic ticket, I pleaded that even small contributions would help.

"None of us want to wake up sick at heart on November 5th," I warned.

Having done what I could for the candidate who seemed to embody the qualities of deliberation and humility my scholarship often referenced as political virtues, I joined Gloria in bearing witness to the Obama family's election night celebration of a once-inconceivable victory in Chicago's Grant Park, the site of bitter antiwar protests forty years earlier.

It felt like the country had dodged a bullet.

It had to be one of the greatest days of my life.

Gloria just smiled.

WAITING FOR #17

every form of refuge has its price
– D. Henley/G. Frey/D. Felder

As I amble along the six-block walk to the bus for the ride to the university on a gray morning early in fall term, I am thinking about my cultural history class, where I plan to introduce Cotton Mather.

"I will show them the graves of their fathers," the Puritan divine declared at the start of a chronicle of New England's seventeenth-century spiritual errand in the wilderness.

Mather sought to implant humility in the coming generation by pointing to the legacy of its predecessors. Yet I wonder once again, as I do every time I teach the course, how I can make the venerable Mather come alive for a cohort of students born after Ronald Reagan left office. In an age of wireless social networking, instant text messaging, Internet blogs, and personalized playlists, is it possible for anyone to gain a sense of a people whose service to God and community demanded the harshest self-scrutiny? Can I really sharpen the tools of intellectual empathy – the ability to understand the circumstances and mindset of remote societies and times from *inside* the experience – when few people can imagine alternatives to our commodity-absorbed, communications-savvy, and self-absorbed lives?

FIFTEEN RULES

At the bus stop, where I spend a few minutes admiring the lush greenery of my Northeast Portland neighborhood, I reflect upon my own dance with technology. I use the university's library computers to survey the Internet for finite tasks such as political poll watching or accessing historical documents. Yet I remain skeptical of cyberspace's plethora of de-contextualized information, rumor, conspiracy, and personal indulgence. The most important thing that college teaches, an English instructor once explained in an article on undergraduate education, is the ability to give reasons for what you believe. Nevertheless, the attempt to convince students that a commitment to disciplined, rather than self-centered, thinking can have relevance to their lives can be challenging. It is so easy to see history as either a compilation of useless facts or a way to provide "lessons" for the future.

Unclear whether my efforts were achieving any result one term, I distributed a handout with the following fifteen rules for cultural and historical study:

1. All societies feature opposing characteristics that engage each other in an ongoing dialectic or cultural dialogue.

2. Particular ideas, values, and practices receive rigorous defense only when they fall under attack and are no longer "self-evident."

3. The louder and more insistent the discourse, the more anxiety and uncertainty it masks.

4. Although human motivations are difficult to ascertain, individual participants in social movements usually act from both specific self-interests and broader notions of moral right or justice.

5. Successful political and social movements emerge from coalitions of diverse parties with distinct interests and values.

6. No social movement can succeed without invoking the perceived will and interests of the majority of the populace and demonstrating respect for the same.

7. The less incremental or gradual social change, the less lasting its impact.

8. The discipline of history studies the past record of societies by employing a fair-minded selection of facts or evidence as the basis for the construction of reasonable interpretations.

9. As location is to real estate, context is to the study of history.

10. As in all endeavors, certainty is the downfall of all fools.

11. When dealing with the use of conceptual tools, areas of specialization, and jargon, the fashions of today most likely become tomorrow's clichés.
12. Historians must not confuse their own sensibilities and aspirations with those of the subjects they study.
13. Historians are not parties to particular disputes but seek to explain the terms of the debate.
14. As a discipline deeply embedded in the humanities, history offers a means to cultural understanding and social healing.
15. Rather than teaching specific lessons or pointing to the "mistakes of the past," history offers the chance to develop general insights and broad perspectives on the human condition.

DOROTHEA

I like to joke with my students that the work of a cultural historian is never done.

An illustrative example occurred when David Milholland and I undertook one of the Oregon Cultural Heritage Commission's most ambitious projects. The idea of exhibiting the work of New Deal documentary photographer Dorothea Lange, who recorded over five hundred images of Oregonians for the Farm Security Administration in 1939, came from a suggestion by Portland radical historian Mike Munk. Calling attention to these portraits of proud and dignified rural families during the Great Depression, Mike pointed out that Lange's original negatives were accessible in the online archives of the Library of Congress. Yet nothing came of the idea until New York University social historian, Lange biographer, and Portland native Linda Gordon referenced the collection in a note following the release of *The People's Voice*.

With two modest foundation grants and private donations from OCHC Board members and others, Milholland arranged to digitize

Getting There

and print nearly fifty enlarged versions of Lange's negatives before having the pictures professionally mounted. Meanwhile, David and I negotiated with Portland State's student-run Littman Gallery for a fall 2009 exhibit. Friends of History then agreed to bring Linda Gordon to campus to serve as the exhibit's keynote speaker.

By now, Munk, Milholland, and OCHC Board member Lois Leonard had cataloged the quotations Lange had transcribed from her Oregon subjects as well as the artist's detailed captions. This gave me the chance to devise a script for a group recitation to accompany a PowerPoint screening of the images. I chose Dory Hylton and Gloria for the female voices and Milholland and me for the males. David and I then approached the Alumni Association about including the reading in PSU Weekend, an annual event for former students scheduled for six days after the opening of the exhibit. Highlighting the gallery show, the Gordon lecture, and the PowerPoint dramatization, *PSU Magazine* did an illustrated cover story on the Lange retrospective, followed by extensive coverage in *The Oregonian* and the *Vanguard*.

Each of the three events attracted large and enthusiastic crowds. Heartened by the response, OCHC subsequently took the exhibit and PowerPoint recital to a number of venues including Bay City, the Washington County Historical Museum, a suburban roadhouse, the University of Oregon, and Malheur County, the eastern Oregon site of many Lange photographs.

10 PRINCIPLES

History department colleagues were incredibly supportive of the Lange project. Nevertheless, my view of our discipline as an integral part of the humanities could leave me feeling somewhat isolated. Instead of devoting so much of teaching and research to complex theoretical constructs and descriptions of dysfunctional policy and behavior, I leaned toward an approach that emphasized a multidimensional assessment of human civilization that, among other things, took into account the fruits of creative thinking and expressive culture. Academic historians were not so much training history scholars, I believed, as helping students apply critical thinking and a fair evaluation of evidence and cultural existence to any number of pursuits. This was why I preferred to have people in my classes summarize the substance and arguments of key interpretive works rather than focus on narrowly defined research projects.

My concerns about the technical and specialized nature of university education coincided with a sense that much of American public discourse seemed to be operating independently of empirical reality and elementary standards of reason. Beyond the influences of the Internet and social media, and beyond the country's intense political polarization, I had to wonder if the constricted fixations of academia had some bearing on the problem. By de-emphasizing the precepts of intellectual discipline and empathy inherent in general education and the humanities, it seemed as if we had we left ourselves in the precarious position of talking to ourselves and to a few like-minded clones. I often wondered if educators had virtually abandoned the public arena to the absolutists that humorist Stephen Colbert once described as "knowing with their heart."

As I mulled over my own discomfort with the state of academia, outside voices were striking a blow at higher learning from an entirely different direction. The financial meltdown of 2007-08 and resulting recession prompted budget-conscious political leaders to hold administrators to quantitative evaluations of university programs and student employment prospects. The stagnating job market also led many parents to question whether escalating tuition and student debt made college a wise investment. Seeking to link the health of the university and professional history to American political vitality, I put together "Thoughts for a New Academic Year," a handout I distributed to students on the first day of the 2010 fall term.

First, I embraced the well-defined goals of liberal arts education: sharpening intellectual faculties, engendering curiosity about the world, expanding the ability to think critically and creatively, developing the facility to learn and grow intellectually, and stimulating the capacity to liberate the mind from habit and custom. Historical studies fit this scheme perfectly, I suggested. The important point, however, lay in the realization that humanistic learning could serve the practical needs of the knowledge-driven economy while simultaneously creating the foundation for personal enlightenment. An evidence-based field of inquiry such as history, I argued, could provide the tools of critical reasoning applicable to *any* endeavor or course of self-development a member of a democratic society might choose to pursue.

Friends of History published an abbreviated version of my commentary in its next newsletter. By then, the Republican Party had regained control of the House of Representatives on a wave of Tea Party rants about Washington's "tyranny" and "socialism." Feeding off hostility to the Affordable Health Care Act, conservatives stepped up opposition to any federal role in regulating finance and the environment or sustaining the economy. In an unpublished letter to *The Oregonian* two months before the 2010 election, I argued that since measures such as infrastructure spending promote business activity, Republican leaders who opposed these appropriations must want to delay recovery to win the votes of disaffected Americans.

Social critics such as Henry A. Giroux have described a "neoliberal" ideology that undermines faith in public institutions and concern for the common good with purely market-oriented strategies. The results include continuing assaults on the remnants of the welfare state, the dominance of corporate money in politics, attacks on employee unions, inequitable distribution of wealth and income, the privatization and de-funding of public education, and the adoption of corporate marketing and management techniques in the university.

During the summer and fall of 2011, the Occupy Wall Street movement offered a constructive counterpart to these developments by highlighting the financial sector's role in the collapse of the home mortgage market and ensuing unemployment, consumer bankruptcy, and student debt. For a time, the movement succeeded in changing the national conversation. Yet it seemed to lose much of its focus when protesters repeatedly took on local authorities in confrontations over the right to camp out in public parks. At the same time, activists never succeeded in fashioning a coherent political agenda, a necessity when democratic elections and the mechanisms of representative government, no matter how compromised they may be, remain the ultimate arbiter of social change in American society.

I had a chance to engage several Oregon Occupy activists the following May when I accepted an invitation to comment on the showing of *The Seventh Day*, a student-made film produced during the Portland State antiwar strike of 1970. The event's sponsor, "Kick-Ass Oregon History," a community group devoted to a spirited review of the local past, had billed the movie as a documentary about Portland's "original Occupiers." It was in this light that much of the ensuing discussion concentrated on organizing strategy. A young woman insisted that the anti-Wall Street coalition would succeed once it "empowered the people." I responded that I had heard that call many times but had learned that saying it was easier than doing it.

Acknowledging that I had no blueprint for progressive social change, I addressed several operating principles I believed essential to a successful movement. Several days later, I organized my thoughts into still another handout:

10 PROPOSED PRINCIPLES FOR EFFECTIVE SOCIAL MOVEMENTS

dedicated to students, friends, and allies in the Occupy Uprising

1. Set tangible and attainable goals.
2. "Serve the people."
3. Move beyond personal agendas.

4. Maintain respect for people outside the movement.
5. Police gratuitous acting-out or violent disruptions within the ranks.
6. Acknowledge that effective and lasting changes ultimately involve all segments of society, even powerful elements that may be part of the problems you identify but whose long-range interests may wind up coinciding with many of your own.
7. Forming strategic coalitions with those who may not share *all* your political and cultural views is essential.
8. Do not be afraid of incremental or gradual change.
9. Adopt a reasonable time line for fulfilling your goals.
10. Sustain hope in the possibility of qualitative change to prevent premature burnout and loss of focus.

ON TIME

As I wait at the bus shelter, I think about the immigrant roots of my family, the struggles of my parents, and my Bronx childhood. I reflect on the transition from earnest liberal to political radical, counterculture days, my awakened sense of political realism, and the evolving populist emphasis of my scholarship, cultural activities, and political sensibilities. Beyond the challenge of transforming the idealism of the "Vietnam" generation into workable forms that still made sense, I have tried my best to fuse a career inside and outside academia with a socially constructive and relevant life philosophy. Although the professoriate did not necessarily have the *answers* to society's problems, I told the PSU convocation in 2007, we at least held out the promise of intelligence and mental discipline in the attempt to resolve common dilemmas.

I remember a game several years ago involving the Wet Sox, our PSU city inter-league softball team. Just after our mediocre crew miraculously took the lead, the opposing pitcher disputed several calls so vehemently that the umpire awarded us a forfeit victory.

I was infuriated. Winning was not the issue. It was getting on with the game.

I just want to be a player.

I want to help people think clearly, free of sterile formulations and fearful mind traps. I want to have a role in empowering those around me to trust their better selves. I want to provide nurture for the *intangibles:* creative beauty, spontaneity, spirituality, the capacity for surprise.

And yes, I want to play some part, however small, in repairing, transforming, and facilitating social justice in the world and the country with which I am so intimately involved. If there is any theme to the convoluted odyssey that has been my life, it lies in the attempt to be an effective human being who makes a socially redeeming contribution to the world.

These aspirations require a fundamental belief in the possibility of change, one of the legacies of the 1960s and early '70s that I most cherish. Certainly, the examples of Louis Filler, Uncle Mickey, and many other people I have cared for and admired have convinced me of the necessity of avoiding bitterness – the blind alley leading nowhere.

Maintaining an optimistic frame of mind often means accepting partial victories. Still, as a politically aware person open to self-scrutiny, I am not immune to moments of doubt.

Although teaching involves an ultimate act of faith, I wonder about encouraging the use of intellect amid shortsighted fixations and a tendency to rely on belief instead of reason.

How long can I reconcile a populist outlook with the life of the mind when embattled resources and declining interest in reflective thought threaten the preservation of mental and spiritual nourishment as a democratic right and impose the most instrumentalist and materialistic goals on the educational experience?

I explained to the convocation audience that I would not retire until I had a compelling reason to do so because I still got a jolt from the challenge of thinking on my feet and inspiring people to experience the pleasures of intellectual reflection. Yet do my classes, presentations, and forums; my desire to clarify issues through writing; and my quest for cultural affirmation and vitality really mean anything in the scheme of things? Am I fooling myself when I sustain a critical approach to ideological fixations of all kinds and still aspire to social progress?

Have I constructed a grand illusion about my self-importance and the idea of contributing to the good of humanity?

Given the continuing Israeli-Palestinian stalemate, festering terror in the Middle East, and political gridlock here at home, are progressive dreams of enlightened politics and aspirations for human improvement additional casualties of my generation's fall from grace?

Do the ingrained habits of my "Rain Man" personality, as Gloria calls it, prevent an adjustment to the world with sufficient plasticity to avoid self-marginality?

What, after all, is the impact of my presence on earth?

If the idea is to become a relevant human being who leaves something worth remembering, are there any hopes of ever getting there?

After all, it is not enough to dream.

These thoughts sometimes keep me awake nights.

Yet it's a beautiful day – the 17 is on time, my lecture notes are in order, and it looks like it's going to rain.

SELECTIVE LIST OF AUTHOR'S PUBLICATIONS

(entries within each category in reverse chronological order of publication)

Books:

The People's Voice: A Populist Cultural History of Modern America. Sloan Publishing, 2008

On the Edge: The United States in the Twentieth Century. Wadsworth, 2005 (coauthor)

America's Political Class under Fire: The Twentieth Century's Great Culture War. Routledge, 2003

Inside the Klavern: The Secret History of a 1920s Ku Klux Klan. Southern Illinois University Press, 1999

Beyond Left and Right: Insurgency and the Establishment. University of Illinois Press, 1997

Academic Journals:

"The Sicuro File: A Personal Perspective on the Struggle over Portland State University's Most Controversial President." *Oregon Historical Quarterly* 112 (Summer 2011)

"The New Deal and People's Art: Market Planners and Radical Artists." *Oregon Historical Quarterly* 109 (Summer 2008)

"Is There a Viable Populist Cultural History of the United States?" *Historically Speaking* (May/June 2008)

"The Normality of Extremism: The Ku Klux Klan Revisited." *Society* 35 (September/October, 1998)

"An Alliance of Convenience: Independent Exhibitors and Purity Crusaders Battle Hollywood, 1920-1940." *The Historian* 59 (Spring 1997)

"Senator Borah's Crusade to Save Small Business from the New Deal." *The Historian* 55 (Summer 1993)

"The Perils of Commodity Fetishism: Tin Pan Alley's Portrait of the Romantic Marketplace, 1920-1942." *Popular Music and Society* 17 (Spring 1993)

"The 'Cross of Culture': La Grande, Oregon in the 1920s." *Oregon Historical Quarterly* 93 (Summer 1992)

"The Klansman as Outsider: Ethnocultural Solidarity and Anti-elitism in the Oregon Ku Klux Klan of the 1920s." *Pacific Northwest Quarterly* 80 (January 1989)

"Social Morality and Personal Revitalization: Oregon's Ku Klux Klan in the 1920s." *Oregon Historical Quarterly* 90 (Winter 1989)

"White Southerners' Alienation and Civil Rights: The Response to Corporate Liberalism, 1956-1965." *Journal of Southern History* 54 (May 1988)

"Independent Merchants and the Chain Stores: Portland, Oregon, 1928-1935." *Oregon Historical Quarterly* 89 (Winter 1988)

"North Dakota Noninterventionists and Corporate Culture." *Heritage of the Plains* 17 (Summer 1984)

Newspapers and Magazines:

"Antioch at the Dawn of the Sixties." *The Antiochian*, Winter 2011

"Peace Activists Must Expand Their Horizons." *Portland Tribune*, November 29, 2002

"Palestinians Can Take Control of Their Future." *The Oregonian*, May 24, 2002

"Does the Tail Wag the Dog?" *Sunday Oregonian Forum*. March 1, 1998

"Vietnam War Tore Nation Along Lines Still Unhealed." *The Oregonian*, May 8, 1995

"New Tactic Can Break Mideast Stalemate." *The Oregonian*, November 27, 1992

"Faith of a Bronx Dreamer." *Back in the Bronx*, Vol. 3 (1991), No. 1

"The Road to Woodstock Went Through Jo-Jeans: A Dialogue on Pop Music." *North Coast Times-Eagle*, September-October 1989

"An Eight-Day Week in Nicaragua: A Personal View," Parts I and II. *North Coast Times-Eagle*, May-June and July 1987

"On Klansmen, History, and Truth: A Response." *North Coast Times-Eagle*, March 15, 1985

"George Touhouliotis: The Passion Behind Satyricon." *Multnomah Monthly*, December 1984

"The Thirty-Year War: A Reconstructed Diary of an MTV Fanatic." *Multnomah Monthly*, November 1984

"New Wave and Rock: Latest Invasion from Britain Repeats Cycle as Music Continues to Sculpt Culture." Sunday Forum, *The Oregonian*, August 12, 1984

"The Capitalist Conspiracy: I'm Left, You're Right, and Wall Street is Just Fine." *Clinton Street Quarterly* 2 (Fall 1980)

"Left Out in the Cold? A Report on the California Delegation at the Democratic National Convention." *San Francisco Bay Guardian*, July 23, 1976

"CIA Intelligence Report: Fortress Washington – Beginning to Breathe the Stench of Empire." *Oregon Times*, November 1975

"CIA Intelligence Report #1: E. Howard Hunt: Laments of a CIA Loyalist." *Oregon Times*, October 1975

"Tracking Down the CIA: Murder and Drugs in the Cathedral." *Portland Scribe*, August 15-21, 1975

Getting There

"Unity and Resistance: Angela Davis in Portland." *Oregon Times*, November 1974.

"Richard Nixon: Paradoxes of a Presidential Pariah." *Oregon Times*, September 1974

Portland State Vanguard:

"The Emperor Has No Clothes," May 11, 2000

"Simpson Trial Prompts Questions of Justice System," February 22, 1995

"Hold Administration Responsible for Trimming Our Fat," April 1, 1993

"Why We Fought," March 1, 1991

"An Open Letter to Chairman Arafat," January 4, 1991

"No 'Good' Choices in Gulf," November 16, 1990

"Talking Mideast Peace at PSU," January 6, 1989

"Big-Time Sports Stifles Academics," October 13, 1987

"Charges Deserving of Serious Investigation," March 3, 1987.

"Recognition of Israel's Sovereignty Vital," January 31, 1986

"High Time to 'Cut' a Deal for Peace," October 30, 1985

"Show Provides Forum for Punks, Parents," October 16, 1985

"Pop Music Parallels Cultural History," October 16, 1984

"Last Freeway," June 6, 1975

"Sixty-Nine," May 23, 1975

"State of the Cathedral," May 16, 1975

"Boy Scouts," May 2, 1975

"Old-time Music," April 18, 1975

"Mirage," April 11, 1975

"Da Nang Saturday Night," April 4, 1975

"Conspiracy," February 28, 1975

"Letter from Laguna," February 14, 1975

"Old Crusaders," January 31, 1975

"Super Sunday," January 17, 1975

"Breakfast at the Hilton," December 13, 1974

"Virtue," December 6, 1974

"Courthouse," October 18, 1974

"Bombing," October 11, 1974

"Two Trials," October 4, 1974

"Mission Blues," September 27, 1974

"Along the Watchtower," May 31, 1974

"The Axe," May 17, 1974

"Governor Evidence," May 10, 1974

"Cover-up," May 3, 1974

"Fatal Flaw," April 26, 1974

"Connections," April 19, 1974

"Top Dog," April 12, 1974

"The Princess," April 5, 1974

"The Exorcist," March 1, 1974

"SLA," February 22, 1974

"Coliseum," February 15, 1974

"Bitter Fruit," February 8, 1974

"Hire Education," February 1, 1974

"Junk People," January 11, 1974

"Faith," December 7, 1973

"Credibility," November 9, 1973

Getting There

"Sweepstakes," October 12, 1973

"The Invisible Man," October 5, 1973

"Judas 'n' Jesus," September 28, 1973

"Worthy Advisor," September 21, 1973

"Real Life and Television," December 8, 1972

"Working-Class Ignored," November 21, 1972

"McGovern Needs Miracle," October 31, 1972

"Radical Professors," October 20, 1972

"The 'Trusted' Word," October 13, 1972

"CIA Link ..." September 29, 1972

"Changing Times," September 22, 1972

CREDITS FOR PHOTOS AND SONG LYRIC EXCERPTS

Front cover photos: author at three years of age, West Bronx, New York, 1944; author at Democratic National Convention, New York, July 1976, Daniel H. Wolf; and author as "Uncle Sam," Portland State University Department of History, June 1995, Gloria E. Myers

Epigraph: Bruce Springsteen, "It's Hard to Be a Saint in the City," Canyon Music, 1972

"Prelude" photo: Arch Cape, Oregon; lyric: Donald Wallace Poythress, "You Remain," BMG Songs Inc., EMI April Music Inc., Sound Island Publishing/Big Daddy's Baby, 2000

"Breaking Away" photo: author at eighteen, Roslyn Heights, New York, 1959; lyric: Bob Dylan, "Lay, Lady, Lay," Big Sky Music, 1969

"Branching Out" photo: author and singing group at Rochester, New York settlement house, February 1961, Baden Street Settlement; lyric: John Lennon and Paul McCartney, "Blackbird," Northern Songs, LTD, EMI Blackwood Music Inc., ATV Music Corp., 1968

"Canopy" photo: author at Foyer Amitié, Loire Valley, France, 1962; lyric: Keith Reid, "A Whiter Shade of Pale," Essex Music Inc., 1967

"Estuaries" photo: author at South Minneapolis railroad yards, 1966, Crystal Gandrud; lyric: Bob Dylan, "All Along the Watchtower," Dwarf Music, 1968

403

"Westwinds" photo: author with antiwar poster, 1969; lyric: John Lennon and Paul McCartney, "The Fool on the Hill," Comet Music Corp., EMI April Music Inc., 1967

"Fireweed" photo: author to left of image of Portland Park Blocks antiwar confrontation, May 1970, *Portland State Vanguard*; lyric: Stephen Stills, "For What It's Worth," Cotillion Music Inc., 1966

"Ferment" photo: "Dandelion Dave" and Beulah, 1973; lyric: Jackson Browne, "Redneck Friend," WB Music, 1973

"Primrose" photo: author with Afro hairstyle, 1974; lyric: Leon Russell, "The Ballad of Mad Dogs and Englishmen," Skyhill Publishing Co., 1971

"Habitat" photo: author at Democratic National Convention, 1976, Daniel H. Wolf; lyric: Sting, "Spirits in the Material World," Virgin Music Inc., 1980

"Crevice" photo: author and Peter Carroll at Muir Woods, California, 1978; lyric: "Ric Ocasek, "You Might Think," Lido Music Inc., 1984

"Foliage" photo: experimental portrait of author in Minneapolis, 1983, Susan Eurich; Paul Fishman, "The Politics of Dancing," Jambo Music Ltd., 1982

"Clearing" photo: author in class, 1984; lyric: Don Henley and Glenn Frey, "After the Thrill is Gone," Benchmark Music, 1975

"Conifers" photo: author at John Reed Centennial Celebration, Portland Pioneer Square, 1987, Ilka Kuznik lyric: Sting, "King of Pain," Magnetic Publishing, 1984

"Meadows" photo: author and Gloria Myers protesting plans for neighborhood incinerator, 1989; lyric: Paul Simon, "The Boy in the Bubble," Paul Simon BMI, 1986

"Leading Edge" photo: author and activist Stew Albert, 1991; lyric: Bruce Springsteen, "For You," Canyon Music, 1972

"Salal" photo: author and longtime debating partner, Bob Williams, Cannon Beach, circa 1991; lyric: Randy Newman, "I think It's Going to Rain Today," January Music, 1970

"Precipice" photo: author, Walt Curtis, and Michael McCusker, 2001; lyric: John Prine, "Hello in There," Sour Grapes Music/Walden Music, Inc., 1971

"Pinnacle" photo: Gloria Myers political placard, 2006; lyric: James Taylor, "Sweet Baby James," Country Road Music/BMI/Blackwood Music, Inc., 1970

"Waiting for #17" photo: N.E. Portland bus shelter, Andrea Janda; lyric: Don Henley and Glenn Frey, "Lyin' Eyes," Benchmark Music, 1975

Back cover photo: Andrea Janda.

INDEX

Abraham Lincoln Battalion, 80, 327
Ace, Johnny, 34
Adderley, Cannonball and Nat, 70
Affirmative action, 319-20, 351
Affordable Health Care Act, 392
Agnew, Spiro, 120, 155
Agricultural Marketing Act of 1929, 215
Albert, Stew and Judy, 258, 318, 319, 328
Aldermaston March (Britain), 48-49
Alinsky, Saul, 73-74, 77, 296
Allen, Penny, 110, 116, 117-18, 180, 182, 303
Allen, Woody, 3
Allende, Salvador, 193
Allison, Mose, 21
Al Qaeda, 347-50, 364-65
Altholz, Josef, 63, 84
Amalgamated Clothing Workers Union, 8
America First Committee, 219, 236
American Association of University Professors (AAUP), 282
American Historical Association (AHA), 90, 194, 216, 302
American Legion, 18, 119, 127
American Studies, 67, 380
American Theater Company, 180
Americans for Democratic Action (ADA), 12
American Veterans Committee (AVC), 12, 18, 339
Anderson, Barry, 353
Anderson, Stu, 35
Antioch College, 3, 7-8, 15-16, 38-39, 127, 195, 209; and Lilienthal nomination, 236-37; reunions, 299; and social protest, 32-33, 36, 60. See also Filler, Louis
Antioch Education Abroad, 39
Aptheker, Herbert, 108
Arafat, Yasir, 311, 312, 328
Arch Cape, Ore., 336-38, 343
Armstrong, Louis, 318
Armstrong, Tony, 264
Aronowitz, Stanley, 82
Art Space Gallery (Bay City), 327-28, 338, 375, 378
"Ashcan" school of art, 38
Atomic Energy Commission (AEC), 213, 236-37
Baden Street Settlement House, 33, 35-37, 43, 69, 84
Baez, Joan, 22
Baja Peninsula, Mexico, 139

Index

Baker, Howard, 194
Baldwin, Jim, 248
Baldwin, Lola, 334-35
Bancroft Library (University of California at Berkeley), 228-29
Band, The, 131
Barnes, Tim, 338
Bates, Tom, 206
Bates, Whitney, 91, 118
Bateson, Gregory, 152
Bay of Pigs Invasion (1961), 36, 56, 191
Beach Boys, 82
Beard, Charles and Mary, 38
Beat Generation, 71
Beatles, 49, 59, 78, 82, 86, 182
Beckwith, David, 189-90, 193
Bell, Daniel, 213, 359
Bellush, Bernie, 339
Bennett, Ade, 31, 67
Bergman, Ingmar, 21
Berkhofer, Robert, Jr., 66-67
Bernstein, Bart, 213, 222
Bernstein, Maury, 66
Berry, Chuck, 34, 201
Bethel, N.Y.
Beyerle, Frank, 138-39, 197
Beyerle, Lynn, 197
Big Al's (Minneapolis), 70-71
Big Julies' discotheque (New York)
bin Laden, Osama, 364
Biolsi, Tom, 356
Birmingham civil rights protests, 56, 60, 234
Black Panther Party, 100, 103, 129, 318, 319
Black Power Movement, 82, 100, 138
Black Studies (Portland State), 320, 351-52, 373-74
Blakely, Judd, 106
Blashfield, Jim, 249-50
Blum, V.O., 303, 334, 362
Blumel, Joseph, 172, 176
B'nai B'rith, 256, 277
Bogart's Joint (Portland), 220
Bolshevik Revolution, 278
Booth, Brian, 278, 310, 331
Borah, William E., 215, 235
Borosage, Robert, 187
Boulé, Margie, 333-34
Bourne, Randolph, 73

407

Bowie, David, 248
Braeman, John, 86
Brandeis University, 62, 83, 95, 115, 340
Brewin, Michael, 280-81, 284, 289, 294-95, 338
Bricker, John W., 237-38, 239
Bridal Veil, Ore., 135-36, 145, 149
Brinkley, Alan, 252, 301, 302
Broadway Books, 329, 335
Brooklyn Dodgers, 19
Brooklyn Paramount Theater, 35
Brooks, Jeff, 40
Brown, Jerry, 201-202
Brown, Mel, 223
Brown Sugar, 131
Browne, Jackson, 131
Bryant, Louise, 374
Buber, Martin, 38
Buddy Holly and the Crickets, 59
Bullfrog II, 104, 119
Burdick, Usher L., 232
Burgess, Michael, 343
Burke, Barney, 275-76
Burns, James M., 174
Burns, Ken, 374
Burns, Marjorie, 275, 290
Bush, George H.W., 313, 314
Bush, George W., 347-48, 349, 360-61, 362, 364-65, 369-71
Cabezas, Omar, 271-72
California Angels, 304
Cambodian incursion, 110, 128
Campbell, Dick, 269
Cannes, France, 47
Cannon Beach, Ore., 116, 125-27, 132, 140, 153, 336, 343
Capehart, Homer E., 238
Carawan, Guy, 27
Carlyle, Thomas, 84, 99, 193
Carmichael, Stokely, 82
Carnegie Foundation for the Advancement of Teaching, 284
Carnegie Hall, 33
Carr, Karen, 349
Carriage Room, 131
Carroll, Peter, 194-95, 200, 207, 211, 327, 342
Carter, Jimmy, 195, 201, 257
Cassavetes, John, 69
Cassidy's (Portland), 303
Castaneda, Carlos, 152

Index

Castro, Fidel, 36, 48, 188, 189, 193
Catskill Mountains, 9, 12, 34, 64, 249, 299
Cease, Ron and Jane, 298
Center for National Security Studies, 187-88
Central Intelligence Agency (CIA), 4, 36, 124, 169-70, 190-91, 214, 297; and Church Committee, 184, 187-91, 193-94; conspiracy theories, 78, 143, 177-78; and Contra war, 269, 271, 274
Cerelli, Bob and Sandy, 336-37
Chaivoe, Nick, 117, 128-29
Chalmers, David, 246
Chambers, Clarke, 84, 89, 130
Chambon sur Cisse, France, 40
Charles, Ray, 21, 59, 318
Chautauqua Program, 253, 278
Cherny, Andrei, 371
Chicago Cubs, 245
Chicago Eight, 117
Chicago White Sox, 299
Chomsky, Norm, 349
Christian Right, 320-21, 349, 362
Church, Frank, 187, 191, 197, 201
Church Committee on Intelligence Activities, 187-91, 193-94, 195, 197
Clark, Bud, 310
Clarke, Arthur C., 138
Clarke, Guy, 196
Clinton, Bill, 328, 339, 360, 369, 379
Cohen, Leonard, 86, 153
Colbert, Stephen, 391
Colby, William E., 188-89
Cold War anticommunism, 80, 229-30, 282; and scholarship, 3, 227, 230-31, 237-38, 240, 358-59; and teaching, 247-48, 350
Cold War noninterventionists, 231-32, 236, 238, 252
Cole, Wayne S., 215, 236, 239, 302
Collins Foundation, 331
Columbia River Gorge, 87, 135-36
Columbia Slough, 298-99
Columbia University antiwar protest, 93
Committee to Re-Elect the President, 151
Committee for a Sane Nuclear Policy (SANE), 83
Communist Party, 61, 230, 248, 376, 377
Comstock, Anthony, 39
Concordia Neighborhood Association, 298
Congress of Industrial Organizations (CIO), 11
Conservative Alliance (Portland State), 320
Contact Center (Portland), 205, 216
Contra war (Nicaragua), 259, 269-75

409

Cooper, D.B., 136
Costa Brava, Spain, 52
Coughlin, Charles, 234, 252
Counter-Progressive historians, 67
Country Joe and the Fish, 78
Crawshaw, Larry, 353, 357
Cream, 86
Crippens, Dave, 26
Cronin, Jim, 172-74
Cronkite, Walter, 57
Crosby, Bing, 33
Crosby, Stills, and Nash, 107
Crosby, Stills, Nash, and Young, 131
Cuban Missile Crisis (1962), 43-44, 56
Curl, Hank, 376
Curtis, Walt, 116, 251-52, 278, 310, 331, 338, 381
Damis, John, 313
Da Nang, South Vietnam, 178
Dash, John, 293
Daughters of the Confederacy, 195
Dave Clark Five, 49
Davis, Angela, 174-75, 374
Davis, Miles, 21, 318
Davis, William ("Bud") E., 280
Dean, John, 151-52, 169, 207
Deane, Teddy, 181, 217
Deinum, Andries, 149
deLay, Paul, 131
Del Mar, Calif., 138, 197
Delkin committee (Portland State), 283-84
Democratic Farmer-Labor Party (DFL), 91-92
Democratic National Convention of 1968, 92-93, 99-100
Democratic National Convention of 1976, 200-202
Dennis, Lawrence, 240
Desmond, Lola, 180
Dexter, Roger, 105
Dietrich, Marlene, 184
Disneyland, 139, 293
Divine, Robert ("Bob"), 227, 228, 263
Division of Continuing Education (Portland State), 123-24, 197
Doenecke, Justus, 301
Domino, Fats, 34
Donaldson, Sam, 194
Doors, The, 86, 95
Dos Passos, John, 193; and John Reed, 279, 310, 340; and *U.S.A.*, 14, 18, 31, 61, 73, 207

Index

Dreiser, Theodore, 14
Duberman, Martin, 115
Duin, Steve, 319-20
Duke, Vernon, 221
Duncan, Isadora, 182
Dunthorpe neighborhood, Portland, 283, 292
Durrell, Lawrence, 52
Duvalier, Jean-Claude ("Papa Doc"), 290
Dye, Eva Emery, 246
Dylan, Bob, 182; as folk and country music artist, 59, 66, 131; and electric rock, 69, 78, 80, 82, 160-61, 209
East Bronx, N.Y., 9, 10
Eastern Oregon College, 278
Eastman, Max, 61
Eberman, Willis, 126
Eddy, Nelson, 11
Edinburgh, Scotland, 49
Edsall, Thomas, 318-19, 351
Eglin Air Force Base, 190-91
Ehrlichman, John, 151-52
Eisenhower, Dwight D., 20, 22, 238
Ellington, Duke, 221
Ellsberg, Daniel, 159
Emerson, Ralph Waldo, 38
Emporia State University, 252
Engle, Laura, 329-30
Erickson, Mike, 280-81
Estes, George, 246
Estes, Jack, 333
Euphoria Tavern, 131, 180
Eurythmics, 249
Evers, Medgar, 60
Fahey, John, 104
Fair Play for Cuba, 36
Fallen Warriors Foundation, 333
Farm Security Administration (FSA), 389
Farr, Grant, 363, 364
Farris, Steve, 187
Fausold, Martin, 214
Federal Bureau of Investigation (FBI), 103, 193, 197, 230
Federal Art Project (WPA), 376
Federation of Jewish Philanthropies of New York, 13, 31, 37, 234
Ferguson, Homer, 237
Ferrary, Jeanette, 327
Filiates, Greece, 50-51

411

Filler, Louis, 341-42; as Antioch history professor, 31-32, 38, 55-56, 59, 61-62, 69, 359; conservative views, 205-206, 208-211, 275-76, 341, 395; as Progressive reform scholar, 31, 38, 67, 73
Fisher, M.F.K., 327
Fitzgerald, Ella, 318
Fitzgerald, F. Scott and Zelda, 46
Florence, Italy, 45
Forbes, Orcilia, 281-82
Fourget, Marcel, 40, 42
Foyer Amitié, 40-42
Free Speech Movement (University of California at Berkeley), 77
Freedom Rides, 36
Flynt, Josiah ("Cigarette"), 32
Ford, Gerald, 172, 190
Ford, Kent, 129
Ford, Susan, 194
Fornara, Peter, 115
Fosnser, Harold R., 342
Foster, Stephen, 380
Fowles, John, 86
Fox News, 363
Franco, Francisco, 327
Frank, Tom, 371
Freed, Alan, 34, 249
Freedom of Information request, 197
Froines, John, 117
French New Wave cinema, 21, 69
Friends of Israel for a Palestinian State (FIPS), 297-98
Fuller, Buckminster, 201-202
Fundamentalism, religious, 211
Gandrud, Crystal, 66, 70, 79, 95
Gangle, Martina, 375-78
Garety, Anne, 180-81, 184
Garland, Judy, 33
Garrison, Tim, 348-49
Garrison, William Lloyd, 38-39
General Union of Palestinian Students (GUPS), 258
Genet, Jean, 180
Genoa, Italy, 45
Genovese, Eugene, 86, 108, 137, 140, 150, 159
Gera Meri, Greece, 51
Gerry and the Pacemakers, 49
Gershwin, George, 221, 318
Gershwin, Ira, 316
Giese, Frank, 172-74
Gilbert, Lucy, 59, 148

Index

Gilman, Catheryne Cooke, 239
Gilmore, Jesse, 117, 123, 149
Ginsberg, Allen, 118
Giroux, Henry A., 392
Gitlin, Todd, 372
Glover, Tony, 70
Goldberg, Robert, 379
Goldstein, Bruce, 148, 152, 197, 231, 232-33, 260-61; as graduate student, 77-78, 86-87, 91-92, 95, 145, 177-78
Goldwater, Barry, 216, 219
Golub, Ben, 196
Golub, Mo and Lil, 177
Gooding, R. Thomas, 278
Goose Hollow student housing controversy (Portland), 127-28, 197
Gordon, Linda, 389-90
Gore, Al, 369-70
Goucher, Candice, 259, 352-53
Gould, Stephen J. ("Steve"), 43
Gouldner, Alvin W., 359
Grand Ronde Valley, 316-17
Grateful Dead, 78
Great Depression, 9, 12, 100, 103, 222, 376, 382, 389
Greek Civil War, 50
Greenwich House, 64
Guenther, Gary, 184
Gulf War. See Persian Gulf War
Guthrie, Woody, 43, 379
Guttman, Herbert, 194
Haggerty, Lee, 353
Haight-Ashbury (San Francisco), 78, 87, 139
Haldeman, H.R., 151
Haley, Bill, 34, 299
Hall, Hazel, 331-32
Halperin, Mort, 187-88
Hamilton, Bill, 149, 155
Hammond, John, Jr., 60
Harlem Race Riots of 1964, 65
Harmon, Rick, 263-64
Harris, Nat, 11
Harris, Nathaniel, 11
Harrison, George, 78, 338
Hart, Lorenz, 316
Hatfield, Mark, 194
Hawley, Ellis, 253
Heaney, Charles, 375
Hearst, Patricia, 165-66

413

Heath, Jim 114
Hertzig, Charlie (maternal great uncle), 10
Hill, Tom, 180-81
Hilliard, Asa, 351
Hiss, Alger, 230, 240
History Channel, 342
Hitler, Adolf, 12, 13, 45, 83, 230
Hoffer, Eric, 18, 31
Hoffman, Abbie, 100, 210, 292
Hoffman, Dustin, 94
Hoffman, George, 123, 149
Hoffman, Nicholas van, 120
Hofstadter, Richard, 216, 222
Holiday, Billie, 318, 374
Hollywood, 10, 239, 248, 382
Holy Modal Rounders, 181
Honesdale, Penn., 9, 299
Hoover, Herbert, 214-15, 252-53, 253
Hoover (Herbert) Presidential Library, 214-15, 239
Hoppe, Arthur, 183
Hornburg, Michael, 248
Horowitz, Barnett (Ariovich) (paternal grandfather), 8
Horowitz, Becky (Rifka Golub), (paternal grandmother), 8-9, 314
Horowitz, David J., 128, 197, 210, 253, 319-20
Horowitz, Dorothy (Levine) (mother): background, 9-11, 103, 229, 394; in California, 229, 256; and cancer, 256-57, 298, 304-305, 329; as creative writer, 256, 304; as educator and guidance counselor, 13, 37-38, 130, 137, 177; and Israel, 94, 138; and Jewish identity, 94, 208, 212, 256; memorial, 309, 315; as parent, 19-20, 24, 94-95, 201, 208, 212, 219, 257
Horowitz, Irving Louis, 341
Horowitz, Michael G. (brother), 245, 256, 264, 299; and academic career, 129-30, 205, 216, 362; as college student, 63, 83, and counterculture, 95, 115, 127, 129-30, 138-40, 150, 205; family relations, 7, 11, 145, 260, 330-31, 339; as graduate student, 95, 115, 216, 218, 223; and journalism, 95, 118, 120, 205, 303, 334, 362; novels, 303, 334, 362; political views, 44, 150, 155, 335, 362. See also Blum, V.O.
Horowitz, Nathan ("Nady") (father): background, 8-11, 103, 394; in California, 177, 229, 256, 277, 304-306; as creative writer, 13, 177, 256; as dialect lyricist, 10-11, 304; health issues, 177, 258, 261, 303-304, 329-30; and Israel, 94, 138, 312; and Jewish identity, 19, 20, 94, 138, 208, 212, 256; as parent, 16-17, 25, 37, 64, 94-95, 208, 212, 219, 336; and Robison Home, 309, 329-31; and suburbia, 13-14, 94, 139; as widower, 305-306; in work force, 9-12, 16, 137, 177. See also Harris, Nat; Harris, Nathaniel
House Committee on Un-American Activities (HUAC), 240, 248
House Select Committee on Intelligence Activities, 188
Houston, Cisco, 14, 200

Index

Houston Rockets, 196
Howells, William Dean, 72-73
Hoyt Hotel, 131
Hubbert, Cork, 180
Hughes, Howard, 188
Hults, Billy, 343
Humphrey, Hubert, 32, 92, 100, 103, 127
Hunt, E. Howard, 190-93
Hunter College (New York), 9
Hüsker Dü, 233
Hussein, Saddam, 310-13, 360-61, 364
Huston Plan, 119
Hylton, Dory, 332-33, 338, 381, 390
Igoumenitsa, Greece, 50
Indiana State Library, 238
Industrial Workers of the World (IWW), 18
Inouye, Daniel, 151
Institute for Judaic Studies, 314
Internal Revenue Service (IRS), 192, 193
Iran-Contra Scandal, 275
Iraq War, 360-65
Israeli-Palestinian conflict, 257-60, 277, 297-98, 312, 314, 335, 349-50, 396; parents' support for Israel, 94, 138, 257; and Persian Gulf War, 311-14
Ivancie, Frank, 113
Ives, Burl, 33
Jackson, Andrew, 38
Jackson, Kenneth, 245-46
Jackson, Michael, 249-50
Jackson State University, 111
James, Henry, 72-73, 99, 193
Jazz Age, 211, 213, 245, 247, 255, 264, 317
Jefferson, Thomas, 38, 130
Jefferson Airplane, 78, 104
Jenkins, Steve, 207
Jennings, Waylon, 196
Jewish Association for Services for the Aged, 329
Jewish Colonization Society, 8
Jewish Historical Society (Brandeis University), 340
Jewish Student Union (JSU), 258-59
John Jay College, 90
John Wayne Clinic (UCLA), 257
Johnson, David, 265, 334-35. 357
Johnson, Hiram W., 215, 228-29
Johnson, Lyndon B., 92-93, 192, 228, 229. See also Vietnam War
Johnson (Lyndon) Presidential Library, 227, 229
Johnson, Magnus, 231

415

Jo-Jeans ice cream stand, 34, 249, 299-300
Jolson, Al, 33
Joplin, Janis, 78
Joplin, Scott, 359, 379
Jordan, Winthrop, 68
Kaiser shipyards (Vancouver, Wash.), 328, 376, 378
Karant-Nunn, Susan, 351-52
Kashmir, 349
Kauffman, Craig and Trisha, 327-28, 375-77
Kaye, Michael, 139-40
Kazantzakis, Nikos, 86
Kazin, Michael, 379
Keillor, Garrison, 231
Kempster, Norm, 188
Kennedy, Billy, 251
Kennedy, John F., 23, 32-33, 43-44, 56-57, 189, 234
Kennedy (John F.) Presidential Library, 234-35
Kennedy, Robert ("Bobby"), 94-95, 100, 151
Kent State University, 110-11, 128, 280
Kerry, John, 370
Kershaw, Doug, 131
Kesselman, Amy, 157
Key, V.O., 17-18
"Kick-Ass Oregon History," 393
Kilgore, Rebecca, 220
King, Martin Luther, Jr., 25, 93, 94, 99
Kingsford, Charles, 11, 34
Kissinger, Henry, 188, 193, 198
Knowles, Eric, 21-22
Koerner, Spider John, 70
Kolko, Gabriel, 84
Kopp, Mike, 85. 232, 260-61
Koppleman, Richard, 35
Kosokoff, Steve, 269, 272, 352
Kowal, Mary, 300, 338
Kraditor, Aileen, 137
Krassner, Paul, 14
Kristofferson, Kris, 125
Krogg, Karl, 252
Kuhn, Thomas, 150, 159
Ku Klux Klan, 3, 211, 213, 215, 261, 277, 310; in La Grande and Pacific Northwest, 245-47, 253, 263-64, 278, 302, 317, 341-42; publication of *Inside the Klavern*, 341-43
Kurds, 311
Kurshan, Nancy, 15, 25
Kuwait, 310-311, 313

Index

Kuznik, Ilka, 279
Labor Arts Forum, 378
Labour Party (British), 43
Ladd's Addition, Portland, 149, 218, 223, 245
LaFeber, Walter, 109
La Follette, Philip, 238-39
La Follette, Robert M., 215, 235, 240, 301
La Jolla, Calif., 139, 197
Lake Huntington, N.Y. 9, 10, 33, 299, 301
Lake of the Isles, Minneapolis, 87
Lakoff, George, 371
Lakota Sioux reservation (Pine Ridge, S. Dakota), 262
Lambert, Joe, 353
Lamont, Corliss, 310
Lang, Bill, 369-70, 381
Lange, Dorothea, 389-90
Langer, Elinor, 372
Langer, "Wild Bill," 232
Lasch, Christopher, 359
Laursen, John, 332
Lawrence, D.H., 62
Lawson, James, 25
Lay, Shawn, 278, 302, 316, 317, 341
League of Nations, 235
Leary, Tim, 85
Lease, Mary Lou, 290
Lederman, Doug, 285
Leeds Folk Music Club, 43, 49
Leflar, Stephen, 332
Le Guin, Ursula and Charles, 323
Leisure World, Calif., 177
Lemisch, Jesse, 102
Lemke, William, 232, 234
Leonard, Lois, 378, 390
Lerner, Michael, 258
Lester, O.H., 36, 84
Levine, Bessie (Hertzig) (maternal grandmother), 9, 12
Levine, Milton D. ("Mickey") (uncle), 95, 138, 201, 212, 257, 279, 305; and civil rights, 12, 25; in Florida, 261, 338-39; health problems, 256, 261; legacy, 339-40, 342, 395; as peace activist, 82-83, 234, 274, 338-39; and social justice, 205, 233-34, 256, 261, 338-39; as young socialist, 9-10, 12-13, 103, 229
Levine, Nat (maternal grandfather), 9, 10, 261
Lewis, John, 25
Lewis, Sinclair, 14
Lewis and Clark College, 312

Getting There

Library of Congress, 235-36, 389
Liddy, G. Gordon, 190
Lilienthal, David E., 236-37
Lindberg, Mike, 274
Linder, Ben, 274
Lineweaver, John, 15
Linstone, Hal, 155, 179
Lissy, Dan, 221
Little Richard, 34
Littman Gallery (Portland State), 390
Living Colour, 299
Lloyd, Charles, 70
Long, Huey, 252
Long Good-bye tavern, 208
Long Island University, 137
Looby, Alexander, 26
Los Angeles Dodgers, 304
Lost Generation, 213
Love, Matt, 378
Lovin' Spoonful, 82
Low, Robert, 117
Lower Columbia College, 129, 216
Lower East Side, Manhattan, 8-9, 233
Lubin, Dave, 35, 83
Luby, Tom, 351-53
Luckett, Tom, 381
Ludlow, Louis, 234
Lutz, Chris, 31-32, 36
Lydia's cocktail lounge, 125
Lynch, Doug, 377
MacArthur, Douglas, 300
Mach, Sue, 331
Mafia, 193
Maheu, Robert, 188
Mailer, "Stormin' Norman", 72
Malamud, Bernard, 102
Malcolm X, 68
Malik, Mazen, 258, 260
Mann, Horace, 8
March on Washington (1963), 60
Marcuse, Herbert, 115, 138
Marjorie, 153-54
Marquez, Gabriel Garcia, 150
Marshall, Burke, 234
Marshall College, 232
Marshall Plan, 232, 236, 238

Index

Marx, Karl, 230, 358
Marx Brothers, 180
Marxism, 44, 80, 108, 168, 358, 374
Masonic Lodge, 353
Mass, Bernie (uncle), 64
Mass, Teddy, (aunt), 8, 10
Mather, Cotton, 387
Maugham, Somerset, 14
Maurer, Frank, 15-16, 60
Maynard, Hugo, 105, 119, 275, 284
McCain, John, 383
McCall, Tom, 119
McCarthy, Eugene, 92-93
McCarthy, Joseph ("Joe") R., 219, 230
McCleery, Mickey, 17-18, 127
McCord, James, 150
McCusker, Mike, 116, 119, 178-79, 253, 273, 302, 303
McGarrity, "Sailor John," 254-55
McGovern, George, 140, 145-47
McLean Hospital (Belmont, Mass.), 37, 39
McLuhan, Marshall, 115, 138
McNamara, Robert, 159
McReynolds, David, 23
McSherry, Robert, 173
Measure 9, 320
Men's Resource Center, 176
Mersereau, John, 336
Metcalfe, Phil, 381-82
Metro on Broadway, 248
Metropolitan Opera (New York), 35
Milholland, David, 219, 249, 278, 310, 331-32, 377, 381; and Lange project, 389-90
Millar, Branford P., 282, 381
Miller, Arthur, 11
Millner, Darrell, 320. 351-52
Mills, C. Wright, 15, 159
Mills, Wilbur, 175
Minnesota Historical Society, 231-32, 239
Minnesota Twins, 91
Minnesota Vikings, 176
Minsk (Russia), 9
Minsky's Burlesque (Miami, Fla.), 10
Mitchell, Joni, 249
Mixers, The (Minneapolis West Bank), 65, 69, 77
Moll, Vic, 24, 31
Money Tree (Minneapolis), 85

419

Monk, Thelonious, 44
Montana Historical Society, 241
Montgomery Street fire, 132-35
Morgan, Arthur E., 8, 236-37
Morgenthau, Jr., Henry, 234
Morgner, Fred, 89
Morris, William, 84
Morrison, Jim, 95, 115
Moseley, Josie, 248
Mt. Hood Community College, 106-107
Mulligan, Kevin, 119
Mundt, Karl, 240
Munich, Germany, 45
Munk, Mike, 389-90
Munro, Sarah Baker, 378
Museum of the History of the Revolution (Nicaragua), 272
Museum of People's Art (Bay City, Ore.), 375-78
Music Men, The, 35
Music Millennium, 104
Music Television (MTV), 245, 249
Mussolini, Benito, 45
Myer, Lynn, 173
Myers, David, 299-301, 381
Myers, Gloria E., 264-65, 298-300, 304, 332-33, 340, 390. 396; and Arch Cape, 335-37; and Lola Baldwin, 334-35, 382; and Obama, 383-84; and people's art, 327, 377; and Popular Culture conferences, 303, 316, 382; and Sicuro campaign, 292, 294; and wedding, 337-38
Nader, Ralph, 370
Nanette, Shirley, 220
Nash, Diane, 25
Nashville lunch counter sit-ins, 24-27, 31
National Endowment of the Humanities (NEH), 214, 227
National Guard, 110, 112
National Press Club, 190
National Recovery Administration (NRA), 235
National Security Administration (NSA), 193
National Student Association (NSA), 110
Navasky, Victor, 248
Nelson, Bobbie, 197
Nelson, Willie, 196, 201, 210
"Nervous Nellies," 83
New Age fiction, 303
New Carissa wreck, 343
New Deal, 89, 103, 375-86, 378, 389; opponents, 193, 234, 235, 237-40, 276, 359
New Era business, 90, 91, 108, 316
New Jewish Agenda (NJA), 258-59, 297, 317, 328

Index

New Left: historiography, 86, 102, 115, 137, 213, 219; activism, 101, 140, 165, 257, 258, 372
Newman, Randy, 131
New Paris Theater (Portland), 217
New School for Social Research, 95, 115
Newton, Jon, 248
New University Conference, 105-106, 109, 110, 119, 124-25, 143
New Wave pop music, 245, 248-50
New York Giants, 19-20
New York Teachers' Strike of 1968, 138
New York Yankees, 19-20
New York World's Fair of 1939, 11
Nicaragua, 240, 259, 269-75
9/11. See September 11th
Nirvana, 251
Nixon, Richard, 103, 111, 127, 145, 146-47, 187. See also Vietnam War; Watergate Scandal
Noble, David W.: Lecture in American Studies, 380; as mentor, 67, 72-73, 90, 102, 130; as scholar, 68, 140, 150, 157, 159, 194; as textbook co-author, 194, 207
Noize, Ronnie, 250
Nonpartisan League, 232
Norbeck, Peter, 229
Norris, George W., 215, 235
Norris, Frank, 62
North Atlantic Treaty Organization (NATO), 232, 236
Novak, Michael, 146, 318
Novick, Peter, 321-22
Nye, Gerald W., 215, 222, 236, 253
Obama, Barack, 383-84
Occupy Wall Street movement, 392-93
Ohio Library Association, 276
Ohio State Historical Society, 233, 237
Olcott, Ben, 246
Olmstead, Roy, 381
Open Door Policy, 80, 128
Operation Phoenix, 189
Oppenheimer, J. Robert, 213
Oregon Alien Land Law of 1923, 254
Oregon Citizens Alliance, 320-21
Oregon Council for the Humanities (OCH), 245, 247, 253
Oregon Cultural Heritage Commission (OCHC), 310, 331-32, 374-75, 377-78, 381, 389-90
Oregon Department of Environmental Quality (DEQ), 298-99
Oregon Historical Society (OHS), 245-46, 255, 278
Oregon State University, 102, 124, 222, 274

Oregon State University Press, 335, 378
Organization of American Historians (OAH), 85-86, 358
Organization of Petroleum Exporting Countries (OPEC), 157
Pacific Northwest History conferences, 316, 320
Pacific Rim Studies Center, 143, 144
Packard, Vance, 14
Packwood, Bob, 194
Paine, Tom, 38, 102
Palestine Liberation Organization (PLO), 257-58, 260, 311, 328
Palestinian National Council, 297
Palin, Sarah, 383
Palomar Observatory, 139
Pander, Arnold and Jacob, 250
Pander, Henk, 181, 334
Pantheon group, 310
Paris, 40, 45, 51-52, 117
Parrish, Maxfield, 136
Passi, Mike, 150, 159, 167, 194, 247, 275; on populism, 145-47, 318
Patriot Act, 349
Paudler, William, 292, 294
PCUN (Piñeros y Campesinos Unidos del Noroeste), 340
Peace Corps, 339, 362
Peace and Freedom Party, 100
Penk, Jerry, 281, 283
Pentagon Papers, 159
People's Army Jamboree, 119-20, 123, 178
Perot, H. Ross, 319
Persian Gulf War, 310-14
Perugia, Italy, 71-72
Pessen, Ed, 316
Phillips, Mike, 105, 106, 113, 130
Piccard-Krone, K.C., 382
Pierce, Walter, 254, 342
Pioneer 10, 157
Pocono Mountains, 9
Poison Idea, 251
Police, The, 249
Polishuk, Sandy, 377
Popular Culture Association, 302, 316, 322, 382
Porter, Cole, 221, 316
Portland Art Museum, 248, 376, 378
Portland-Corinto Sister City Association, 269
"Portland Pledge," 259-60
Portland State Alumni Association, 292, 333, 390
Portland State College, 3, 87, 90-91, 101
Portland State Convocation, 381, 394-95

Portland State Foundation, 289-90, 292, 295
Portland State Friends of History, 321, 359, 379, 381, 382, 390, 392
Portland State Strike of 1970, 110-17, 123-24, 178, 332-34, 371, 393
Portland State University, 104, 282; athletics controversies, 175-76, 283-85; budget cuts, 167-68; history department, 123-25, 130, 148-49, 167-68, 348-49, 372-74; Middle East forums, 258-60, 297-98, 312, 348-50, 361-62, 363-65; military recruiting disputes, 110, 124; publications controversies, 182-83, 281-83. See also New University Conference; Portland State Foundation; Portland State Friends of History; Portland State Strike of 1970; PSU Weekend; Radical Social Science Union; Radical Studies Center; Sicuro, Natale; University Studies; Vital Partners Conference
Powell's Books, 340
Price, Lloyd, 21
Progressive reform era, 31, 67, 73, 90, 334
Prohibition, 211
Proudhon, Pierre, 165
PSU Weekend, 390
Puerto Vallarta, Mexico, 198
Rabin, Yitzhak, 328
Radical Social Science Union, 109-110, 117, 124
Radical Studies Center, 104-105, 108, 197
Radun, Belarus, 8, 314-15
Raitt, Bonnie, 131
Ramaley, Judith, 322, 353
Ray, Dave, 70
Reagan, Ronald, 219-20, 256, 259, 271, 273, 275, 276; and "Reagan Democrats," 319
Red Cross, 135
Reed, John, 278-79, 374, 376
Reed College, 314-15, 374
Reedy, George, 228
Reich, Charles, 105, 137
Reiner, Rob, 147
Replacements, 233
Reserve Officer Training Corps (ROTC), 274-75
Reubens Five tavern, 116
Reyes, Karen, 279
Ribuffo, Leo, 302
Riis, Jacob, 32
Risley, Terri, 181
Roberts, Betty, 206
Robbins, Bill, 222, 378
Robinson, Dan, 375
Robison Jewish Home, 309-310, 316, 329-30
Roche, John, 68
Rockefeller Foundation, 209

Rodgers (Richard) and Hart (Lorenz), 217, 221
Roger Williams College, 300
Rolland, Romain, 42
Rolling Stones, 82
Rome, Italy, 47, 51
Ron Steen Trio, 220
Roosevelt, Eleanor, 12, 64
Roosevelt, Franklin D., 89, 234, 236, 240, 300
Roosevelt (Franklin D.) Presidential Library, 234
Roosevelt, Theodore ("Theo"), 32, 379
Rosario, Mexico, 139
Rose City Grade School mural, 376
Ross, Amy, 381
Ross, Margie, 36
Ross, Mike, 43
Rubin, Jerry, 100, 210, 292
Runquist, Albert and Arthur, 327-28, 375-78
Ruskin, John, 84
Russell, Leon, 201
Russian Tea Room, 34
Ruth, Babe, 304
Rutman, Darret, 89-90
Ruuttila, Julia, 377
San Blas, Mexico, 198
Sandgren, Nelson, 375
Sandinistas (Nicaragua), 269-72
Sarasohn, David, 249
Satyricon, 251-52
Saudi Arabia, 349
Schaefer, Phil, 32, 45-46
Schechter, Patricia, 372
Schorr, Dan, 189
Schumacher, Tommy, 34, 315
Schwab, Herb, 338
Scully, Vince, 304
Seeger, Pete, 14
Seegmuller, Fred, 250
Segal, Bernie, 257
Sellwood district, Portland, 208, 272
September 11th, 8, 55, 347, 349, 364-65
Sheperd, Jean, 14, 69
Shiites, 311
Shipstead, Henrik, 231-32
Sibley, Mulford Q., 73, 77, 80
Sicuro, Natale, 280-85, 289-97, 300
Silberman, Charles, 68

Index

Simon, Paul, 299
Simon and Garfunkel, 82, 86
Simpson, O.J., 335
Sirica, John, 190
Six Day War of 1967, 257
Slater, Philip, 173, 175
Smith, Al, 214
Smithsonian Institution, 236
Social Welfare Archives, University of Minnesota, 84
Socialist Party, 9, 23
Socialist Scholars Conference, 108
Socialist Workers Party (SWP), 9, 229
Southern Illinois University Press, 342
Southern Oregon College, 280
Spanish Civil War, 61, 80, 327
Spear, Allan, 68-69, 77, 80, 90, 130
Stalin, Josef, 9, 13, 229-30, 261
Stampfer, Joshua, 297-98, 314
Stanford University, 213, 222
Stansell, Christine, 375
Steffens, Lincoln, 32
Stein, Ira, 35
Steward, Larry, 269, 270
Stewart, Rod, 131, 136
Stills, Stephen, 107, 131, 211
Storefront Theater, 128, 180-81, 184, 187, 217, 264-65
Storm, Howard, 14
Stroheim, Erich von, 62
Student Coalition for Responsible Administrative Policies (SCRAP), 290
Student Peace Union, 23
Students for a Democratic Society (SDS), 101, 105, 110
Sudbury, Canada, 83
Summer of Love (1967), 87
Sun and Rosie's tavern, 176
Survey Research Center, University of Michigan, 21-22, 36
Suzanne, 125-27, 131-36, 140, 149-50, 152-54, 158, 171-72
Sweeny, Susan, 180-81
Swift, Dan, 280
Symbionese Liberation Army (SLA), 165-66
Tactical Operation Patrol (TAC Squad), 113-14
Taft, Robert, 236
Taliban, 347, 349
Talking Heads, 249
Tanner, Bill, 252
Tawney, R.H., 46
Taylor, James, 131

425

Getting There

Taylor, Levi, 258-59
Tea Party, 392
Teapot Dome scandal, 240
Tennessee Valley Authority (TVA), 38, 236-37
Tet Offensive of 1968, 91
Third Reich, 20, 45
Thomas, Norman, 9
Thompson, William Irvin, 149, 156, 179-80
Thomson, Bobby, 20, 304
Thoreau, Henry David, 38
Timberline Lodge (Oregon), 376
Times Eagle Books, 303, 334
Tin Pan Alley, 182, 316, 374
Tone Loc, 299
Toll, William, 247
Tonga, 339, 362
Touhouliotis, George, 251-52
Town Hall program, 250-51
Toy, Eckard, 278, 320
Trevelyan, George M., 43
Triangle Bar (Minneapolis), 78-79
Triple Revolution, 23
Trotsky, Leon, 9, 11
Trotskyists, 9-10, 45, 340
Truman, Harry S., 230-31, 237
Truman (Harry S.) Presidential Library, 229-31
Tselos, George and Gretchen, 66, 70, 93, 94
Twain, Mark, 72-73, 380
Tyler, Richard, 181
United Federation of Teachers, 13
United Jewish Appeal (UJA), 257
United Nations Organization, 50
University of Alabama, 60
University of California at Berkeley, 77, 228
University of California at San Diego, 155
University of Illinois Press, 302, 340
University of Leeds, 39, 42-43, 45-47, 49
University of Minnesota, 87, 194, 380; graduate school, 63, 66-69, 72-74, 84, 130, 177
University of Missouri, 229
University of Nevada, 247
University of North Carolina, 101, 195
University of North Dakota Library, 232
University of Portland, 275, 311
University of Rochester, 36
University Studies (Portland State), 322-23, 352-58

University of Texas, 227
University of Washington, 275
University of Wisconsin, 79
Urban Noize club, 250
Uris, Charlotte, 298
Uris, Joe, 101-102, 105, 116, 144, 233, 298, 313, 369-70, 381
Usual Suspects, The, 248
Vanderbilt University, 26
Van Heusen, Jimmy, 221
Vanport Extension Service, 101, 282
Vatter, Barbara, 87, 90, 102, 113, 123, 135
Vatter, Ethel, 103
Vatter, Harold, 87, 90, 100-102, 135
Vatter, Rita, 85-86, 91, 94-95, 100, 104, 117, 129
Venice, Italy, 45
Versailles Peace Treaty, 235
Vets for Common Sense, 361
Viet Cong, 178-79, 189
Vietnam Moratorium, 106-107
Vietnam Veterans Against the War (VVAW), 178
Vietnam War, 127, 166, 178-79, 191, 312, 332-33; in courses, 80, 275-76; and Johnson policy, 72, 82, 89, 159; and Nixon policy, 110, 119, 128, 140, 172-73, 188; protest in Johnson era, 82-83, 93; protest in Nixon era, 103, 106-107, 110-15, 118, 128, 172, 202, 332-34; protest legacy, 312-14, 332-34, 358, 363, 371-72, 394; and veterans, 116, 119, 178-79, 312, 333-34. See also Cambodian incursion; Pentagon Papers; Portland State Strike of 1970
Vital Partners Conference, 180, 183
Vortex rock festival, 119
Waits, Tom, 211
Wallace, George, 156, 216, 219, 234, 276
Waller, Gary, 101, 105, 109, 233
Wallets, The, 233
Wall Street, 222, 232, 238, 392-93
Walton, Linda, 374
Warhol, Andy, 95
Warren, Earl, 228
War Resisters League, 23
Washington, Ed, 298
Washington, George, 16
Washington County Historical Museum, 390
Watergate Scandal, 4, 150-52, 169-71, 173-74, 188, 189, 207; in *freeway* columns, 153-155, 158, 166, 168-69; and Hunt, 190-92
Wavy Gravy, 139-40
Wayne, John, 178
Weavers, The, 14

Webber, Bill, 378-80
Weikel, Ann, 90
Weiskopf, Doug, 113
Wendeborn, John, 221
Wentworth, Richard. 302
Wentz, Harry, 375
West, Frank, 113, 175
West, Mae, 155
West Bank (Minneapolis), 65-66, 70-72, 78-79, 85
West Bank and Gaza (Middle East), 257, 259, 297, 350
West Bronx, 7, 11, 217, 315, 394
West Chemical, 11, 177
Western Historical Manuscripts (University of Missouri), 229
Westerwelle, Wendy, 217
Wheatley High School, 7, 15, 139
Wheeler, Burton K., 240-41, 272
White, Charles ("Charlie") M., 117, 290
White Lake, N.Y., 34, 299
White Panthers, 110
Whitman, Walt, 380
Wholly Cats, 220
Wick, Grace, 246
Wild Bill Lucas, 78
Wilde, Oscar, 166
Williams, Bob, 118, 127-28, 130-31, 132-33, 245, 260, 347; and debate over Iraq War, 362-64, 371
Williams, Katy and Cody, 245
Williams, William ("Bill") Appleman, 104, 124, 150, 156, 159, 222; as radical historian, 80, 84, 86, 89-90, 99, 101, 140, 215
Wilson, August 264
Wilson, Woodrow, 80
Winningstad Theater (Portland), 278
Win Without War, 361
Wirt, William A., 359
Wisconsin State Historical Society, 238, 340
Wise, Gene, 159
Wittenberg College, 32
Wolf, Dan, 202, 206
Wolfe, Gregory B., 101, 105, 124, 143, 144, 150, 172; response to campus antiwar activity, 110-12, 123
Wolfe, Marianne, 149-50
Wood, Cathy (Wyrick), 115, 116, 333-34
Wood, Charles Erskine Scott, 374
Wood (Robert E.) Papers, 239-40
Woodstock, Conn., 300
Woodstock Nation, 301

Woodstock rock festival, 104, 299-301
Works Progress Administration (WPA), 375-76
World Court, 234, 235
World Trade Center, 347, 349, 364
World War I opponents, 235
World War II, 11, 300, 327; noninterventionists, 236, 240
Wright-Patterson Air Force Base, Ohio, 23
Yellow Springs, Ohio, 15, 20, 209
YIVO Institute for Jewish Research, 314
Young, G.M., 46-47
Young, Ric, 181, 184, 217
Youth International Party (Yippies), 100, 127, 171, 318
Ypsilanti County, Mich., 22-23
Zagone, John, 181, 184, 187, 217, 264
Zihuatanejo, Mexico, 197-200
Zinn, Howard, 379

CPSIA information can be obtained
at www.ICGtesting.com
Printed in the USA
FSOW01n0357130515
7071FS